Lacanian Psychoanalysi in Practice

M000267199

In this book, fourteen Lacanian psychoanalysts from Italy and France present how they listen and understand clinical questions, and how they operate in session. More than a theoretical 'introduction to Lacan', this book stems from clinical issues, is written by practicing psychoanalysts and not only presents theoretical concepts, but also their use in practice.

Psychoanalytic listening is the leitmotif of this book. How, and what, does a psychoanalyst listen to/for? How to effectively listen, and thus understand, something from the unconscious? Further, this book examines the evolution of psychic symptoms since Freud's *Studies on Hysteria* to today, and how the clinical work has changed. It introduces the differences between 'classic' discourses and 'modern' symptoms, with also a spotlight on some transversal issues. Chapters include hysteria, obsessive discourse and phobia, paranoia, panic disorder, anorexia, bulimia, binge-eating and obesity, depressions, addictions, borderline cases, the relationship with the mother, perversion, clinic of the void, and jealousy.

Despite possessing the same theoretical reference of Sigmund Freud and Jacques Lacan, the contributors of this book belong to different associations and groups, and each of them provides several examples taken from their own practice. *Lacanian Psychoanalysis in Practice* is of great interest to psychoanalysts, psychotherapists, students, and academics from the international psychoanalytic community.

Diego Busiol is a licensed psychologist and licensed psychotherapist in his native country of Italy and obtained his PhD from City University of Hong Kong. As a psychoanalyst, he has maintained a private practice in Hong Kong for several years.

Lacanian Psychoanalysis in Practice

Insights from Fourteen Psychoanalysts

Edited by Diego Busiol

Routledge
Taylor & Francis Group

LONDON AND NEW YORK

First published 2022
by Routledge
2 Park Square, Milton Park, Abingdon, Oxon OX14 4RN

and by Routledge
605 Third Avenue, New York, NY 10158

Routledge is an imprint of the Taylor & Francis Group, an informa business

British Library Cataloguing-in-Publication Data
A catalogue record for this book is available from the British Library

Library of Congress Cataloging-in-Publication Data
A catalog record for this book has been requested

ISBN: 978-1-138-36246-8 (hbk)
ISBN: 978-1-138-36247-5 (pbk)
ISBN: 978-0-429-43206-4 (ebk)

DOI: 10.4324/9780429432064

Typeset in Times New Roman
by Apex CoVantage, LLC

Contents

Acknowledgments

This book is the result of many years of practice of psychoanalysis – as an analysand, a member of various psychoanalytic groups and associations, and a psychoanalyst. I am grateful to everyone – teachers, patients, and analysands – who have taught me along the way. I would like to thank all the contributors to this book, who enthusiastically agreed to participate in this project. I was impressed by their generosity and level of participation. Firstly, I want to thank Michael Holosko, who helped me imagine, conceptualize, and design this book. Secondly, I want to thank Gabriele Lodari and Renata Miletto, who discussed this project with me from the beginning, providing me with important feedback and ideas, and contributing to its realization.

This book was originally written in Italian and French, and then translated into English. It has been a long process, but a very interesting one. Translating and proofreading a text is very close to the work of a psychoanalyst, as in the process of translation all the assumptions, equivocity, and contradictions of a text emerge. I am indeed very grateful to all of those who helped me translate: Esther Leong, William Heidbreder, Alma Buholzer, and Sam Warren Miell. A very special thanks to Kazuo Hope for reading all the chapters drafts and for his important feedbacks on the readability of the text. And thanks to all of those who I have not named, but who never failed to offer me their advice and continuous support to improve this book.

Glossary

Castration: The term castration is used by Lacan in several senses: for the purposes of this work, I refer to Lacan's use of it to describe the effect of the intervention of the (symbolic) Law on a living being. It is to be understood, therefore, not in reference to the purely imaginary aspect of the Oedipal story reduced to narration, which is now outdated (the father who threatens to evirate his son), but as a product of the very action of language (of which the symbolic father is the representative) on the body, action of libidinal emptying that installs a structural lack. Castration, in this sense, designates the mechanism of production of a *béance* (gap) from which desire will originate as a tension to its filling (F. Lolli).

Clinic: The term 'clinic' has, in Italian, French, Spanish, and Portuguese a sense which is broader than a building, or a type of practice within a building. Generally, 'clinical' is opposed to 'theoretical'. A clinician is someone who sees patients, whereas someone who conducts laboratory studies is a researcher or an academic. However, in psychoanalysis theory and practice are intertwined; practice is not simply the application of a theory. Then, in psychoanalysis 'clinic' does not only refer to the clinical work, or treatment, but *also* to a clinical understanding of a certain phenomenon. To some extent, 'clinic' is related to psychopathology, which is commonly understood as the study of the origin, development, diagnosis, and treatment of mental and behavioral disorders. But psychopathology has a negative connotation. In psychopathology, symptoms (and everything that is an expression of the unconscious) are understood in terms of deviance from normality, disorders, malfunctioning, thus pathology. This is not the case with psychoanalysis. The word clinic comes from Ancient Greek κλίνειν *klinein* meaning to slope, lean or recline. κλίνη *klinē* is the bed and κλινικός *klinikos* is a physician who visits his patients in their beds. In Latin, this became *clīnicus*. In Italian, 'clinic' indicates the observation, testing, examination, diagnosis, and treatment of patients. The etymology of clinic is interesting. However, in psychoanalysis, we do not study/observe the patient, his/her behaviors, or the sign of illness, as in medicine, but instead, we focus on his/her speech. In psychoanalysis, we analyze how a person's speech/word slopes, lean, turns, bends. How it is biased. Clinic is the analysis of *how the speech/word unfolds*. This includes the study of symptoms, the (social, cultural, temporal) context in which they originate, and how they change through time, their course, how can they be understood; the analysis of the unconscious fantasy; the analysis of transference; the development of psychoanalytic technique and practice over time (D. Busiol).

Enjoyment: A typical human experience that language is, structurally, unable to say. Intimately connected to the concepts of death drive and compulsion to repeat, it indicates the presence in the living being of a type of unconscious satisfaction that escapes the pleasure principle and manifests itself in the body in the paroxysmal (and anti-hedonistic) forms of the accumulation of excitement. It, therefore, indicates the insistence of a tension to unconscious satisfaction unrelated to pleasure (understood as a reduction in the level of excitement of the system): its manifestation has the characteristics of trauma, surprise, an unexpected encounter, impersonal (*ça jouit*, says Lacan) that the subject, who is crossed without being aware of it, experiences as estranging (F. Lolli).

Fading: Referring to the structure of the fantasy (as described in this glossary), the logic with which Lacan articulates the fantasy would suggest that there can never be co-presence of the subject with the object. When the subject is present the object subtracts itself, and when the object emerges the subject fades away in a fading movement, as when a record, instead of ending on a final chord, fades away little by little (M. Focchi).

Fantasy, or phantasm (*fantasme* in French):   this is the operative way in which each person relates to the world. In its original form, it is the idea (Lacan), that is to say, the mode of the relation to the object. (G. Lodari) The fantasy is an imaginary scenario that depicts a peculiar pattern of satisfaction of the desire for the subject. In Lacan, it is described as a logical articulation where the subject vanishes before the emergence of the object of desire. (M. Focchi).

Fantasy of mastery: this is the way in which the maternal fantasy deals with things of the world, subtracting them from the word, in the belief that it is able to grasp and dominate them (G. Lodari).

Gaze: Lacan adds the two objects' gaze and voice to the Freudian series of drive objects (which includes breast and feces). These are intangible objects, which are essentially subtractive in nature. The gaze is a glimmer, a flash of something that has disappeared as soon as it is glimpsed, just as the voice emerges from what is inaudible in the word (M. Focchi).

Hole/Lack: what for Freud was castration is formalized and generalized by Lacan as lack. The symbolic is not complete; something is missing, and this is what mobilizes desire. The lack, precisely because it refers to the symbolic, is related to a concept of order: something is missing, not in an absolute sense, but it is missing from its place. The hole is not related to a concept of order; it is something more radical. If we refer to what we said about the Real, we can say that because it is never reabsorbed by the symbolic, the Real is what constitutes a hole in the symbolic (M. Focchi).

Interval: time has no autonomous or independent existence from the word; it is 'time' in the word. In the interval, by doing, time settles. Therefore, the interval does not take place between two 'times' and is not even included in a place. The interval is the structure in which the Other (the unconscious) is operating. It is the 'time' other, where things happen in contingency, in the act. The narrative, just like the act, belongs to the interval; they occur in the interval. Certainly, they do not develop in chronological time, understood as duration, as it happens for the account of facts (G. Lodari).

Logic of the word: ultimately, it is a matter of transforming the Aristotelian predicative logic, which informs not only the obsessive discourse but also the discourse that claims to cure it, into logic of the word. This logic is, then, the logic of the unconscious. The logic of the word requires the tripartition of the sign: name, signifier, and Other (or the Freudian unconscious) since it does not sustain itself on any foundation other than the act of speech itself. For this logic, in fact, no element is valid by itself; each one is a reference that allows one to move on to the next element. With the tripartition of the sign, the Aristotelian principles of identity, non-contradiction, and the excluded third also falter. The logic of the word has been extraordinarily elaborated and studied in the cyphermatics (G. Lodari).

Maternal fantasy: when the world is represented and believed to be already given rather than *in actu*, the fantasy (fantasme) risks degrading itself into maternal fantasy and fantasy of mastery. The act, which dwells free and arbitrary in the word, becomes a passage to the act. The maternal fantasy proceeds from the belief that fantasy can act rather than operate (G. Lodari).

Mirror, gaze, and voice: in the logic of the word, Freudian objects can only be understood as the object in the word: mirror, gaze, and voice. These are also originary conditions of syntax, phrase, and pragma, respectively. The mirror function, condition of the equivocal (or, of the slip) with which the signification starts, excludes any principle of identity. The gaze function, condition of the phrase with its lie, against any principle of non-contradiction. And the voice function, function "third", condition of the doing, therefore against the principle of the excluded third (G. Lodari).

Name of the name: a name that no longer functions in the repression, hence no longer opens to the equivocal, but keeps repeating identical to itself. A 'name of the name' blocks the signification and imposes an absolute sense. It consecrates the universal and the substance as a foundation; and prefers certainty over doubt (doubt that allows continuation). The name of the name is such in the maternal fantasy (G. Lodari).

Name, signifier, and Other: these are elements that pertain to the tripartition of the sign. A name is a signifier that functions in the repression, adjacent to another signifier. In psychoanalysis, unlike in theology (where it is rather the name that functions as name of the name), the condition for the name to function, thus starting the signification, is precisely the Other. Any signifying element, as long as it is unconscious, can function as a name and account for the variety of the word and reality. Thus, reality does not precede the word itself (G. Lodari).

Narrative (in Italian: *racconto*): the narrative is not the account of the facts, as both the obsessive person and common sense believe. The narrative is originary and happens; it has never (already) 'happened'. Facts are always fantasmatic constructions. The obsessive person, in his account, tends to favor the single memory, eradicating the phrase and isolating it from the narrative and making it a concept, always in an attempt to control things through the fantasy of mastery. But such operation of impoverishment of the narrative, which should remain originary and authentic, that is, pragmatic, is, in hindsight, consequent to any classification system. Instead of the narrative, which allows the doing, in the chronicle of the obsessive person the sterile account of the facts prevails. Memories prevail at the expense of the memory. Only the narrative and poetry allow an authentic and originary relationship with the world. The world is never already given, but every time it is necessary to invent it (G. Lodari).

Other: Lacan distinguishes the figure of the other (with a lowercase o) from that of the Other (with a capital O). In the first case, the other is to be understood as the subject's interlocutor on the plane of reality, the set of partners in flesh and bones with whom s/he interacts. Feelings and emotions (regardless of their emotional tone) are projected onto the similar person. The Other with a capital O is considered by Lacan as the symbolic place from which the subject takes the material s/he uses (through identifying mechanisms) to represent him/herself in the world: it designates, therefore, the sum of expectations and signifiers that anticipate and prepare his/her coming into the world and, more generally, the world of representations that structure his/her universe of meaning (F. Lolli).

Phallus: this indicates a lack (on the symbolic level) and the object supposed to be able to fill it (on the imaginary level) at the same time. The phallus is, in Lacanian terminology, the object that the child identifies him/herself as, capable, imaginarily indeed, of completely satisfying the maternal desire. This identification with the phallus represents one of the ways in which secondary narcissism is affirmed within the evolutionary history of the child. The failure of the project to fully satisfy the maternal desire constitutes the experience of phallic trauma: in other words, the verification of one's own inadequacy in relation to the grandeur of the task assigned (F. Lolli).

Phantasm: see Fantasy.

Real: for Lacan, the human world is essentially symbolic, and from the beginning of the orientation he gives for conducting the cure he presents the coordinates of the symbolic and the imaginary as bearings. However, the network of the symbolic does not cover the totality of the psychoanalytic experience, especially with regard to sexuality. The Real is therefore what remains undetermined by the laws of the symbolic (M. Focchi).

Semblant: the semblant is the object within the word. From the Freudian object of desire to Lacan's object a – object cause of desire – to the semblant, that is, the object that is non-final cause (that has no purpose), and object with no origin. Object without place and elusive. Object of provocation and obstacle, it is necessary for the journey to start. Experience and formation lead the analyst to inhabit this non-place from which the act originates. Theorized by Armando Verdiglione, the semblant is characterized by its functions of mirror, gaze, and voice (G. Lodari).

Universal quantifier: in logic, it is the universal property that is believed could be assigned to every element of a system. Considering death as a universal quantifier means accepting it as an absolute value, according to the well-known Aristotelian syllogism: all men are mortal, Socrates is a man, therefore Socrates is mortal. In the logic of the word, there are no longer universal quantifiers. Each element can function as a name and can, therefore, be equivocated. The word and the narrative do not end, even things do not end (G. Lodari).

Contributors

It is not my intention here to revisit all the evolutions of Lacanian psychoanalysis in Italy over the last forty years. I just want to point out that this is a rather heterogeneous field, within which different associations coexist, and sometime even in contrast with each other. Some associations refer to Miller's *École de la Cause freudienne*, others to Melman's *Association Lacanienne Internationale*, and others were founded by psychoanalysts who trained in these associations then left them. When writing this book, I was able to collect the contributions of various psychoanalysts belonging to different associations, and I thank them for having participated despite the differences, not only theoretical, that separate them. I believe that the richness of this book also lies in this diversity. I think that for the purposes of this book it would be too complex for me, and perhaps misleading for the reader, to describe the landscape of all Lacanian associations and groups in Italy. I find it far more interesting and practical to let each author briefly present him/herself and his/her formation: the associations in which s/he trained and grew, his/her teachers and reference points, the groups s/he attended and/or founded, the initiatives s/he took part in, the contexts in which s/he currently operates.

Perhaps in this way the reader can better appreciate that there is not only one (or, The) Lacanian psychoanalysis. In fact, there is no psychoanalytic theory that one could simply apply to the case, in session: this would be a doctrine. Theory and practice are interconnected; one originates from and clarifies itself in the other. And when I talk about the practice of psychoanalysis, I do not just refer to the patients an analyst has had and has. I also refer to one's own personal analysis, and therefore to the transference towards psychoanalysis, towards one's psychoanalyst (sometimes more than one), towards one's teachers (those met in person, or through texts). And I refer to the vicissitudes of the transference: ruptures, detachments, distances, returns. Therefore, each one has a personal and unrepeatable journey. After a brief note about my journey, I will leave it to the Italian psychoanalysts to say something about their formation and their practice (please note that all are autobiographical, but some are in the first and others in the third person).

About the editor

Busiol, Diego: In 1997 I enrolled in the faculty of psychology (in Turin, Italy), even though I knew that there was little room for psychoanalysis (Lacanian in particular) at university. During my university years I certainly devoted more time to attending study groups, conferences, and seminars about psychoanalysis, than to my academic course. In particular, my psychoanalytic formation began within the association *Tracce Freudiane* [Freudian Traces] founded by Gabriele Lodari (Chapter 7 of this book). With this association I also took my first steps as a speaker at some conferences, and I published my first writings. Since 2002 I have been working as an educator in various psychiatric community residences. From 2006 to 2010 I trained as a psychotherapist at *Laboratorio Freudiano per la formazione degli psicoterapeuti di Milano* [Freudian Laboratory for the formation of psychotherapists, Milan] and at *Associazione lacaniana internazionale (ALI) di Torino* [International Lacanian Association, Turin], following the teachings of Renata Miletto (Chapter 14) and Fabrizio Gambini (Chapter 8). I have been living in Hong Kong since 2010, where I moved to do a PhD. The desire for the unknown, for what is foreign, that is, that same desire that led me to encounter psychoanalysis, has led me to a place where there is no psychoanalysis. I wrote about this unique experience in the book: *Psychoanalysis in Hong Kong: The Absent, the Present, and the Reinvented* (Routledge, 2016). After completing my doctorate, I worked in a university as a researcher, but above all I dedicated myself to clinical practice. Today I am one of the very few (if not the only) psychoanalysts in Hong Kong. Personal website: www.drbusiol.com

The Italian Contributors

Benvenuto, Sergio is a psychoanalyst and philosopher, living in Rome. He is a researcher at the National Council for Scientific Research (CNR) in Rome, Italy, at the former Institute of Psychology. He is the president of the Institute for Advanced Studies in Psychoanalysis (ISAP) in Italy. From 1995 to the present he has been the editor of *EJP. European Journal of Psychoanalysis*, and he is a member of the Editorial Board of *American Imago*. He is a contributor to journals such as *Telos, Lettre Internationale* (Berlin), *Journal for Lacanian Studies, L'évolution psychiatrique, Division/Review, Psychoanalytic Discourse, Journal of American Psychoanalytic Association*. He has worked on Freud and Lacan, Wittgenstein and ethics, Plato's philosophy of Eros, Theory of Fashion, Theory of populism, and Monotheisms (with J.-L. Nancy). His publications, in many different languages, include: Perversion and charity: an ethical approach, in D. Nobus & L. Downing eds., *Perversion. Psychoanalytic Perspectives/Perspectives on Psychoanalysis* (London: Karnac, 2006, pp. 59–78); with A. Molino, *In Freud's Tracks* (New York: Aronson, 2008); Ethics, Wonder and Real in Wittgenstein, in Y. Gustafsson,

C. Kronqvist, H. Nykänen, eds., *Ethics and the Philosophy of Culture: Wittgensteinian Approaches*, (Cambridge Scholar Publishing, 2013, pp. 137–159); *What Are Perversions?* (London: Karnac, 2016); *Conversations with Lacan* (London: Routledge, 2020). Personal site and Bibliography: www.sergiobenvenuto.it./

Calciolari, Giancarlo has a background in psychoanalysis. He graduated in psychology in 1982 and is a writer of culture, art, and science. He has written several books, including *Teoria della cucina* [Theory of cuisine] and *L'oro della balbuzie* [The gold of stuttering].

Cosenza, Domenico, psychologist and psychotherapist, PhD in psychoanalysis from the University of Paris 8. He is a psychoanalyst in a private practice in Milan, Italy. He is an Analyst Member (AME) and past President of the Lacanian School of Psychoanalysis (SLP) (2013–2016) and member of the World Association of Psychoanalysis (WAP). In 2017 he was elected President of the Euro Federation of Psychoanalysis (EFP). He teaches at the Clinical Section of Milan and is frequently invited to teach in other clinical sections in Spain, France, and Italy. He also teaches developmental psychopathology in the Department of Psychology at Pavia University. He has extensive experience working in clinical institutions for eating disorders in Italy (ABA, therapeutic community residence "La Vela"), and was member of the board of the FIDA (*Federazione Italiana Disturbi Alimentari*, [Italian Federation of Eating Disorders]). He is president of Kliné, Milanese center of FIDA. He is the author of several books, among them: *Jacques Lacan e il problema della tecnica in psicoanalisi* [Jacques Lacan and the problem of technique in psychoanalysis] (Astrolabio 2003), *Il muro dell'anoressia* [The wall of anorexia] (Astrolabio 2008), *Le refus dans l'anorexie* [Refusal in anorexia] (Presses Universitaires de Rennes 2014), and *Il cibo e l'inconscio* [The food and the unconscious] (FrancoAngeli 2018).

Focchi, Marco: Milan has always been a place for the intertwining of encounters and cultural possibilities, and Lacan began to spend time there during his early years and make his mark in the field. In my first year of university, in 1972, in a psychology exam with Prof. Enzo Funari, well-known pupil of Cesare Musatti, the founder of psychoanalysis in Italy, in the list of complementary texts was indicated *La cosa freudiana*, the first collection of Lacan's texts published in Italy. For a first-year student it was not an easy reading, but it hooked me, and it was from there that my relationship with Lacan began, which led me to Jacques Alain Miller's couch. All the following stages that have led to the creation of the Lacanian Institution in Italy developed from this encounter with him. First I founded, in 1980, with some colleagues and friends, the *Centro Culturale Agalma* [Agalma Cultural Center], which later merged into GISEP, the study group that prepared the creation of the *Scuola Lacaniana di Psicoanalisi (SLP)* [Lacanian School of Psychoanalysis], of which I was president, and which is part of the *Associazione Mondiale di Psicoanalisi (AMP)*

[World Association of Psychoanalysis, WAP]. I was a member of the Board of Directors of the latter for a few years. I am currently director of the *Istituto freudiano per la clinica, la terapia e la scienza* [Freudian Institute for Clinic, Therapy and Science], an institution that provides the legal title for the practice of psychotherapy in Italy.

Gambini, Fabrizio: Born in Piombino (LI) on 31 July 1953, he graduated in Medicine and Surgery at the *Prima Facoltà di Medicina e Chirurgia* with a thesis (Supervisor Prof. Dargut Kemali) on "The mental illness as a disorder of nature from the French Revolution to 1860". He specialized in psychiatry at the *Clinica Psichiatrica della Prima Facoltà di Medicina e Chirurgia dell'Università di Napoli* [Psychiatric Clinic of the First Faculty of Medicine and Surgery of the University of Naples] with a thesis on "The psychiatric concept of crisis" (Supervisor Prof. Dargut Kemali). He attended the Leonardo Bianchi Psychiatric Hospital in Naples as a volunteer student, and the Furlone Psychiatric Hospital in Naples, directed by Prof. Sergio Piro, as a Volunteer Medical Assistant. He was a member of the Operational Unit of the CNR (National Research Center) "Sub-project aimed at the prevention of Mental Illness" directed by prof. Sergio Piro. Since 1982 he has worked in Collegno (TO), initially at the former Psychiatric Hospital and then at the CSM (Center for Mental Health). Later, he directed the District 1 (Mental Health Center and Day Hospital) of the DSM (Department of Mental Health) of ASSL 2 and the SPDC (Psychiatric Diagnosis and Care Service) of the Mauriziano Umberto I Hospital, in Turin. He is a member (AMA, *Analyste Membre de l'Association*) of the ALI (*Association Lacanienne Internationale*) and lecturer at the School of Specialization in Psychotherapy *Laboratorio Freudiano* [Freudian Laboratory] in Rome and Milan. He has published numerous essays in psychoanalysis and psychiatry journals and is the author of *L'acredine pungitiva. La follia come disturbo di natura dal Rinascimento al 1860* [Stinging bitterness. Madness as a disturbance of nature from the Renaissance to 1860] (in collaboration with Paolo Schettino), Tempi Moderni, Salerno 1980; *Freud e Lacan in psichiatria* [Freud and Lacan in psychiatry], Raffaello Cortina, Milan, 2006; *L'ora del falso sentire. Psicoanalisi e disturbi dell'umore* [The hour of false feeling. Psychoanalysis and mood disorders], Franco Angeli, Milan, 2011; *Paranoie. Tra psichiatria e psicoanalisi: saperci fare con la psicosi* [Paranoia. Between psychiatry and psychoanalysis: knowing how to deal with psychosis], Franco Angeli, Milan, 2015; *Dodici luoghi lacaniani della psicoanalisi* [Twelve Lacanian places of psychoanalysis], Franco Angeli, Milan, 2018. Together with Mauro Milanaccio he edited the collective volume: *Perché la topologia* [Why topology], Galaad, Milan 2019.

Lodari, Gabriele: My mother tongue is French. I have always been interested in literature, philosophy, linguistics, and social sciences. I graduated in Milan with Professor Carlo Sini with a thesis on the text that remains fundamental for me, by Paul Ricoeur, *Freud and Philosophy: An Essay on Interpretation*.

After my discovery of psychoanalysis, and in particular of Jacques Lacan's *Écrits*, I decided to get a degree in psychotherapy (there was no other way to practice as a psychoanalyst, without being denounced for illegal practice of the profession) by attending the *Istituto Freudiano di Roma* [Freudian Institute of Rome]. I have participated in numerous conferences in Italy and abroad. Later, I founded my association, *Tracce Freudiane* [Freudian Traces], organizing multiple annual conferences, "cartels", and study groups, and continuing, with a weekly frequency never interrupted until today, the seminar I conduct around different theoretical and clinical themes. I have published books, monographs, and various articles. As for my professional profile, I was a teacher of community psychology at the University of Eastern Piedmont for a few years, and currently I am still a consultant and trainer of educators in the psychomedical team of three institutes that host severe psychotics and young autistic people. My last published book, *Il sogno e la voce* [The dream and the voice], collects reflections on my experience with autism.

Lolli, Franco: My training in psychoanalysis began in the early 1990s within the then-called *Sezione Italiana della Scuola Europea di Psicoanalisi* [Italian Section of the European School of Psychoanalysis] (SISEP), which later became the *Scuola Lacaniana di Psicoanalisi* [Lacanian School of Psychoanalysis] (SLP), an institution belonging to the World Association of Psychoanalysis (WAP). My experience of psychoanalysis and the many experiences of supervision took place between Rome and Paris. Since the end of the 1990s, I have progressively reduced my participation in the activities of the SLP and decided to leave it to join *Espace Analytique*, to which I still belong. I am an analyst member of *Associazione Lacaniana Italiana di Psicoanalisi* [Italian Lacanian Association of Psychoanalysis] (ALIPsi) and president of *Litorale – Associazione di Ricerca, Cultura e Formazione in Psicoanalisi* [Litorale – Association for Research, Culture and Training in Psychoanalysis]. I participated in helping to build up a network of Psychoanalytic Clinic Centers which extended throughout Italy and built a Psychotherapy Training School of which for eight years I was director. I am the author of many psychoanalysis essays and contributor to several journals and a national newspaper. I am a supervisor at numerous public and private bodies, and scientific consultant of various social and health cooperatives.

Miletto, Renata lives and works as a psychoanalyst in Turin. Born in 1949, she first graduated in philosophy and then, in 1981, in psychology. She first approached psychoanalysis in the early 1980s, with a long internship at the child psychiatry department of a city hospital, which had a Kleinian orientation. In that same period, she discovered Lacan and was struck by him, sensing, beyond the complexity of his style, a conception of the unconscious and of the transference which was in line with her first clinical experiences. She then started attending the seminars of Dr. Costantino Gilardi, who brought back to Turin the teachings and working style of the *Association freudienne*

[Freudian Association] of Paris, founded in 1982 by Charles Melman. In this context, in 1989 she participated in the foundation (in Italy) of the *Associazione freudiana* [Freudian Association], which a few years later became the *Associazione lacaniana internazionale* [International Lacanian Association] (ALI), following the path of the French ALI, where her continuing formation as a psychoanalyst took place. She accompanies clinical practice with training activities, organizes seminars and study days, and participates in the teachings of the *Laboratorio freudiano* [Freudian Laboratory], School of Psychotherapy in Rome and Milan. In 2010 she participated in the foundation of ALI in Italy, which brings together the ALI associations of Milan, Rome, Naples, and Turin with the aim of encouraging exchange and comparison and therefore promoting the transmission of psychoanalysis according to Lacan's teachings.

Recalcati, Massimo teaches at the universities of Pavia and Verona. He is scientific director of the Research Institute of Applied Psychoanalysis (IRPA). His books have been translated into several languages.

The French Contributors

Chassaing, Jean-Louis; psychoanalyst and psychiatrist. He practices in the center of France (Auvergne) in Clermont-Ferrand. He completed his psychoanalytic training in Paris and has maintained many links with the capital. He is a member and currently the Secretary of the *Association Lacanienne internationale* [International Lacanian Association, ALI] and was one of the few founders of the *Fondation Européenne pour la Psychanalyse* [European Psychoanalytic Federation]. He is the former Assistant in the psychiatry department of the University Hospital Centre of Clermont-Ferrand, and a former Hospital Practitioner of this department. He taught psychiatry at the Clermont-Ferrand University of Medicine. He now teaches at *EPhEP*, a practical school for advanced studies in psychopathologies in Paris. He is a member of the editorial board of *La Revue Lacanienne* [The Lacanian Review]. His numerous publications on psychiatry and psychoanalysis mainly concern toxicomanias and addictions, borderline states, and the history of concepts. Among others, we can cite *Écrits psychanalytiques classiques sur les toxicomanies* [Classic Psychoanalytic Writings on toxicomania], coordinated by Chassaing, Jean-Louis, with the help of Balbure, B, Dufour, A & Petit, P, C. Paris: Éditions de l'Association freudienne (today the ALI), 1998; *Drogue et langage –du corps et de la langue* [The drug and language – the body and the language], published in 2011; Erès editions; *Présentation* [Presentation] (coll. P. Maugeais) republication *Les Morphinomanes* [Morphine Addictions] by Ernest Chambard, Frénésie editions, coll. Insania, 1988; *Jeu, dette et repetition. Les rapports de la cure psychanalytique avec le jeu* [Gambling, debt and repetition. The relationship between psychoanalytic treatment and gambling] (coord. with C. Bucher and C. Melman), editions from ALI, 2005; *Psychanalyse et* *psychiatrie. Demandes et réponses contemporaines* [Psychoanalysis and Psychiatry. Contemporary demands and responses], érès editions, collection *Point Hors ligne.*

Cacciali, Jean-Luc; psychiatrist, psychoanalyst in Grenoble. AMA member of the *Association Lacanienne internationale* [International Lacanian Association, ALI] (member of its Board of Directors, its Bureau Committee, and its Teaching Commission). Author of articles, conferences, and teachings.

Cacciali, Paule; psychoanalyst in Grenoble. AMA member of the *Association Lacanienne internationale* [International Lacanian Association, ALI]. Practitioner of Psychoanalysis. DESS (Diploma of Specialized Higher Studies) in Clinical Psychology. Member of the ALI Research Circle on the prevention of autistic risks in babies.

Melman, Charles; psychoanalyst and writer. In 1982, he founded the *Association Freudienne*, which a few years later became the *Association Lacanienne internationale* (ALI).

Introduction

Diego Busiol

From the moment my own personal psychoanalysis began – in the mid-1990s – the way I listen to and understand various issues in the world, and in life, has changed. For me, psychoanalysis has never represented only a therapy, something that occurs in a specific time and place, but is first and foremost a way of thinking, a way of examining and analyzing things. As I started to regularly lay on my psychoanalyst's couch, I started reading the writings of the great psychoanalysts of the past (and also about philosophy, anthropology, linguistics, poetry, and much more) and attending various conferences, seminars, and psychoanalytic study groups (which Lacanians call "cartels"). Analyzing the unconscious immediately seemed to me the most obvious thing to do, and the most pragmatic, but also the most fun. This is how my psychoanalytic journey began.

Soon after obtaining a master's degree in clinical psychology, I started working in the field of so-called mental health, where I could finally become acquainted with psychosis and psychiatry. These were very formative years. Later, I completed my formal training in psychotherapy (in Italy, like in many other countries, the practice of psychotherapy and/or psychoanalysis is regulated by law. I will speak more about this in Chapter 5), and I started to see my first patients in a private practice. In 2010, I moved to Hong Kong to do a PhD (that revolved around the question: why there is no psychoanalysis in Hong Kong?), and I have lived there ever since. I then continued working in a university as a researcher, and parallel to this, I resumed my activity as a psychoanalyst in a private practice.

In Hong Kong, I have had the opportunity to work with a very diverse population. This has included not only Chinese people, but also Italians like me, and foreigners from all over the world: Europeans, Americans (North, South, Caribbean), Australians, and Asians (India, Bangladesh, Korea, and others). People come to me with different motives. Normally, Italians contact me because they are looking for a psychologist and prefer to speak in their native language; often, they do not even know that I am a psychoanalyst. On the contrary, most Chinese people who contact me do so precisely because I am a psychoanalyst; they are young, they have often studied abroad where they have heard about psychoanalysis and feel that it is something unique that could be right for them. People from other countries have had different motivations to come and see me. Some people

DOI: 10.4324/9780429432064-1

contact me because they're looking for a psychoanalyst and are not interested in other types of psychotherapy. Others come to me simply by word of mouth. Others have found my name on the internet, so come quite casually. With these people in particular, it is not always clear what they are looking for, but it is easy to feel that they are in a hurry; and often, after a quick appearance, they disappear again.

Hong Kong is a fast-paced city, a city that never stops: materialistic, always oriented around business, profit, very practical. All of this comes at the expense of thinking, talking, listening to the unconscious. It is a place with a lot of coming and going. It is beautiful and unique, yet historically it has always been a transit place, maybe even more so in recent years. Some of my patients have even called it a "non-place". All of this is reflected in the kind of demand for treatment that I receive. Many patients report being disoriented, without direction in life. These are often people who lead a particular life, away from their country of origin. A life that can be full of extreme freedom, comfort, continuous possibilities of encounters, trips, and entertainment. But this freedom (from the family, cultural, social context of origin; from social ties, norms; from the Other) sometimes results precisely in a loss of reference points (Where do I come from? Where am I going? What do I want?), in being uprooted from the world, adrift. At some point, being nomadic no longer sounds like a dream. The feeling of being a "citizen of the world", which is initially liberating for some people, shows its bitter flip side and now sounds more like a curse, as the feelings of not being based on anything solid, having no foundations or structure, not really feeling "at home" anywhere, and being really lost settle in. This raises various questions for a psychoanalyst. And it is inevitably reflected in the practice: as to how patients' demands are re-formulated, what issues they bring into the session, how they "stay" in therapy (often, with one foot in and one out), how the analyses start (if and when they start), and also how they end.

While I have been thinking a lot about what kind of clinical work can be done in a place like Hong Kong, I have also wondered how it is possible that there is no echo of psychoanalysis in an international city like this, even among those who work as counselors or psychotherapists. In Hong Kong there are many counselors and psychologists (both local and foreigners) and many of them have trained abroad. Most of them have an eclectic approach, informed by the most diverse orientations or techniques (some, I must confess, I had never heard of before I came here), but only a few of them have received psychoanalytic training or report being inspired by psychoanalysis in their clinical practice. I often ask myself: what guides these counsellors and therapists in their clinical work? I have not found a definitive answer to this question. I have the impression, however, that many counselors and therapists could benefit from reading clinic psychoanalytic literature, if it were available to them.

These are some of the observations that made me realize there was a need for me to write this book. A book that – through a dialogue with expert psychoanalysts – could help me rethink and address some questions that arose from my clinical practice; a book that could then be of help to other psychotherapists, who may not be so familiar with psychoanalysis; but also a book that could help Lacanian psychoanalysis become more accessible (to therapists of different orientation, but also more generally to anyone interested in psychoanalysis), and thus a book that could give a glimpse of how psychoanalysis works in practice. The present book is then intended to: 1) rethink the clinic with patients; 2) provide a useful tool to counselors/psychotherapists of other orientations, and for less experienced analysts in training; and 3) present the Lacanian clinic orientation (especially Italian) to an international audience.

To rethink the clinic with patients

Psychoanalytic listening is the leitmotif of this book. First of all, how and what does a psychoanalyst listen to/for? How to effectively listen, and thus understand, something from the unconscious? And subsequently, how to make the patient listen, and feel, something from the unconscious? That is to say, how to make a patient understand that there is something else in what s/he is saying, and that this is exactly what s/he needs to pay attention to? The first part of this book (Chapters 1 to 4 in particular) aims to address these questions more explicitly.

It is even more of a challenge today with patients who present "new" forms of the symptom – meaning new forms of expression of discomfort that have their roots in a social discourse deeply different from that circulating at Freud's times – such as anorexia and bulimia, panic attacks, addictions, with borderline patients, and those who are lost, adrift, without direction (Not to mention all the economic and technological changes that have so deeply affected our lifestyle throughout these years, including how the food is produced and consumed, our relation with work and leisure time, the advancements in medicine; And also all those objects and those substances – from drugs to psychotropic drugs, from the Internet to mobile phones – that did not exist a century ago and that have a big impact on the formation and the expression of symptoms today). Some of these factors will be further discussed in chapter 1. They are often people with complex, rich, and interesting lives, but who seem to find it very difficult to think of a dimension *of word* (indeed, the new symptoms have to do with *substances*, not words). They talk, but they do not listen; they act, but they don't feel. They generally show little curiosity about their symptoms, which in fact seem foreign to them, devoid of meaning, and not of relation to their own lives. Lacking this curiosity for what they do not know or understand (curiosity that to a certain extent the "classic" neurotic had), they focus on answers, solutions, remedies. And they enter a vicious circle: between the urgency of having immediate answers (they have very little patience, do not tolerate waiting, imagine they can receive textbook answers, and often if they do not receive prompt answers they quit therapy), the frustration resulting from each answer (because each answer can only be partial, temporary, and therefore never entirely satisfactory), but also and importantly *the deep anxiety of really discovering something about themselves*, of approaching what they feel as a dangerous internal void into which they risk falling.

Apparently, they want more knowledge, but of a universal kind, for example how to deal with their symptoms. They may not always be interested (or ready) to know about themselves. And often, they quit psychoanalysis *when the analysis progresses – not when it stagnates*. They leave very little room for maneuver. Then I asked myself: how do I intercept them in their wandering, and how can I help them to *stay*? And how can I involve them in psychoanalysis, without necessarily promising quick solutions and without acting as a coach or teacher, but at the same time providing some effective intervention that allows them to engage in the process and ask themselves some questions. That is to say, how to keep them on a word level and prevent them from passing to the act, meaning how to help them analyzing and dissolving their fantasies, rather than acting them out?

Chapters 6 to 17 focus on the differences between "classic" and "modern" symptoms, with also a spotlight on some "transversal" issues, that is to say, issues that do not belong only to a specific discourse, but that we find frequently in the clinic today. The clinic has changed a lot since Freud's time. Today we no longer see "classic" cases of hysteria such as those described by Freud. This does not mean that the hysteria has disappeared; more likely, it manifests itself in different ways, which it is important to recognize. In Part 2, therefore, some forms of hysteria, obsessional neurosis, and paranoia are analyzed, as they may present themselves today. Part 3 explores the symptoms we most frequently see today: anxiety and panic attacks; anorexia, bulimia, binge eating, and obesity; depressions; addictions; and borderline states. Many people may mistakenly think that psychoanalysis is not effective in listening to and treating these "modern" symptoms (modern in the sense that they are, at least in part, a product of modernity). In these chapters, however, the characteristics of these symptoms are examined, as well as the critical issues they pose to clinical work, and how they can be addressed in the session. Finally, Part 4 deals with a series of "transversal" issues. The social changes taking place today have led to what Lacan called the "evaporation of the father's name". This has its consequences. First of all, it means a strengthening of the maternal dimension. In this section some issues that reflect this greater incidence of the maternal dimension and this evaporation of the father's name are presented: the relationship with the mother; perversions; the clinic of the void; and jealousy.

To provide a useful tool to counselors/ psychotherapists of other orientations and for less experienced analysts in training

For many, psychoanalysis is something out of date. However, seeing how most counselors work has further convinced me to write this book, because I think that psychoanalysis really has something unique and innovative compared to all the other orientations. Speaking with some counselors, I was asked what I specialize in. At first, I didn't understand what this meant. Then I realized that counselors "specialize" in treating a certain/specific symptom or disorder. In some ways it also seems reasonable; after all, this is how medicine works. But my clinical experience seems to suggest the opposite, namely that the same symptom can have an absolutely different weight and meaning in the psychic economy and in the history of different people. Being able to specialize in the treatment of a particular symptom seems to me more like a way of controlling the therapist's own anxiety when faced with an unfamiliar situation/symptom. And thinking that everything that is said can be interpreted on the basis of general, academic knowledge does not encourage listening.

It is not only patients who lack the ability to listen (this can be expected from them), but also many therapists (and this is a big problem). Taken by the anxiety to find answers and solutions, they do not listen and instead resort immediately to this or that theory or technique, or to providing advice, suggestions, explanations, or interpretations (according to their own comprehension, thus their fantasy*, without being aware of it, of course).[1] Giving generic answers can temporarily relieve the anxiety of both the therapist and the patient. But it does not lead to discovering much of the functioning of one's own unconscious; it does not allow for any advancement with respect to one's own issues. Therefore, I think that honing the listening skills in this profession is fundamental, regardless of the theoretical orientation of the therapist.

To present the Lacanian clinic orientation (especially Italian) to an international audience

There are too many "introductions to Lacan". They are often vague texts, based on repetitions of out-of-context formulas, slogans, and concepts. Most importantly, they are often written by people with no clinical experience. Particularly in anglophone countries, Lacan is known more among intellectuals and academics than among practitioners. But Lacan was a psychoanalyst, not a philosopher. What he said might seem abstract to those who do not have an analytical experience, but in reality it is very concrete. Unfortunately, today there are too many stereotypes and myths about psychoanalytic practice, especially Lacanian practice. This is why I asked various analysts to talk about how they operate in sessions, without technicalities and jargon. This book stems from clinical issues, is written by practicing psychoanalysts, and does not only present theoretical concepts, but their actual use in practice.

In particular, living abroad, I realized how little of the psychoanalysis that I know (mainly Italian) is available in English. It is a pity, because in Italy there is an important psychoanalytic tradition, which is largely unknown outside national borders. I therefore thought of collecting in a book the contributions of some expert psychoanalysts, who have published books, teach in psychoanalytic institutes, and/or regularly hold conferences and seminars. Chapters 4 and 6–17 collect the contributions of these psychoanalysts.

Writing this book, I encountered a number of significant difficulties. For example, as I was planning to interview several authors on different topics, I first thought to submit all authors a similar list of questions. Ideally, this would have helped obtain similar chapters, in terms of structure, length, and style. However, I soon realized my naivety in this idea. In fact, none of the contributors to this book took my questions into account, and each of them answered in their own way, different from each other: some reported a single clinical case, others started from Freud's writing before presenting their own practice, others presented many short clinical cases, and so on. I find there is something exquisitely psychoanalytic in this.

It is in some ways impossible to say how an analyst should operate in a session, because a standard cannot be set. It is not possible to describe a procedure to be followed step-by-step, as happens in other professions (e.g., social workers, counselors, behavioral therapists), because the analysis follows the patient's word – his/her memories, free associations, forgetfulness – and not the therapist's word. Therefore, the direction that an analysis will take cannot be decided a priori. Freud said that in analysis, as in chess, it is possible to describe only the opening moves. Of course, in psychoanalysis we speak of *structures* or *discourses*, and therefore we can identify or isolate some issues, some figures of speech; but then, each case is unique, it is described by a particular trait and it is precisely on that trait that the analysis is played out. Then, the unfolding of an analysis, with its vicissitudes, depends more on the encounter of two desires than on the application of a technique. Therefore, it has more to do with ethics, than with technique (although there is a technique too). If there were a universal technique, only to be applied each time, analyst and analysand would both be in the position of object (object of a manual to be followed, for example; or object of treatment). Instead, in analysis it is first of all a question of desire. Consequently, it is impossible to say in advance what the intervention "to do" will be. The effective intervention is a word that is animated by the analyst's desire, and touches something of the analysand's desire, making something resonate in him/her. Without the analysand's speech, one could not imagine what to say. Indeed, effective intervention comes as a non-intervention; not as something external to what one is saying, but as something organic. It is something that has to do with improvisation, with wit. As such, it cannot be planned, codified, manualized. An analyst intervenes in the session according to his/her own style; not without the Other, however, that is, according to what the analysand says, in the contingency, and therefore in the invention.

Similarly, even the formation of an analyst cannot follow a path that is already outlined. Everyone becomes an analyst by having different experiences, with different teachers, listening to different patients, and cultivating their own style. Becoming a psychoanalyst is not limited to acquiring a technique, and certainly not a codified, standardized technique. In fact, this book is not a manual, and should not be taken as such. As you will see, each contributor thinks and writes differently (while a manual gives indications, information; in a manual the author does not count). And each chapter of this book is not representative of the way in which Lacanism has developed, but only of the particular journey of its author, that is to say, how that analyst has combined theory and clinical practice and continued his/her own formation. My hope is that this book will not set a standard (thus a limit) for each reader but will instead help each one to continue.

Last, but not least, most of this book has been translated by me (apart from Chapters 6 and 13, which have been translated by William Heidbreder and Sam Warren Miell, respectively, and Chapters 8 and 15, which have been translated by their authors). This has been a very difficult undertaking, and I am not at all sure

I have done justice to the authors. Translating is in some ways impossible, all the more so when writing about psychoanalysis, given the importance that we give to words, to signifiers. It is not just a matter of translating from one language into another. Thus, some passages may remain unclear. At times, it may be that my translation is not perfect. Other times, it may be that understanding what is being said is difficult because the subject we are dealing with is difficult. It is not necessary to understand everything with one read; some things may be understood later. I hope the reader will consider this.

Note

1 The * highlights terms that are listed in the glossary.

Part 1

Chapter 1

The evolution of psychic symptoms from Freud's *Studies on Hysteria* to today

Diego Busiol

The unconscious, this unknown

When I first arrived in Hong Kong in 2010, I was very surprised to see how little psychoanalysis was known here. Something that in Italy and in many Western countries has long been part of common knowledge (the psychoanalyst has been represented, even caricatured, in many movies; today, there are even many *memes* circulating on the internet depicting the psychoanalyst at work in his office, next to his couch), seemed to never have arrived in Hong Kong. I then decided to conduct research into what has hindered the reception and practice of psychoanalysis in this city (especially among local counselors, psychologists, and psychiatrists), and I discovered that one of the main reasons, although not the only one, was a difficulty in understanding what we mean when we talk about the unconscious: what it is, how it shows itself, and also how to use it in therapy (Busiol, 2016).

What can we say about the unconscious? The unconscious is not a concept, but something alive. Therefore, it cannot be explained, but only experienced first-hand. This is what makes psychoanalysis untransmissible to some extent. There are many psychoanalysis manuals; these may provide some form of knowledge *about* the unconscious. But one can only discover something that is unconscious through one's own lapses, free associations, slips of tongue, dreams, or forgetfulness. This is a knowledge that comes *from* the unconscious; as such, it is not universal, but unique for each person, and can be accessed primarily through one's own personal analysis. It is rather the scientific discourse that proceeds by accumulation of knowledge: a universal knowledge to which everyone can add a little piece, like when completing a puzzle. But an analysis does not continue from what others have discovered in their analyses. The unconscious is precisely a hole in the knowledge. What one discovers in an analysis are associations of words, fragments of memories. These discoveries can be illuminating for the speaker, but not necessarily for others. It is common for an analysand to be asked, "what do you talk about in session?" But it would be impossible to answer. The unconscious works for associations of signifiers, which is precisely what subverts the manifest, intended meaning. Therefore, it is impossible to generalize or decontextualize what is said in session. Any answer might only be disappointing.

DOI: 10.4324/9780429432064-3

There is no psychoanalytic knowledge that goes without analytical practice, unlike other psychologies/psychotherapies. Psychoanalysis is a primarily a practice of speech. Thus, there can be psychoanalysis only if there is practice of psychoanalysis. It is not a coincidence that in a place like Hong Kong only psychoanalysis is missing, while dozens of other psychologies, psychotherapies, and forms of counseling are practiced.

Practicing psychoanalysis in Hong Kong, with patients from all over the world, I realized that regardless of the country in question, the unconscious is always more unknown, misunderstood, and ignored. This is quite surprising after more than a century of psychoanalysis. There are probably several factors that can explain this phenomenon. These are not only individual, cultural, and economic factors, but also social and environmental factors that have to do with modernity. Today, the scientific discourse, which reduces the language to a tool for communicating and the signifier to sign, also dominates in Europe. But then, if distinctions are lost, if everything becomes univocal, the unconscious will also be lost. Conformism will prevail, and therefore: where is the unconscious, if everything means the same for everyone?

Hong Kong is a modern, business-oriented city with a very fast pace of life; a vertical city, full of skyscrapers and with a very high population density. It is a society that mixes capitalism and traditional Chinese values. And like any capitalist society, Hong Kong is a city that rewards efficiency, long working hours, and the ability to "function" smoothly. In this sense, it is a paradigmatic society of today. Indeed, in some ways it anticipates the times, and therefore can represent a privileged point of observation. Historically, it is a city built on business and commerce, and much less on arts and culture. We could say that in Hong Kong material values have always prevailed over immaterial and spiritual ones. It is not surprising that in such a context the space to think, to articulate a question, is limited. This obviously affects the reception and practice of psychoanalysis: I am one of the very few analysts in town. Conversely, there is a wide range of practices for the "well-being" of the individual: physical and mental. Once the question of the word[1] has been expunged, what remains is the dualism of body/mind, the first being the prerogative of medicine, the second being left to new-age practices, yoga, mindfulness, meditation, and to a various range of psychotherapies, but not psychoanalysis. This means that the response to the 'discomfort of civilization' takes place on two levels: reducing or removing the symptom, so as to get back to work as soon as possible, and promoting new enjoyment, fun, and carefreeness, so as to contrast the cause of discomfort and regain a good level of comfort. What is wrong on a personal level is fixed with some technique. What is not known on a social level, is sought in the discourse of science: procedures, standardized research, statistics. Science applied to commercial and human relations.

Today's patients

Working in this context, I soon noticed the lack of a demand for analysis in many patients. Some people came to my office asking to "try"; a bit like one can try a first class in the gym, before signing up. Others canceled appointments at the last moment, as if it were not something they are really committed to. Or, as if psychoanalysis could be an activity to do in their spare time. Initially, I was very surprised by this "one foot in and one foot out" or "seeing how it goes" approach. In the last century, patients went to analysis four or even five times a week. Today, one session a week seems already a lot. Things have changed a lot since Freud's time!

Melman (in Melman and Lebrun, 2018) notes that young people who go to therapy today do not know where they have come from or where they are going. He speaks of *atopic* subjects, who cannot find their place or their voice. Their path is fragmented, hesitant, and their identity (even sexual) restless. They carry with them a discomfort that they can hardly express in words. Costa and Lang (2016) observe that a large part of their patients "can hardly move past the complaint. Their demand is scattered, lacks implication, and people that seek psychotherapy almost never reach the level of communicating their desire" (p. 119). Verhaeghe (2008) compares yesterday's patients with those of today: "About 30 years ago I saw my first patient. My classic education and training meant that the following clinical characteristics were to be expected: a patient would have symptoms that can be interpreted; these symptoms are meaningful constructions, although the patient is unaware of this meaning due to defense mechanisms; the patient would be aware that these symptoms were connected with a life history"; today, however, "we meet with an absent-minded, indifferent attitude, together with distrust and a generally negative transference" (p. 1). At the same time, these patients may show excessive attachment, separation anxiety, and difficulty entering into a meaningful relationship. He then observes how this can frustrate the therapist who expects a patient with a certain psychological mindedness and that, not finding it, he can label the patient as resistant or oppositional (Verhaeghe, 2008). According to Hartocollis (2002), since the second half of the century, psychoanalysts have begun to see an increasing number of patients with poor symbolization skills, who struggle to link their symptoms to their story, are unable to process conflict on a psychic level, and find it difficult to express themselves, or perhaps do not have the words to do so.

Vienna in the late nineteenth century and the world presently

Psychoanalysis was born in a context different from the current one. Vienna in the late nineteenth century was an aristocratic, bourgeois, patriarchal, conservative, and counter-reformist society. At the same time, however, it was also a city of artists, musicians, philosophers, architects, intellectuals (beside Freud: Karl Kraus, Arthur Schnitzler, Robert Musil, Egon Schiele, Gustav Klimt, and Arnold Schoenberg, to name just a few). A city that appreciated culture and scientific knowledge, and that was famous for its cafés, where men and women of different social classes met to read, discuss, and converse (Schorske, 1981). The vibrant intellectual life was counterbalanced by the immobility of the administration, the bureaucracy, the social compromise to quell any hypothesis of revolution and prolong the life of the empire (it would be interesting to analyze this, knowing that Hitler was raised here precisely in these years). Freud (1914) denounced "the hostile indifference of the learned and educated" (p. 40) for psychoanalysis that he found in Vienna as nowhere else (he was probably mainly referring to medical societies). However, it was in this context that he operated, treating mainly patients of the rich bourgeoisie. And the research allowed Freud to describe the unconscious and transference, as well as hysteria, obsessional neuroses, and phobias.

Since then, there have been huge changes in our societies. What we witness today would have been unimaginable in Freud's Vienna: a family crisis, a change in parental roles, an increase in adoptive families (Irtelli, 2018); continuous technological and media development (the internet and mobile phones in particular), continuous growth of markets and the supply of consumer goods (especially online), climate change, environmental disasters, greater pollution, global migration, an aging population (Cianconi et al., 2015); artificial insemination techniques, loosening of borders (Melman and Lebrun, 2018). The scenario has changed radically, and today we find ourselves listening to a different population. According to several studies (Kessler et. al., 2007; Steel et al., 2014), the most common symptoms in today's population, worldwide, are: anxiety disorders (panic disorder, agoraphobia without panic disorder, specific phobia, social phobia, generalized anxiety disorder, post-traumatic stress disorder, and separation anxiety disorder), mood disorders (major depressive disorder, dysthymic disorder, bipolar disorder I or II, or subthreshold bipolar disorder), impulse control disorders (intermittent explosive disorder, oppositional-defiant disorder, conduct disorder, attention-deficit/hyperactivity disorder), and substance use disorders (alcohol and drug abuse with or without dependence). These studies also report a higher frequency of anxiety and mood disorders among women, and a higher incidence of dependence on alcohol or other substances among men. Less frequent symptoms include anorexia and bulimia, which are relatively low among the general population, but more frequent among young people, especially women (Qian et al., 2013), psychosomatic disorders, social isolation, aggressiveness and anger, and various types of addictions (e.g., gambling, shopping, sex).

My first consideration is that today we live in a society of symptoms. While for most of the last century we reasoned in terms of psychic structures (e.g., hysteria, obsessional neurosis, perversion, psychosis) or discourses, today we focus on symptoms, but without questioning their function for the subject, and without being able to read them as part of a personal story. That is to say that the reading/construction of the case, as Freud did, has been replaced by the medical-statistical model, the list of symptoms. Not only among mental health professionals, but also among patients. Many patients today do not seem to be able to link their symptoms to their personal history; to most of them, symptoms seem to occur in an absolutely random and unpredictable way. Today, we refer to symptoms as if they have universal meaning, as if they all speak the same "organ language". But psychoanalytic practice shows that each case is unique and comes with its own logic, different from that of the previous one. And each chapter of this book testifies the attempt to grasp (through psychoanalytic listening, which is listening to the unconscious) precisely the uniqueness of each case, and to reinvent the practice each time, starting from that case.

Another interesting consideration is that modern symptoms or disorders encompass for the most part enactments ('passages to the act' or acting-out), often together with abuse of substances and (acts of) self-harm. This may be a consequence of what was said above: if the word is expunged, then we have enactments (passages to the act and acting-out are not really actions; they are the non-reflective playing out of a mental scenario). And if the word is expunged, then it is replaced by the substance.

One may say that alcohol, drugs, substances have always existed, yet the phenomenon of addictions is relatively recent. How is this possible? Svolos (2018) observes that the use of drugs in antiquity or in some Aboriginal cultures is ritualized and takes place within a particular symbolic context; therefore, it supports the Other and the social structure, it does not break with them. For Canabarro and D'Agord (2012) "drug addictions resist social ties because they refuse to participate and denounce the illusion contained in social ties. The capitalist discourse sells the promise that lost enjoyment can be recovered, so that the subject, by acquiring an object, becomes self-sufficient without having to establish any other type of relationship" (p. 490). The symptom is co-constructed according to the dominant social discourse. It is therefore essential to listen and analyze what is the dominant social discourse today, and what are some of the most recurring signifiers.

The dominant social discourse today and its clinical consequences

I have found it interesting to take a look at the phrases we hear every day in commercials, slogans, the most common slang expressions: "just do it", "no limits", "the sky is the limit", "work hard, play hard", "if you want, you can", "believe in yourself". There is an emphasis on the individual, and on the infinite possibilities of doing, without limits of space and time: if you want, you can, at any time. It seems to me that this lack of limits is reflected in modern symptoms. While the "classic" neurotic person had problems transgressing the limit, modern symptoms (substance abuse, eating disorders, panic, self-harm behaviors, anger, impulsiveness, just to name a few) rather show the absence of limits. Another very common problem today is the lack of direction in life. It is probably another consequence of the fact that "there are no limits" and that "everything is possible". If everything is possible, if everything is at hand, it is also less desirable. If there is no law (even a law to go against; a law to fight), there is no direction. A society is "rigid" when it limits the expression of individual desire for the benefit of the group. But if on one hand this seems to limit the freedom of individuals, on the other it is what anchors them to a group or a place and gives them direction in life. It is possible that a century ago, in many societies, people occupied more clearly defined positions than they do today; their goals and purposes in life were clear from birth and were rarely questioned. Today there is much more freedom, but at a price: it is much more difficult to find something that gives one direction. In an age where everything is possible, only a few know what drives them.

Many people complain about the lack of *vocation*. Vocation is a voice that literally calls you and tells you where to go, and what to do. It is a voice that comes from elsewhere; it is not the ego. It is not the "I do what I want", but rather the "I do what I am called to do". Vocation is not an initiative of the subject who chooses for him/herself. Indeed, it is something that decentralizes the person from himself. It is a call that needs to be answered. It requires one to rely on this voice, thus on the Other, rather than the ego. Therefore, it implies a loss of autonomy and individualism. But in an age where individual freedom is the absolute value, the price to pay is precisely the loss of vocation. Similarly, we do not often hear talk of *fate* nowadays. The ancients had a strong sense of fate (from Latin *fari*, meaning 'to speak'). One's fate, destiny, and destination were spoken. One could go against it, fight it, but it was spoken. Instead, what we see today (Hong Kong is a good example, but not an exclusive one), is that many people are uprooted, as if they are escaping their fate. But this has a consequence: being a castaway, going adrift.

This is also and above all the era of panic. Often, panic attacks come when one is confronted with one's own solitude; when the symbolic landmarks are lost; when one feels that s/he cannot rely neither on him/herself nor on others; when something no longer holds the subject together. Panic can come when one is alone in open spaces, in a large square, for example. But it can also come when one is among others, for example in a crowded underground at peak time. What matters is not the number of people around, but the feeling of loneliness that the subject experiences in that moment and the sense of helplessness (and despair) faced with a situation that is perceived as overwhelming. And in fact, what does the panicked subject do? S/he isolates him/herself within four walls. And if s/he really has to go out, s/he does it with a companion, someone trusted who will not leave him/her alone. Panic attacks can also occur in situations of pleasure, that is when one may relax and loosen/lose control. The subject fears that if s/he loses control, then anything can happen, as if that were a tipping point. Panic, like many of today's symptoms, reveals *the lack of the lack*. That is, it reveals that there is too much offer from the Other, something that cannot be stemmed. *Whereas the "classic" symptoms were the product of a strong censorship, of a prohibition, panic and modern symptoms show that what is missing is a "not", an interdict, a bulwark.*

"Happiness" is another word that astonishes me. Happiness is not a very popular term in Europe. I think it is more popular in North America, and I was surprised to hear it so frequently in Hong Kong. Probably, the European philosophical tradition (characterized by existentialism, nihilism, even pessimism) has focused on the finitude of the subject rather than its full realization. Likely, North American culture more than others emphasize the achievement of goals, self-realization, will, and autonomy, and these seem to be the values that are spreading across societies today (in my opinion, what is commonly named Westernization might be named Americanization). Happiness seems to reflect an ideal of plentitude and fullness that the subject can enjoy, uninterrupted and undisturbed. A few patients said in session: "I just want to be happy, why the hell can't I?" And they complain a lot that they cannot be "happy", as if this full, continuous happiness were their right, and they don't understand why this right would be denied to them. Every lack is experienced in frustration (which is imaginary) because there is no castration* (which is symbolic), that is, lack is not symbolized. They experience frustration because they feel they have not received something that was promised to them, something they were owed. They demand happiness, and therefore want to get rid of the symptoms. *It is no coincidence that in a world that pursues the ideal of happiness and enjoyment, depression and lack of desire are among the most frequent symptoms.*

Self-sufficiency, autonomy, and independence are other recurring words in the dominant discourse. These signifiers well describe anorexia, which relies completely on willpower (thus, the ego). Anorexia does not contemplate the possibility that there is something that escapes the ego, that the ego is not master. I have never met anyone more determined, focused, and driven than a person with anorexic traits. The anorexic finds enjoyment in thinking that everything is in his/her hands, that no one and nothing else is needed. They can talk about not needing to eat as an orgasmic experience. "I've been without food for 10 days", they can proudly say, to show how strong are, only to later fall into despair if the anorexic phase turns into the bulimic phase, where they cannot stop eating. Normally, these people ask us to help them strengthen their willpower, that is, to help them to remain in the anorexic phase, preventing it from turning into bulimia.

Then there's the myth of the 'self-made man'. Interestingly enough, many people today complain of being lonely, isolated from the world, incapable of being in relationships. The myth of self-making is also the myth of doing without the Other (autonomy, autarchy, and self-reliance are very common terms today), as all these "modern" symptoms show. Self-make, or "to make oneself" is also linked to addictions (in Italian language the expressions "self-make" and "to make oneself" can also mean "do drugs" or take drugs). It is also interesting to note that another term to indicate some form of substance abuse is 'dependence'. There are many kinds of addictions (e.g., drugs, alcohol, gambling), but one thing they have in common is that the addict ultimately finds him/herself alone, isolated. Then, we see how many of today's symptoms are the flip side of the coin of the current dominant discourse, a sort of Dante's *counterpass* (a principle that regulates the punishment of offenders by the opposite of their sin or by analogy to it. For example, in Dante's Hell, sorcerers, astrologers, and false prophets had their heads turned back on their bodies and they could not see "ahead of them"). And the problem is that many therapies and practices that are popular today (those mentioned above) lean towards strengthening the ego of the subject and his/her fantasy of mastery, rather than helping him/her to get rid of some of his/her certainties, question some of his fantasies about him/herself and others, and help him/her face his/her own issues.

Social changes and New Psychic Economy

Formica and colleagues (2018) describe the post-modern man as in constant rush, always on the move, but without direction, like a spinning top. This state of perennial agitation leaves neither time nor room for reflection, only for enactments. According to the authors, we have shifted from a society of discipline (and therefore also of guilt) to a society of efficiency (and therefore of inadequacy). The hysteria described by Freud found fertile ground in the conflict between rules and derogations; however, in a society that focuses less on rules, we may expect other symptomatic manifestations. In particular, Formica and colleagues identify four traits that describe (Western) societies today: 1) social precariousness; 2) consumerism; 3) nihilism; and 4) individualism. According to these authors, the clinical consequence of precariousness is panic, that is, the loss of references, of orientation. Consumerism, which is based on the myths of image and consumption, results in anorexia and bulimia. The nihilism and the sense of emptiness (of ideals, of values) it produces create fertile ground for new addictions (substances, internet, shopping, gambling, sex). Finally, individualism is the root cause of growing narcissism.

Melman (in Melman and Lebrun, 2018) speaks of a "New Psychic Economy" which would be different from what we have known in past centuries. If the "old economy" was based on the repression of sexual desire, causing neuroses, the "new economy" is based on "enjoyment at all costs", causing a *generalized perversion.* In particular, "the new psychic economy is not the result of the disappearance of patriarchy but of the end of a father-centered psychic economy. By disappearing, it leaves no room for an economy centered on the mother, unlike what one might think, but for an economy that, being able to rely only on a mother that cannot be numbered, finds itself without a center . . . without gravity" (p. 11). There are a couple of considerations. First, a father intervenes in a ternary structure (mother-father-child); then, once the father is removed, only the dyad mother-child remains. This makes it more difficult for interdiction, lack, and castration to happen. But it is precisely these functions that, by preventing the access to the mother, promote sexuality. Once the father is removed, the object is immediately available: "wholly at once"; but it is a mortiferous enjoyment, without desire. It is the enjoyment of substances. Second, for Melman, the logic of a mother differs from that of a father. Whereas a father generally refers to the authority of ancestors (in this sense it would be numerable: George I, George II, George III . . .), the mother refers only to her own authority, and therefore is an arbitrary, unlimited, capricious authority. Being inserted into a genealogy also means being inserted into a destiny, into a history; to represent the authority is not only to command, but also to insert the child into a story. In maternal logic nothing is impossible, which indicates that there is no reference text: "it is as if she herself continually creates a text that the child must decipher" (p. 181). But the child, unable to refer to a stable law, struggles to find coordinates that can give direction to their own life: they are without gravity. This decline of the father, in a world without borders, produces subjects adrift. Melman also observes that there is more and more abandonment of the home, that is, a house, a place with which bonds are established, and not just a transitory residence, such as a hotel room.

Where has hysteria gone?

At present, we no longer see the hysterical manifestations that were described by Charcot at the Salpêtrière Hospital in Paris. Is this enough to say that hysteria has disappeared; or does it manifest differently at present? A general question not specific to psychoanalysis: is hysteria a constant in the history of humanity, or is it specific to a particular context? According to Trimble and Reynolds (2016) the first descriptions of symptoms that we could define as hysterical date back to the Assyrians and Babylonians, about 4000 years ago, and the term hysteria derives from the ancient Greek ὑστέρα (*hustéra*, 'womb'), although King (2019) specifies that hysteria is not a Hippocratic term or diagnosis, but a very modern one. With such a long history, why then has the diagnosis of hysteria almost completely disappeared today, and why is it limited to (Lacanian) psychoanalysis?

Historically, we have seen changes in diagnostic categories over time, depending on the social context. For example, at the beginning of the last century and during the First World War, hysteria received a lot of attention, whereas interest in psychosis was limited. Between the two wars, interest in psychosomatics and narcissistic pathologies grew. In the second half of the century, the focus shifted again to psychosis and borderline states (Irtelli, 2018). The question is: do changing living conditions trigger new pathologies or different manifestations of similar structures? A premise of this book is that the structures identified by Freud present themselves today in different ways; thus, it is important to identify the underlying structure.

According to some, changes in affectivity (increased dysphoria, shame, irritability, restlessness, boredom, feelings of emptiness, etc.) and behavior (reduction of impulse control capacity, interpersonal skills, reflective function, etc.) indicate a shift towards borderline levels of personality functioning (Ferraro et al., 2016). According to these authors, even the modern "depressive states" would be different from the "classic depression" in that they are not based on a sense of guilt, but on a sense of inadequacy (with regards to the demands of society). The new depressive states would therefore reveal a borderline-narcissistic background, in which narcissistic strategies would be ways to keep borderline experiences (feeling of emptiness, irritation, boredom) at bay. However, according to Bollas (2000), the concept of borderline is hyper-inclusive, and many of the cases commonly diagnosed as borderline are clearly cases of hysteria. Similarly, also many diagnoses of anorexia, attention-deficit/hyperactivity disorder, multiple personality disorder, chronic fatigue disorder, and even some diagnoses of schizophrenia would be examples of hysteria. According to Bollas, interest in hysteria had reduced so much by the early 1990s, that this term had disappeared from most diagnostic manuals; but this does not mean that hysterical patients have disappeared. And because a trait of the structure of hysteria is to situate itself in the desire of the Other, it is possible that these hysterical patients have begun to present symptoms, problems, and various clinical situations (borderline in particular) that fall within the field of official, recognized pathologies. Also, according to Ávila and Terra (2012), hysteria has not disappeared at all, and presents itself in forms other than traditional ones. The authors observe that many symptoms of borderline disorder are compatible with manifestations of hysteria, to the point that "if pure cases of borderline personality disorder did not exist, the majority of patients would simply be considered as suffering from hysteria" (p. 33). According to these authors, several current diagnoses would simply be manifestations of hysteria: insomnia, incurable headaches, dysphonia, walking coordination disorders, pain and spasms, paresthesia, digestive disturbances, sexual dysfunction, prostatitis, gynecological disorders, gastrointestinal complaints, fibromyalgia, chronic fatigue syndrome, and irritable bowel syndrome, to name a few. Finally, other diagnostic categories (e.g., somatization, psychosomatization) have been preferred to hysteria, which was considered unsatisfactory and stigmatizing. Having said that, it is also important to clarify that not everything is attributable to hysteria. For example, some diagnoses of borderline can be psychosis.

Old and new symptoms

Are these symptoms new, or have they always existed, but were earlier unseen/undiscovered, as these patients did not come to the therapist? Verhaeghe (2007) argues that some of the new symptoms overlap with the Freudian category of current neurosis. Initially, Freud distinguished *psychoneuroses* (hysteria, obsessional neurosis, phobias; later he divided the *psychoneuroses* into *transference* and *narcissistic psychoneuroses*) and *actual neuroses* (anxiety neurosis, neurasthenia, and hypochondria). The former were understood as an expression of an internal conflict, precisely the repression of a sexual or aggressive desire, and were linked to the patient's past. The latter seemed to be unrelated to any internal conflict, but rather caused by the present living conditions, and were understood as the expression of a free and unprocessed anxiety, which expressed itself in somatic symptoms. According to Verhaeghe (2004), actual neuroses include modern panic attacks, panic disorders, somatization and somatoform disorders, but also the entire borderline spectrum and most traumatic neuroses. He suggests using the term *psychopathology* for classic symptoms, since it emphasizes the psychological and temporal dimension (the patient's past history; the meaning), and *actual neurosis* for modern symptoms, as these seem circumscribed to a more limited temporal and spatial dimension (the present moment, rather than the past; the patient's body, more than his history).

According to Verhaeghe (2008), the so-called new symptoms present three characteristics that distinguish them from the classic symptoms:

1   *They involve the real of the body*: at present we see various forms of self-harm, self-mutilation, cutting, substance abuse, eating disorders, and/or somatization that directly alter the body. Conversely, "classic" neuroses involve the imaginary of the body, which was then not altered permanently.
2   *They imply a concrete action*: whereas the classic symptoms (with the exception of obsessive-compulsive behaviors) remained on an imaginary level (in fantasies), modern symptoms manifest through enactments. Whereas the classic patient had to be accompanied up to a certain threshold before s/he took a step, it is the opposite with the new symptoms.
3   *They seem to lack meaning and connection with the patient's history*: symptoms are often presented without particularly significant content.

Pozzetti (2007) lists a series of differences in the clinical practice of classic and new symptoms:

1   Repression was the mechanism at the base of classic symptoms, whereas the new symptoms show a prevalence of narcissism and an attempt to cancel the distance between what one is and how one would like to be;
2   Whereas the classic neurotic symptoms are formations of the unconscious, the body image and drugs (typically related to new symptoms) are not;
3   Whereas the classic neurotic patient shows some interest in deciphering his own unconscious and discovering what he does not know and manifests in his dreams, forgetfulness, and lapses, with the new symptoms the patient is less driven by a desire to know. Indeed, drug addicts and anorexics possess an enormous amount of knowledge (of drugs, of food);
4   the new symptoms guarantee an identity (e.g.: "I am an anorexic", "I am a drug addict") and therefore provide patients a sense of belonging to a group; and
5   whereas the Freudian theory and practice was centered around the figure of a strong father, the new symptoms often refer to a weak, insufficient father, unable to take on his responsibilities and his parental function (even a humiliated father, not recognized in his function).

How can psychoanalysis help today?

Over the last 20 years I have had the opportunity to work in different contexts and in different roles: as an educator in psychiatric community residences, as a researcher at a university (Department of Social and Behavioral Sciences), as a psychoanalyst in a private practice. It seems to me that psychoanalysis is generally better known and more appreciated in many clinical settings within the so-called field of mental health than in most academic departments of psychology, where traditionally it encounters some resistance. In psychology departments, most professors and researchers conduct quantitative research, but they generally have little or no clinical experience, and even if they wanted to, they would still not have time to practice because they have to submit one research project after another and publish articles in order to survive in the academic world. For some years I have inhabited these two worlds, working as a psychoanalyst in my office and doing quantitative research at a university. It was a very enriching and formative experience. But I have also experienced how difficult it is to straddle these two worlds. Many psychoanalysts distrust statistical methods, which instead have helped me to address and refine my research. Conversely, researchers build complex and rigorous statistical models, but having no clinical experience they conduct studies that are often trivial and without any relevance for clinicians. I therefore agree with Jonathan Shedler, also a psychoanalyst in a private practice and university researcher, when he writes that:

> Most academic researchers do not practice clinically. . . . But they are the ones writing treatment manuals and promoting eight- or 12-session instruction-manual therapy. The push for protocol-driven therapy is coming from academic researchers, not working clinicians. . . . They are promoting treatments that fail vast numbers of people – that's an empirical fact – and that a great many people do not actually want. So here we have got these parallel universes. One universe is the real world; the other is an academic bubble of artificial laboratory experiments. It creates a real problem because when journalists and policy makers look for experts, they look to the academic world, not realizing that the people doing academic research are not experts at therapy. They are operating in a parallel universe that has little to do with meaningful psychotherapy.
>
> (in Howes, 2019)

Having both clinical and academic research experience, I think I can say that psychoanalysis has something unique compared to any other psychotherapy. In particular, I believe that all other practices are even "pre-Freudian" because they have not yet discovered the unconscious. Nonetheless, psychoanalysis has been attacked from all fronts since its inception.

Stereotypes about psychoanalysis

Much has been said against psychoanalysis: that it reduces everything to sex, that it only works if you believe in it, that it is only for the rich, that it takes too long, that psychoanalytic concepts and treatments lack empirical support, that it is an obsolete and obscure method, that psychoanalytic technique is not as developed as other forms of psychotherapy, that it is not good for everyone, that it does not offer concrete solutions; the list is endlessly tedious, yet familiar to any psychoanalyst. In most cases these criticisms come from people who have no experience of psychoanalysis and have never read Freud. These criticisms are often based on secondary sources, impressions, hearsay. Personally, I have been used to hearing these criticisms (always the same) since my first year of university. I often get the impression that they only serve to display some sort of empty knowledge, or to fuel the controversy. There are not only theoretical questions behind these criticisms. There are also often ideological reasons, prejudice; other times it is a matter of convenience (some have built an academic career on criticizing Freud and psychoanalysis); sometimes there are "commercial" issues, that is, to gain market share, attract new customers, marketing strategies. I have no interest in debating these stereotypes here. However, I am interested in analyzing some of the premise from which they move.

Psychoanalysis has gone out of fashion. Psychoanalysis has never really been in fashion. Indeed, it has always met with resistance. This may have several causes. First, psychoanalysis, by investigating the unconscious, has revealed to people their less pleasant side, their baseness: precisely what causes embarrassment and what normally one does not want to know. Second, psychoanalysis has revealed the complexity of the human, and what escapes one's control. This is something that many are not willing to accept. Freud wrote: "the ego is not master in its own house". This does not attract patients, who instead (even more so today) want to be masters in their own house. Other psychotherapies are more "at the service" of the individual, promising targeted and effective strategies to get rid of the symptoms. It is not surprising that these therapies are more fashionable (although they may only last until one realizes that they do not keep their promises). Third, there is the idea that psychoanalysis is an old (and thus unfashionably unscientific) practice, simply because it was chronologically the first. Other therapies may be perceived as more advanced and effective just because they are more recent. And what would be "the new" today? When I read authors of other orientations I find that most of them try to define themselves with respect to psychoanalysis. They still use psychoanalysis as a term of comparison (even if they try to discredit it). They have not really gone *beyond* psychoanalysis. And most of the criticisms these authors raise against psychoanalysis are issues that Freud had already addressed over a hundred years ago. It would be enough to read Freud. Fourth, some think that psychoanalysis is irremediably tied to the historical period in which it was born and that it cannot work in a different context. But psychoanalysis was born precisely as a critic of its time. And it has always maintained a position of alterity with regards to the dominant discourse in society. In fact, psychoanalysis has had an enormous influence on cultural studies in general, unlike the great majority of other psychotherapies, which have found application only in the clinical psychology/psychiatric field. Since its inception, psychoanalysis has studied the individual in relation to its Other (i.e., family, culture, society. The mOther is usually the first person to occupy the position of Other for the baby). We can say that in the unconscious we find both the individual and the o/Other. This is why Freud did not limit his interest within the consultation room, but developed his theories based on the study of myths, religions, languages, art, history, science, cultures, literature, and social practices, as all of this can shed light on the functioning of the unconscious. Studying the unconscious is always *punctual*. No one lives in a vacuum, in a timeless dimension. Some think that the unconscious is only about the past, but in the unconscious we actually find the past, present, and future (just think of the dream, which mixes different worlds and times). The time of desire is the future perfect, that is, something that is past, but that is constituted at the moment when the subject speaks. The time of the subject is not chronological but logical. Finally, there is perhaps the idea that psychoanalysis is too slow as a therapy for modern times. For many, dealing with the unconscious is a waste of time. They prefer to look for shortcuts. But not considering the unconscious (which is one's own specific logic) means relying on abstract, universal rules (supposed to work for everyone). At present there are many diets, lifestyles, philosophies, sports, and practices that promise to fill the void the subject perceives (a void that is felt but not fully recognized; it is not taken as an existential void, but as something that has to be filled), and to give a direction to those who do not have one. But these are all passing fads, which change every few months because none of them really work. And these people keep turning in circles, but believing they are moving towards a final destination; the idea of saving time actually leads to time being wasted and not making any progress. Presently, the unconscious is misunderstood and forgotten, and it is essential to restore it at the center of our theory and practice. Nowadays, more than before, the unconscious is "the new".

Psychoanalysis is not very effective. Although psychoanalysis was born as a therapy, it is more than that. For Freud, psychoanalysis (psychoanalysis as a science, but also every single analysis) was primarily a process of seeking the truth and knowledge of the unconscious, that is, a knowledge that is not known (because it is unconscious), but that can be said through the analysis. This knowledge, Freud found, could subsequently also have therapeutic effects. Conversely, Freud (1933) observed that the other psychotherapies that produced therapeutic effects by using the power of suggestion could help neither the patient nor the therapist to shed light upon unconscious processes, and they could not produce lost-lasting changes. We can therefore say that *psychoanalysis is also a psychotherapy, but other psychotherapies are not also psychoanalysis*. Furthermore, we can also note that since psychoanalysis aims at gaining some form of knowledge, it requires at least one question to begin. Even something as simple as: why is this happening to me, now? Instead, the other psychotherapies, which focus mainly on the symptom, do not necessarily need any questions.

But then, how to evaluate the effectiveness of a therapy? Most research measures the effectiveness of a treatment in terms of symptom reduction. This, besides reducing psychoanalysis only to a therapy (which means ignoring all the benefits that an analysis can have, beyond the symptom reduction), also means reducing the sample only to those patients who have measurable symptoms and excluding those who do not have a symptom which is definable according to a psychiatric classification. But not every patient we see is simply asking us to reduce symptoms; thankfully, they present broader questions. For example, some people question what it means to become a father, others are looking for a direction in life, others feel troubled by their sexual desire (too little, or excessive, or aimed at something they are not comfortable with). The list is long.

How do we take into account these patients, who are likely the majority? Most academic research is based on a rather limited and specific sample, which then cannot be representative of the entire population of people who are in therapy. Furthermore, it is also quite doubtful how these measurements are conducted. Many studies evaluate the effectiveness of therapies simply with questionnaires and self-assessment scales. These tools do not allow one to measure any unconscious dimension, and instead measure only what one believes about oneself, or the frequency with which that specific initial symptom reappears (they cannot assess, for example, if an older symptom has been replaced by a new one), or other rather superficial dimensions. It is therefore not clear if, and how, these tools can really be useful and informative for psychotherapy research. And yet, despite all these limitations, there is currently a lot of research showing that psychoanalysis is not second to other therapies in terms of symptoms reduction (for a review see Leuzinger-Bohleber et al., 2020; Shedler, 2010).

Finally, we should say that in psychoanalysis the goal is not necessarily to remove the symptom, as if the symptom were the real and ultimate problem. Conversely, a symptom is valuable because it indicates that there is an impasse somewhere, and this is what needs attention. The symptom is like the petrol warning light, which comes on when there is no fuel. It may disappear when the conditions that are causing it disappear.

Then, what is the effectiveness of psychoanalysis? Psychoanalysis is effective when it fills up the tank of desire, which is our fuel. It is effective if it makes one think differently. If it creates the premises for thinking something that previously could only express itself through a symptom. If it makes one start living again. If it leads one to ask questions about things s/he does not understand about him/herself, to do with the world, life. If it helps one to discover something from his/her own unconscious desire and make something of it. My personal and professional experience leads me to say that if these premises occur, each symptom can diminish or even disappear. In this sense, I don't think that cases can be labelled as easier or more difficult. When an analysis *really* begins, each case reaches some concrete and tangible results.

Psychoanalytic treatments are not supported by empirical research. 'Evidence-based' empirical research originates in the medical field, in which symptoms are signs (for all patients, they indicate the same cause of disease) and the cure is based on a *method* (etymologically: systematic treatment of the disease) that is as reliable and replicable as possible, in the sense that the same treatment for the same disease should bring the same results for everyone. Given these premises, psychoanalysis is not a method; and it is not simply "applicable". As mentioned above, the psychic symptom is not a sign, that is to say it does not refer to the same thing for everyone. Then, an analysis cannot simply repeat what others have discovered or said in their analyses; each analysis has its unique development.

Finally, psychoanalysis cannot be reduced to a technique. The observer is part of the observed phenomenon, and deeply affects it. Psychoanalysis shows that desire and transference are more important than technique alone. And therefore, there is no guarantee that repetition of the technique will lead to the same results. So, one can do research in psychoanalysis, but the analysis is the encounter between two singularities, analyst and analysand, and this cannot be replicated, just as no conversation can be replicated. It is as if we wanted to "manualize" friendship, or love. There are many books that teach what to say to win over a woman, but obviously these strategies are not effective. There are also many books that explain what to say at a job interview, how to present yourself, and what questions to ask, so as to show that you are interested (even if most likely you are not). These strategies reflect a fantasy of mastery, meaning the attempt to manage or control the conversation. However, when one has a script in mind most likely it will fail, because it is not in the contingency, in the relationship *in actu*. It is not driven by an authentic act of speech.

The analysis develops in the *transference*. The transference is normally ignored by those who imagine the therapy as a cognitive exercise. Recently, various psychotherapies have started to consider some aspects of the transference, even though they do not call it 'transference'. Even the so-called evidence-based therapies must finally admit that the relationship (and therefore the transference) is among the most important treatment factors of the therapy, and in doing so they partially disprove the premises from which evidence-based research starts.

Finally, it must be said that a therapist with some experience works to elaborate and dissolve the transference, and not to hold it back through suggestion. Those who ignore the transference will not be able to work to dissolve it.

Psychoanalysis is too difficult to learn, and psychoanalytical training takes too long. This is partially true. Psychoanalysis is not just a technique that can be mastered once and for all. Psychoanalysis is partly a science and partly an art. Freud said it is an impossible profession, like educating and governing. Lacan said that psychoanalysis is primarily based on the analyst's desire (which is a desire to do analysis, a desire "for absolute difference", as put by Lacan; not a desire to do good). The formation of the analyst does not take "little" or "much" time: it is continuous, never-ending. But most importantly, the formation of an analyst does not purely come from academic training. There are at least three devices that contribute to the formation of an analyst: 1) one's own personal analysis; 2) clinical supervision, when one begins to see patients; and 3) reading texts, attending reading groups (*cartels*, in the Lacanian tradition), seminars, writing theses, articles, books, etc.

Although the teaching of psychoanalysis also includes academic teaching, it is primarily a teaching that comes from one's own personal analysis (as an analysand), and later from occupying the position of the analyst. That is, it is not only a teaching about the unconscious (texts, theories, what has been written by others), but also and above all a teaching that comes from the unconscious. Being in analysis is a necessary condition to become an analyst, it could not be otherwise. This is not necessarily true for other psychotherapies. Many of them do not require their students to have been in therapy to become therapists. They separate the moment of the theory from that of practice, whereas in psychoanalysis theory and practice proceed together; there is no one before the other.

Psychoanalysis is too expensive. There is a stereotype that psychoanalysis is only for the rich; for those who have plenty of money and time. Perhaps at the beginning psychoanalysis was practiced by an elite group of people. Freud was an established doctor, and many of his patients were part of the wealthy bourgeoisie. But many psychoanalysts were, and are, socially committed and active in the community. Psychoanalysis is no longer something elitist. Instead, I believe that psychoanalysts, more than many other practitioners, have tried to address the issue of the price of sessions in pragmatic terms. Not in abstract terms, as the professional boards do, imagining that they can determine an intrinsic value of sessions and then fix the price of the sessions for everyone. Many psychoanalysts consider the fees precisely in relation to the treatment and the patient.

Psychoanalysis is costly. However, what is actually the *cost* of an analysis? What is the price to pay, so to speak? And what is instead the cost of being in pain? When we talk about the cost of a therapy, we often forget that it is not simply an asset that can be purchased as if it were a bag, a gym membership, or another product. It is important that there is a price and that it is not done completely for free. Money is the symbolic element *par excellence* and by charging a fee we can limit the imaginary aspects of the transference. That is, through payment we make sure that there is no debt of gratitude, recognition, love, guilt, reproach, or else. And it is important that a patient invests (money, time, effort) in a treatment. However, the investment amount cannot be the same for everyone; it differs case by case. Nonetheless, there is something that is not simply extinguishable by payment. Even if a person has the means to pay for his/her therapy, this does not mean that s/he can come as and when s/he wants. Also, for this reason I don't like to use the words 'client' or 'user'. Other therapeutic orientations use them, but in my opinion, not all aspects of an analysis can be resolved through a monetary transaction. One is not paying for a product or a service; not even for the professional's expertise or his/her time. *The cost of an analysis is the renunciation to the symptom and its secondary benefits.*

Some people who ask for therapy immediately ask for a discount. This rings a bell for me. In most cases it is not a question of price. There is something else at stake. What discount are they asking for? Is it a reduction of the work they do not want to commit to? In my experience, these people normally will not come for long, even if I agree on a lower fee. They are not investing in their own personal analysis. Then, there are people who come because they are reimbursed by their insurance, so do not pay at all. But precisely for this reason, normally after a few sessions they stop coming. They are not in the best position to start an analysis. They are consumers. They are customers, who expect to receive a service. And who are deeply disappointed when they realize that they have to work in analysis. They cannot simply wait for the analyst to provide them with answers.

Psychoanalysis is not a service for the well-being of the individual, or a hobby to do in one's spare time. Psychoanalysis works when a person is in a state of necessity, or even desperation. When a question is to be addressed urgently and cannot be further postponed. Psychoanalysis is a practice that requires a decisive involvement.

The representation of the end of time

What do these stereotypes have in common? They reveal a representation of the end of time, of death. For instance, if someone says that psychoanalysis takes too long, it is as if they have first imagined the time for therapy and only in the end, when they are finally "ready", can they imagine the time for living. As if the time spent for the therapy is time taken to life. This separation is completely imaginary. When a psychoanalysis begins, little by little life becomes part of the analysis. Then, through the analysis, one's personal history, which initially is fragmented and has many blank spaces, starts unfolding. This new narrative, this new storytelling begins to produce effects in life, outside of the analyst's office. Life enters analysis, which in turn becomes part of life, and together they originate something else. Similarly, both concepts of efficacy and effectiveness of psychotherapies reflect a representation of the end of time. But this is a representation of death. Time does not end; and in fact, most of this research does not stand the test of time, as demonstrated by the poor results of many follow-up studies.

Psychotherapy is normally understood as a tool for solving some issue or symptom. After all, most of the time this is what triggers a demand for treatment. Thus, most people think that therapy ends when the symptom disappears or the issue is solved. However, psychoanalysis starts from different premises. Although people do come with a symptom in analysis, often they start talking of something else and do not even mention the symptom for quite some time. At times, it may diminish or even disappear by itself. A symptom can be an excellent pretext for starting therapy. Nevertheless, some people continue to come to analysis even after the symptom disappears because there are other things they want to understand or discover. Some people quickly realize that there is more beyond the symptom. For instance, that a symptom could be just a screen for some unconscious conflict. Then, the question is: how can the symptom become a starting point, rather than an ending point, for a patient? Beyond the symptom, there is a plot (i.e., the *fantasy* or *phantasm**) from which this symptom emerged as a symptom; a plot that one may wish to know, review, reconstruct. Then, has the patient any curiosity or questions that allows him/her to continue? How can we support this question?

Therapy may respond to the urgency of the moment, but an analysis requires a logic other than that of symptom reduction. Only when it is possible to speak of Other can an analysis begin. The analysis has to do with quality of life, not just with getting back to being functional, productive, adapted to one's social/family/ work context. Sometimes during the first interview patients ask me: "how long will it take?" With some irony I may ask back: "you just arrived and you want to leave already?" When things start, it is impossible to know how they will unfold. And the effectiveness of the analysis should be in every session, not after one, five or ten years. If the analysis is effective, we immediately feel it in our lives. And if it is effective, why finish something that is beneficial? Many people ask how long they will have to stay in analysis. Freud asked himself this question and said that a psychoanalysis can end, but the analysis itself is endless. As long as we are alive the unconscious will produce something, and one may wish to analyze it. Lacan gives some indications about the end of the analysis. In the 1960s (Lacan, 1979), he argued that the analysis ends *when the fantasy has been crossed*. When the object *a* detaches itself from the forms of identification. That is: one can continue to desire but is no longer stuck to that initial representation of his/her object of desire. Further on, Lacan (1977, p. 7) says that "knowing how to deal with your symptom, that is the end of analysis". He speaks of the end of the analysis as identification to the symptom. And he theorizes the end of the analysis with shifting from the symptom, source of suffering, to the *sinthome*, source of creation.

In some cases, people ask how long therapy will take because they are afraid of becoming dependent on the analysis, or on the figure of the analyst, and they try to set an imaginary limit. The idea of the end, the idea of having a *dead*line can be of help for some; it is the limit that often is lacking today, and that is necessary for doing. In analysis (as in life) it is also important to have an idea of a time frame, of introducing a cut in time, and concluding; without any of these, there is the impasse of the symptom, or the immobility of those who cannot take a step because they are never "ready" or because "who knows where you can end up". There is the eternity of things that never happen. It is common for one to be more productive nearer a deadline. But the end cannot be represented. And what will happen at the end, when the task is completed? If one begins university thinking that it must come to an end, in the end one will find oneself lost, not knowing how to proceed. In life, in relationships, and in business one cannot focus on the end. It is a matter of taking the first step, but after this step there will be another one.

What contribution can psychoanalysis give in this "liquid" context? I believe that psychoanalysis, and precisely the psychoanalytic listening is our best option for understanding something of both the unconscious and the discomfort of civilization (and thus of the individual). I don't see any valid alternatives. However, psychoanalytic listening is very different from listening as it is understood in everyday language. In the next two chapters I will try to examine in detail *how to listen*, and *what to listen to/for* in analysis.

Note

1 I am not referring here to any particular word, but to the speech act, to the word *in actu*, to the enunciation. I could also have said 'language', but I prefer to refer to 'word' because language can be confused with language as a system, or with a particular language (e.g., English, Italian). Why is the question of the word important in psychoanalysis? The word, and not reality, is original. In Lacanian terms we could say that the signifiers are original, not the meanings. Initially, the word has no meaning; it takes on

meaning by difference from other words. The commonplace has it that there is a substantial, ontological, factual reality that the word should simply name. As if there were objects on one side and words on the other. The word would therefore be a label to be placed on the nameless object. Conversely, the experience of analysis leads us to reconsider the so-called reality as rather the effect of language. Lacan follows the teaching of Ferdinand de Saussure but reversing the relationship between signified and signifier. But even this reversal would still remain caught up in dualism, were it not for Lacan to introduce a third element (the Other), which prevents the identity between signifier and signified.

References

Ávila, L. A., & Terra, J. R. (2012). Hysteria and its metamorphoses. *Revista Latinoamericana de Psicopatologia Fundamental, 15*(1), 27–41.

Bollas, C. (2000). *Hysteria*. London: Routledge.

Busiol, D. (2016). *Psychoanalysis in Hong Kong: The absent, the present, and the reinvented*. Abingdon, UK: Routledge.

Canabarro, R. D. C. D. S., & D'Agord, M. R. D. L. (2012). Drug addiction and social discourses. *Revista Latinoamericana de Psicopatologia Fundamental, 15*(3), 482–496.

Cianconi, P., Tarricone, I., Ventriglio, A., De Rosa, C., Fiorillo, A., Saito, T., & Bhugra, D. (2015). Psychopathology in postmodern societies. *Journal of Psychopathology, 21*(4), 431–439.

Costa, D. S., & Lang, C. E. (2016). Hysteria today, why? *Psicologia USP, 27*(1), 115–124.

Ferraro, A., Guarnaccia, C., Iacolino, C., & Giannone, F. (2016). Postmodernity: Clinical and social reflections about new forms of psychopathology. *Journal of Psychopathology, 22*, 229–235.

Formica, I., Branca, M. C., Mento, C., Di Giorgio, A., Iacolino, C., & Pellerone, M. (2018). A life with no direction: New frontiers in psychopathology. *World Futures, 74*(5), 282–296.

Freud, S. (1914). *On the history of the psycho-analytic movement. The standard edition of the complete psychological works of Sigmund Freud* (Vol. XIV). London: Hogarth Press and the Institute of Psycho-Analysis.

Freud, S. (1933). New introductory lectures on psychoanalysis. In *Standard edition* (Vol. 22, pp. 5–182). London: Hogarth Press.

Hartocollis, P. (2002). "Actual neurosis" and psychosomatic medicine. *International Journal of Psychoanalysis, 83*, 1361–1373.

Howes, R. (2019, November–December). *Point of view. Research or reality? The flawed science of psychotherapy*. Retrieved from www.psychotherapynetworker.org/magazine/article/2414/point-of-view

Irtelli, F. (2018). Iper-modern paradoxes and Iper-modern symptoms. *Perspective, 3*(8).

Kessler, R. C., Angermeyer, M., Anthony, J. C., Demyttenaere, K., Gasquet, I., Gluzman, S., Gureje, O., Haro, J. M., Kawakami, N., Karam, A., Levinson, D., Medina Mora, M. E., Oakle y Browne, M. A., Posada-Villa, J., Stein, D. J., Adley Tsang, C. H., Aguilar-Gaxiola, S., Alonso, J., Lee, S., Heeringa, S., Pennell, B. E., Berglund, P., Gruber, M. J., Petukhova, M., Chatterji, S., & Üstün, T. B. (2007). Lifetime prevalen ce and age-of-onset distributions of mental disorders in the world health organization's world mental health survey initiative. *World Psychiatry, 6*(3), 168–176.

King, H. (2019). *Hippocrates now: The 'father of medicine' in the internet age*. London: Bloomsbury Publishing.

Lacan, J. (1977). *Le séminaire. Livre XXIV. L'insu que sait de l'une-bévue s'aile a mourre*, lezione del 16 novembre 1976, Ornicar?, n.12/13, décembre, p. 7.

Lacan, J. (1979). *Il seminario. Libro XI. I quattro concetti fondamentali della psicoanalisi. (1964)*. Torino: Einaudi.

Leuzinger-Bohleber, M., Solms, M., & Arnold, S. E. (Eds.). (2020). *Outcome research and the future of psychoanalysis: Clinicians and researchers in dialogue*. Abingdon, UK: Routledge.

Melman, C., & Lebrun, J. P. (2018). *La nuova economia psichica: Il modo di pensare e di godere oggi*. Milano: Mimesis.

Pozzetti, R. (2007). *Senza confini. Considerazioni psicoanalitiche sulle crisi di panico*. Milano: FrancoAngeli.

Qian, J., Hu, Q., Wan, Y., Li, T., Wu, M., Ren, Z., & Yu, D. (2013). Prevalence of eating disorders in the general population: A systematic review. *Shanghai Archives of Psychiatry, 25*(4), 212.

Schorske, C. E. (1981). *Fin-de-Siecle Vienna: Politics and culture*. New York: Vintage/ Random House.

Shedler, J. (2010). The efficacy of psychodynamic psychotherapy. *American Psychologist, 65*(2), 98–109.

Steel, Z., Marnane, C., Iranpour, C., Chey, T., Jackson, J. W., Patel, V., & Silove, D. (2014). The global prevalence of common mental disorders: A systematic review and meta-analysis 1980–2013. *International Journal of Epidemiology, 43*(2), 476–493.

Svolos, T. (2018). Introducing the "new symptoms". In Y. G. Baldwin, K. Malone, & T. Svolos (eds.), *Lacan and addiction* (pp. 75–88). Abingdon, UK: Routledge.

Trimble, M., & Reynolds, E. H. (2016). A brief history of hysteria: From the ancient to the modern. *Handbook of Clinical Neurology, 139*, 3–10.

Verhaeghe, P. (2004). *On being normal and other disorders*. New York: Other Press.

Verhaeghe, P. (2008). A combination that has to fail: New patients, old therapists. *EISTEACH (Dun Laoghaire), 8*(4), 4–8.

Verhaeghe, P., Vanheule, S., & De Rick, A. (2007). Actual neurosis as the underlying psychic structure of panic disorder, somatization, and somatoform disorder: An integration of Freudian and attachment perspectives. *The Psychoanalytic Quarterly, 76*(4), 1317–1350.

Chapter 2

How to listen in analysis

Diego Busiol

The question of listening should be at the center of any practice of speech. It is surprising, therefore, that this is often overlooked, especially given that there is such extensive literature on what to say or do in session. It is true that psychoanalysis was first born as a "talking cure". Freud soon realized that the body of hysterics "spoke", in the sense that the physical symptoms came in place of something that could not be said. Later, he found that talking could free the body from the symptoms. Hence why psychoanalysis was called "talking cure" by one of Freud's first patients, Bertha Pappenheim, known in case studies by the alias Anna O. But psychoanalysis is also a "listening cure". Freud did not stop at the cathartic method: if the patient is required to speak, the analyst has to be capable of a particular type of listening, a listening that goes beyond what the patient intentionally communicated. That is to say that *the analyst has to listen to the unconscious*. At the beginning of an analysis, it is mostly the analyst who practices this type of listening; however, it is possible, and indeed desirable, that the patient also develops this type of listening. This also marks the transition from being a *patient* to becoming an *analysand*.

Presently, there are several "talking cures", but it is precisely this type of listening that distinguishes psychoanalysis from any other form of psychotherapy or counseling. And now more than ever, listening can make a difference in the clinical practice of the "new symptoms". In the classic clinic of neuroses, based on the psychic mechanisms of censorship and repression, talking alone may be enough to alleviate most symptoms. But today in many modern societies, the mechanism of repression is no longer so central on a social and, therefore, individual level. This is reflected in today's clinic*. Presently, many patients feel empty, lost, and with a lack of direction in life. They do not show a particular resistance to the unconscious. If they do not speak about their personal issues it is not out of reticence, rejection of the unconscious, or fear of what they may discover, but because they feel disconnected from their unconscious. They literally feel a void inside themselves. So, they do not see their symptoms (or any other manifestations of the unconscious, e.g., dreams, slips) as being of any relation to them. They may talk a lot (more precisely, they may complain or lament), *but they do not listen to what they are saying*. There is not much that seems to surprise or lead them to question. The word seems to have lost value for them. They do not seem

DOI: 10.4324/9780429432064-4

to be driven by any question or curiosity about themselves or the world (thus, it is not surprising that they have not yet found a direction in life). And this is why today more than ever it is necessary to rediscover the unconscious and practice psychoanalytic listening.

How does psychoanalytic listening work? What distinguishes psychoanalytical listening from listening as it is commonly understood? In a previous study (Busiol, 2016) I identified three components that describe listening as conceptualized and practiced among most psychoanalytic orientations (*free-floating attention*, the *unconscious*, and the *transference*), and three components that describe listening as generally practiced in psychotherapy/counseling (*focused attention*, as opposed to the psychoanalytic free-floating attention; a rather *active role of the therapist* to direct the patient, through suggestions, advice, even homework; and an inclination to *aim at solutions* to problems rather than analyzing questions). In addition, I reviewed the main theoretical developments of psychoanalytic listening from Freud to the present day. After Freud, different schools have developed very different perspectives: some have suggested that the psychoanalyst should listen to the patient's unconscious through his own countertransference and his own subjectivity; others instead have emphasized intersubjectivity; some believe that listening can only happen through empathy, whereas others suggest that there is no difference between listening and interpretation. A reader who is interested in knowing more may refer to this earlier publication (Busiol, 2016).

My impression, however, is that the proliferation of all these different orientations stems from a fundamental problem: after Freud, language lost its centrality because it was no longer considered by most analysts to be what truly founds the human experience. Gradually, language was reduced to simply a means of communication. Putting language aside, these analysts thought they could base psychoanalysis on concepts or principles. Or that they could replace the analysis of language with the analysis of affects. But can there really be listening if the patient's speech is forcefully understood/reduced on the basis of a pre-established interpretative grid? Theory (any theory: Freudian, Lacanian, Kleinian) cannot precede listening. If we imagine that there is an a priori theory, before the analysand's word – a theory to which everything can be traced back, a theory that should explain everything the patient says – then there is no listening.

The analytic listening, or as we could also call it, the listening *tout-court*, is at the same time something very simple and very difficult. In this chapter, I will try to show why. To begin with, I think it is important to ask: what is the object of analysis, and therefore of listening? *The object of listening is the unconscious. And the object of analysis is the word/speech of the person talking, not their personality or behavior.*

The word in Freud

Freud may not have explicitly addressed the question of the word, but it was central in his work from the beginning. In fact, already in 1891, he wrote *On Aphasia*.

Later, with *The Interpretation of Dreams*, published in 1900, and considered by many to be the founding text of psychoanalysis, Freud begins to describe in more detail the mechanisms of the unconscious and their relationship with language. According to Freud, the dream operates by condensation and displacement (or, as Lacan later said, by metaphor (e.g., the lake is a mirror) and metonymy (e.g., lend me your ears)). Some dream images may seem absurd. But the dream is like a rebus, that is, a riddle to be deciphered, which mixes letters and figures. Therefore, *it is not the images that interest us, but the words that name them*. It is possible to understand elements of a dream only by putting it into words, by recounting it. An image can begin to *say* something if it is read, if it is put into words, because at this point the words reveal a polysemy, a multiplicity of meanings that the image cannot show. In Italian, if we say that someone "has lost his head", this can refer to someone who was beheaded during the French Revolution, someone who is very much in love, or someone who has gone mad. But only words (signifiers) can maintain such equivocity. Conversely, an image can only represent one of these cases, so the image fixes a meaning. For us, the image is acoustic, in the sense that it is made of words, and therefore in analysis it is a question of listening to the images. That is what we do with dreams, but also with certain symptoms: we turn these images back into words.

Shortly after *The Interpretation of Dreams*, Freud wrote *The Psychopathology of Everyday Life* (published in 1901) and *Jokes and Their Relation to the Unconscious* (published in 1905). These three texts form a sort of trilogy, in the sense that Freud demonstrates that dreams, forgetfulness, slips, wit, and even symptoms are all formations of the unconscious and share broad characteristics. In most cases, they represent an unconscious conflict (between a wish and an attempt to repress it). Freud shows us that we can grasp some understanding of them if we pay attention to the exact words adopted in telling them. Freud (1901/1975) cites the case of the judge who at the opening of the session exclaimed: "Gentlemen: I take notice that a full quorum of members is present and herewith declare the sitting closed!" (p. 101). That is, instead of declaring the session open, he declares it closed. Freud's comment is that evidently that slip was not just an error, but that it revealed something of his desire to be there. That is to say that a slip of tongue is never trivial, it is never innocent, because it reveals something (unconscious) that cannot be said otherwise. The comic effect produced makes the communication lighter (it makes the embarrassment of revealing one's own desire bearable), but this does not mean that we should not take the lapses seriously. Quite the opposite. Whereas in most situations in life we tend to dismiss such lapses as 'just a mistake' (overlooking it), in analysis we consider them very meaningful, and we underline them enthusiastically when they happen in session. After all, it is through joking that one can let the truth out.

Finally, several years later Freud (1925) wrote *Negation*, where he shows that negation is nothing more than a mechanism for overcoming internal censorship. The negation of a sentence does not make it any less true. That "not" placed in front of a thought, which in any case the person speaking has formulated, only serves to say something unacceptable, taking distance from it: "Now you'll think I mean to say something insulting, but really I've no such intention" (p. 235; in this case the use of negation is also preceded by projection).

Listening to the letter

My clinical experience shows me that when listening to a patient, the most important and at the same time the most difficult thing to do is to follow 'to the letter' what is being said. This means paying extra-careful attention to the patient's words: stick to the exact signifiers uttered, avoid using synonyms, and avoid referring to what (one imagines) the speaker intended to say. A clinical vignette will help to understand this.

An analysand complains about his lover, who is not available when he needs him. He says that he has always gone out of his way to help him, support him, serve him, while the other is cold and repulsive. Then he recounts a moment of intimacy: "when I am with H. I always give him foot massages, and I love being between his legs. It does not matter if he looks at his phone in the meantime, I like to touch him there. I could spend hours holding his balls". As he speaks, the analysand himself, now somewhat trained in psychoanalytic listening, realizes that "holding his balls" is very similar (especially in Italian, the language we speak in session) to the expression "have someone by the balls", which does not express submission at all, but rather having total control over the other: exactly the contrary. And by listening to what he has said, he can recognize something of his unconscious desire, something he has not yet considered. And this revives him because it allows him to stop seeing himself as a servant or victim.

Another vignette:

G: I met my former boss yesterday because I was curious to know about his new job. It's something I'd like to do, and I wanted to see if it was possible to work in this new company. I felt a lot of "frenesia" (frenzy) prior to this meeting.

DB: Frenesia?

G: Mhmm yeah . . . isn't that a synonym for excitement?

DB: Oh yes?

G: Hm

DB: It is interesting that this word came to your mind. Last session you talked about a situation in bed where you were overexcited and sweating.

G: Hm yeah, it's like when I'm driving and I have the feeling that I cannot slow down. I am anxious, I feel that I have to complete the task . . . (then, talking again about the job interview) a question that my father would ask me in these cases is: what are the expectations of the other?

Frenzy is not exactly the same as excitement, and it is appropriate to stop the patient on this term. Interestingly enough, *frenesia* in Italian sounds similar to the verb *frenare*, meaning to brake or slow down (despite its etymology being from

Latin *phrenesis*, from Greek *phrēn* 'mind', so unrelated to slowing down). The patient associates this state of frenesia precisely to driving a car (and difficulty slowing down). There is a constant push to do (frenzy), but also a braking issue. A failure to brake, but also a failure to lose brakes (he says he feels like he has the handbrake on).

These nuances can only be understood through this type of listening "to the letter". Moreover, we have to say that synonyms do not exist: saying one word or another is not the same thing. Saying: "I like to hold his balls" is not at all the same as saying "I like to put my hands in his pants". We have to stick to the exact signifiers used, because we are aiming to understand unconscious desire, which we can only access through the equivocity of words and misunderstanding the manifest or obvious meaning, the intentional speech. Playing with the equivocity of the word opens up other possible understandings. It may also allude to the analysand's feeling of "not having the balls" (to do something). Balls that the other has (literally and figuratively), and that have become so beautiful and desirable.

Then, we understand why it is fundamental to remain anchored to the exact signifiers that are said and not to the presumed general sense of what one is saying. Analytical listening does not take place on the level of sense or meaning (that we imagine), but by placing one letter after another, one signifier after another, as is done when solving a puzzle. It is precisely the choice of words that informs us about one's unconscious desire. This is the essential aspect of analytical listening, and it is surprising that this is not commonly practiced in the "psych" world. It is also surprising how many therapists pay very little attention to the terms adopted by their patients, *not realizing how their speech/narration clearly revolves around some specific signifiers*. I often hear presentations of clinical cases from which the patient's speech is completely absent; the whole case is built not on what the patient said, but on what the therapist understood, or remembers, or thinks the other intended to say.

An analysis can only proceed by listening to that word that the patient did not think s/he was going to say, but which nevertheless came out of his/her mouth. Only through rigorous observance of this type of listening, and not through the acquisition of any psychoanalytic "knowledge", can allow a patient to become an analyst him/herself, that is to say that this kind of listening allows one to analyze any discourse, including his/her own.

What I am saying here was not made explicit in these terms by Freud. It is Lacan, who reread Freud in light of the contribution of de Saussure's linguistics, who introduced, for example, the distinction between signifier and signified. Lacan started from a radical consideration, namely that language pre-exists us, that the human being is a *parlêtre*, a being of speech. We are born into a world that is primarily a world of words. And the observations made by Freud about slips, dreams, and wit indicate precisely this: that we have no control over language, and that language comes before us.

The fundamental rule

Freud wrote extensively throughout his life but gave relatively little technical information on "what to do" in the session. Instead, he indicated what *not* to do, so as not to preclude listening. After abandoning the cathartic method and suggestion, he in fact established only one rule to give to patients before they start talking, namely to say "whatever comes into their heads, even if they think it unimportant or irrelevant or nonsensical or embarrassing or distressing" (Freud, 1904, p. 251). This very important indication later became "the fundamental rule". Later, in *Recommendations to Physicians Practicing Psychoanalysis* (Freud, 1912), Freud lists a series of recommendations for the analyst. In fact, even these indications are attributable to the fundamental rule:

1   "not directing one's notice to anything in particular and in maintaining the same 'evenly-suspended attention'" (Freud, 1912, p. 110). This is the counterpart to the demand made to the patient to obey the fundamental rule of free association.
2   avoid taking notes during analytical sessions;
3   the analyst should maintain emotional coldness "and concentrate his mental forces on the single aim of performing the operation as skillfully as possible" (p. 114);
4   the analyst should do everything not to become a censor of his own in selecting the patient's material (metaphor of the receiver);
5   educative ambition is of as little use as therapeutic ambition; every doctor should "take the patient's capacities rather than his own desires as guide" (p. 118); and
6   avoid intellectualizing the psychoanalytic conversation as "mental activities such as thinking something over or concentrating the attention solve none of the riddles of a neurosis"; instead one should patiently obey "the psychoanalytic rule, which enjoins the exclusion of all criticism of the unconscious or of its derivatives" (p. 118).

Freud says that it is not necessary to talk about something in particular, but simply to talk ("as you would do in a conversation in which you were rambling on quite disconnectedly and at random", Freud, 1904, p. 251). It is not a question of digging into the past in search of the repressed trauma or the unspeakable secret (it would be naive to think that something does not remain secret to the analyst). For the analysand, it is a question of saying what comes to mind in the moment, and for the analyst a question of listening without thinking that s/he has already understood what the other is saying.

There is often some anxiety among less experienced psychotherapists about what to say in the session, how to respond to the patient, how to guide him/her. There is an anxiety about not knowing what *to do*. Similarly, some patients ask for indications on what they should say, what is expected of them, or how therapy is supposed to work; as if there is a standard, a rule to follow. Some patients imagine that they have to say "everything" in the first session; then, they make the conscious effort to provide as many details as possible about their situation (literally overflooding the therapist with words), thinking that this is enough for the therapist to understand their problem and finally give them the solution. Freud completely reversed this logic. The fundamental rule implies that it is not necessary to prepare what to say before the session. "What am I going to talk about in today's session?" is a question that patients often ask themselves. However, Freud urged his patients not to prepare any sort of speech, because he knew that it would only obstruct the emergence of something truly significant, and then he invited them to put aside any thoughts and simply say what was going through their head in that given moment. With this simple rule, Freud placed the unconscious, and not the intention of the speaker's ego, at the center of listening. He used an effective metaphor: "act as though, for instance, you were a traveler sitting next to the window of a railway carriage and describing to someone inside the carriage the changing views which you see outside" (Freud, 1913, p. 135). The Freudian hypothesis is that *there is a logic, which is unconscious and that will clarify itself later.*

A patient begins the session by saying that he has seen a play, in the theater, which describes the vicissitudes of a European family. He says that he found this representation interesting because this family belongs to a society that for historical, political, and religious reasons has always defined itself by contrast with the neighboring country, that is to say that it has built its identity on the difference from, or even on contempt for, the inhabitants of the neighboring country. "Without the others", the patient observes, "they are nothing". This might seem like a simple historical/social observation, a way to break the ice. It might seem that this person, after all, is just talking about a play seen at the theater. It might even seem like a way of avoiding the "real" issues he should be talking about. But we keep on listening. This person continues talking, and wonders why the ethnic minorities in his country have not united with each other and have not rebelled against the oppressor. What is this person talking about? What is he referring to? Maybe he cannot explain an identity that is not built on the contempt for the other, and therefore outside of a dependence on the other? I don't have enough elements yet, but in the meantime I welcome what he is saying and suggest that perhaps there is something here that relates to him. But how, I ask him. What has struck him? He says he has always felt like someone who struggles at work and in life, one who fights, alone, basically always in competition with other people, others whom he despises and by whom he feels despised, devalued. And at the same time, others he cannot do without. Little by little, it becomes clear what he is talking about. It does not matter what the theater play was about. This is what resonated with this person. Competition with the other, contempt, devaluation, but ultimately also dependence on the other are issues that he can relate to, to the point that it is difficult for him to imagine someone who would not represent himself as either a victim or an oppressor.

The free-floating attention

Free-floating attention is the counterpart for the analyst to free association for the patient. That is to say, if the patient simply has to say what comes to mind, the analyst will simply have to listen, without worrying about understanding (putting his judgment before listening) or will have to listen to something in particular (selectively), but follow the chain of thoughts and signifiers, as they unfold, as they present themselves. Many psychologists and counselors think that listening to patients is tiring and takes a lot of energy because it requires one to be focused. To them, listening is a cognitive effort (Busiol, 2016). They practice what they call 'active listening'. Freud's position is rather different, as he theorizes instead the free-floating attention: "in this way we spare ourselves a strain on our attention which could not in any case be kept up for several hours daily, and we avoid a danger which is inseparable from the exercise of deliberate attention. For as soon as anyone deliberately concentrates his attention to a certain degree, he begins to select from the material before him; one point will be fixed in his mind with particular clearness and some other will be correspondingly disregarded, and in making this selection he will be following his expectations or inclinations. This, however, is precisely what must not be done. In making the selection, if he follows his expectations, he is in danger of never finding anything but what he already knows; and if he follows his inclinations, he will certainly falsify what he may perceive. It must not be forgotten that the things one hears are for the most part things whose meaning is only recognized later on" (Freud, 1913, pp. 133–134). The 'evenly-suspended attention' is suspended particularly with respect to the manifest content of what is said and the obvious meaning. Not focusing on anything in particular may allow us to find something new, grasp some words that are being repeated in the patient's speech, spot the inconsistencies of the narrative, focus on what remains unspoken, as well as to the particular use of some terms. The analytical listening is not heavy or cognitively draining at all. Freud suggested not even taking notes in sessions. What is surprisingly unique about analytic listening is that one does not need to make an effort to remember anything. Freud already noted how he happened to remember the essential, despite having so many patients who every day told him many details of their lives.

When we listen, attention has to be "fluctuating". This is something we all experience. If someone begins a sentence by saying "the corner" we know that this signifier can take different meanings. It could be the corner of the room, or the corner of the street, by metaphor that corner of paradise; the list goes on. So, it is only when the speaker continues talking and adds the signifier "kick" that we understand that he is talking about a football match. That is to say that it is only what follows that, retroactively, will give meaning to the sentence; therefore, we are continually required to suspend judgment, so as to understand what is being said.

In the example above, one may assume that there is a communicative intention on the side of the person speaking. In such cases, one just has to wait and the message will clarify itself. But in session this becomes more complicated, in the sense that what we are trying to listen to and understand escapes, at least partially, any patient's (communicative) intention. What one thinks s/he is saying does not necessarily reduce to what s/he says. At best, the speaker does not know what s/he is saying. When we speak – unless we just read a speech we have prepared in advance – we don't know exactly where we're headed. We also hear ourselves for the first time, so may be surprised by what we happen to say. Then, the analyst must resist the idea of knowing what the patient is saying; the judgment must remain suspended.

Associations of thoughts

Just like how each signifier gives meaning to the previous ones, each new element that is said in session (a memory, an association, a comment) is linked to what was said before and is to be understood in a sequence. This sequence is in itself a free association. Even when we think that we are changing topic, actually most of the times we are not really changing topic. What links these elements together, the common thread, is often opaque, and that is what we need to discover. However, it takes some time for a sequence to emerge. One should resist the temptation to interpret everything the moment it is said. Things will be understood in the *après-coup*, in retrospective, in light of what comes next. Oliver recounts in session:

O: I had a meeting with another bank. They seem smarter than the first bank. But let's see, I don't know what they want. [. . .] My sex life is zero right now. My girlfriend does not want me, she does not seem interested in sex at all. I tried to ask her why, yesterday. . . . My business partner, well I don't understand him. We need to find clients, and I am doing this kind of search job. But him, and actually all the people in my office seem to be just followers. If I tell them to do something, they will do it. But otherwise, they won't.

DB: It is difficult to understand what the other wants: the bank people, your girl-friend, your colleagues.

O: Hmmm yes, this seems to be the common thread.

Oliver is not aware of what links these apparently disparate situations to each other, but listening to the sequence, a common question seems to emerge. We are not interested in ascertaining the truthfulness of what is being reported. But *we are interested in grasping the (unconscious) question underlying his speech*, what he is wondering about, what troubles him. For example, his relationship with the Other, whose desire he cannot read. The Other, which escapes his representations, beliefs, and he feels he cannot control. What does the Other want? For Oliver, this is a mystery. Oliver finds it hard to recognize and accept the Other as really other than himself, as someone with a desire and a logic different from his own. Thus, the Other becomes unintelligible.

How does an analysis begin?

An analysis can only take place through the patient's word. There is no universal knowledge about the unconscious that the analyst can master and dispense to a passive patient, or worse, a client or a user as some say. Knowledge is not on the analyst's side, but on the patient's side; however, it is an unconscious knowledge. We can say that the patient does not know that s/he knows. The analyst's responsibility is to make the analysand hear that there is more in the folds of his/her speech, and that this is what must interest him/her. The patient should orient his/her interest towards what is in the folds of his/her speech, what remains unsaid, or between the lines of his/her conscious speech. Of course, the analyst's formation is important, and his/her desire to analyze is even more fundamental. But ultimately, it is the word that heals, more than the analyst (the analyst does not possess all the power accredited to them). Therefore, it is essential that the patient develops some desire to do analysis. It is essential to respect the appointments and the fundamental rule. In short, it is essential that there is some transference towards the analysis (more than the analyst). What can guarantee the success of an analysis, if not the desire to do analysis (i.e., desire to discover something new; to understand something; to find a direction in life)? It does not really matter what the symptom is. It is not like in medicine, where one "heals" more or less rapidly depending on the severity of the symptom. Desire for analysis, questioning, and listening are three interrelated issues. The success of an analysis depends on the level of one's active engagement in the process. The desire (to know, to discover) leads to the development of questions, which in turn enhance the listening, and this in turn revamps the desire, and so on.

Freud compared the analyst's work to that of the archaeologist (in *Constructions in Analysis*, 1937), but not in the sense that the unconscious is something deep, which should be unearthed. The idea of the unconscious as a well, as something that can be localized (in the depths) is misleading. Lacan specifies this when he refers to E. A. Poe's *The Purloined Letter*. We could say that the unconscious is always under our eyes, only we don't always notice it. The unconscious manifests itself continuously, but we don't always grasp it because understanding something other than what is said requires some practice. *An analysis begins only when the patient puts aside his/her beliefs, reasoning, and intentional speech, and gives in to a spontaneous speech and narration.* When s/he begins to associate, tells dreams, when s/he no longer feel the need to prepare a list of things to say. Only at this point may one find something unexpected and surprising (and interesting) in what s/he happens to say.

In my experience, this step is not easy and can take quite some time. When my patients talk, I always try to repeat or emphasize some signifier they said that could be understood differently. Not all of them immediately get it. And it's not a matter of education, age, or intelligence. It is a sensitivity that some have early on, that for others takes a long time, and that some seem never to have (to some, the equivocity of the signifier troubles them, they cannot stand it, they defend themselves from it).

A patient, who has a lot of difficulty in saying what he wants (he enjoys contradicting what others say, and silences them; but he finds it very hard to express his own opinion and say something that is not in opposition to others, for fear of being criticized), suddenly began to study how to make masks to protect against Covid-19. In particular, he developed an innovative and very economical filter, and then contacted several NGOs and research institutes offering them his idea, for free. He cannot quite understand why he is so passionate about this project. Indeed, he is a carpenter by profession. I notice, however, that a *mask* is perfect for hiding the face, for covering the mouth. And the *filter* is a great idea for filtering . . . words, maybe? Indeed, a great solution for someone who is conflicted about getting his voice out and making himself heard (or for silencing others).

Another patient, a lawyer, comes to see me because she lost any interest in her profession. She tells that for some time she has been interested in interior design, although she cannot explain why. She asks me if she should continue on this path, despite not having received any formal training. I ask her to tell me more, and she tells me that she is particularly fascinated by 'decluttering' which, she explains to me, is the art of tidying up the house, getting rid of clutter, so as to have a simple lifestyle. It is amazing, isn't it? It is a matter of understanding 'interior design' and 'decluttering' in the equivocity, that is, not as much referring to architecture as to the internal world of the patient. As a desire to get rid of the hindrances in her life, to lighten or ease her path, to relieve her from some pressure (this person first finds this decluttering externally, with regards to the spaces she lives in and shares with others, but also finds it internally with me, in session). This kind of (mis)understanding of the signifier is light, ironic, touches the essence of the question, and tells which signifiers (interior, lighten, simplify, cut out, decorating) are orienting the patient's life. Not everyone develops the sensitivity to listen/understand these other leads, but if this happens it is normally a turning point in the analysis.

Psychoanalysis is not the theory of communication

The theory of communication, developed in the field of psychology, is very simple: there is one person (A) who sends a message to another (B) who receives it, and who in turn sends feedback to signal that s/he has understood. The message is encoded by the sender and decoded by the receiver: that's all. The experience of analysis shows us instead that nothing is as clear as it seems. To begin with, it is not clear who is speaking, since what the patient says partially escapes his/her own understanding. Language is not just a tool that we use to transmit thought. Thought itself is made of words, and we ourselves are spectators, or better an audience, of what we happen to say. We ourselves have to talk (even just to ourselves) to tell us what we think. Some people even complain that they have some intrusive thoughts, which they would rather not have but that take over. The unconscious precedes the ego. So, who is speaking? This is the great mystery of the word. Where does the word come from? And who is it addressed to?

In the psychoanalytic setting, the patient's speech is addressed to the analyst. However, it is probably more correct to say that it is addressed to the place (temporarily) occupied by the analyst, rather that the analyst himself. This is not easy to understand. In most cases, it is not at all clear to patients; often, not even to the analyst. In the analytic setting, the analyst acts as a receiver (B), only because s/he occupies the place of the Other. And his/her job is to point out that the analysand is actually referring to the Other.

And what about the message of the communication? If even the emittent A does not have full control over what s/he says (because there's something in his/her speech that escapes him/her), what will the receiver B understand? The experience of the analysis shows that communication fails continuously, and that the misunderstanding – due to the equivocity of the word – is inevitable. No one can be in control of the word. We communicate through signifiers, but then for each of us the meaning of these can be slightly different. It is not entirely shared. It is therefore somehow surprising that despite all these limitations, we manage to understand each other from time to time, or so it seems to us.

For example, imagine a person who is thinking of a tree, and who wants to talk about this tree to another person. According to the theory of communication, the image of the tree must be translated by the emittent A into the signifier 'tree', then the word will be received by B, who will then translate it again into the image of the tree. It seems a very simple process, but in reality, it is almost certain that the sender and the receiver have two very different images of a tree in their minds, even if they have the impression that they have understood what is in the other's mind.

If you ask 10 people to draw a home, you will most likely have ten different drawings. Someone will draw an apartment, someone a villa, someone the house where s/he grew up, someone the house of his dreams, someone will draw it from the outside, someone will draw the plan of the house from above, and so on. Yet, when we talk, we seem to know exactly what the other is talking about. This misunderstanding is inevitable, and indeed it is what allows the interaction. If no misunderstanding was possible, then no conversation would be possible. Then, it is good to remember, especially if we are analysts who see patients, that the same signifier does not have the same meaning for everyone. We cannot take for granted what the other is saying. It is important to "make use" of the misunderstanding, for example, by asking: what is this home you are talking about like, who is inside, how is it made, what characteristics does it have, what can be said about it, what is unique about it, what makes it a home?

Why is it essential to follow the signifiers and not the meanings? Think, for example, of a conversation between a patient and a doctor. The patient says "Doctor, please help me I'm addicted to Twitter". And the doctor replies "Excuse me, I don't follow you . . .". This is clearly a joke, and we find it funny precisely because "I don't follow you" plays with the equivocal and opens up another possible understanding. If the doctor had answered "I don't understand you" instead of "I don't follow you" – thus eliminating the ambiguity – this story would not only not be funny anymore, but it would reduce everything to a rather insignificant communication. *We can think of some symptoms in similar terms: as a translation that is too concrete, which has eliminated the equivocity, and that is therefore incomprehensible.* I am thinking, for example, about Freud's first patients, for whom the impossibility to say or do something (an impasse, a paralysis in some areas of their life) literally became a physical paralysis of the body (the arm, for example). Of course, the problem was not in the body, but at the level of the speech. Psychoanalysis was born to translate these physical symptoms into words. Recovering the misunderstanding, the equivocity, thus playing with words, with the signifiers. Sticking to meanings would be in the logic of the symptom itself. Then, the symptom is a resource, and as such we must not be in a hurry to remove it. The symptom is already an attempt at a solution (a compromise solution, Freud said). Of course, the symptom can be distressing and painful for the patient. The symptom indicates an unconscious fantasy, and this is what should interest us.

If the unconscious manifests itself through the misunderstanding, it is not a question of aiming at the "deep" meaning, building on what is said, or explaining. Conversely, it is a question of subverting, breaking the meaning. Freud suggested avoiding intellectualization in the session, as this is a resistance to the unconscious. And Lacan said that an analyst should do crosswords, because these are not based so much on erudition or knowledge, but on knowing how to play with words, with the ambiguity of definitions, while also paying attention to the letters that are already in the table.

Limits of comprehending

I'm trying to question the idea that it would be possible to *comprehend* everything that is being said. Etymologically, comprehend refers to "to grasp + together". It therefore refers to obtaining a 'full grasp of a meaning'. Most psychology attempts to comprehend uncertainty by definition, explanation, and clarification. The experience of analysis shows us that this is not possible. The very hypothesis that something is unconscious implies that we cannot come to a definitive and full comprehension. The unconscious is limitless and therefore an ultimate meaning of it does not exist. There is no signification that is ultimately true. To clarify, we must repress the ambiguity, the misunderstanding, and therefore the unconscious. But if we do this, then we do not "comprehend", precisely because we are leaving something out.

The word cannot be fully explained because it inevitably refers to other words. The unconscious is produced continuously, as an effect of words. But this is not a limit for the analysis; indeed, it is this reference to other that allows something to be said. But finally, what would comprehension be for, if it were even possible: to heal; to solve problems? What should happen once we have comprehended: enlightenment; insight? Or, perhaps the comprehension of the "original trauma" that would make the long-awaited change possible? Psychoanalysis is not an orthopedics, a direction of conscience, or counseling. Furthermore, the limit of comprehending is that *we comprehend with regard to our standards or beliefs.* Cognition is recognition of the already known; it is bringing the unknown back to the already known. It illuminates what is obscure, but adds nothing new.

Comprehending is making the Other familiar, the strange similar. Conversely, through speaking (and listening to what we happen to say and to what is being said), we find the strange in what we believed familiar. We find difference in what we imagined similar. Comprehending is a way to reduce the distance between oneself and the Other, to make the Other similar to oneself, a way to master the object, to make it more manageable. When attempting comprehension, however, the two most likely outcomes are: 1) we do not understand what the other is saying, and so the other is perceived as deviant, stupid, unreasonable, incapable; or, 2) we have the impression that we clearly understand everything the other is saying. In both cases, the other is not perceived as radically different (to oneself). In the first case nothing the other says makes sense; in the second case, everything is clear even before the other speaks, as if words were not needed. And in fact, words are not needed in order to comprehend, because comprehension is not in the register of listening. If we listened, sooner or later we would realize that the other does not say *exactly* what we thought s/he was saying. If we listened, sooner or later we would realize that the other also has a logic of his/her own, and that perhaps s/he is not stupid.

Trying to comprehend is an obstacle to listening, since, as we have said, listening requires a certain suspension of judgment. The anxiety to comprehend is common among new therapists, who are so attentive to every communication from their patients. What does what the other is telling me mean? And what do I answer now? The urge to understand is linked to the urge to respond, to elucidate, to explain, to give instructions, to clarify, to eliminate the cognitive distortions of the other, to straighten his errors of understanding. This turns out to be a boomerang. As a psychologist – who was trying hard to read what her patients told her based on the few concepts she learned at university – once told me: "I realize that I often remain on a very superficial level, I cannot go beyond".

Even if it is not possible to comprehend *everything*, it is still possible to understand *something*. The misunderstanding in communication is inevitable because the word/signifier is equivocal and can take on different meanings depending on the sentence in which it is placed, the context, the speaker, the tone of the voice, and many other variables. However, this is not what causes incomprehension. Rather, incomprehension originates from supposing that we all share universal meanings, whereas the signification is partly unconscious, and therefore singular, slightly different for each person. Paradoxically, it is precisely the misunderstanding that allows us to understand something of the speaker's speech, and of our own; only when one encounters a misunderstanding one can (retroactively) become aware of the assumptions of his/her own speech and logic. So, clarity is not an alternative to misunderstanding, quite the contrary. The experience of the analysis shows us that something is clarified only by passing through a misunderstanding, and only *thanks* to this misunderstanding.

Make the misunderstanding work

Some analysands are not ready to accept the equivocity of what they say, that is, that what they say can be understood differently to what they meant. It happens that some people immediately try to correct themselves, or to correct the analyst, saying "I didn't mean that, but this . . .". When this happens, I usually do not insist. But I repeat the term they used, and I remark that the interest for us lies precisely in this word choice rather than another. I stress the positive value of the equivocity of words, and thus the misunderstanding, for the analysis. For us, this is gold because it opens up another possible understanding.

Focusing on signifiers also allows us to disconnect from the level of affects. The content of a conversation can be very painful, heavy. Remaining anchored to the content can have two consequences: empathy (from Greek *pathos*, meaning 'passion' or 'suffering'), or antipathy ('opposed in feeling'). It is certainly not a question of being cold or rude with the other, but it is also not a case of getting stuck at the level of affects, as this may not lead very far. Affects are effects of the speech (effects of a closed, circular discourse, rather than an authentic act of speech), and therefore are not original. As such, the level of affects is largely imaginary. It is therefore a question of welcoming what the other has to say, but at the same time listening to another possible understanding, which is the only way to alleviate suffering. What is pain, if not a way of telling a story that cannot be said otherwise? What causes pain, if not the repetition of the identical? Or a story that cannot be told, that remains interrupted because words fail? Or the fixation on a meaning that cannot be overcome? This is the fixed idea, the obsession. It is painful when we cannot move on "in the speech", that is, when we cannot change narrative. So, perhaps in analysis it is not a question of adding more meaning (comprehending, finding the explanations, the causes), but rather a matter of *finding some new elements* (a few words) that allows one to get out of the impasse, which allows the narrative to unfold, to take a new turn.

Some people think that psychoanalytic listening is difficult but personally, I think a listening that aims at manifesting a meaning and empathizing is actually more taxing. Analytical listening proceeds from lightness, from irony. It is not heavy because it aims at the essential. It is not a question of saying everything in analysis, or remembering everything, but one of freeing oneself from the weight of memories (which are screen memories, that is, reconstructions); it is a question of losing the thread of the discussion. If we take the discussion for granted, then yes, it is heavy, because the discourse is closed, it does not lead to anything new.

Psychology recommends a form of listening that defines 'active listening', the purpose of which would be to reach full comprehension of what the interlocutor is saying. But imagine following the speech of a person who complains that the world sucks and says that he has tried everything but nothing works. How can a full comprehension help us and our interlocutor in any way? What should one say when faced with such a speech (which is rather common, to tell the truth), if our "active" listening aims to understand the point of view of our interlocutor? In the end, we can do nothing but agree with his/her reasons: "it's a difficult world; it's the system's fault; you could not do otherwise"; but in this case we can only give some encouragement to persist, not to give up, like in those slogans "if you believe, it comes true", "the fall is not as important as how you get up", or to recommend other survival strategies. Because that is where this kind of active listening leads.

On the contrary, we realize that there is always Other, beyond what is said. What is said must be listened to in the misunderstanding, because it opens to another scene and says something about an unconscious desire. A patient of mine complains that he does not understand what his wife wants: "you do not listen to me", she repeats to him, while he is convinced that s/he has done his utmost to satisfy her requests. And it is true; he does not listen precisely because he is committed to satisfying her requests. The other's desire makes him extremely anxious. Then, he tries to satisfy such desire, so as to suffocate it, silence it, to reduce it to zero. He fails to metaphorize what the other says, everything is taken literally. For him, the other's speech is an order that he cannot escape and which he must fulfill. He fails to question the value of those requests: what does the other want? There is listening when there is no image (the meaning; the representation of the object), when the message remains partly mysterious. It is not about becoming paranoid, imagining that behind what is said there is another (and only that) meaning. Lacan (1974) said that psychoanalysis is "a controlled paranoia" (p. 103). The paranoid knows that the truth is not all in that is said, it is elsewhere. The paranoid knows that no communication is neutral, that nothing is just said without meaning, and therefore s/he pays attention to every little detail and does not underestimate any element. Then, however, the paranoid is wrong because s/he imagines that every gesture, every sentence means precisely something else; there is no mystery for the paranoid, everything is a sign and therefore each element is brought back to a predetermined meaning.

Jacques Lacan

Jacques Lacan's name often evokes the image of a dark, baroque thinker, difficult to understand. Some are fascinated by him and consider him a master of thought, while to others he is a charlatan. Lacan certainly spoke an articulate, evocative, dense, cryptic language – a language far from common sense – but this was also very much in line with the object of his discourse: the unconscious. In other words, Lacan made good use of the signifier's equivocity and the misunderstanding to prevent the listener from thinking that s/he could come to a quick comprehension. This equivocity intrigues some, because something seems to continually escape full understanding, and bothers others, who instead would like clear, explicit answers, without mincing words. Lacan wanted to 'speak well', but speaking well does not come to an end because there is always a distance between 'speaking' and the thing said. Yet, 40 years after Lacan's death there are still many who read and study his teachings (mainly seminars transcribed by his students, and not revised by Lacan), which perhaps owe their richness precisely to the opacity of his word, since at each reading they seem to be opened up to a different interpretation, and in this sense they are truly inexhaustible. On the contrary, it seems to me that the various attempts to clarify, explain, and define 'Psychoanalysis' have not had the same following as Lacan had. As if to say that imagining preserving orthodoxy leads to sterile repetition of the identical, therefore to closure, marginality, and even extinction.

Lacan is known for some dense and enigmatic expressions, aphorisms, and maxims. For example, he spoke of the divided subject, written as $ or S /, that is, S indicating the subject and the bar indicating the division. Traditionally the subject of philosophy was the Cartesian subject: "I think". But psychoanalysis shows that since there is an unconscious, which is something that is "inside" us, but also "beyond" us, the subject is no longer the transparent subject of the philosophical reflection but is crossed by something that is foreign to them. Something imposes itself on the subject. We can say "I speak", but we don't really have control over what we say, and in fact we do experience lapses, forgetfulness. Thought itself is already a sort of inner conversation, what we use to listen to ourselves, to hear the voice, which is 'ours' but nevertheless precedes us. Where does the voice come from? The voice is not localizable. So, perhaps it is more correct to say that "we are spoken".

Lacan introduced the notion of *'fantasme'* (in French; translated into English as fantasy or phantasm), which is different to fantasy as it is commonly understood. We can say that the *fantasme* describes the subject's relationship with the object. Lacan wrote the formula of the *fantasme*: "$ <> a" to describe the way in which the subject ($) poses itself towards the lost object, the object cause of desire (a). Basically, the *fantasme* is the veil through which the subject sees and represents the world, that is, how one understands and gives meaning to things.

Another of Lacan's famous phrases is "the analyst is the subject supposed to know". The analyst, but also the therapist, are often in this position when they are addressed a question from a patient, who does not know what makes him/her suffer and turns to them, supposing they know and therefore are able to help. It is important that there is such supposition, because this is what allows a demand to be formulated. It is the precondition for transference. However, an analyst must not fall into the trap of believing that s/he knows anything, because this may become an obstacle to analysis. Younger therapists/analysts may get a little anxious about not knowing what to say or how to answer patients, and perhaps this indicates that they also suppose they should know this before the other speaks. But this is not possible, and not due to some insufficiency or incapacity of the analyst, but because for each person the chain of signifiers (i.e., the sequence of associations of words, memories, fantasies, etc.) develops in a unique and unpredictable way. To some, the term 'home' may bring to mind 'family', and therefore 'dog', and then 'tree', because the dog pees on the tree. For another, 'home' can be associated with 'investment', and therefore the material sense of the word, the four walls. There is no way to know about this sequence if not through speaking, because it is the word that imposes itself on the speaker, in an original, arbitrary way, mixing elements of the past and the present, as in a dream. Going back to what we said before, we can say that this idea of being able to build knowledge about the Other (the stranger we have in front of us, but ultimately the Other who speaks within us) is already a fantasy. Knowledge becomes a way to try to master the always elusive object. This is also what happens outside of the analytic setting. Uncertainty provokes anxiety, and humans tend to resort to knowledge to make the world more intelligible and reduce anxiety. But in psychoanalysis, knowledge is unconscious; and it should not come from the analyst, but the analysand, who, however, "does not know to know". The analyst may be *supposed to know* (although this was truer in Lacan's time, likely less so at present), but he must handle this supposition with care. Teachers, professors, coaches, trainers, medical doctors know; and they do not need to listen. But one who wants to call himself an analyst must listen, and to begin listening s/he must not imagine that s/he already knows. An analyst cannot rely on universal or academic knowledge. It does not mean that s/he does not have to know anything. An analyst's formation is both theoretical and experiential and therefore his/her own analysis must be rigorous, but it is not starting from there that an analyst listens. His/her formation and knowledge must remain suspended.

Another famous maxim from Lacan is "there is no sexual rapport" (in French: "Il n'y a pas de rapport sexuel", which can be both understood as "there is no sexual intercourse" and "there is no sexual rapport"). Lacan loved to provoke, and he certainly succeeded in this. Of course, the sexual act exists, but here Lacan stresses that the *rapport* does not exist (the Merriam-Webster dictionary defines rapport as a "harmonious relationship. A relationship characterized by agreement, mutual understanding, or empathy that makes communication possible or easy"), meaning that a relationship in which two subjects can be together as one does not exist. Becoming one with the other is a fantasy. Yet quite often we hear people say, "we understand each other so well that we don't even need to talk". Only on an imaginary level can one think of being in a direct, immediate relationship with the other. However, the relationship with the other and the world is always, inevitably mediated by the word. Each person speaks a slightly different language. *The signifier introduces the difference.* The fantasy of a relationship not mediated by words, that abolishes difference and misunderstanding, is a childhood fantasy, which however persists even through to adulthood, and we also find it in many organizations. To say that sexual rapport does not exist means that one does not get to experience the same enjoyment as the other, but that basically everyone enjoys his own fantasy – sexually too, one enjoys his/her own body and not that of the other – and that between the two there will always be a gap, an unbridgeable distance.

The L schema

Lacan invented the L schema (Figure 2.1) to formalize the relationship with the other in the intertwining of the symbolic and imaginary dimension. At first glance it may seem a bit complex, yet I find it enlightening and helpful to understand some clinical issues.

- A (Autre) = Other
- S = subject of the unconscious
- a = ego
- a' (autre) = other (the similar person; all the others one sees around)
- a-a' = imaginary axis
- A-S = symbolic axis

In the lower left corner of Figure 2.1 we have a person speaking, the one who emits the message; it is an ego, and Lacan calls it little other (a). In the top left corner, we have the subject of the unconscious; a subject that is not yet represented here as a crossed subject (S). It is interesting, because we already see two subjects, and therefore it is not so easy to say "who is speaking". At the top right is the recipient of the message, the similar other, that is, another small a (a'). At the bottom right is the big Other (A). Lacan distinguishes the other with a lowercase letter from the Other with an upper-case letter. The other could be a friend, a relative, someone we have met on the street and to whom we speak. But the Other, what we actually relate to, beyond the imaginary relationship, does not have a face, it cannot be represented. It is the 'bath of language' in which we are born, culture, society; it is where the word comes from. Each person is born within the Other

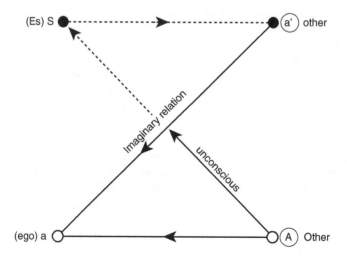

Figure 2.1 The L schema

that precedes him/her. We can say that the mother is generally the first person to occupy this position, since she introduces one to the world, to language. It is then important to distinguish the person from the position s/he occupies in a discourse. Subsequently, it is also very important to try to understand what Other the speaker is addressing: what characteristics does it have? How is it experienced? Who may it represent?

If we consider the classic scheme of communication mentioned above, we find it along the a-a' axis, the axis that Lacan calls an imaginary relation because it is between two egos. But in this L schema, which takes the unconscious into account, we see that it is not so easy to isolate emittent and receiver. Who is talking? Who is it really aimed at? The question becomes more complicated if we take into account the axis that goes from A to S, which is the axis of the unconscious. The imaginary axis is the axis of chatter, discourse, intentionality, answer, and therefore also of incomprehension, confrontation, bickering. An analysis can work only if the analyst is not in a'; that is to say that even if the analysand address him/her, the analyst does not respond in a personal capacity with his/her ideas or opinions. The analyst should listen knowing that s/he occupies a place in the Other. Therefore, the analyst understands what the analysand is saying as the analyst takes the place of the Other during speech. If the analyst is able to operate this distinction (if s/he is in A), then s/he will hardly be represented, and then his/her intervention will be in the symbolic rather than the imaginary register. This type of intervention can make the speaker falter, it can make him question what s/he is saying, it can open up questions. This is the meaning of the arrow that goes from A to a: "the sender receives his own message back from the receiver in an inverted form" (Lacan, 1977, p. 85).

I do not want you to think that the imaginary is something negative, however. The imaginary is essential; if we did not have imaginary, we would not address speech to anyone, including the analyst. Let's have a look at the schema. It is only by positioning on the imaginary axis (a-a') that we notice the other axis (A-S). At the same time, however, the former is also an obstacle to the latter. The a-a' axis acts as a barrier to the A-S axis, hence why the line is partly dashed. Behind the ego there is S. The imaginary is inevitable, but it is not the only dimension on which we are placed. This schema designed by Lacan is also partly imaginary, and should be taken as such, but helps us to reflect on the clinical practice, and allows us to invent something new.

Comprehension, which we mentioned above, lies along the imaginary axis. We can make other examples. In the following table I have tried to distinguish how listening changes depending on whether we are on the imaginary or on the symbolic axis (Table 2.1). This list is partial, incomplete. I have only considered some of the most common terms, but one could continue.

Ego Vs unconscious. Listening, as understood in psychoanalysis, is not simply listening to the friend, psychiatrist, therapist, or in general the person in front of us. In such cases, we would still be on the imaginary level, listening to the speaker's ego. *Psychoanalytic listening is listening to the unconscious.* If we do

Table 2.1 Listening along the two axes

Imaginary axis (a-a')	Symbolic axis (A-S)
Ego	Unconscious
Dialogue	Free associations
Empty speech	Full speech
Psychiatric, psychological, interpersonal, intersubjective, friendly, psychotherapeutic listening	Psychoanalytic listening
Vision	Listening
Natural language	Language of the Other
Me-centered attention	Free-floating attention
Empathy	Kindness, generosity
Eroticism and aggressivity	Alterity
Representations of the other (e.g., defensive, oppositional)	The Other is radically different
Comprehension	(Mis)Understanding
Explanation	Revelation
Intended meaning	Other meaning
Clarity	Opacity
Univocal meaning, obsession, certainty, delusion	Equivocity
Technique	Setting/dispositive/device
General/universal	Singularity
Knowledge about the other	Knowledge from the Other
Loneliness, isolation	Solitude

not take into account the unconscious (the element *third*) there is judgment, everything is reduced to the dualism: right/wrong, true/false, agree/disagree, yes/no, rational/irrational. Dualism is implicit in the meaning: such as, "right" brings with it its opposite "wrong". Conversely, listening to signifiers is listening to pure difference.

The analytic listening subverts the classic scheme of communication because analyst and analysand are not simply emittent and recipient. Something is said in the session, but the patient is required to listen to what s/he says, and to analyze it her/himself, becoming her/himself an analyst of her/his own speech. The attention is oriented towards the unconscious, thus, psychoanalysis does not occur *between* two people. Further, since the moment Freud set the fundamental rule, there is no *dialogue* in analysis because there is no logos, that is, discourse, reasoning. Psychoanalysis occurs at the level of the signifiers (expressed by the analysand). And the analyst can only take up the signifiers used by the analysand, being careful not to add any of his/her own.

The analyst analyzes. Freud said that the analyst must operate as a mirror. In chatter, complaint, or recrimination, one is completely alienated in the other, but without realizing it. One argues with the other, without realizing that s/he is actually fighting his own image, for example what s/he would or would not like to be.

Lacan defined chatter or lament as an *empty speech*, that is, a speech that does not engage the speaker in the first person because he does not recognize her/himself in it, one does not feel involved in what s/he says, it does not concern him/her; one really thinks s/he is just talking about others. The empty speech operates on the imaginary axis because it excludes – it does not lead to recognize – the subject of the unconscious (S). In this sense, the analyst acts as a mirror, making the analysand question what s/he is saying: *how does what you are saying implicate you? How is what happens to you the effect of what you say?*

An analysand complains of being surrounded by people who are unable to take any initiative and who turn to her for everything: "My daughter calls me for everything, even when I'm at work. My ex says it's my fault if he cannot see my kids". She reports several similar examples. However, one may ask: how does this person support the other's desire to turn to her? It seems paradoxical, because it is what the person complains of, yet in some way she is part of it, to begin with by always responding to the other's requests. How does she elicit the other's demands toward herself? This person talks about how much she likes to be the center of attention and be loved by everyone: "I like doing for others", she says. She then talks about her fear of being alone (without people around her, or with people with whom there is no connection, nothing to say), and how she is full of energy when she is among others. Here, the story takes a completely new turn: if it is true that others do not take any initiative, it is also true that she does not let them take it, for fear of remaining alone.

There is no symmetry in analysis, and not because the "cold" analyst does not speak. If the analyst is careful about what s/he says, it is because s/he is trying not to add elements of his/her own, extraneous to the analysand's discourse, which would only cause confusion. The analyst must try not to give answers. Not for questions of principle, but because each answer given is a lost opportunity to do analysis, because an answer works as a closure to the question, and therefore interrupts one's questioning. Then, the analyst asks, possibly trying to ask open ended questions, and not artfully crafted questions to guide the patient towards the answer s/he wants to obtain. The closed ended question is suggestion, and as such it can work (perhaps) for the authority granted to the therapist, therefore still limited to the imaginary level, but it does not go in the direction of an unconscious truth.

Psychiatric/psychological Vs psychoanalytic listening. Medical analysis is carried out through the collection of signs, therefore through vision rather than listening. Psychiatric and psychological listening are affected by this medical approach, that is, this search for signs of disease. The signs are interpreted on the basis of a shared and general knowledge. In medicine and psychology there is no listening to the uniqueness of the case, because the statistical model – and therefore the norm and the idea of normality – prevails. The patient is required to comply with the doctor's cure and prescriptions. The question remains between two individuals, one of whom is in the position of an object.

Natural language Vs language of the Other. Along the imaginary axis, language is imagined simply as a tool for communicating. Meanings may be taken for granted, especially when two persons speak the same mother tongue. Linguists tell us that we all speak a natural-historical language, which is the language of the dictionary, such as English, Italian, Chinese. For many linguists it is then possible to translate from one language to another without major difficulties. Conversely, the experience of analysis shows us that everyone speaks a slightly different language. What we call mother tongue is the language in which we were raised, which is not the language of the dictionary. Indeed, no one's language is reducible to the natural language. Therefore, a perfect translation from one language to another is very unlikely, if not impossible.

Among friends, but also in certain psychotherapies we may hear: "I understand you perfectly, this happened to me too". This sort of (imaginary) identification with the other does not guarantee that one understands what the other is actually saying. This is listening to one's own fantasies, nothing more. It is literally a *me-centered attention*. We all speak different languages. Speaking/listening to one's own language (one's own understanding) only leads to Babel, to chaos. Conversely, speaking/listening the language of the Other (the pragmatic, diplomatic language; the language that considers the misunderstanding) might lead to the miracle of Pentecost.

Empathy Vs kindness/generosity. Empathy is a widely used term today. The idea of "putting yourself in the other's shoes" to experience what the other feels sounds very generous. In reality, based on a representation of the Other, empathy may be an obstacle to listening, because the dimension of the unconscious is eliminated. Empathy, like sympathy, can easily turn into apathy, if not antipathy, when the other does not conform to the representation. The analyst's transference is very different and is not based on the representation of the other. Rather than empathy, I think an analyst should cultivate generosity and kindness. These are qualities that are independent from the other and from any presumed state (e.g., of need, suffering).

Eroticism and aggressiveness Vs alterity. If we do not listen to the unconscious, we remain on the imaginary level. If the Other is expunged, then the relationship is established with the other who is in front of us. With the represented other – caught in an imaginary capture – the relationship can easily oscillate between the opposite poles of eroticism and aggressiveness. The other can be represented as a friend or enemy, a lover or persecutor, a good or bad object. What are eroticism and aggressiveness, if not fantasies of mastery over the other?

Representations of the other Vs the Other is radically different. We happen to hear therapists, parents, and teachers describing some of their patients, children, or students as being defensive or oppositional. They may say: "he does it on purpose, he doesn't listen to me". Especially in analysis, it is imperative not to lapse on a personal level, that is to say, not to feed the imaginary transference by placing oneself in a' (in the L schema). The Other is not stupid but has its own logic that goes beyond the manifest behavior, and cannot be reduced to a deviance, deficit, or lack of commitment. Saying that the other is oppositional or defensive indicates more easily a lack of listening on the part of the therapist, parent, or teacher, that is, them being imposing (indeed, if there is an opposition, first there is something that is perceived as an imposition).

One can also be oppositional, but then being oppositional has its own value in the psychic economy of the speaker that needs to be verified; it probably serves a cause, according to a particular logic. What is the function of being oppositional? It is not a case of brandishing something as nonsense because it escapes one's understanding. Some therapeutic orientations speak of "irrational beliefs" that need to be restructured through therapy. But again, labeling something as an "irrational belief" means a failure to grasp the logic behind it. Even a phobia may seem like an "irrational belief", yet the so-called reality check is of little use in these cases. When a child is afraid of monsters it may be useless to tell him that monsters do not exist. For him, they do exist. In this example, it is a case of letting these monsters enter into a story, so that they become speakable, take other appearances, and maybe are no longer monsters who can haunt you.

The fantasy of making One

A person tells me about her insomnia. Insomnia is very interesting. Typically, it was found in soldiers in the trenches who could not sleep because the enemy could have attacked at any moment, and therefore they had to always be alert, on guard. Our sessions became very important for this person, to the point that she was afraid of becoming dependent on them, not being able to do without them anymore, and therefore occasionally she was trying to reduce the frequency of appointments. One day she meets an old friend of hers, who she describes as a complex, sensitive, intellectually stimulating man. She is enthusiastic about this friendship that now fills her days: "what a beautiful relationship, we understand each other without the need to talk". Soon, this (imaginary) closeness turns the friendship into a strong sexual attraction for the other. A desire to unite, not only metaphorically. In fact, this analysand begins to complain of not being able to think of anything but this person. It should also be noted that the beginning of this friendship also coincided with a disinvestment from the analysis, as if this person had finally found what she was looking for. In analysis this imaginary plan cannot prevail, it would be the end of the analysis. The analyst functions as a *semblant*: something that seems, but it is *not*. The function of this *not* preserves the difference (on the speech plane, the distance with the object remains inexhaustible). Therefore, there can be no agreement or disagreement, no fusion or abandonment in analysis. With this person, her unconscious desire to make 'one' with the Other also revealed its opposite, that is,. the obsession of the other, the impossibility to find a difference (thus a symbolic separation) from the other. Insomnia in this case could be understood like this: the resistance to the desire to abandon oneself to the Other, a desire perceived as threatening because it is imagined as a point of no return. In her dreams, she was often falling into the void. Sleeping itself implies a fall: to fall asleep. As in loving: to fall in love.

Another analysand tells me about her fusional relationship with her mother: "When I was little, we were always hand in hand. One day, when I was 15, I enter my room and see my mother reading my diary: it was a shock, I felt betrayed". The fantasy of this fusional relationship with the mother had suddenly cracked. Not only had her mother betrayed her trust, but her mother probably didn't even know her too well if she felt the need to read her diary. The night before our first session she has a dream: "I go to a psychotherapist, we look into each other's eyes, and I have the feeling that he understands me without the need for words". This is the fantasy of being able to reproduce that fusional couple. A fantasy of this kind, if not analyzed, that is, if it remains imaginary, if it is not put into words, can only have two outcomes: one remains together in fusionality with the other, in tacit agreement, at the price of not growing, not going anywhere, or at some point there is a breakup, a physical separation, a goodbye.

The psychoanalytic intervention

Initially, Freud thought of analytic intervention essentially in terms of interpretation. He imagined being able to find the Rosetta Stone, that is, the key to access the meaning of dreams. Similarly, he thought it was enough to provide patients with an interpretation of the meaning of their symptoms to dissolve them. But the symptom itself is an interpretation, which we need to dissolve. Presently, the clinical practice with the new forms of symptoms shows us the limits of interpretation understood as an explanation or translation of a symptom. It is not the "clarifying" intervention that produces any advancement in the treatment. As we mentioned above, it is rather the misunderstanding and the equivocity of the word that work.

Then, how does one understand the interpretation? How an actor interprets a role, a character, just as a musician interprets a song. And the beauty of the interpretation does not lie in the reproduction or repetition of the original text, but in what is new compared to the original, the new version that is produced thanks to the rereading or misreading operated by the artist. Interpretation produces effects, has consequences, if it allows one to understand differently something that was already there, but that had never been valued; a detail, an element that is seen in another light, that receives greater emphasis, or is said in a different tone.

It is important that the interpretation take into account the axis of the unconscious (in the L schema), S and A, meaning that no interpretation can be definitive: there is always the Other. An interpretation that imagines being able to say everything, to reveal the enigma of the patient's speech, or to say "how things actually are", is an interpretation that remains on the imaginary level. An interpretation that does not introduce a bit of doubt and does not open to other possible understandings presents several problems. Lacan (1987) says: "it provokes smiles at a certain use of interpretation, as the sleight of hand of comprehension. An interpretation whose effects are understood is not a psychoanalytic interpretation. It is enough to have been analyzed or to be an analyst to realize that" (p. 113).

An interpretation that fixes a meaning, in addition to being theoretically wrong, is also counterproductive with patients with a hypertrophic ego, or who are overly self-centered, such as narcissists; or people with strong paranoid traits, as these people are already engaged in a grueling process of interpretation with no way out. Here, there is the risk of falling into the other's representation, becoming for example a persecutor in the eyes of the other, who may feel judged and counterattack, so unleash all his/her aggression. Interpreting may also be a problem with people with strong obsessive traits, people strongly anchored to logic and reasoning, who will do everything to dismantle an interpretation, since they are masters in this.

It is necessary to displace the other, to draw his/her attention elsewhere. The best intervention does not even present itself as an intervention; it can be a question that displaces the patient, that makes him/her talk about something else, or something that confuses him/her, leaves him/her perplexed for a moment, makes him/her lose the thread of the discussion. For Lacan, our interpretation of the unconscious should sit between *citation* and *enigma* (Lacan, 2007, p. 37). The citation brings the patient his/her own word back: a word s/he previously said, or a signifier that returns in his/her story. But it could also be a citation from someone else; for example, "Goethe would say . . .". The enigma is a non-univocal interpretation, and therefore a way to leave the question open.

Who is the therapist? As analysts, we stick to the analysand's speech, we rely on the logic of the signifier. We can underline some signifiers, we can highlight some contradictions, we can raise questions, but in the end it is not us who imposes the direction of the treatment, but the word itself. How many times has an intervention that we believed to be precise, on the spot, and delivered at the right time instead not been received, or been received in a completely unexpected way? The opposite can also happen: sometimes a banal comment, even a "wrong" one can open unexpected scenarios.

More than once I have heard an analysand say "the other time you told me that thing (and mention something I have absolutely no memory of saying, and which I probably didn't even say, at least not with those words) and it did make me think a lot . . .". But even the "success" of an intervention should not make us believe that we have understood everything:

> Ce n'est pas parce que le sens de leur interprétation a eu des effets que les analystes sont dans le vrai, puisque même serait-elle juste, ses effets sont incalculables. Elle ne témoigne de nul savoir, puisqu'à le prendre dans sa définition classique, le savoir s'assure d'une possible prévision [It is not because the meaning of their interpretation has had effects that analysts are in the true, since even if it were correct, its effects are incalculable. It bears witness to no knowledge, since if we consider it according to its classic definition, knowledge guarantees some possible predictability].
>
> (Lacan, 2001, p. 558; My translation)

We do not have much control over what we say, and even less so over what the other understands, and the effects that the word produces. Lacan himself tells us that the analytic interpretation "n'est pas faite pour être comprise; elle est faite pour produire des vagues" [It is not made to be understood; it is made to produce waves] (1976, p. 35; My translation). This is to say that it is not important to explain or clarify. Etymologically, to explain means to make everything plain, flat: "to deprive of significance by explanation, nullify or get rid of the apparent import of".[1] But in this case, we come to a halt, the narration stops, it is no longer possible to continue, we are stuck. Furthermore, an explanation risks being only a belief that replaces an old one, and therefore produces fixity (a fixed idea is an obsession). Rather, it is necessary to short-circuit the meaning to free speech, to restart the narration. The paradox is this: a deliberately clarifying intervention, an explanation, a pedagogical intervention often leads to many more doubts than it resolves, only increasing the confusion. Conversely, a brief, equivocal intervention, which plays with the misunderstanding, can result in absolute clarity, and in a moment may subvert any rumination and doubt.

Psychoanalysis: a path to solitude

It is only in the commonplace (the common thought, chatter, discourse) that everything seems clear, transparent. In analysis we do not take meanings for granted, indeed we question what seems obvious. This can be destabilizing for some people. Some patients express disappointment because they came to reach clarity, and after a few sessions they do not seem to understand anything any more than they did before their first session. They are more confused than before. Very well, that's a good sign. Later, with some practice of analytical listening, they might understand something from the unconscious.

In analysis, each case is unique and not a repetition of a previous case. In the same way, each session is unique and does not replicate what has been said before. One may find that various people find themselves asking similar questions, but for each of them the answer may be different. Every analysis unfolds differently. Every analysand walks his/her own path and is then faced with the question of solitude (which is not loneliness or isolation). Psychoanalysis has never promoted the single thought, neither in session nor outside; it is perhaps no coincidence that the history of psychoanalysis is a history of divisions and splits, and that in different countries it has had such different developments.

In analysis, one has the chance to face one's own speech. This is a radical confrontation with the Other, rather than with the whole series of other "little" others around us. One of my patients was easily annoyed by the presence of other people, so he had the tendency to isolate himself. Once, he went camping alone in a national park in a remote area. Around him, only nature, within miles of anybody else. He could not sleep at night, because of tremendous nightmares, fears, anxieties. Only being there alone could he realize that the Other he was trying to escape is within and not outside of him.

Most patients, at least initially, do not realize that it is a question of their relationship with the unconscious (therefore a symbolic question) and not their relationship with others (an imaginary relationship). And therefore, they confuse isolation (from others) with loneliness (in the word). We can say that being alone with oneself is being in bad company, because being alone one gets easily trapped in thought, ruminates, tend to give reason for oneself, confirms his/her own beliefs.

We have said that language comes first, and that misunderstanding is unavoidable: here lies the distance from the other, that is to say that there is no universal truth and each one advances along a path that is their own, a unique itinerary. The question of solitude means that everyone must try to speak in the first person; there are no others who can be responsible, or who could be guarantors, for one's own speech. It is only by restoring the relationship with the word, and therefore with the Other, that we can finally recognize the "little" others that surround us as not-me. Being in relation with the Other is the precondition for relating to others, for listening to what is being said, abandoning the language of the litigants (i.e., when everyone listens in their own language, rather than in the language of the Other). The relationship is not between just *two* parties. There is also the unconscious, which makes three.

Analysis allows us to experience this absolute difference, and therefore confront this solitude. Rediscovering solitude means also recognizing one's own solitude among others, which is the condition that allows one an encounter.

Note

1 www.etymonline.com/word/explain

References

Busiol, D. (2016). *Psychoanalysis in Hong Kong: The absent, the present, and the reinvented*. Abingdon, UK: Routledge.

Freud, S. (1904). Freud's psycho-analytic procedure. In J. Strachey (ed. and trans.), *The standard edition of the complete psychological works of Sigmund Freud* (Vol. 7, pp. 247–254). London: Hogarth Press.

Freud, S. (1912). Recommendations to physicians practicing psycho-analysis. In J. Strachey (ed. and trans.), *The standard edition of the complete psychological works of Sigmund Freud* (Vol. 12, pp. 111–120). London: Hogarth Press.

Freud, S. (1913). On the beginning of treatment, Further recommendations on the technique of psychoanalysis. In J. Strachey (ed. and trans.), *The standard edition of the complete psychological works of Sigmund Freud* (Vol. 12, pp. 122–144). London: Hogarth Press.

Freud, S. (1925). Negation. In J. Strachey (ed. and trans.), *The standard edition of the complete psychological works of Sigmund Freud* (Vol. 19, pp. 235–239). London: Hogarth Press.

Freud, S. (1975). *The psychopathology of everyday life*. Harmondsworth: Penguin (Originally published 1901).

Lacan, J. (1974). *L'aggressività in psicoanalisi, Scritti* (Vol. I). Torino: Einaudi.

Lacan, J. (1976). *Conférences et entretiens dans des universités nord-américaines, entretien du 24 novembre 1975, Scilicet* (Vol. 6/7). Pa ris: Seuil.

Lacan, J. (1977). *Écrits: A selection*. London: Tavistock.

Lacan, J. (1987, October). Responses to students of philosophy concerning the object of psychoanalysis. *40*, 106–113. doi:10.2307/778346.

Lacan, J. (2001). *Autres Écrits*. Pa ris: Seuil.

Lacan, J. (2007). *The seminar. Book XVII: The other side of psychoanalysis*. New York: W. W. Norton & Company.

Chapter 3

Desire and enjoyment in psychoanalysis

Diego Busiol

Despite being the great Freudian discovery, the unconscious still encounters a great deal of resistance. But what do we mean when we talk about the unconscious? What are we listening to/for when we listen to the unconscious? In other words: what makes humans unique and distinguishes them from computers?

I recently saw a photo of a mural that says "Soy un buen error. Cométeme", which we can roughly translate as "I'm a good mistake. Make a mistake with me". I found it very poetic because it plays with the ambiguity of the word 'error', suggesting that it could be good. It is an invitation to make a mistake that is actually positive, fruitful. This sounds paradoxical. In psychoanalysis, errors are not errors at all; the so-called (Freudian) slips[1] are indeed not faulty but very successful acts. *Lapses*, as we prefer to call what are normally called errors, are absolutely significant, because they reveal a repressed desire. So, I thought: what distinguishes human beings from computers, if not the possibility of making a slip? Computers cannot make slips: it is terrible. They can make mistakes, but these are not mistakes that inform us of the uniqueness of the machine. They are programming errors, or absolutely random and contingent errors. We could say that computers lack the Imaginary register (the machine code is purely symbolic), thus lack imagination, pleasure, and desire. The machine error does not refer to an Other. Conversely, for humans it is precisely desire that introduces the possibility of "error"; here, the error refers to Other, and that is why a slip is interesting for us.

Desire and enjoyment are central issues in everyone's life, as well as in psychoanalytic theory and clinical practice. Indeed, they are what distinguish psychoanalysis from other psychotherapies. I would like to highlight some points that seem essential to me.

Desire: Freud uses the German term *Wunsch* to describe what would be the basis of psychic life, and which would reveal itself through dreams, slips, wit, forgetfulness, etc. The term *Wunsch* was translated into English as *Wish*, while in French it became *désir* [desire, which later became central to Lacan's elaboration] and in Italian *desiderio* [desire]. The German term *Wunsch* can indicate a wish made intentionally (e.g., Ich wünsche dir einen schönen Tag!, meaning (I wish you to) have a nice day!), however Freud refers to an unconscious desire. In the *Interpretation of dreams* there are constant references to the *unbewußte Wunsch*

DOI: 10.4324/9780429432064-5

[unconscious wish, or unconscious desire]. Listening to the unconscious is, therefore, listening to a desire that is not expressed openly (for Freud, repression is the cornerstone of psychoanalysis). Therefore, Freud not only tells us that we must listen with evenly-suspended or free-floating attention, which responds to the *how* of listening, he also gives us some indication of *what* to listen to/for, that is to say, the unconscious desire. The research around the unconscious desire runs through the whole Freudian reflection. After all, it was when he was trying to find an answer to this question that Freud got stuck, admitting that he was unable to find one: "*Was will das Weib?*", which means "what does a woman want?"

The encounter with desire raises many questions, because desire is what exceeds the ego, what displaces it, and therefore what disrupts its serenity. We are not masters of our desire; at some point, we simply find ourselves desiring. It is something beyond our will. Desire causes instability; this can be positive, in the sense that it promotes growth, advancement, social interactions; but it is also what leaves behind a hint of restlessness because it always leaves something unsolved: a question that never ceases to probe, an idea that does not let one sleep. Desire prevents stillness, tranquility, *and therefore nullifies any ideal of full and continuous happiness*. Desire is also what causes envy and jealousy between individuals. Desire is a cross and a delight. But at the same time one cannot do without it: what sort of life is a life without desire?

Death drive/enjoyment: Desire is intimately linked to pleasure, and enjoyment would seem to be the logical consequence of desire. Freud, however, realized that sometimes men "suffer" from an excess of enjoyment, they cannot do without it (for example: substance abuse, addictions, or repetition of apparently unpleasant experiences). He hypothesized that this drive, which he called the "death drive", served to "extinguish" the desire – with all the inconveniences and frustrations that this sometimes entails – restoring stability, homeostasis. This seems to me to be logically flawless: if desire introduces life, life necessarily introduces death as well. Nevertheless, many psychoanalysts on this issue have turned away from Freud, not recognizing the conceptual and clinical usefulness of the death drive. Conversely, Lacan takes up the question of the death drive in terms of *jouissance*, or enjoyment*.

Desire is the fuel of life, but the discovery and the encounter with (one's own and others') desire can be uncanny, alienating, traumatic, even painful. On a social level, different cultures and religions have tried in various ways to stem, limit, and regulate desire. On an individual level, we can also understand neurosis, perversion, and psychosis as attempts to defend oneself from desire, to free oneself from it, or to silence it, also through enjoyment. In this chapter, I will try to show how listening to unconscious desire can become our compass, both in life and in the clinic. To begin with, I want to examine some aporias of desire:

1   "My" desire originates elsewhere, outside of me.
2   Desire is the necessary superfluous. It cannot be reduced to need, instinct, or intention.

3 Desire arises from a lack and is therefore closely linked to dissatisfaction.
4 Access to desire passes through castration, thus through a renunciation of being/having/knowing everything.
5 Desire is not "right", "democratic", "balanced", "altruistic". It should be taken without ifs and buts.
6 Desire is on the side of the Law. But pure, full enjoyment of the object (of capitalism, substances, perversion) is found outside of the Law. Taken in repetition, the enjoyment is always the same and deadly.

"My" desire originates elsewhere, outside of me

It is quite common to hear someone say: "I do not know what I want". One's own desire can be absolutely foreign to oneself. We cannot know much about our desire through reasoning. Desire is unconscious, and we can only know something about it through its manifestations, such as dreams, slips, free associations, forgetfulness, fantasies, fears. This indicates something of our relationship with the unconscious desire: it is something of our own, but at the same time something that comes from elsewhere. Words, thoughts, memories, and fantasies *come to mind*. Where do they come from? And *who* is speaking? The Freudian experience starts from these fundamental questions. As much as we believe we are in control of what we say, the experience of psychoanalysis leads us instead to say that we are spoken by language. Indeed, the less we are present as conscious subjects, the more an unconscious desire can manifest itself. For instance, it is precisely when we sleep, that is to say when we do not think, that something unconscious can manifest itself, in dreams.

Desire seems rather paradoxical because it belongs to me, but at the same time goes beyond me. This shows one of the greatest illusions to human beings, which is that life coincides with myself, and therefore that it can be reduced to what "I" want. But no one is self-generating; each person is born in the Other, that is to say in a family, social, and cultural system, and therefore from a desire that – as little or as much as it is – precedes him/her and prepares his/her life. We are born in the word, that is to say in a narrative, such as the story of a pregnancy (intentional or accidental), in the parents' choice of the name, in their fantasies about the sex of the unborn child, their expectations about his/her future and profession as an adult, and so on. Desire is essential to psychic life. Indeed, children who are raised in orphanages or institutions where only basic needs are met and where the dimension of desire is lacking, have limited social, relational, and cognitive development, and develop autistic-like problems (Merz & McCall, 2010; Lionetti et al., 2015).

Desire anticipates life, it precedes the subject. It is a desire that in a way one inherits, receives. And therefore, it is a desire that is mine, because it inhabits me, but that comes from elsewhere, from outside of me. This is why desire is always a little alienating, elusive, mysterious, unknown. It is a desire made of words, signifiers received from others, and therefore it is also partly the desire of someone else who precedes us. It is important however that the desire of the other becomes the desire for Other. There is life if there is desire *for Other*, for something new, for the unknown. Conversely, if one's desire remains only a *desire that belongs to someone else*, it is a desire that suffocates life. I am thinking, for example, about children who have to fulfill their parents' desire, and for this reason are not able to have a life of their own; this is not a desire that renews itself and gives life. That is why some children are 'the symptom of their parents', because they take on a desire that is not theirs.

To say that we are born in the field of the Other means that there is no one who could simply become "him/herself". Also, the ego is constituted based on what comes from others; indeed, in the beginning there is not even this distinction between ego and other. In this regard Lacan speaks of "alienating identity".[2] The assumption of desire, precisely because it can only take place by passing through the o/Other, involves what Lacan calls *alienation.* For example, I may want to be an engineer, like my father. It is a way of assuming the desire (of the other) through identification, and therefore it is an alienation in the desire of the other. It is not something negative. It is a first step, but after this the next step is needed, which Lacan calls *separation*. When I identify with the words of the other, I do not necessarily identify with the desire of the other. There is, however, Other in those signifiers. Even when I identify myself with the word "engineer", this carries with it meanings that do not necessarily correspond to what I desire. And therefore it is a question of carrying out a work of separation from identification to these meanings so that perhaps in the end I can be an engineer according to my desire, in my own way.

Desire is therefore not a faculty of the individual, that is to say, something that one can fully possess and master. This is how desire is commonly understood, although it would be more correct to say that this is the *will*. We could attempt to make a distinction here: the will belongs to the ego and the desire originates from the Other. One can say, "I want . . .", but to say "I desire" is already more problematic because desire does not entirely belong to the ego. There is a big difference between what one wants and what one desires. In fact, *a desire can be absolutely unwanted.* For example, a desire can present itself in an enigmatic, incomprehensible (why did I say that thing?), disturbing (a sexual desire that is felt as inappropriate or wrong), unpleasant way (a desire that seems to backfire on the subject, e.g., that is self-destructive). Desire *divides* the subject. It comes from elsewhere and it is aimed elsewhere, towards something external to the subject, something that is *missing*. This cut or division is what opens up a lack in the subject. This is what causes so many problems for humans – who struggle so hard trying to get rid of it, fill it, or substituting the will for the desire – but in the end it is precisely this lack that allows interaction among people.

A famous phrase from Lacan is "*man's desire is the desire of the Other*"(Lacan, 1964, p. 235). Firstly, this suggests that the Other pre-exists the individual.

Secondly, as we said above, it suggests that men are crossed by desire. The "desire of the Other" could be understood in various ways. Man's desire is:

- *What the other desires* – one desires what others find desirable. Those who work in marketing know this well: it is important to show the object as highly desirable (by others, by everyone) so that it is desired by the individual. For example, a car is all the more desirable the more it is desired by the major-ity of people (and thus, it becomes a *symbol* of desire). We all experience this from an early age: it is the object of the friend's desire (the toy, the dress, the partner) that is immediately desired, precisely because it is desired by the other, and not for the intrinsic qualities of the object. One desires what the other desires. This also means that *desire generates desire*; that desire is transmitted, it is contagious. And therefore, it is important to be desiring, alive, because desire transmits life.
- *The desire of the other* – one desires the desire of the other, that is to say: that the other desires (me), and that s/he continues to desire. For example, the child wants to be the mother's phallus*, he wants to be everything for her, that is to say that he desires her desire.
- *The desire for other/the Other* – Desire (the *drive* as Freud would say) does not have a specific object, and therefore it can shift from one object to another. However, this does not mean that every object is equally good, as desire emerges in the field of the Other, in the unconscious. We can identify some specific characteristics of the object of desire. The object of desire is the object that is missing, and for which all substitute objects can only partially fill this lack. It is good that there may be this shifting, and that we may wish for something new. When this is not possible, when desire cannot pin itself on a new object, depression occurs (a question that will be taken up again in Chapter 11 of this book). Or, when the desire shifts continuously it is prob-ably because we are in hysterical discourse and in anorexia (as we will see better in Chapters 6 and 10 of this book); ultimately, the hysteric's desire is a desire for *nothing*.

Desire is the necessary superfluous. It cannot be reduced to need, instinct, or intention

Desire is often considered *superfluous*, because it is imagined as something unre-lated to "basic" needs (food, water, sleep), and therefore something not vital, not strictly necessary for life. In psychology, Maslow proposed, in 1943, a theory of human motivation based on a hierarchy of needs (represented as a pyramid) according to which the satisfaction of the most basic (physiological) needs is a necessary condition to bring out those of a higher order (i.e., psychological and self-fulfillment needs). This may sound like common sense (and in fact this theory has become extremely popular, despite having no scientific support), however it seems to me that clinical experience shows that it is not at all easy to separate a purely physiological need from desire. It would be very difficult to understand anything of anorexia, bulimia, addictions, depression, or insomnia in the light of this common sense. Most psychology has separated desire from the body. With the body/mind division, the body was conceived as the seat of "basic" instincts and needs, and the mind as the seat of intentions and will. We can say that desire has no physical seat, it is not localizable, but at the same time it affects both the body – therefore the needs – and the mind – therefore the intentions and the will. But if we neglect the dimension of desire, we have responses to needs that turn out to be unsatisfactory, off-target, or unnecessary. In fact, without desire not even the so-called basic needs are guaranteed. As such, desire is superfluous and also very *necessary*.

Desire often presents itself as an obstacle to the "natural" flow of events. If there were no desire, as is the case with computers, life would be in some ways much more linear. Instincts, for example, are similar for all members of the same species, making animals' behaviors quite predictable. Instead, desire is built for each person around a narrative, a fantasy (thus, language). Desire is interwoven with imaginary, and therefore exceeds reason, rule, or purely symbolic calculation (the machine language); this is why one's desire often remains incomprehensible. Desire is linked to pleasure, it is what gives life flavor and color. Also, for this reason, it is necessary for life. The renunciation of desire is the flattening of life. This would be a reduction of the body to a machine: artificial life.

Michael: the fleeting passion. Michael is a computer programmer. He likes to write in machine code because it is an unambiguous, clear language. It is a language made up of commands and instructions that the machine processes and executes. He complains because, he says, his passions do not last. For example, he decides he has to wake up at 6:00 every morning to go for a run, but after two weeks he no longer has the strength to stick to his plans. He starts taking up a language, or a finance course, but after a short time this passion fades; and he thinks there is something wrong with him. He does not allow himself something that is not in the logic of profit, or a goal to be achieved. He imagines being able to program his life like he programs a computer, only to realize later that he cannot carry out what he has imposed on himself.

He comes to see me because he says he is depressed. He says in the morning it is particularly hard to get out of bed; this is a common trait in cases of depression. After all, what is desire, if not what makes us get out of bed in the morning? As the analysis proceeds, Michael begins to cultivate interests purely for the pleasure of doing, without specific goals to achieve, without bringing them back to a production logic. Little by little, he lets some pleasure seep into his life, he rediscovers the pleasure of the word (he talks about the trips he would like to go on, the adventures he would like to have, he even makes jokes), and after a long time he remembers dreams he had during the night. He also starts dating girls, which sometimes frightens him because he feels he can succumb to this desire and become addicted to it. He starts to finally feel alive.

Desire arises from a lack and is therefore closely linked to dissatisfaction

The etymology of the word desire[3] refers to the stars, to waiting for something or someone, to looking at the stars waiting for a sign, or an answer. Thus, desire originates from a lack, from something that escapes understanding, from something that is sought outside of oneself, perhaps with a gaze fixed upward.

Etymologically 'to desire' and 'to consider' share the reference to the stars, but with an important difference. While considering would mean choosing based on what the stars say (in the past many decisions were taken by consulting the stars), desiring (which has the prefix de, privative) represents the act of deciding without worrying about what the stars say. One can consider (choose) when he is in front of an alternative (this, or that?) or a series of possible options, but one can desire also the impossible, what is missing, what is not available.[4]

It is a state of precariousness and uncertainty that feeds desire, and this is the creative side of the lack. *It may seem counterintuitive, but desire is closely linked with lack and partial dissatisfaction, rather than with happiness and the fullness of being*. In order for desire to be renewed, fulfillment and satisfaction must remain in some way transitory, partial. One can feel accomplished, believing to have everything, but this may come at the price of no longer feeling desire.

In neurotic discourses this lack creates a lot of inconvenience. Freud isolated two great neuroses: hysterical and obsessive. Later, Lacan described four discourses: the discourse of the master, the discourse of the hysteric, the discourse of the university, and the discourse of the analyst. Lacan does not distinguish an 'obsessive discourse' per se, and various traits of obsessional neurosis can be found in the discourse of the hysteric, the master, and the university. Personally, I find it useful to refer to hysteria and obsessive neurosis as *discourses* because this allows us to identify some particular linguistic elements, some rhetorical figures, rather than hypothetical personality traits. So, from now on I will try to distinguish hysterical and obsessive discourses. As we will see, the hysterical discourse aims at preserving the lack, so that the desire is continually renewed, but without reaching enjoyment. The fundamental fantasy of the hysterical discourse is keeping the desire *unsatisfied*. Almost in opposition, the obsessive discourse makes every effort to try to destroy the lack, imagining being able to reach a state of fullness, completeness, wholeness, or full happiness; only, it does not realize that it is exactly this lack (that fortunately can never really be filled) that allows him to go on, to continue. The fundamental fantasy of the obsessive discourse is keeping the desire *impossible*.

Hysterical and obsessive discourse are two ways of dealing with the unconscious desire and the enjoyment. When we say hysterical and obsessive discourse, we must not imagine two clearly defined and distinct or opposite categories; there is some continuity between one discourse and another, indeed one can pass from one discourse to another.

Desire in hysterical discourse

In principle, I would say that hysterical discourse – which is closely linked with femininity,[5] although we can find it also among men – aims at making the other desiring and being desired by the other; it provokes the desire of the other. There-fore, the other's desire becomes more important than one's own desire. "Being desired" becomes more important than desiring, or at least it becomes the neces-sary condition for it: "I can desire only when I am desired". It is an unconscious strategy. The other's desire would describe "who I am", how much I am worth, what my qualities are, and so on. The hysteric wants to know, s/he wants to hear "why me"; it is not enough for her to be desired, s/he wants to discover the secret of desire, and that of her "nature" of a woman: "what have you seen in me that makes me special?" Because hysteria is about the question of femininity: *what does it mean to be a woman?* Am I, or am I not a woman? It is easy to describe a man, in fact it is said that "men are all the same", and also "men all want the same thing". Men normally get along well in groups, they like hierarchies. Men look at each other, they engage in pissing contests (in reality as children, figura-tively as adults), they try to figure out "who has it longer", so as to understand who of them is the boss, because men function more likely in the register of *hav-ing*, therefore of those who have more; it is quantifiable. Large groups such as the army and the Church are typically only male groups, which function as one; they are *uni*-form. It is much more difficult to form a group of women, because women do not work in uniformity but instead prefer to emphasize differences and singularity: "I am not like the others", a woman might say. They are in the register of *being*, rather than having. Of course, there can also be a female boss . . . but then, it is easily a woman who makes the parody of the (imaginary) man, as they say, "with balls". In the end, it is difficult to say what constitutes a woman, and the hysteric seeks the answer to this question in the other, in what the other wants. This is why the hysteric says, "I am as you want me". The hys-teric exists as long as she is desired, and therefore she must continually revive the desire of the other. How? For example, by becoming indispensable to the other. The hysteric is extremely good at understanding exactly what the other wants, his preferences, his weaknesses, and his shortcomings. And she gives him everything he needs, only to then . . . escape, making her absence felt, so that the other will miss her, and thus be desired. But to do this she must never give herself up. As mentioned above, the desire (of the other) in hysterical discourse remains mostly unsatisfied. This is one of the fundamental traits of hysteria. The dissatisfaction is primarily on a sexual level. We could say that the hysterical game revolves all around seduction, but without ever moving on to the sexual act. From a young age the hysteric shows him/herself to be attractive, even pro-vocative, and gives off an image of her/himself as an ideal person, but refuses to enter into sexuality, s/he is almost disinterested in it. We have said that hysterical discourse is typically feminine, but it does not only concern women; cases of male hysteria are not infrequent.

Andrew: seduction Vs sexuality. Andrew, born into a middle-class family, was sent to study at a rather difficult boarding school, which was attended by older, sometimes violent boys. Having relatively little hair on his body, as a young boy, he questioned his own masculinity. As a result of this, he says he soon developed a macho, bully attitude. Perhaps being a bully was his way of answering the question: am I a man or am I a woman? He says that in sports, as in life, he doesn't like to let his true intentions leak; he loves to hide them and then surprise the others when they least expect it. He plays to hide his desire from others, and perhaps he also hides it from himself. Tall, with long blond hair, he has kind and gentle manners. Women fall at his feet, or rather at the feet of his ideal and seductive image. He has had sex with some of them but prefers the feat of conquering the other, feeling that the other is at his disposal, at his service. He complains that on several occasions some girls have literally jumped on him, forcing him to have sex with them. He does not even suspect that he has provoked the other's desire, that is to say that he does not recognize when he is fulfilling his own desire, and therefore experiences the enjoyment of the other as a form of abuse.

Sex is often experienced as an abuse in the hysterical discourse, at most as a (marital) duty, something that must be done, but without much pleasure. The hysteric does not accept making him/herself an object, that is, s/he does not accept placing herself in a passive position with respect to the other, because hysterical discourse is basically a fantasy of mastery over the Other (the hysteric does not want to know about her own subjective division. S/he does not want to know about his/her own unconscious desire. S/he experience what happens to him/her as something that does not concern him/her. S/he has the face of a *beautiful soul*), and therefore also on the other. Nor does s/he accept becoming the object of the other's enjoyment (e.g., s/he may have physical blocks, lose sensitivity, even nausea), because *what matters is the other's desire; and if the other enjoys, then the desire can run out.* This is a difference between hysteria and feminine position: a (non-hysteric) woman does not refuse enjoyment, nor does she refuse to become, at least temporarily, the object of enjoyment for the other.

The hysteric wonders so much about the other's desire (but ultimately "what does the other desire?" is the main question of neuroses) that in the end she knows nothing about her own desire. The hysteric wonders if the other wants her, imagining that this could answer the question: who am I? Am I man enough, or am I woman enough? But what the other desires does not say much about one's own desire. Also, because when the hysteric gets what s/he imagined s/he wanted, the object of desire (e.g., that lover, that relationship) soon turns out to be disappointing. Disappointment is often the result of hysterical desire, which then slides towards a new object that is imagined (again) as the right one.

Desire in the obsessive discourse

Unlike the hysteric, the obsessive person cannot bear the other's desire, so s/he must continually mortify it. The hysteric aims to provoke the other's desire, but defends her/himself from her/his own unconscious desire through repression. Instead, the obsessive operates a continuous resistance to desire, and can go so far as to deny it, to annihilate it. If you share an idea with an obsessive person, s/he will try to dismantle any enthusiasm, and will make a large effort to show that the project will fail and therefore that it is better to give up. The obsessive person is generally not a dreamer, he is more into thinking and reasoning. He wants to avoid the risk, which he thinks he can avoid with continuous programming (he could be an excellent employee, one of those who will do overtime every day, therefore very attractive to companies). The obsessive does not want to know about the other's desire, nor does s/he have a strong desire for other: s/he finds comfort in the routine, the already known, the same object. The hysteric wants to be desired, and continually demands the other for more, to test if his/her desire is solid, or if it shows uncertainties. Oppositely, in order to avoid any encounter with a lack, the obsessive person tries to anticipate every request even before the other asks anything, or precisely in order to avoid being asked anything, as this may give way to something unexpected, something that cannot be fulfilled or that he is not ready to give, something on a more personal level. The obsessive may offer advice, favors, or assistance, as long as s/he is not too implicated: "I'll do everything you want, but then leave me in peace". The obsessive cannot stand the dimension of lack, that is, that something is missing, or is out of place, so s/he makes sure that the other does not need anything, that everything is settled, that everything is in order. But this is not out of generosity; it is a strategy for keeping distance, for suffocating the other's desire, for nipping any possible desire in the bud, finally for not knowing about it.

The obsessive person experiences, with annoyance, the dimension of upheaval, uncertainty, and loss of control that lack and desire necessarily entail. An analysand of mine who has always been very afraid of approaching girls and asking them out, tells me: "I am not so afraid of rejection, quite the contrary. I'm afraid they will say yes! Then, at that point what happens, what do I do?" Then, it is better not to ask, and not to know. Then, the obsessive estranges him/herself from life, observes it from the outside, comments on it, pontificates about it, but does not come into play. The obsessive is constantly preparing, but never begins. S/he packs the bags, but s/he never leaves. When s/he has to take the first step, s/he finds a reason to cancel, to postpone. It is never the right time, something is always missing. S/he never takes the first step because at that point s/he will not be able to turn back, and that is what scares him/her the most. S/he is terrified of losing. And therefore s/he lives in a suspended, frozen time, in perpetual waiting. S/he prefers to sacrifice his/her life than to play and risk losing. Whereas the hysteric does and undoes, constantly changes her mind, constantly upsets the course of her life, and can rebel against the world and its rules, the obsessive seems frozen, petrified, and finds comfort in a regulated life, in routine, in repetition, in the already known.

The existence of the obsessive is strongly impregnated with death; it is the mortification of desire and of life, by definition. The obsessive is very attracted to death, especially that of others. On the one hand, this is an expression of the repressed aggression and anger he feels towards others (e.g., parents, bosses, colleagues); on the other hand, it is the obsessive tendency to deal with things that end, that die, such as his relationships, his projects, his activities.

Master and slave

It is said that the hysteric "wants a *master over* whom she can *reign*" (Lacan, 2007, p. 129), and in fact she can be attracted to someone powerful, rich, at the top of the hierarchy, but never comes to recognize him as a master. After all, she knows that the other is not as powerful as it seems, and indeed her whole game is aimed at revealing his powerlessness. The hysteric is a master in identifying the lack of the other, that is to say, the other's desire, and therefore also his weaknesses. Through this game she secures her place with the other, she becomes irreplaceable for him. She chooses someone who shows some lack and who, thanks to her, can eventually become someone important. This gives the hysteric power. It is also true that the hysteric makes a parody, a caricature of the master; she tries to impose herself, she gets angry, makes a scene, and often goes away slamming the door, as she wants to have the last word. Hysteria is a fantasy of mastery. In fact, hysteria can easily develop into paranoia, that is, the fear that this master really exists and that he could harm her. As if this paranoia is saying: the master really exists, but it is not me, it is the other! Here, one's own desire to dominate is repressed and projected onto the other, whereby it becomes the fantasy of being dominated. *If hysteria is on the side of the master, the obsessive remains in the position of a servant.* The obsessive hides behind a boss, which he hates, but who is necessary for him. He serves him and awaits his death. But when the boss dies, he finds it very hard to take his place, he is terrified of occupying this position; he may prefer to find another leader to serve.

Enjoyment in hysterical and obsessive discourse

One might simply think that desire leads to enjoyment, to the fulfilment of desire. However, it seems that in neuroses there is an irremediable separation between desire and enjoyment. For example, in the obsessive discourse enjoyment seems to be a defense from desire, while in hysteric discourse (unsatisfied) desire is a defense from enjoyment.

In hysteric discourse, the desire (of the other) must remain unsatisfied, that is, not reaching complete enjoyment. Indeed, only the postponement of enjoyment would allow the desire not to be exhausted, keeping it alive, in a postponement which, however, proves to be endless. Therefore, the hysteric does not enjoy, *although she could enjoy, and despite the fact that everyone encourages her to enjoy.* In Victorian times there was some degree of sexual repression, and some thought that maybe hysterics did not feel entitled to enjoy. In reality, in hysterical discourse there is an overestimation of enjoyment as a point of no return.

Enjoyment is fantasized as absolute and overflowing; often, in a hysteric's discourse the enjoyment is imagined as an endless precipice, a loss of control that would lead to madness, a fall into the void, and it is not uncommon for a hysteric subject to develop severe vertigo.

This absolute enjoyment is not extraneous to the obsessive discourse, but here the enjoyment is idealized and continuously pursued, and in fact it remains unattainable. Whereas in hysteria the object of desire changes continuously, in obsessive discourse the object is fixed (e.g., that girl or that boy, or that job, or that objective) so that it seems as if only that object will guarantee full enjoyment. The enjoyment imagined by the obsessive is therefore always to come, in an eternal tomorrow; it requires a continuous preparation, and therefore a continuous renunciation, a continuous sacrifice of other pleasures (in the present) which would be only partial enjoyments, and therefore wastes of time. "Work today to enjoy (unlimitedly) tomorrow": this could be a slogan of the obsessive discourse. In fact, it is also the discourse of some religions, which promise future enjoyment in the hereafter, in exchange for renunciations and sacrifices today. Freud actually said that religion is at the collective level what obsessional neurosis is at the individual level: "Religion would thus be the universal obsessional neurosis of humanity" (Freud, 1927, p. 43).

Access to desire passes through castration, thus through a renunciation of being/having/knowing everything

Castration is a term introduced by Freud. It has nothing to do with emasculation, that is to say that castration is not a loss. Castration simply means not everything is possible. We can distinguish an imaginary castration from a symbolic one. Imaginary castration is castration understood as loss, as personal incapacity, as sacrifice, as punishment. It is the limit assumed subjectively; it is impotence. Symbolic castration is simply the limit to which we are all subjected; it is the confrontation with the impossible. The fear of castration, for little Hans, was the fear of punishment from his father; this is the imaginary aspect. But actually, Hans's father is also subject to that same law, so he too is subject to castration. And by passing on castration, Hans's father does not limit Hans, but on the contrary frees him from maternal desire and allows him to go his own way. Therefore, it is precisely the limit imposed by the law (the impossible) that ensures that there is life; this is the symbolic aspect. Therefore, only by passing through (symbolic) castration can one access one's own desire.

The neurotic person does not surrender to this idea and still thinks that everything would be possible *if only it were not forbidden to him/her* (e.g., by the father, the boss, or others). Then s/he blames the other; s/he fights against what s/he feels to be forbidden as a reaction, but this does not lead him/her to discover anything of his/her unconscious desire. Indeed, the more s/he sees something as forbidden, the more s/he thinks s/he wants it. If Hans realizes instead that he is confronted with the impossible – that is, a symbolic rather than imaginary castration – he then has the possibility of leaving the specular relationship with the other; because it is a question between him and his desire, his speech. In this sense castration is not a loss: if *everything* is *not* possible, *not everything* (and therefore at least *something*) is possible. It is however a question of trying to say. The neurotic (obsessive, in particular) finds it hard to *ask*, because in doing so he would show his lack. And he finds it hard to *say*, to *tell* because when he speaks he realizes that he cannot say everything, since saying one thing implies excluding some others, it implies taking a stance. The risk here is not only the judgment or censorship of the other (i.e., the imaginary castration), but realizing precisely that there is nothing objective and unquestionable that supports one's narrative, except only desire – desire that the obsessive person feel s/he cannot sustain.

Trevor: avoid castration. Trevor teaches, and he is very good at summarizing what others have said, but fails to develop his own theory. When he is forced to write down a thought of his own, he fails; it seems to him that nothing is absolute, irrefutable. He starts a sentence, but then realizes that no sentence is objectively true, and so he cancels it. He can only write when there is no more time left, always at the last moment, when there is no longer the possibility of a choice. It seems to him that everything is the same, and then he ends up doing nothing. Trevor imagines he can avoid castration by keeping himself on the sidelines. But by never taking that step (i.e., not saying, not taking risks, not choosing) he does not participate in the game of life, he continually postpones, but in fact he complains that nothing new ever happens; he is a spectator of life.

Symbolic castration cannot be bypassed because everyone is subjected to the laws of language. To speak is always to say something that is partial. Every sentence or utterance turns out to be incomplete. Then, everyone is faced with the impossibility of completely knowing what they want, who they are, how they function. Nevertheless, one only has to pass through the lie or untruth of a sentence in order to recognize at least something of one's own desire. We cannot know anything about our desire if not by speaking; it is not possible to know anything a priori. Castration is not loss, because the whole, the fullness, is imaginary. But desire (like the devil) is not everywhere: it is in the details, in the unique characteristics that we seem to find only in that particular object. One can only proceed by making distinctions: what catches my attention? Under what conditions does this work, or not, for me? What does not leave me indifferent? What makes me talk?

Castration for a neurotic has already occurred: either one accepts it, or one rejects it. The paradox is that by refusing castration, paradoxically, it is doubled. That is, we find ourselves unable to do anything. For Freud (1937), the analysis finds its limits in the rock of castration, which would be attributable to castration anxiety in men and to *penisneid*, the phallic envy in women. For Lacan, however, this does not represent a limit to psychoanalysis because once the object that causes the desire has been recognized (once the fantasy has been crossed), the desire continues to be present as a force. The point is that now one continues to desire "in vain", in the sense that there is no longer the presumption to achieve one's desire as something positive that makes one feel accomplished, arrived.

Desire is not "right", "democratic", "balanced", "altruistic". It should be taken without ifs and buts

As we said above, there is a gap between what one desires and the desire of another, that is to say that one's desire is unlikely to completely coincide with the desire of someone else. Desire is by definition eccentric to the subject. The same subject feels already crossed, divided by a desire that goes in multiple directions. Desiring already signals tending towards something, therefore it indicates an imbalance. Thus, there can be no desire that it is moderate, or "balanced it not to mention the enjoyment, which also implicates use of the other, even a reduction of the other to an object – just like one enjoys a property, a right, an asset). Some patients complain that they would like a less pressing desire, which would leave them more at peace. This is the idea that the ideal life would be a harmonized, balanced life. But desire is precisely what subverts tranquility, inertia, balance. Either there is desire, or there isn't: either we go forward, or we go back. Only a dead body is a body in perfect balance: without desire, but also without life.

Catherine: the desire that breaks the balances. Catherine is frightened of her own desire, which she feels is violent, excessive, uncontrollable. As a young girl she kissed a boy one year younger than her, and she wonders, even now, if in doing this she committed an act of abuse. She never got her driver's license because, she says, she is afraid of killing someone while driving. Catherine received an education deeply inspired by strong religious values, and she imagines the relationship with the other as a relationship between equals, symmetrical or reciprocal. There can be no secrets in relationships, no distances, no desires that aren't shared. She is therefore committed to eliminating any trace of a desire that seems to exclude (even only partially) the other. This leads her to live very close, exclusive relationships (family, friends), in which, however, she feels suffocated because she cannot manifest a desire other than what she imagines to be the other person's desire. And therefore, either she suffers the desire of the other (she represents herself as a victim) or she suffers her own desire (she represents her as a perpetrator), but always in the abuse.

The encounter with sex and sexuality is often traumatic, because it is something absolutely out of our control. And in fact, we do not consciously choose our sexuality; at some point we find ourselves desiring a certain type of object, a certain type of encounter. We find ourselves hetero/homosexual, or something else. For some people, the discovery of a (own) homosexual desire can be met with disappointment. It can also be experienced with embarrassment or shame, if it is something that is not accepted at a family and/or social level. Even if accepted on a personal level, it can still be something to hide from others. This is an important question, because the relationship with one's own sexual desire can influence the relationship with one's own desire *tout-court*. This is something I have found in many homosexual patients. None of them demanded an analysis to change their sexual orientation; maybe it could have happened in the past that someone wanted to "become heterosexual", but much less today. Yet, a trait that I have found in many homosexual patients is a difficulty in taking a clear position in the presence of others, in expressing their own thoughts and beliefs openly. Several homosexual analysands have told me "I always try to avoid conflict". Starting a conflict means exposing oneself to attacks (right or wrong) by the other, and this puts into question one's relationship with one's own desire. To sustain a conflict with the other, one must not feel at fault; that is to say, one must be able to support one's own Other, first of all. It is therefore possible that those who have had to hide an important part of themselves from a young age still face difficulties in publicly supporting and defending their own desire.

There is more. It is not just a question of homosexuality being more or less accepted on a social, cultural, and family level. Rather, in homosexuality that conflict between being desired by the other, the desire for other, and the desire of the other that we have mentioned above seems to be amplified. For psychoanalysis, homosexuality originates in a pre-Oedipal phase, therefore in a relationship between two people. This is a specific avoidance of castration. It is the position of the child who wants to be the mother's phallus. Thus, there is great emphasis on the desire of the other, on seeking the desire of the other, to provoke it, to serve the other, at the price of not desiring. Hence the great difficulty in expressing one's own desire, a desire different from that of the other. And it is not uncommon to see in these people a split between an anonymous practice of the drive with occasional partners, and a stable, official relationship with a permanent partner.

One should try to say something about one's own desire, however uncomfortable it may seem. An analysand tells me: "but if I really follow my desire, I will find myself alone". But no, articulating one's own desire is the only condition for an encounter. There is encounter only in the Other. Otherwise, without the Other there is only the relationship with the semblable, with the similar person, that is, the other who is separate from me, but who does not differ from me – my specular me.

It is not a question of administering or taming desire, as the various psychotherapies promise. Desire is by definition an excess. It is necessary for something to be said about one's own desire, and for one to recognize it, because the unconscious desire operates, even if it is not spoken. And a desire that cannot be put into words is a desire that is *acted out* (through behaviors, actions, or better re-actions, passages to the act), or that is translated into affects (frustration, anger, aggression, embarrassment), or into fantasies (of revenge, for example). For everyone, the relationship with the Other anticipates and makes the relationship with the other possible. Not the other way around.

re is on the side of the Law. But pure, enjoyment of the object (of capitalism, suꞵstances, perversion) is found outside of the Law. Taken in repetition, the enjoyment is always the same and deadly

The law is functional to desire. One can desire where there is a law, where there is a limit, an interdict. Conversely, enjoyment knows no bounds. It may seem paradoxical, but we realize that desire is on the side (it is an effect, we could say) of what Freud called the reality principle (the principle that regulates enjoyment according to external conditions), while enjoyment (as Lacan reinterprets Freud's death drive) is at the service of the pleasure principle.

Recently, I happened to see a very funny cartoon: a patient on the couch exclaiming: "honestly, it seems to me easier to suffer than to solve all my problems". This funny meme reveals in its raw simplicity something which is very true, and which presents itself easily in the session: complaining brings great enjoyment, and it is not easy to give it up and change the subject. Complaint is a protest against something that would be rightfully right and that (the subject feels) has been taken away from him/her. It is typical in pre-Oedipal structures, for example among narcissists or in perversions. More precisely, the idea of a "full", "pure" enjoyment refers to the memory of a fusional, inseparable relationship with the mother. This absolutely pre-Oedipal position is supported by the pleasure principle: a fusional pleasure that, however, prevents personal development, growth. Without separation there is no birth, no word, no difference, and thus no desire. It is a form of thanatological and repetitive enjoyment that leads to endless suffering and lamentation. On the contrary, desire originates from the interdiction posed by the paternal function. It is the law of language that makes it possible to desire; and thus, it makes it possible to access some satisfaction, even a substitute, even partial satisfaction. This is in line with the reality principle, which takes into account lack and castration, which are instead unknown to the pleasure principle. Desire and satisfaction therefore require an ethical position, and constant work over time.

From the sentence (the ego) to the narrative (the Other)

Hysterical and obsessive discourse are two ways to try to control the word. In some ways, both discourses propose strategies to get rid of the unconscious, which however results in a loss of coordination and direction in life. Not wanting to know about the unconscious means not wanting to know about the unconscious desire that guides us in life, and so it is easy to drift away. Neurotic discourse tries to replace desire (which can be intermittent, which requires continuous articulation) with the rule, the sentence. We can understand neuroses as this: *replacing the free-association of words, the narrative, the storytelling, and poetry (which is metaphorical, ironic, light) with discourses, sentences, statements, and certainties (which are heavy, definitive, peremptory).*

Hysteria and obsessional neurosis try to handle the open question of desire respectively with *being* (who am I for the other; what makes me desirable?) or *having* (quantity, length, size, rather than quality). If, as we have said, desire originates from a lack, then the analysis begins from here, that is, from the *not* of being and the *not* of having. From what I do *not* understand, for example. From what I can*not* grasp, I do *not* have, from what I am missing. We identify something of our desire when we miss something, or someone. This is a lack that is anything but unpleasant, since normally falling in love gives one a lot of energy, it makes one feel alive.

For the obsessive, it will be very necessary to be able to admit a lack of one's own – a lack and not a deficiency. The obsessive is all centered around the ego, in an attempt to re-establish a full ego. So, he ends up blaming himself, complaining, denouncing his shortcomings and deficiencies (with respect to an ideal), feeling sorry for himself because "he is not up to par", because he has low self-esteem. Or, exactly on the contrary, he may feel that he is the only one who is 'up to par', the only one who is capable, the only smart one, the best one, and therefore he can become absolutely aggressive and arrogant. High or low, best or worst are only two sides of the same coin, that is, one's image of oneself, the representation of oneself. The obsessive imagines solving the lack with a fantasy of mastery, a fantasy of control of the object. The more the obsessive perceives a lack (i.e., an openness to the Other) the more s/he tries to exert control (therefore trying to strengthen his/her ego and shut the Other out). Recognizing a lack would then mean recognizing not being able: to say everything, to do or have everything, to build knowledge on the Other, thus not having all the answers; recognizing that it may not be what one thinks.

An analysand who experienced failure perhaps too late in life was desperate to be unable to control his life. Yet, only starting from the failure of his fantasy of mastery was he able to deflate his ego a little, and gradually make room for an Other. And after many tormented, poignant love stories, in which his relationships were sustained through fighting and clashes, he finally finds a woman with whom he sets a relationship in a new register, no longer picking fights, no longer under the control of the ego, but perhaps involving a little more listening to the Other (a woman, in her uniqueness, is a figure of difference) and gets married. The ego needs to be deflated to make room for the o/Other.

The obsessive thinks he must know/do everything, and therefore for him the *impossible* becomes a sort of salvation; if something cannot be done because others prevent him from doing it (e.g., the situation, the boss), he is safe. But this is a paradoxical solution, since he will only be able to deal with things that fail, with projects or tasks that are impossible, which will lead him to yearning and frustration. Then, the *non*, that is, the obstacle, must be found in the word, and not represented in reality, such as the impossible. For example, it could become "*not*-everything" – that is to say that it is not necessary to know everything or do everything – in order not to know about one's own lack. On the contrary, this very lack can become the strength, what gives direction in one's life. It is from this *not* that we are guided, meaning we are attracted by what (we imagine) we do not have, or what we miss. We could say that, after castration, there are two paths. Fear it, and in this way remain in a position of obedience, rivalry, but always deeply dependent on, for example, the father. Or take it as a lack and make it a starting point to try to direct one's own desire elsewhere with respect to the paternal ideal.

Joseph: knowing vs. doing. Joseph is a pilot with many hours of flight, but he is still a first officer, and just cannot seem to pass the exam to become a captain. He has always been the best on the pilot course, and all his classmates turn to him before exams. He has read and reread the manuals hundreds of times, he knows them by heart, perhaps better than his instructors. He is one who "knows". He comes from a family of professors and school principals, of people 'who know', who know more than others, and who teach. But as he knows a lot already, he struggles to occupy the position of a student (he didn't even finish university); he also wants to teach his instructors, with whom he inevitably quarrels, and whom he deeply hates. But he imagines that once he becomes a captain he will finally be free from all constraints and will no longer have to obey to anyone. He imagines he knows everything; then, in session it is very difficult to make him stop on his own slips, to make him listen to what he says. He does not listen because he thinks he knows everything already. But without listening, the 'one who knows' cannot become the 'one who does'. That knowledge remains imaginary, impersonal, therefore sterile, and leads nowhere.

A captain is not someone who commands. Far from it! A captain is simply the one who is in charge of running the machine. A captain is not the non-castrated one who would do what he wants; on the contrary, he is the first who must take into account the laws of physics, mechanics, currents, the rules of navigation, that is, what sets the limits; this is what gives direction to what he can do or not, certainly not his will. The captain is the last to get off the boat, as if to say that driving is an ethical question, there is no room for selfishness or complaints. Becoming a captain means running the machine, not so much by taking control of it as by taking care of it. *Complaints are nothing more than expressions of the maternal fantasy,* for which one should be able to do what one wants, or should be awarded, recognized for being special. This is not the case. And after all, Lacan's invitation to "not give in on one's desire" does not mean that one can or should do whatever one wants (this would be pure enjoyment rather than desire). It rather means "taking care of the machine", making sure that the conditions for which one's desire can be expressed are respected, so that this can also lead to satisfaction.

The hysteric deals more easily than the obsessive with the lack, and in fact she can easily talk to others, she can ask others things, and she can make encounters quite easily. However, she often finds herself in a state of dissatisfaction. There is nothing or no one who completes her, who gives her what she wants, who defines her. Then, she constantly changes object, or she wallows in complaining. For the hysteric, it is a question of finding that behind this *not* ("it is not this", "I prefer not", "not this one" are some of the hysteric's statements) there is not "nothing", but there is already something, there is desire, even if it is perhaps linked to an ideal, hence the frustration and dissatisfaction. After all, every psychoanalysis begins with a lament, with a protest. It is not a question of stifling the protests, but neither of making the revolution and burning everything down (as the hysteric would rather do). It is necessary that an intellectual device is established, that is, that each statement, every sentence taken seriously, listened to, analyzed, and every belief dissipated. It is not a question of correcting, of rectifying. It is a question of making these elements work in a new, different narrative, that is that they take a new turn. There is not a hidden secret to discover in hysteria. As one of my patients says: "my desire is there . . . I just have to decide what to do with it".

The direction

An analysand complains of having no certainties in life. He feels he just goes where the wind blows, while it seems to him that everyone else around him has clear ideas. But why would it be better to have certainties in life? Why not keep a little doubt instead? If, as we have said, there is an irreducible Other, how would it be possible to have certainties (in this regard, also Gödel's theorems of incompleteness come to mind)? Certainties are representations of the ego. The idea is the representation of what Lacan calls the *fantasme* (fantasy or phantasm). What one *wants* is not necessarily what one *desires*; and what one believes is not necessarily what gives one direction in life. In fact, all the certainties that one builds generally collapse at the first breeze. Then, it is not a question of having certainties (i.e., the ego, without the Other) nor of going where the wind blows (following what others say; seeking the so-called empathy), but of listening to the Other. The Other *in the word*.

What gives direction in life? It is not the *subject* who gives a direction (neither the I nor the other), but the *word*. It is *signifiers* that lead us in our lives; but in order to understand this, we must take them in the equivocity. For example, someone who feels 'empty inside' just happens to have become an 'interior designer', that is, someone who designs, builds, furnishes, and decorates indoor spaces. Spaces that are *empty*. Is it a way to deal with his own emptiness? Is it a way to see what others have *inside*? Another analysand feels she does not have a *structure*. And she complains of behaving like an *earthquake* in her life, scaring others away, or being pushed away from them. She graduated in *structural* engineering and has further specialized in the design and construction of *earthquake-resistant* houses, which include, for example, assessing structural *breaking loads*, *fragility curves*, *flexibility*, and so on. Only in session she can finally hear that there is Other in what she says, and that obviously it has to do with her life and her relationships, before engineering; however, in the past she never grasped such connections. Thus, even we are not aware of it – and regardless if one has certainties, or not – *there is* something that guides us. And one can name it. *It is not true that there is nothing guiding us, or that everything we do is the same.* Often, a professional path can be an attempt to articulate an absolutely personal (and largely unconscious) question. This question, which operates in the background, must be read on another level. Another analysand says she is fascinated by men who have stories to tell, men who have rich, even mysterious lives. However, she wonders why she feels an irresistible sexual attraction for a guy whose life is not particularly interesting or eventful. A guy she describes as "stubborn, straightforward". I observe that this man's job title includes the word 'master', and that in the past she had been attracted to other 'masters' (even from very different professional fields). Remarkably, there is this signifier that is repeating: *master*. But who is a master: someone in control, someone with a clear mind, straightforward, or even a bit stubborn, who tells you what to do? Then, it is not surprising that there is no fun on the side of the master; yet, there is a strong attraction. And in fact this person speaks of her sexual fantasies of being dominated . . . by whom, if not by a *master*? Then, what is this attraction for a master; is it about discovering what a master likes, or desires? Is it about having a master; or becoming one? This is something that should be explored.

It is necessary to find the metaphors in one's own speech. Only in this way can we inhabit the Other. Certainty is rather the repression, or better the displacement of the Other from the word. *Not recognizing the Other in the word leads one to act it out, or look for it externally, such as in concrete objects.* An analysand says she had flooded one of her ex-boyfriends with postcards from several cities in the world. Later, about the same boyfriend, she says that "there was no *correspondence* with him" (meaning, there was no reciprocity). Postcards were then *the concrete object* to establish a reciprocity/correspondence. The concrete had replaced the metaphorical, in an attempt to make it real. But in doing so, the initial and main question is lost. In analysis we go the opposite way, we follow the signifiers, taking them in the equivocity. *To identify the signifiers that give direction to our lives* is the fundamental step to be taken in analysis. But this passage is very difficult, because it is very difficult to think that there is no *subject* (as centuries of philosophy have instead postulated) and that the direction is instead impressed simply by words, by language. However, this is something that can be *experienced* in analysis, and when a person can experience this, the analysis can really begin.

The examples are endless. Another person says she feels "inferior to others", whom she sees as being "higher" than her. Then, she makes an effort to get to their level, by studying more and more. She "aims high", she says. So high that she developed an interest for rockets and satellites and became an aerospace engineer. Only to realize later that it was not exactly what she was looking for. What she imagined was above her, now she seeks it inside of her. She asks me for an analysis, and she would like to come every day because "it's faster, it's quicker". For her, the object can be defined numerically (e.g., number of sessions, hours). However, the Other is within the word; it is Other than what one thinks one wants.

There is not a concrete, quantifiable object outside that could finally represent the Other. In this sense, Lacan said that "there is no Other of the Other", meaning there is no meta-language that could provide a guarantee to our meanings or any form of truth. *Inferiority* and *superiority* are figures of speech, and not something to be found in the (outer or inner) space. There is nothing outside the language (as is the case in conspiracy theories); if this was the case, psychoanalysis would not even be possible.

The intellectual and narrative device

It is now clearer that in analysis it is not so much a question of solving a series of problems or finding answers. Life does not simply resolve itself. Imagining to resolve, to find the solution, is still a neurotic fantasy, a way to avoid desire and enjoyment, thus another way not to join the game. In analysis, it is a question of saying, and of hearing in that saying what drives one to speak. It is a question of reintroducing the play into life, that is to say, to listen to a double meaning, to something else. There has to be some play, as there has to be some play between screw and bolt, which is what allows the screw to slide in both directions. Only if we can hear another possible understanding we have the possibility of making the narrative take new turns, so that life can take new directions.

Personally, I do not think that there are cases that are more "difficult" than others. Regardless of the "severity" of the symptoms, *there are analyses that begin because somehow an intellectual and narrative device is established; and there are analyses that never begin.* And if an intellectual and narrative device is established, then surely there will be positive outcomes. An analysis works if there is curiosity, if one wants to discover something (and is not just expecting answers from the analyst), if there is research, if there is authentic word, that is, word *in actu*, if the goal is not to simply arrive (at a solution, for example). If one is in this disposition, one is also in a position for steps to be made and milestones to be reached every time. What matters is that something does not cease to question, that is, that there is an open question, even a doubt, and not certainties, which function as closures. The adventure, the discovery, the lucky encounter, the novelty proceeds from the encounter with the unknown. Direction is found by *saying*, *going*, *doing*, in the gerund.

Many people turn to a therapist because they want to change. But change what? There is in fact no trauma, intended as the event at the origin of all problems, and likewise there is no single solution that would put everything back in place. In analysis it is not a question of digging into the past, or retracing life in reverse to discover some lost memories or a secret. Analysis is also not so much a matter of comprehending or reflecting. There is analysis if there is a transformative (performative) word, which opens up something new and engages whoever is speaking. A certain psychoanalysis has thought of patients (which is etymologically linked to: suffering) only in terms of conflicts, defenses, and resistances, and therefore has limited itself to being just a therapy, with the idea of having to straighten out what is crooked. Freud instead bets that even nightmares conceal a desire, even if it is a desire that the ego cannot accept, from which the fears and conflicts with which it defends itself. So I propose that our listening is guided by *desire* (the analyst's desire, i.e. the desire to analyze. And the analysand's desire, which is unconscious: how is it manifesting? Around what questions it revolves?) and by the *valorization of the word.*

Carl says he is very angry with two of his friends to whom he lent a lot of money when they were in trouble, and they never paid him back despite his constant requests. Indeed, mutual friends have also revealed to him that as soon as they have a little money they spend it all in nightclubs. Yet, he acknowledges that in the period he was seeing these so "desperate" friends, things were going well for him; he had a more regular life than he has now, and he was trying to give direction to others. That is to say, he occupied a position that was positive, beneficial for him. What he had not considered was that his own desire to educate, to grow, and to elevate others probably did not correspond to an equal desire, on the part of those he lent to, to be educated, to be raised, or to be elevated by others (if anything, this revealed his desire to be educated, in turn, by others). What he was met with were people who simply wanted to enjoy life, possibly without paying. Nothing wrong with that. In complaining about these friends, Carl did not consider that probably giving them money corresponded to his desire, rather than a favor for others. And therefore there is nothing to correct in his behavior, and there is no need to feel stupid for having believed that they would return his money; rather it is a question of recognizing one's own desire, and recognizing that it is not necessarily the desire of the other. And it can also be an uncomfortable desire, but it is part of one's own desire, and at that point one can do something about it, without blaming the other.

Listening to desire is both an *ethical* and *clinical* question. Ethical, because even in adversity it is a question of asking "what part do I have in what happens to me, in what I complain about?"; even in difficulties it is a question of not representing oneself as a victim, because in becoming a victim one's own desire is hidden. And it is clinical, because the Other is not stupid, but is the place of a desire that always seeks different ways to express itself. Even the symptom is a substitute for enjoyment, that is, also a symptom that aims to accomplish something. Then, it is necessary to abandon a theory of deficit, for which the symptoms would be indicators of malfunctions to be corrected. Rather than looking for "what is wrong" (i.e., the deficit, the pathology), our listening should be oriented around questions like: what unconscious desire is driving the patient in what s/he is doing? What (unconscious) question is s/he trying to address, or to avoid? What leads him/her to put him/herself in an uncomfortable, even painful position? What function does this symptom have for him/her? Ultimately, a theory of deficit only leads to finding the deficit, the problem, the error, so it is already without perspective: it is an autopsy. On the contrary, listening to desire is listening to something that is trying to come out, something that cannot be expressed otherwise, something that is trying to be said in an enigmatic, painful way, but still something that is something vital and positive, which is to be valued, something that can take shape when put into words.

Notes

1 Freud used the German word *Fehlleistungen*, which can be understood as "faulty functions", "faulty actions", faulty achievements, or "misperformances". However, Freud's translators mainly used the terms 'Freudian slips' or parapraxis (from the Greek term *parapraxes*, composed by 'another' and 'action').
2 The very concept of identity is overrated in modern psychology and social discourse. After all, even to define one's identity one must necessarily refer to something else (e.g., I'm Italian, I'm the son of . . . , I like . . . , I write about . . .).
3 https://www.etymonline.com/word/desire
4 Le Corps Sur Le Divan. Les Pathologies Minées Par L'inconscient (Bodies on the couch. Pathologies undermined by the unconscious, my translation.) https://ephep.com/fr/content/texte/grande-conference-de-lephep-charles-melman-le-corps-sur-le-divan-les-pathologies-2
5 For this reason, I tend to use the pronoun "she" when referring to the hysteric's discourse, and the pronoun "he" when referring to the obsessive discourse. However, this does not mean that we do not find cases of men in the hysteric's discourse or women in the obsessive's discourse.

References

Freud, S. (1927). Future of an illusion. In J. Starchey (ed. and trans.), *Standard edition of the complete psychological works of Sigmund Freud*. London: Hogarth Press.

Freud, S. (1937). Analysis terminable and interminable. In *Standard edition* (Vol. 23). London: Hogarth.

Lacan, J. (1964). *The seminar. Book XI: The four fundamental concepts of psychoanalysis*. London: Hogarth Press.

Lacan, J. (2007). *The seminar of Jacques Lacan, Book XVII: The other side of psychoanalysis*. New York: W. W. Norton & Company.

Lionetti, F., Pastore, M., & Barone, L. (2015). Attachment in institutionalized children: A review and meta-analysis. *Child Abuse & Neglect*, *42*, 135–145.

Merz, E. C., & McCall, R. B. (2010). Behavior problems in children adopted from psychosocially depriving institutions. *Journal of Abnormal Child Psychology*, *38*(4), 459–470.

Chapter 4

The listening, the linguistic precision, the intervention

Giancarlo Calciolari

Listening is not a matter of hearing; it is not a matter of the senses, but of intellectuality. Listening is not established without the echo** of the image in the semblance**.[1] The image, different from itself and divided by itself releases the echo: then, things are understood in the labyrinth** and in the paradise** of the word. Without the echo of the image there is instead the still image, the image to either love or hate.

The controversy of iconoclasm and iconodulism proceeds from the 'one' representing a subject for another 'one', without the 'other', which is also the other 'time' and not only other than 'zero'** and 'one'**, that is, name and signifier, and its indexes: the father and the son. The ideal image, denied, presumes its fixity and is closed to difference and variation, and to cinema and theatre. Repetition without difference is the repetition of the identical, and this is the nineteenth-century notion of symptom. A symptom that is being demonized must then be eliminated; until the "weak" demonization of Jacques Lacan that spurs coexistence with the symptom.

Yet in the word, the symptom is the method, an aspect of each person's intellectual journey: an element of the particularity of the word and not a representation of the subject, even if "divided" for Jacques Lacan. The other aspects are the exodus and the synod: aspects of the impasse and the schism, respectively. And the image is not what one sees, but what one listens to: the image is the mark of the signifier in the dimension of semblance. Then the representation of the symptom as an impossible economy of the method is not to be eliminated but to be read: the reading device in turn is tripartite in conversation, narration, and reading. If instead one accepts the suppression of the symptom, one only gets its caricature: the "cured" stutterer, psychotherapist of other stutterers cannot help but trumpet at the beginning of each sentence.

What is the importance of the symptom, or of each linguistic element? Its dignity as the standard-bearer of the question of life, even in common thinking may seem a useless, banal, negligible, unimportant, anomalous, and disturbing element. Jacques Lacan (so Armando Verdiglione narrates) reports the testimony of a psychoanalyst in New York: a lady is referred to him by a friend and at the first session she doesn't lie down on the couch. When asked why, she replies that she

DOI: 10.4324/9780429432064-6

is afraid of the crocodile hiding under the couch. The psychoanalyst, like a good realist, gets up from his armchair and lifts up the couch to show her that there is no crocodile underneath. This was the first and last session. When after some time the psychoanalyst meets his friend again, he asks him about the lady who had gone to see him. "What, you do not know?" the friend replies: "she is dead. She was walking in the zoo and inadvertently slipped into the crocodile pit".

It is not the symptom that devours the impatient,[2] but its negation that governs the presumed subject of the phantasm*. The crocodile is a way of formulating a totemic phantasm and it is necessary, not only in analysis but also in life, that the articulation of the phantasm leads to its dissipation. Freud wondered how much the military secret (as well as the religious secret) prevented, if maintained, the analysis. In each case, the phantasm, even if barely touched in the fairy tale of the conversation, is megalomaniac, unimaginable: always personally, socially, and politically incorrect. A crocodile under the couch? Unbelievable, crazy: absolutely not! Conversely, it is that linguistic element that, although "wrong", starts the itinerary: the account and the narrative. In this sense it is a structural account error, an equivocal, a quid pro quo that does not accept the status, the social connotative system.

Of course, there can be a formation and a teaching in which the question of the fantasy animal is always addressed in the analysis, but it is not an absolute knowledge for directing the cure. The direction of the cure is indicated by each linguistic element, which no psychoanalyst can take to govern his phantasm: what Freud called the countertransference.

When the linguistic element "crocodile" as a signifier does not signify, but differs from itself and divides itself, then the image, its mark in the dimension of images, releases an echo that is affected by the function of signifier and the variation of time. So, "crocodile" is not – as in psychoanalytically oriented psychotherapy – the totemic substitute of the dead father, but the element that initiates a new fable, one that responds to the need of the other life to be invented, of which there is also a trace in Luigi Pirandello's narration.

The psychoanalyst's listening requires not assuming the phantasm that may show up in his/her clinical practice. The analysand's listening is not the result of the masterful practice of "his/her" psychoanalyst, but requires precisely that the risk be intellectual: risk of understanding the quality of the word, of one's own experience, of one's own case, and not to succumb to the phantasm that governs him/her and from which s/he draws that substitute enjoyment that chains him/her to the desire of the other (which Lacan and Verdiglione write with the capital O), precisely when s/he presumes to do freely what s/he wants, and absolutely not to give in on his/her own desire.

Oedipus, not Oedipism, is nothing but the matter of the word, of the journey, of the itinerary: of the cultural journey and the artistic journey. Dad, mom, brother, sister, grandfather, grandmother, tree, house, crocodile, horse, mouse, wolf, lamb, oak, beech, fir, stone, coin, scandal, god, idol, and demon are not institutional and universal signifiers, but in each line (or verse or phrase): it is precisely that line that counts, of which Ludovico Ariosto sings the daring feats. Each linguistic element thus enters the conversation and narration; and then through the reading comes to its cipher, to its effect of truth, to the quality of the word.

There is not a single demon whose signification Socrates has fixed with his *daímon*. Here is our gymnastics that led us to the dissipation of the representation of the symptom. We aim for this each time but can never achieve it once and for all: the linguistic element as a name, as a signifier and as other than name and signifier. In the fairy tale of the invention of the cyphermatics, the science of the word by Armando Verdiglione, the *functional tripartition of the sign*** should be called the milestone, as Freud called the "repression". And the 'name' function is the repression function. The other two functions are the resistance function and the empty function or time function, which is an invention of Verdiglione's clinical experience, not found in Freud or in Lacan, where time is logical and does not concern the pragma, the doing.

Each element as A, as non-A and as other than A and non-A. *Crocodile, non-crocodile* and other than *crocodile* and *non-crocodile*. And parodying the supposed knowledge that might overlap with what we write: *crocodile* is everything one knows about crocodile, *non-crocodile* is what one does not know about what crocodile is, and other than *crocodile* and *non-crocodile* can read as the implication of this linguisteria[3] (linguistricks or linguistrickery) in the action, rather than in the doing. There are those who mortally embrace the crocodile like the lady impeded by the couch and those who skin the crocodiles to get rich with bags, shoes, wallets . . . To this "crocodile" we do not owe tears but some cues of this narration, beyond comedy and tragedy.

The intervention requires linguistic precision and not imprecision of the discourses, which still entangle psychoanalysis, to the point that various psychoanalysts are concerned about the disappearance of the originary word. Paranoia, obsessional neurosis, hysteria, and schizophrenia are discourses of nineteenth-century psychiatry that today have changed because the business reasons have changed. Hysteria has been taken out of the international psychiatric manual and depression has incorporated other aspects of other discourses to pave the way to the increasing advance of the psychopharmacological ocean, which by comparison makes the business of drugs pale, without getting one's hands dirty or slipping into the criminal and penitentiary process.

Linguistic precision is the other name for the science of the word: for each linguistic element the journey goes from the milk to the honey of life, from the openness to the cipher of the word. It is gold when a linguistic element reaches the cipher, the extreme quality, the capital of life. And that is why I wrote *L'oro della balbuzie* (*The gold of stuttering*, Transfinito Edizioni, 2008): if we had removed, undermined, suppressed or demolished the symptom of stuttering, by using one of the four hundred psychotherapies, which are also body therapies, we would still be making the caricature of the cured stutterer, *homo metronomicus*, the man of the chant, the man of the least common last *nodus linguæ*. Instead, it happens not to stutter, not for a super control, but for its absence.

Clinical intervention requires linguistic precision, also with regard to the phantasm, to the idea that everyone has of the idea, which in the biblical narration is the idol. The rhetoric of the unconscious, explored by Lacan with metaphor and metonymy and by Verdiglione also with catachresis, is even greater than the infinite rules of the Midrash. And the intervention does not come from someone: neither the psychoanalyst not the analysand intervene.

The intervention comes from the object and the time. The mirror (point of distraction and cause of enjoyment) intervenes between the name taken in the function and the name not taken in the function. The gaze* (point of subtraction and cause of desire) intervenes between the signifier taken in the function and the signifier not taken in the function. The voice (point of abstraction and cause of truth) intervenes between the two functions: both between the paths and between the borders. And time does not overlap itself on the object, it does not split it into two in terms of good and bad as in Melanie Klein, or in Lacan's clinic of the phallus. For Freud the object of the drive is unrelated, whereas for Lacan, the phallus is the foundation of the male and female genealogy. In the conversation the mirror intervenes as "you", the gaze intervenes as "I", and the voice intervenes as "it". This is the triality and singularity of the object and cause in the word.

We can say that irony is received as sarcasm in the paranoid phantasm, in its ideal negation of the two, of openness (a question that leads to prison in Plato and to system in Aristotle) or that severity provokes the escape in the schizophrenic phantasm, which practices the death of the family enunciated by David Cooper in the book of the same name. It is the linguistic context, the Freudian matter of the case and the linguistic precision, as well as the reception of each emerging linguistic element, that provide the bait to grasp the direction of the case, which is never the patient's direction as in psychotherapy: criminal and penitentiary therapy as a cure.

Linguistic precision does not belong to discourse as a cause, which is resolved in categorical taxonomy from Aristotle to Peirce. And for this reason, precision does not precede the act of speech; it is not the prerogative of the mimicry of professionals or officials of standard linguistics, or cultivators of universal grammar and the hypothesis of the ungrammatical enemy. Each element enters the journey as a question and instance of life, and dispels every impossible cover, also because every "representation" of the symptom is unacceptable and does not hold up the gerund of life: doing, living, dreaming, writing. The intellectual non-acceptance of representation is called anorexia, and here the linguistic precision, by parody, leaves mental anorexia at the antipodes, anorexia denied, ideal for substantial business. Intellectual anorexia does not crave the linguistic imprecision of the perplexed and the lost, both at the top and at the bottom of the social pyramid, which exists only as a windmill in the West and as a paper tiger in the East. Intellectual anorexia is not for or against the power of the other, it is a simple lack of appetite for mimicry, pseudo life, and inauthentic life. The devices in place in conversation, narration and reading are clinical, intellectual interventions. The intervention is not a saving action by the prestigious analyst. The intervention dissipates the magical and hypnotic circle, even Lacan's "rotating order" (of discourses).

Glossary

Echo: the image is not made or built and it is neither visible nor flat. The movement (cinema) and the otherness (theater) of the image release an echo, different for each one. The image does not speak in the social language.

Functional tripartition of the sign: De Saussure introduces a bipartition of the sign between signifier and signified; and he will remain indebted to the system, although his work goes in the direction of *l'alangue*. The non-spatialization of the word in Verdiglione makes him move away from Lacan (to whom he was perhaps initially close for the clinical practice and not for the theory), in the sense that the Other is not the place of the treasure of signifiers and not even the treasure itself. The tripartition of the sign is between name, signifier and Other. And these are three functions, as I wrote in the text: repression function, resistance function and empty function.

Labyrinth: this is the insubstantial and non-mental inferno: it is not infernal! It is the research, and is played between metaphor and metonymy, between the function of the name and the function of the signifier.

One: Complexity appears as infinite, between theology and philosophy, between Aristotle and Plotinus, and from Duns Scotus to the cauldron of German philosophers. Freud discovers the absence of non-contradiction in the dream, where also the principle of identity is not obvious, nor is the principle of the excluded third. The 'one' through a false connection with the ego is divided from Laing to Lacan, in which it is the unconscious divided subject. And here the term "unconscious" also wobbles. It is a question of the "one" not being divided into two but dividing itself and also differing from itself: this as a result of the analysis, in the sense of what is formulated or enunciated around the 'one'. The function of 'one' is not the function of someone but that of resistance. What does the 'one' resist? Ontology. What does the 'zero' repress? The havingology.[4] This is Armando Verdiglione's elaboration of the *not* of having and the *not* of being. And this is how I came to write: having is a property of the name not taken in the function and being is a property of the signifier not taken in the function. Inhuman linguistic property, that is, of the word in its blasphemy. Despite billions of attempts, no one has ever become the owner of the word; no tyrant, no despot, no vampire.

Paradise: this is pragmatic and requires the temporal function, the interval between the path of names and the path of signifiers. It is the paradise of the doing, the sexual paradise, and has nothing erotic about it. The industry of the word.

Phantasm: see fantasy in the glossary of terms.

Semblance: this is the dimension of images. It cannot be reduced to Lacan's imaginary and even less to that of Sartre, who in 1939 wrote a book entitled *L'Imaginaire* [The Imaginary], but translated into Italian as *Immagine e coscienza* [Image and consciousness].

Zero: This is perhaps the most difficult question, because it is very slippery. There is a point in the seminars where Lacan mentions the father as zero, but by having the 'Name of the Father' and not the father as a name, he could only leave this lead pending. I went on a reading journey into mathematics and logic, where there is a meta-zero or zero of zero, as mentioned by Brian Rotman's interesting book *Signifying Nothing: The Semiotics of Zero*, 1987, which, unsurprisingly, was translated into Italian by Spirali.

Reference

Calciolari, G. (2008). *L'oro della balbuzie* (*The gold of stuttering*). Transfinito Edizioni. Retrieved from https://www.lulu.com/it/it/shop/giancarlo-calciolari/loro-della-balbuzie/ebook/product-17544271.html?page=1&pageSize=4

Notes

1 The ** highlights terms that are listed in the glossary in this chapter.
2 It refers to a patient. However, this pun is to suggest that it is not a question of *pathos*, to which the etymology of the word 'patient' refers.
3 The term was coined by Lacan.
4 It is a neologism, to indicate, rather than having, the discourse of having.

Chapter 5

Timeline of Lacan in Italy, and further developments of psychoanalysis in Italy

Diego Busiol

It seems useful to me to trace a timeline of Lacan's most important dates in Italy, the conferences he held, and who his Italian interlocutors were (based on: Contri, 1978; Quesito, 2017; Vegetti Finzi & Lodovichi, 2019). This may help us understand something about Lacan's relationship with Italy and with his Italian analysands and followers, his expectations and hopes, and how (Lacanian) psychoanalysis then actually evolved after Lacan's death. It is important for us to also remember that the practice of psychoanalysis (of any theoretical orientation) in Italy has been profoundly influenced by Law 56/89 "Organization of the profession of psychologist", which I will briefly present below.

Lacan in Italy

1953

- 26/27 September, Rome, International Congress of Psychoanalysis. Lacan, who is still a member of the International Psychoanalytic Association (IPA), presents *Fonction et champ de la parole et du langage* [The function and field of speech and language in psychoanalysis], also known as *Le discours de Rome* [The Rome discourse]. (Lacan will later be expelled from the IPA, in 1963, for clinical reasons: the IPA did not accept his "short sessions". A year later, in 1964 in Paris, Lacan founded his school: *École freudienne de Paris*).

1967

- 14 December, Naples, Institut Culturel Français: *La méprise du sujet supposé savoir* [The mistaking of the subject supposed to know].
- 15 December, Rome, Faculty of Education: *De Rome 53 à Rome 67: La psychanalyse. Raison d'un échec* [From Rome'53 to Rome'67: psychoanalysis. Reason for a defeat].
- 16 December, Pisa, Normale University.
- 18 December, Milan, Institut Culturel Français: *De la psychanalyse dans ses rapports avec la réalité* [On psychoanalysis in its relation[ships] to reality].

DOI: 10.4324/9780429432064-7

1969

- 1 August, Rome, press conference on the sidelines of the 26th International Congress of Psychoanalysis (27 July – 1 August) and the counter-congress that was held in parallel (organized by the Italian Elvio Fachinelli and Berthold Rothschild from Zurich).
- 6 November, Turin, Centre Culturel Franç ais: *Incompréhensible à quelqu'un de normalement constitué* [Incomprehensible to someone normally constituted].
- 7 November, Florence, Institut Culturel Franç ais: *Conférence mondaine du Docteur Lacan* [Social conference of Doctor Lacan].

1972

- First partial translation of the *Écrits* (completed in 1974, translation by Giacomo Contri), and formation of the first Lacanian groups in Italy.
- 12 May, Milan, University of Milan, conference titled *Du discours psychanalytique* [On the psychoanalytic discourse].

1973

- 3 February, Milan, Museum of Science and Technology: *La psychanalyse dans sa référesnce au rapport sexuel* [Psychoanalysis in its reference to the sexual relationship].
- In this same year three psychoanalytic groups are formed, on the initiative of three Lacan's analysands. In Milan, A. Verdiglione founds the *Semiotica e Psicoanalisi* [Semiotics and Psychoanalysis] group and G.B. Contri *La Scuola Freudiana* [The Freudian School]. In Rome, M. Drazien founds *La Cosa Freudiana* [The Freudian Thing]. Other groups are formed in various Italian cities.

1974

- 22 March, Rome (at the invitation of M. Drazien), Clinic of nervous and mental diseases: *La logique et l'amour*. The next day Lacan goes to the Centre Culturel Français to answer questions from the public.
- 30 March, Lacan meets the group of G.B. Contri, at the Centre Culturel Français in Milan. He delivers a speech entitled: *Alla Scuola Freudiana* [To the Freudian School].
- 31 March, Lacan meets the group of A. Verdiglione, in Milan.
- 1 April, Lacan proposes to Contri, Drazien, and Verdiglione that together they form a legally constituted association to offer a common place against the fragmentation of groups (Lacan had first asked Elvio Fachinelli, an analyst of the Italian Psychoanalytic Society, to lead the Lacanian school in Italy, but Fachinelli had declined). Lacan suggests that the association be called: *La Cosa Freudiana*. The letter that Lacan

addresses to the three (towards the end of April) is entitled *Note Italienne* [Italian Note, also known as Note to the Italians].

- 1 June, Milan, Centre Culturel Français. Meeting with about fifty people coming mainly from the two Milanese groups *Scuola Freudiana* and *Semiotica e Psicoanalisi*. Lacan again presents his idea of association (*La Cosa Freudiana*) and tries to mediate between the positions of the members of the various groups. The following day Lacan meets Contri, Verdiglione, and Drazien in his hotel in Milan.
- 31 October – 3 November, Rome, Congress of the *École freudienne de Paris*. Lacan presents *La Troisième* [The Third].
- 4 December, the association *La Cosa Freudiana* is established and Lacan himself signs the Statute. However, the three members of the so-called *tripod* take different paths and the project is abandoned the following year.

1981

- 9 September, Lacan dies in Paris.

After Lacan

First of all, it is necessary to remind ourselves that one year before his death, on January 5, 1980, Lacan dissolves the *École freudienne de Paris* (EFP), the school he founded in 1964. In France, after Lacan's death, it is Jacques-Alain Miller, his pupil and son-in-law, who becomes the editor of all his writings (as ordered by Lacan in his will). In 1981, Jacques-Alain Miller founds the *École de la Cause freudienne*, in an attempt to continue the legacy of the EFP. Others, however, give life to other associations. In 1982, Charles Melman founds the *Association freudienne*, which a few years later would become the *Association Lacanienne Internationale* (ALI), which today is present in 17 countries.

In Italy, Lacan's pupils take different paths and gradually there is a fragmentation of the psychoanalytic (Lacanian) scene into numerous small groups and associations. The so-called tripod would never really work. In 1983, Muriel Drazien founds the *Associazione Psicoanalitica Cosa Freudiana* [Cosa Freudiana Psychoanalytic Association]. Giacomo Contri continues with a new psychoanalytic association (called *Il lavoro Psicoanalitico*). Armando Verdiglione founds the Spirali publishing house in Milan and organizes conferences, in Italy and abroad, ranging from culture to politics, economics, finance, and art. Thousands of people attend his conferences, numbers that would be unthinkable today. He remains a very controversial figure. In 1986, he is convicted of extortion and condemned to four and a half years in prison.

It must be said that psychoanalysis has encountered various resistances in Italy. Edoardo Weiss officially founded the *Società Psicoanalitica Italiana* [Italian Psychoanalytic Society] (SPI) in 1932, but it was closed after six years due to racial laws (Diazzi, 2012). In the following years, the three main obstacles for psychoanalysis were: Fascism, the Church, and cultural idealism (David, 1966). The year 1966 marked a turning point, as the translation of Freud's complete works began. In the late 1960s and 1970s psychoanalysis became extremely popular, also given the historical period in which Italy found itself, between the economic boom, the youth protest, and the years of political terrorism (the "years of lead"). In this context, however, psychoanalysis started to be subject to ideological criticism (Benvenuto, 1997; Diazzi, 2012). Lacan, who was himself a heretic of psychoanalysis, has in some ways fueled these controversies. On the one hand he has given a fundamental boost to psychoanalysis in Italy, but on the other he has contributed to fueling a certain mistrust and resistance towards it. Later, the judicial events of Verdiglione caused a lot of clamor and scandal and divided the public into those who thought he was guilty and those who thought he was innocent and the victim of either a miscarriage of justice or a targeted persecution. In any case, these events have contributed to the acceleration of the debate on the regulation of the profession of psychologist/psychotherapist, which in 1989 led to the "Ossicini law" (law no. 56).

1989

The year 1989 marks a very important date for Italian psychoanalytic associations. On February 18, Law 56/89 "Organization of the profession of psychologist", also known as the Ossicini law, was approved. This law aimed to regulate the profession of psychologist and the practice of psychotherapy. Adriano Ossicini, a university professor and Freudian psychoanalyst, was the communist party senator who wrote the law, after a long mediation between the national medical board (strongly opposed to the law), psychoanalytic societies (some against it, others favorable), and psychologists (largely favorable, because a legal recognition would have allowed them to enter the National Health Service like the medical professions). Law 56/89 includes 36 articles. In particular, article 2 specifies that "to practice the profession of psychologist it is necessary to have obtained a qualification in psychology through the State exam and be registered in the professional register" (therefore the law also establishes the register of psychologists). Article 3, on the other hand, says that "the practice of psychotherapy is subject to specific professional training, to be acquired, after obtaining a university MA degree in psychology or medicine, through at least four-year specialization courses that provide adequate training and formation in psychotherapy . . . at post-graduate specialization schools or institutions recognized for this purpose".

Law 56/89 essentially marks a turning point for psychoanalysis in Italy. It is true that this law does not explicitly mention psychoanalysis. Ossicini said that it was the psychoanalysts themselves who asked him to keep them out of the text of the law because they did not want to be confused with other psychotherapists. As a matter of fact, however, with this law and the new institution of the National Board of Psychologists, many psychoanalysts found themselves at a crossroads: either they continue to operate as psychoanalysts outside the law (with the risk of being accused of illegal practice of the profession of psychotherapist, as indeed did happened to many), or adapt and join the professional board of psychologists and psychotherapists. Furthermore, the law specifies that psychotherapy training (postgraduate, four-year) can only be provided by schools or institutes recognized by the Ministry of University. Most psychoanalytic associations, including Lacanian ones, had no choice but to transform themselves into recognized schools for the training of psychotherapists, conforming to the curricular indications provided by the State. This has had significant consequences. On the one hand, this meant that everything wasn't left to other psychotherapeutic orientations (e.g., behaviorists, cognitivists, family therapists, and so on). But on the other hand, however, it limited the practice of psychoanalysis, and the way psychoanalysts associated. Firstly, this law has practically eliminated the so-called lay analysis (from the German *Laieneanalyse*: basically, psychoanalysis conducted by non-medical doctors and non-psychologists), since it has limited access to the profession only to psychologists and medical doctors. This is not a secondary issue, if we think that in the past many psychoanalysts were neither medical doctors nor psychologists, but were graduates in literature (Otto Rank), law (Emilio Servadio, one of the founders of the Italian Psychoanalytic Society in the postwar period), philosophy (Theodor Reik, but also many of the first Italian psychoanalysts, including Cesare Musatti, who acted as editor for the translation of Freud's complete works), or were not even graduates at all (for example, fMelanie Klein and Anna Freud).

I will not enter here into a debate on whether this law is fair or not. However, I will observe that this law has had significant repercussions: first, before the law was passed, the formation of psychoanalysts above all came from personal *desire* but since 1989 it has increasingly become a formal matter, dictated by the need to comply with the law. This is a need that Freud did not feel (Freud indeed expressed himself in defense of lay analysis), and which seems to respond to the State's need for control (which in turn seems to respond to a growing demand from "consumers", who expect the State to guarantee who is a "good" therapist. Then, it is the "users" who ask for state control), rather than purely theoretical issues. Second, it has facilitated the confusion between psychoanalysis and psychotherapy, and has overshadowed the specificity of psychoanalytic training, leading some people to think that it is enough to attend a psychotherapy school (even psychoanalytically oriented) to become a psychoanalyst. This is not enough. Psychoanalytic formation cannot be separate from one's own personal analysis. And it is a continuous, never-ending formation. Additionally, it must be said that legally recognized psychotherapy institutes train registered psychotherapists, but then each single psychoanalytic association decides who is a "colleague", "school analyst", "training analyst", or "supervisor", and who is not. Third, making psychoanalysis more and more a *job* for "certified professionals" has partially contributed to an impoverishment of the psychoanalytic debate. That is to say, not all of those who enroll in a recognized training institute are moved by the interest for psychoanalytic theory (although one could also claim that even before this law there were people who professed themselves psychoanalysts without actually any psychoanalytic experience or training, and without having undergone their own personal analysis); some people might be simply interested in obtaining a professional title, to secure a job, for monetary reasons, or else. These motivations can translate into a type and level of participation in training institutes that is different (not necessarily always lower) than that which occurs in more informal psychoanalytic groups that do not issue a professional degree (on this regard, we should also consider that in a training institute/school one is still a "student", that is to say, in a more passive position than in another groups of peers). This is my observation, based on my personal experience within both a training institute and in various psychoanalysis associations and groups over the years. Another observation is that towards the end of the 1980s, therefore right after the Ossicini law, the psychoanalytic debate partly declined. However, this may be just a coincidence, as in those years psychoanalysis was under attack globally and not just in Italy. It is also true that in recent years the interest in psychoanalysis has been revived in Italy, especially following the large media presence (i.e., internet, tv, newspapers) of some psychoanalysts Finally, it has outlawed those who practiced as psychoanalysts before the approval of the law and who for various reasons (theoretical, ideological, personal) decided not to adapt and not be recognized as psychotherapists.

References

Benvenuto, S. (1997). A glimpse at psychoanalysis in Italy. *Journal of European Psychoanalysis*, *5*, 33–50. Retrieved from www.psychomedia.it/jep/nithersnvenuto.htm

Contri, G. B. (Ed.). (1978). *Lacan in Italia/En Italie Lacan (1953–1978)*. Milan, Italy: La Salamandra.

David, M. (1966). *La psicoanalisi nella cultura italiana*. Torino: Boringhieri.

Diazzi, A. (2012). Il sapere inquietante di Elvio Fachinelli: una psicoanalisi 'anni Settanta'. *Enthymema* (7), 360–371.

Quesito, F. (2017). *Da Lacan a SpazioZero*. Sacile, Italy: Polimnia Digital Editions.

Vegetti Finzi, S., & Lodovichi, M. V. (2019). *Stato della psicoanalisi in Italia*. Retrieved from www.journal-psychoanalysis.eu/stato-della-psicoanalisi-in-italia

Part 2

Classic discourses

Chapter 6

With Freud and Lacan

Hysteria, anorexia/bulimia, and other contemporary clinical questions

Jean-Luc Cacciali

Translation from the French by William Heidbreder

My discussion will be quite clinical, but only in order to understand what Lacan has brought to us that is new in European psychoanalysis. I have chosen not to avoid some relevant difficulties.

The human being can be defined as a being that speaks. This being is constituted by language, which is to say the discourses by which he is always surrounded, and his singularity is the particular manner in which he inscribes himself within them. What can make this also an illness is that it is being among speaking beings that makes life difficult, because we cannot master language in its totality. The clinic involves this difficult rapport, full of failures, sufferings, and impasses that each person establishes with language, be it with what is said or what is heard or understood. We could even say that our thoughts, and our sentiments, but also our acts, and corporeal behaviors, are determined most often by the way in which language has fabricated us, and in whose terms we have taken our place.

Lacan has approached language as something material, but in the manner not of a linguist but a psychoanalyst. The unit element of language is the signifier, which can be a word but also some letters or an entire sentence. The most scientific way of studying this material is to derive the laws that direct it and push it towards a reliance on logic and also mathematics, and it is from this that the difficulty for us derives.

I have taken the opportunity to speak rapidly, alas, of the support that Lacan will take from the Borromean Knot to account for the very constitution of language. And also the support of Charles Melman with regard to the real numbers between 1 and 0, in order to account in a logical manner for the hysterical symptom.

My intention is essentially to indicate that Lacanian psychoanalysis, if it is not to reduce man to a neuroscientific mechanism, does not search any less to study his functioning, his sufferings, his personal and relational difficulties, or his pathology in the most scientific way possible; and as physics shows for the world around us, mathematics has an important place in this study. This may well be surprising, but it is an ethical position.

DOI: 10.4324/9780429432064-9

Hysterical neurosis

Freud founded psychoanalysis while listening to hysterics. His book, *Studies on Hysteria*, was published in 1895; that is, a long time ago. Nonetheless, his studies are always of the present moment. They are always of the present, because hysteria is always of the present, but it has changed. It is always changing. I draw your attention to this point, that hysteria is always new.

Lacan would ask himself with much humor where were these hysterias of time past, those of these marvelous women, those who are presented in *Studies on Hysteria*. Hysteria is always new, but it advances masked.

Recognizing hysteria under its mask

There is always with hysteria this particular difficulty of knowing how to recognize it behind its mask, and of knowing what mask it is wearing. It can change masks, for it responds to the social demands of its time. And the era of Lacan is not that of Freud, nor is ours any longer that of Lacan. The symptoms are different.

There is thus a clinical polymorphism specific to hysteria, but beyond this there is nonetheless a common clinical structure that we are always able to rediscover as the same one behind the mask. And though there are of course always men who may be hysterics, we nonetheless speak of hysteria in the feminine because it is more often women who suffer from it. And when it is a man who is hysterical, it remains no less true that the clinical structure is the same as it is in the case of a woman.

What characterizes the hysteric is the absence for her of a point of psychical anchoring. We shall return to this in the most precise manner. This absence of mooring explains why it can manifest itself in a very different manner. This is the polymorphism of its symptoms. And it is also because it presents an extreme lability of its affects and humors. This is what is called the versatility of the hysteric.

The nature of hysterical symptoms and their interpretation

Its symptoms, which can be very different from one case to another, nonetheless have in common that they are manifestations of the unconscious, and the unconscious is an affair of words. It can be words, it can be some letters, or it can even be a single letter: it is what the slip of the tongue shows us. A single letter, which arises from a statement, can give us to understand everything else that the speaker is saying.

And if the hysterical symptom is a matter of words, the symptom can thus be analyzed and resolved with words. Nonetheless, it is in the body that the unconscious manifests itself. This is a very important point; there exists a conflict that is by nature unconscious in the order of language, but it manifests itself in the body.

Freud relates the case of a young woman who suffers from paralysis following the death of her father; it is, precisely, an inability to stand or walk, which is to say that she could not hold herself upright with equilibrium. This is a symptom that is called conversion: a psychical conflict is converted into a physical paralysis.

The symptom is written on the body, but it is the expression of a desire, a desire for her half-brother who has become a widower, a desire that she refuses and that thus will be repressed in the unconscious because she cannot admit consciously to having such a desire. But this repressed desire will all the same succeed in manifesting itself in the form of a physical symptom, the paralysis.

She behaves like the family's elder son, like the heir of the father who had told her earlier that she could not marry him. And when her desire for her half-brother emerged, it could not be repressed.

In this analysis, the first element to appear is the attachment to her father and he to her, and the fact that he had put her in the place of a son and a friend. His father had assigned to her a fixed position. He attributed to her a place that was impossible for her to inhabit, that of the son whom he had never had and that of a friend. Thus, there was the word of the father who had assigned to her an impossible position, and this is what explains the complaint that she would repeat unceasingly, the complaint that she could not advance, that she could not leave the place where her father has placed her. She is imprisoned by the word of his father; she is paralyzed by this word.

This makes it possible to understand the formation of the symptom. A symptom can be formed through symbolization. This is to say that the symptom can be fabricated out of language, even if it the symptom is somatic. The mechanism of conversion means that in the place of psychical sufferings, physical sufferings will arise.

And this also gives us the direction of treatment. If the mechanism of the symptom is activated through language, it is thus through language that it must be resolved. And Freud insisted on the fact that hysteria is not an emotional discharge; it is not a manifestation of emotions but a message, and this message is in fact a plea, a plea with an addressee. This discovery is essential, not only for the understanding of hysteria, but also for its treatment. The message, which has an addressee, is nevertheless not said directly; it must be deciphered.

Regarding the case of this young woman, today, we will say that the interpretation of Freud rests on the meaning; it gives a sense of the symptom, the problem being, as he himself stated, that these interpretations are not efficacious over the course of time. We will see that hysteria is able to oppose itself to the knowledge of the master, who here is Freud. Such are the resistances to treatment.

To overcome these resistances, Lacan allows taking things up in a slightly different way, less one of searching to decipher the symptom in explicating it, but coming to understand what the patient wants to say beyond what he says, and for this purpose to bring attention more to the signifier than to the meaning. For this patient, the analyst will understand in insisting on what she herself said: "Since my father is dead, I have no more support."

This small example enables us to insist on a fundamental point of Lacanian analytic practice. Interpretation does not aim at explication; it does not search to give meaning to the symptom; it aims to untangle through language what is not constructed through language. Interpretation aims to cause to understand, to cause to understand what the analyst understands beyond what is said, in founding it on what is equivocal in the signifier. Here, to cause to understand what, after the death of the father, is the absence that she suffers from, of the moral support of her father, and this is what is manifested in the default of support at the physical level: paralysis.

Some elements of the structure of hysterical neurosis

I will now bring out some essential points that will permit us to elucidate at once the transferential movements of hysteria with regard to the psychoanalyst or therapist, but equally in the manner in which the psychoanalyst or therapist is able to conduct the work, and also to take into account their own transferential movements with regard to the patient.

The patient addresses herself to the psychoanalyst in as much as he is supposed to know what she is suffering from and can thus comfort her. This is transference. It rests on a knowledge that is attributed to the psychoanalyst, the analyst not being simply a person but someone who represents a knowledge and thus an authority; he is in the position of the big Other. The symptom is thus a message addressed to the big Other. The big Other is a figure, a representative of symbolic authority, and this is beyond the person of the analyst himself; and he is the representative of the authority to whom the hysteric addresses herself, indeed beyond the analyst. He can certainly be a father, can be a master, can be any figure of authority.

In the hysteric's unconscious, there is always love for the father. This is a love, as it is a question of saving the father. Thus, it is what enables us to understand this unconscious wish, wanting to save the father. It is a question of saving him from castration in order to maintain him as an ideal figure. And it is also for this reason that she may want to propose a world which is not denatured by the law of castration, which is to say by the law of the father. She wishes for a world that would be more authentic, a world that would not be factitious, a true world and not one of semblance.

And if she would save the father from castration, this is because she has an interpretation of it that is proper to her. For her, castration is not a symbolic operation, which is to say an operation of language such that, by the fact of language, the object desired is inaccessible, so that there will always be a lack; satisfaction will not be able to be perfect. For the hysteric, castration is an operation in reality; it deprives her of something of the real. And this is why she considers herself injured in relation to the boy, because she is deprived of something of the real in relation to him. This is an operation in reality that wounds her in relation to the boy and that constitutes her dissatisfaction. The subjective position of the hysteric is to be dissatisfied.

This point is important, as it will be revealed as a difficulty in the treatment, since dissatisfaction is also the habitual position of every subject. A subject, in the sense of the subject of the unconscious, in order to express itself, passes most often through complaint; one complains of what does not work; that is to say, by speaking of dissatisfaction. We will speak more about this, for beyond the difficulty of treating hysteria, this is a point that Lacan will bring to the distinction between hysterical neurosis and what he will call the discourse of the hysteric.

A discourse, which is to say the speech of the subject, whatever he may be speaking about, is animated by the complaint, even without his being afflicted by a hysterical neurosis; that is, without being pathological.

This is the subject's manner of speaking in order to establish a social relationship. On the couch, for example, the analysand, even if he is not hysterical, will borrow a hysterical discourse in order to express what does not work for him, and he will do this in the form of a complaint. The subject will manifest himself through the complaint, by his dissatisfaction, and this is in addition the entire difficulty of curing an obsessional, as he has great difficulty passing through the hysterical discourse. He has difficulty in allowing himself to express his subjectivity, in complaining and saying that this does not work; besides, most often he comes to consult the analyst because those around him, his family, are troubled, but not him. He prefers to rely on rationalizations. He prefers to remain in rational thoughts.

One could say that the hysteric suffers in her body and the obsessional suffers in his thoughts.

And then, always in terms of the message and its address. There is the figure of the father, but Lacan will make it precise. He will distinguish the paternal function and the master: the master, this is not the father. If she wants to save the father, there is another point that is central, and that is that of her relationship to the master and his knowledge. This is a very important point. What the hysteric aims at is the master's knowledge, and today the master wears the clothes of science. The master is not the power of force, but the power of the symbol.

She addresses herself to the master, putting his back against a wall, to produce a knowledge. What animates her is addressing herself to the master, to admire or scorn him, and essentially to show that it is she who has the knowledge and she who reigns over the master. But the hysteric is of her time: she addresses herself to the master and the knowledge of his epoch. And we must insist on this point in order to seize its contemporary relevance, if we want to know what has become of the hysteric today.

Power is what she indeed holds, for this it that of knowledge, but she does not want to take the place of the master; she wants to make of her own place, this place without an anchoring, the master place – to which the master himself will be invited to submit.

These days, she addresses herself to doctors in their clothes of science, outfitted with new forms of knowledge, be they those of neurobiology, those of technology, or those of pharmacology. These are the sciences that she addresses herself to, and for this she can put on different masks. I recall the epidemic that has taken place in the United States of multiple personalities, and which are most often not of a psychotic nature. And these rather surprising questions which arise for the master, such as, for example: if a personality committed a criminal act, without the other personalities knowing, is it then responsible?

The problem is that doctors, in their apparels of science, treat it (this hysteria) in a manner that is more and more surgical; let us say, in any case, more and more scientifically. They no longer understand the message. They no longer hear the plea that is addressed to them. They respond in a way that is pragmatic and scientific. The symptom must be stopped, one must silence the symptom, and it doesn't matter what it signifies. This is why often the recourse from the beginning is to pharmaceutical treatment.

Today, in relationship to the imposing knowledge of science, which can even take on the particular mask of objection to it, the elementary mask of simple objection. Everything you say is quite nice, but what do you make of me? The hysteric will object to the knowledge of science, and make herself understood by saying: and what about me, what do you make of me, whom you seem to be forgetting, I who suffer? We could interpret this ultimate expression as an effect of the extremely rapid propagation of scientific knowledge. The hysteric objects not to this or that scientific knowledge, which is constantly changing with its incessant progress. That is too simple; rather, she will oppose herself to scientific knowledge itself.

In our age of incessant technological discovery, the phallic instance, that is to say the instance that represents the law of the father in a symbolic way, loses its character of referring. This law has its constraints, but it also permits the subject to have a subjective domicile, one almost assured, which organizes itself in relationship to this reference. If this reference no longer exists, he remains only a wandering subject, disarmed, who has no more references, except ones that are real and no longer symbolic. And the discourse of science will only accentuate this position, leaving him merely chained to the real of force or that of death.

A place without ties

But this is a place without ties, without any limit being articulated in his complaint or objection, and which will be able to take on forms that are entirely contradictory. Forms that at once express a confusion of yes and no, but a confusion that has no importance, and never realizes itself in an action. She can object at once to a thing and its contrary.

How then can we account for this particular clinical phenomenon of the hysteric who can emit complaints that have no apparent logic and are even wholly contradictory, without this being of any importance whatever for her? For it means that an infinite number of objects of complaint are possible.

In response to this, I suggest we look at a passage from a talk given recently by Charles Melman. He presented in Paris a cycle of three seminars under the title, "The body on the couch: pathologies uncovered by the unconscious" ("Le corps sur le divan, les pathologies minées par l'inconscient"), and in one of them he evokes this difficult point. During the talk he proposes to account for the logical character of this particular kind of hysterical symptom, which involves [the hysteric's] objecting to everything, and even to both a thing and its contrary, without this being a source of difficulties for her.

We will find here some points that I have already evoked. I have left these because they seem worth repeating, and because among them is a point that is difficult to grasp, or account for in a way that is logical, and not intuitive nor philosophical.

This is a bit difficult and perhaps surprising. To make the point, I make reference to the real numbers between 0 and 1, which are unlimited in quantity. The largest only tends towards the number 1 without reaching it, because there is always another possible decimal beyond it; and the smallest tends towards 0, without reaching it either. This impossibility of reaching the 1 or the 0 suggests the notion that each time a number can be found that will be even closer to the limit. This effort reveals itself in fact to be without end, the entirely real numbers between 0 and 1 being like the unlimited complaints of the hysteric. This recourse to the real numbers may seem surprising, but let us note that already we can understand the One and the Zero as two boundaries, two limits.

Charles Melman has held a number of seminars, and has written elsewhere, notably in a book titled *Les nosuvelles études sur l'hystérie* (New Studies on Hysteria), in implied reference to Freud's *Studies on Hysteria*. I shall recount in detail the moment of his talk by using a spoken style.

Excerpt From the talk by Charles Melman[1]

"I would like, albeit at this late moment, to take again a few quick moments, before being able next time to develop what I believe to be a new approach to the question of organic pathology, in evoking another pathology, which is familiar to us, and which at the same time has become so familiar that we are living with it, without any longer interrogating it, such that it is also rich in how it can instruct us. And I am in the process of evoking for us hysteria. That hysteria, on the basis of which, as we know, was born the history of psychoanalysis, on the basis of this phenomenon that is the body that speaks, and what it says, which is that is suffering.

I will just go over very rapidly, just to give you an idea of this somewhat novel manner of approaching the subject and underlining certain points.

What the hysteric says, is that her body is not within the service of goods, and at the same time, and perhaps in this same place, she will be able to reveal herself to be in total devotion to it.

She will say that her body is not Other, but that it is foreign. And she will give as proof of this the fact that, like Breuer's first patient, she expresses herself in a foreign language, English for example. But at the same time, or successively, it will also be of an absolute nationalism, wild.

She will show that she has the most extreme modesty, but can also be immodest, stripped naked in the extreme. She will manifest herself as having no voice, being rendered mute, speechless, or having trouble speaking, but also engaging in cries and screams, in a voice of extreme intensity.

What is peculiar is that her symptom is what is thus believed to have spoken; her symptom in fact avers itself as if written on a tablet, and as if she herself were to do this in making her symptom a matter of blind obedience, without any need to decipher what is written, yet making herself obey what this writing commands.

Let us note that the symptom is always an address. This is why psychiatrists eventually would claim that isolation as a way of treating hysterics is a bit excessive. One will suppress the address, and in this way one will suppress the symptom, which itself is not idiotic, as can effectively be seen.

The symptom always has an addressee; it is usually addressed to the father but can be to any representative of authority. It could be the analyst. It is to be deciphered as a demand, and one that is a kind of complaint. It is the complaint that the subject is castrated like the boy, that of being a girl but nonetheless just like the boy, not in appearance but at the level of the symbolic. For castration is a symbolic operation. To have the symbolic phallus*, one must renounce the imaginary phallus; that is to say, the organ. It is not the penis that makes the boy, but the phallus as signifier, which is to say as a symbol, and one to which within a culture different significations may be given. At the symbolic level, a woman thus does not have it, but she can be it; she herself can, in her person as it were, represent it. A man has it but not by being it. A woman may thus find it an injustice to not have it as the boy does. The hysteric wants to correct this injustice; but her wish to have it like the boy does is impossible symbolically, as this is a matter of transmission from father to son, in, and here we must insist, in a symbolic manner. She will, therefore, try to accomplish this in reality. She will make, of some of her actions, provocative situations, that, for her, are equivalent to ones of castration, as she, in any case, does not have the penis. This is what we find in the clinic: the hysteric makes the man. The difficulty is that this does not hold because it is not in the symbolic; and so it is always necessary to start again in making the man.

And then this last thing, which may seem enigmatic: why was interpretation at the time confirmed as healing, if not that it was thought to respond to an exigency proper to the hysteric, which is that of the subject as recognized? And what better way to testify to the success of this demand than deciphering, precisely, what she recounts, and which otherwise is evidently enigmatic?

What is notable for us is this healing faculty of interpretation, which is limited to psychoanalysis's first period, and this is a point that is not entirely without significance, but about which there is evidently much to be explained.

Finally, and this is what will enable me to conclude, it is clear that all of this has animated since then a very precise place that the hysteric considers that to which she is relegated, which is the place of the Other. This is because she considers herself in the "Other" place, with the task of placing her body at the service of *jouissance* and also of maternity. It is indeed from this place that she expresses a complaint, which has the contradictory character of confusing the yes and the no. What makes the yes and the no of strictly no importance is that this question is not decided within hysteria. This leads us to this bizarre engagement, with this bizarre reference for valorizing the opportunity to theorize, if one hopes to interpret correctly these clinical manifestations.

If we retain the notion that in the Other there is a deposit that is constituted, the literal deposit that is constituted by what has been repressed, this has thus the peculiarity of not having separated the frontiers of this space by any limit, not of castration, a particularity that is a sort of appeal precisely to the expansion without limit of the demands for recognition that are produced from this place.

If we retain the notion of an image or equivalent of the real numbers that are comprised between 0 and 1, what is limiting, for this literal content (an affair of the letter) of the Other that constitutes the tissue of the unconscious, is also the 0 and the 1; and as with the real numbers between 0 and 1, the inability to arrive at these limits, due to the fact that there will always be a gap between [this position and] the largest number or the smallest, it is tempting, and this has therapeutic effects, to see in this condition the source of these contradictory manifestations, which are otherwise incomprehensible.

They reveal the effort, albeit from one side, to rejoin at last the One, the Master, and to be with him, realizing with him the hoped-for community of belonging; and then, if one supposes that this One is only the expression, the numerical figuration of the Zero that this One supports, and this attraction towards what is the supreme sacrifice, which I would say of this illness, otherwise incomprehensible, that is called anorexia, that is quite frequent today.

Anorexia is simply the refusal of an attraction towards the phallic One in order realize this aspiration towards the Zero. That is to say, to substitute for the absolute the master, the absolute of death. This clinic finds what, I think, is not merely the imagery of the situation, but truly a support, if not of what would remain contradictory, bizarre, in this manner of responding to an ideal, he who challenges her position as woman, the phallic ideal, by responding by way of this other ideal that is infinitely more powerful and that is the original Zero.

This can end with its power of attraction, and illuminate for us the aspect otherwise baroque, colorful, and bizarre character of this clinic that considers itself strictly logical."

The hysteric's failure of anchoring is such that she will be unable to rely upon either of the two symbolic limits, the One and the Zero. The One, which symbolizes God, is the father, the master. But these logically are only the representatives of the Zero, of an empty place. They come to occupy this empty place in order to represent authority. If these two limits are not symbolized, they will only remain limits in a recourse to real limits, that of the power of force on the one side and of death on the other.

And that is important in treatment because the hysteric belongs to her time, as we have said, and the interpretations that were efficacious in Freud's time no longer are today, whence derives the interest in bringing out the logical structure

absolute of death [margin annotation]

of the symptom, which is not dependent on the historical moment. This may permit us to orient our interventions, again beyond explanation; aspiring to rejoin the Absolute Master or to substitute for it that of death from anorexia.

I will insist on what the unconscious is said to be, following Lacan. Charles Melman reminds us of this. The unconscious is the big Other, the Other of language. It is constituted by the deposit of letters that are repressed. It is thus without limits, and we can therefore comprehend how the hysteric who clings to this place of the Other will be able to express an unlimited quantity of complaints.

The distinction between hysterical neurosis and hysterical discourse

I have said that Lacan will make a distinction between hysterical neurosis and hysterical discourse. If the hysterical subject is the dissatisfied subject, we have seen that this is also the habitual position of the subject who speaks and not only of hysterical neurosis.

Hysterical discourse is also the discourse that will keep an analysand on the couch, even if he is obsessional. In the cure of the obsessional, this is even an important tipping point in the resolution of analysis, when the obsessional speaks on the couch from a hysterical position, for this indicates that he is sending a message, making a plea.

With hysterical discourse, we are no longer in pathology; we are in a kind of personal relationship, a social bond. What Lacan calls a discourse is a mode of social tie, a type of human relationship, that is to say, something structured. It is not just a way of speaking.

Lacan formalizes a certain number of discourses. The discourse of the master, the discourse of the university, the discourse of the psychoanalyst, and he wondered if there were a discourse of the capitalist; and thus the discourse that he called the discourse of the hysteric. The discourse of the hysteric, this is the discourse that is characterized by placing at the forefront the subject, but the subject insofar as he is divided. There is the subject of the statement and there is the subject of the unconscious; that is to say, there is always a part of our subjectivity that escapes the "I," that escapes the subject who speaks. A part that is unknown. And for the divided subject, there is only one way to express himself, there is only one way to make himself understood, and that is with the complaint, that is, with his suffering. It is in this regard that we can say that he is a subject who is fundamentally dissatisfied. And this is the discourse that places the subject in the forefront, and that institutes a kind of social relationship, starting from what Lacan calls discourse of the hysteric. I insist that this is a modality of discourse and not a pathology.

Collective hysteria

Another point, often forgotten, concerns collective hysteria. This is a form of hysteria that can be generalized as that of an entire group of people.

The mechanism of this is the following. In a community, an identification through psychical contagion is possible, in such a way that it becomes the source of a new social bond among the community's members. This is, for example, undoubtedly what happens in the case of those adolescents who open fire in schools and kill a great number of persons, to the point that what is called killing in the environment of a school is a phenomenon that today has become quite common.

We will be able in this way to understand the importance today of quests for identity as an objection to the discourse of science, which reduces all subjects to uniformity. Only this time it is no longer in an individual mode that this quest is conducted, but in a mode that is collective. That is to say, hysteria has passed into the social field. There is in this case an identification of each of the members of the group with the same symptom: here, the search for identity.

This is not a matter of a sexual drive between two persons, but of community. And the more significant is this community, the more this partial identification can succeed. It is a phenomenon of identification, we will call it imitation among killers, in the case of school killings in particular, who however do not know each other.

We have evoked the refusal of science, but there is also a refusal of the political. There is a refusal of globalization, of the political or financial system, and to various institutions that are intermediate bodies, in particular the system of justice. People are victims of the system, a system of all kinds of exploitation. And this is the driving force behind the epidemic of collective hysteria that can take the form of a dramatic and spectacular quest appealing to the assistance of a sovereign master who will come to reestablish order, justice, and equality. This is the image of the quest for a father who will treat the daughter as the equal of the son. And today with our social networks, with our technological capacities, the psychological contagion can propagate itself at great speed. Religious fanaticism, like political fanaticism, can easily be expressed in a collective hysteria and propagate itself also at a great speed. We may consider that in modernity, hysteria is a messenger of the political.

The question of hysteria

The question of hysteria is: what is a woman? The question that poses itself beyond this question of a woman is, what is a feminine sexual organ? There is only an absence. The difficulty for a woman is that there is, properly speaking, no symbolization of her sex, as such a possibility; or rather, she does not access it in the same manner as the boy because in her case it has no prominent image.

And the social prevalence of the phallic form requires her passing through identification with the father; that is to say, a detour wherein she is obliged to play the role of the boy. When the question of what is a woman takes, for a woman, the form of hysteria, the shortest and easiest way is that of identification with the father, which allows the possibility and ease of a relationship and with the phallic image.

If the hysteric, to take up again Lacan's expression, makes the man, this is the man insofar as he knows what is a woman. She tries to respond to this question by identifying with the other sex.

Anorexia-bulimia

Today there is, in the clinic, another ailment that is very common, and that also often strikes women and poses the question of femininity. This is anorexia, considered first of all in its clinical form, that of the anorexia of the young woman, the anorexia that we have already evoked, a substitute for the absolute master, the absolute of death, from whence derives the extremely serious character that this ailment can take.

I write "anorexia-bulimia" in this way, even if we recognize that there are the pure forms of anorexia and bulimia, for they both often appear together, or are produced in alternation. And the two forms, anorexia and bulimia, respond to the same logic, a binary logic and not a ternary one, a logic in which there is no third term, a logic of all or nothing.

Anorexia itself attempts to respond to the same question as hysteria: what is a woman? But it does this in a different way. If the hysteric complains about the law of the father, because she has not been treated in the same way as the son, of the law of which she is deprived, she will in response oppose herself to it. She will do this by being not entirely within this law, yet nonetheless being there in part.

Anorexia tries to respond to the same question as that of the hysteric, but it does this in an entirely different way. In this case, it is a question of owing nothing to the father; it places itself entirely outside the phallic law, outside the law of the father. What the anorexic wants is an identity that will be specifically feminine; she wants to be able to define a feminine identity without a relationship between the sexes. There is also the place of men and that of women. We could say that for the anorexic-bulimic, men make men and women make women.

We may consider this as an attempt at a contemporary response to the question, what is a woman? Feminism today seems to me to be searching to determine what a specifically feminine identity might be. But the two identities are totally separated, and thus as we said, women will make women and men will make men. The point in this? That there is no more problem of sex?

This attempt is deployed in the field of orality with the clinical characteristic of being an addiction. Does not this ailment respond to a state of society? Is ours a consumer society with the omnipresence of food and its chefs that confers a veritable social advantage on knowing how to become thin?

Lacan made of nothingness an object and was able to say that the anorexic does not eat nothing, but eats the nothing itself. She eats the object that is nothingness. Does this addiction to nothingness, like an object of *jouissance* (enjoyment*), permit one to understand not only the difficulty of treatment as with other addictions, but further to understand why the result can even be the tragic one of death itself, as the supreme nothing?

Is she searching to demonstrate her freedom? A freedom with regard to the nourishing, breastfeeding mother, freedom with regard to a voracious society with pointless norms for representing woman, because she is considered superficial, leaving her the forced choice of death to demonstrate her freedom? Why also the failure of a hunger to get well?

Clinical cases in analysis

To illustrate this clinically, I will cite some significant statements from patients who suffer from this ailment; in each case, it will be a different patient. This makes it possible to understand certain things that characterize the structure of anorexia-bulimia and to propose dealing with them in a certain way.

"I have a biological way of thinking. I understand what people say to me, when I am depleted of blood sugar in my liver but when someone says that I am thin, I cannot understand."

"With regard to her body, she wants to attain a mental perfection."

"My body and mind are completely separate."

"Her body is foreign to her; she wants to control it like an enemy."

"She is addicted to the mirror; muscles, not fat."

"What I refuse is to look at men. What troubles me is that nonetheless men exist."

"Why am I afraid of being pregnant? Am I afraid it will make me pregnant/fat?" The writing is our own, but we feel authorized by what she said, which makes us think that she herself has understood what she said. In front of the shelves that her father has just filled-up before her arrival, she wonders "Does he make me pregnant?"

"All the pleasures now, I will deprive myself later."

"I am not hungry, but the idea obsesses me more and more, and if I begin, it doesn't stop."

"Filling oneself and emptying oneself." *— fuss/sup eration*

"I do not have a code, I never know what I must do, which is good."

"With the addiction, I throw myself into my mother's arms."

In these statements from several patients, we find the characteristic of a relationship to the body that is very direct, a body that reduces itself to an organic mechanism. This is no longer a body seized in language as in hysteria, with its mysteries, its surprises, which can signify, which necessarily escapes one in her relationship with it, and which will inscribe on her body the message that she wants to send about what no longer works for her.

In these statements, we understand that the body is a mechanism, to manage, or subject to oneself, and if it does not respond, it will very quickly become persecuting. The body is considered as like a foreigner and quite readily as an enemy.

What the hysteric refuses in one way, which may be very radical, is the aspiration towards the phallic One. What she refuses is also a sexed body.

In our responses we thus will try to make it understood that the body is not simply an organic mechanism, that it can also be considered as a body that speaks, with all the difficulties that that brings with it for each of us. The body is not a foreigner, it is Other. It cannot be apprehended directly as it if it were a simple organism. It needs to be understood but not to combat it, as total mastery of it is impossible, but rather to demand that it manifest itself.

And I will illustrate with an example to indicate what this can lead us to propose anew in our practice. For example, proposing to make a sound, which is a way of establishing a relationship to a body that is different from that which establishes anorexia-bulimia. A relationship that can no longer be reduced to a mechanical one.

Some clinical examples that exemplify our epoch

The analyst must respond to what is said, but in a way that is proper to him, which is not as master of morality, nor a coach, nor as if psychoanalysis were a wisdom. And he must not forget that what is said is linked to the historical moment in which it is said. I propose to you several contemporary clinical examples to illustrate what the analyst can understand of [the analysand's speech] in what it is said about it.

A vision of the future

A young man says that when he thinks about what he calls a vision of the future, he has none. He says that he can think about the present or the past, but as to the future he can now only think two weeks ahead. And what he thinks of these two weeks, is only like a copy and paste. This is to say, each day is the same.

We suggested to him that he think about the future, and not the present, because what he said was that he thought of the future only as a reduplication of the present. We proposed instead that he think about the future the way he thinks about the past.

Why would this happen in transference?

First, we note that his immediate response was that this was not a problem, and he agreed to do it. And we will equally note that that has had some effects. So, why this proposal? And why has it had these effects?

In our proposal to think about the future in the same way as the past, it was a matter of proposing that he knot together the present, past, and future, linking all the three, since he could easily think about them, but he could only think them two at a time. That is to say, in a duality, or, indeed, a reduplication. The linking together of three elements introduces a third. It is no longer a matter of a duality. It is a matter of a ternarity, with three elements. The ternary, that is to say, the three, is very important. It is also very present in Chinese thought: earth, sky, and an emptiness in the middle.

It is also very interesting to consider that the founder of Huawei, in the course of a long interview that he gave to a French newspaper, made the following remark: "In fact, we have understood for a long time that the world has a need for three supporting points to maintain its balance. . . . Today, there are only two: China and Europe. Thus, it is unstable. The problem will explode sooner or later." Beyond economic considerations, certainly, and political ones, it is interesting to note that this same person himself remarked long ago that the world needs three supporting points to maintain its balance.

In the West, what we call the ternary, this three, is very present, because it comes from the Christian trinity: the Father, the Son, and the Holy Spirit, which are a three, but a religious three this time. Nonetheless, Lacan was very interested in this Christian trinity.

We find this again in a simple way, with the father, the mother, and the child. And Freud, took this up again, basing upon the myth of Oedipus what he called the Oedipus complex. The child hopes to eliminate the father, including by his death, in order to be able to be alone with the mother. The love for the mother drives him to want to eliminate the father. This is incest and its interdiction. But we can note that in incest it is a question of a relationship exclusively of two; the three prevents this exclusive relationship between a two that consists only of the One and the Other. The father enters as a third between an exclusive relationship between mother and child.

Lacan will take up a new language itself, and no longer at the level of myth. He will support this with a mathematical figure that he calls the Borromean Knot, which has this particularity of being a link of three circles, such that when one is cut, the three fall apart; there are not two that remain linked and one that vanishes. The three come apart, whichever of the three is cut. And he goes on to propose that there are three dimensions of language: the real, the symbolic, and the imaginary, and that they are linked in the Borromean manner. There are of course different ways of following the story of each of them, of following the subjectivity of each; there are different ways to link these three dimensions of language, which are real, symbolic, and imaginary.

But what matters is that they are linked. When I propose to this young man to think of the future as like the past, I am proposing that he try to link the three, to link the present, the past, and the future, and no longer consider them in pairs.

Today, with our technological methods of communication, and in our individualistic and essentially consumerist society, it is the Two that prevails to the detriment of the Three. When the relationship consists essentially in a relationship of two, what we call a relationship in the imaginary, what always comes forth is that the relationship becomes that of the One and the Other; it is no longer the One *and* the Other, but the One *or* the Other; the One remains only One, the One prevailing in relationship to the Other. When the relationship is ternary, even if there are only two persons speaking with each other, there is between the two a reference to a third: a reference to a common third such that, on the one hand, they can speak together and then this will have an effect of appeasement, because no longer will there will be only the One and the Other. There is, on the other hand, between the two, in the relationship between the two, an empty middle. That is to say, a middle term. Beyond the case of the young man, this is a direction for the work of the psychoanalyst.

The lack of the word

A young man who is responsible for the computer system in a medical structure, and whose education was in communication systems, speaks about a meeting that he has had with the company's boss, and in which he made use of knowledge that he had acquired in his education. In the course of this education, he notably learned how to conduct an interview; a knowledge that he thus used in the interview that he was having with the boss. And he said that he was very satisfied with this interview, but that nonetheless he had found himself searching for words. And he hoped that during the work he was doing with me, I would propose a method for ameliorating this problem, which is to say that I would teach him how to solve this problem of a word that he might lack.

I have said that beyond his methods for learning to communicate, in the course of this interview he had to speak [in French, *prendre la parole*] and address himself to someone in authority. It was not a question merely of an interview but of one with someone in authority, in the course of which he had to speak, and this perhaps was not without difficulties for him. And he then evokes the fact that beyond the word that is lacking, which does not come immediately, this not only produces a malaise, but launches in him a veritable panic. Which made it possible to open up these matters beyond the simple technique of communication, and of, rather, his subjective relationship both to lack and to authority, which is to say an instance that represents authority. And as a result, the ability to consider these difficulties as being difficulties in speaking in certain circumstances, in the true sense of speaking and not only of difficulties in transmitting information.

We find this very often today in the clinic. Because the technological means of communication privilege direct expression, an expression that is immediate and in a certain way devalorizes the word in itself. The word in itself makes it such that one cannot say things in a way that is immediate and completely satisfying, as there is always a lack with speech. And a misrecognition causes us to not be surprised that when a subject finds himself in the position of having truly spoken in the relationship to a superior, speaking in public, in an amorous relationship, where the subject can find herself again caught up in anxiety at the very idea of the word that can be lacking.

A little boy who wants to be a princess

There is the question of the little boy who says to his parents that he wants to be a princess. He does not say that he wants to be a prince, but rather to be a princess.

And his parents do not understand that what their child wants is organized by his subjective world; rather, they understand him directly as wanting to be a girl, as wanting to be transformed into a girl, that is to say directly.

What can we tell them?

Properly, that they do not understand the language and its metaphors, and before throwing themselves into it, it would make sense that they let the child express his concern and make it clear. So much that if he wants to be a princess, this is really in order to realize his mother's wish to be a princess. It is a vocation like any other for the little boy to want to realize his mother's wish. I believe that the parents understand above all the desire of the child as a testimony to modernity, because it now happens frequently enough that someone really wants to change their sex. Thus, here also one must allow the parents themselves the time to verbalize a bit their concern and accept that they must renounce being, for example, like a royal couple.

A radical questioning of the model from another perspective

There is a norm of psychical economy, a norm that is or was determined by what we may call the law of the father, the symbolic law with its duties, its interdictions, and what was authorized, but which has the peculiarity of drawing its efficacity from a symbolic power, which is to say a power of the order of speech and not of reality. A symbolic order, which is tied to tradition, to culture, and to moral rules, and that operates through discourse.

Today the prevailing social tendencies are towards the tentative, liberal, or liberatory, towards freeing us of limits to enjoyment; and inasmuch as these limits are necessary, to be faithful to our culture, since we participate it in whether we want to or not, this limitation is evidently attributed to the processes of filiation and debt, which we would have in the place of an original father. And the clinic of today shows us that this has among its effects great changes in subjectivity.

To illustrate this, I will evoke a report of a discussion that I had with Charles Melman, during which I spoke to him of several clinical cases that seemed to me rather characteristic of the clinic that we will be encountering.

There is the case of a young girl who calls into question the exemplary manner in which this symbolic paternal law awaits her. Today we frequently encounter young people who call into question the traditional model, the only one that they have known, with a difficulty that quite quickly appears, which is that they have nothing else to propose replacing it with, and, finding themselves lost, address themselves to the psychoanalyst.

There are also questions of sexual identity, which today is radically called into question. To deliver oneself from constraining habitual norms, exposes one to a confusion of sexual identity that is at once claimed and exposes one to psychical difficulties.

Interview with Charles Melman

What is expected of her that she does not want

Jean-Luc Cacciali (J-L C): A young woman told me that she did not want to have a child, but that she was expected to have a child who would succeed at school, find work and a partner, and himself have children. She has quite well figured out what is expected of her, beyond her own desire, which is to satisfy a symbolic order, directing, let us say, or that has directed, our social organization as well as our psychical one. How can you make precise the nature of this expectation, that she does not want to satisfy, and what will you tell her?

Charles Melman (CM): I would say that the film (so to speak) in which she has been offered to be an actress, is a film that has been so well seen, so well repeated, so [much] performed, and in which one has explored all the combinations, all the emotions, all the pleasure that one could expect in it, since for a young woman, to be a mother is a promotion par excellence. And this film, despite the progress in the technique of film writing, has lost its colors. And that then, this young woman, with much audacity, hopes for something else: the only problem being that she will be incapable of drawing the map of this other thing.

J-L C: Absolutely, and at the same time she comes to see me. So, this something else is a question for her.

CM: Yes, and this is the effective originality of the approach of psychoanalysis today. What one expects of it is no longer to relieve one of the interdiction of a desire, but to specify what there would be to desire. For it is quite evident that psychoanalysis in such a matter contains no image-book of new satisfactions that could be prescribed, and that psychoanalysis is forced to return this young woman to what she herself can expect, can hope for, which is to say to engage oneself with her in the path of a reciprocal disagreement.

J-L C: What do you mean by engaging oneself with her in a reciprocal disagreement? It is uncommon to say these things like that, since we would rather say the contrary, a search for an accord. Do you want to underline that in the encounter there is a misunderstanding?

CM: In the precise case that you evoke, the destiny that seems prescribed, is to speak of having to undertake a labor of reproduction, to have children, who themselves will be delivered to a work of reproduction, not to take up for herself this pathological feature that in measure as this progress finds her deprived of what until now not only justified it, but blessed it, that is to say the relationship to a father, the Father of religion. And this is because this relationship finds itself interrupted or suppressed, that abruptly we see that this destiny to have to have children, who themselves will have children, appears to her pathological.

In fact, what she demands at one given moment is that another referent besides that of the father, and thus at the same another possible destiny. And this is the psychoanalyst, who today seems to be the possible representative of such a mission. But as you see, the disagreement is there, at the beginning since it is not likely in the least that she can find this in an analyst, that is to say the referent that substitutes for this father, who today is found to be destitute.

Why should young women be desired?

J-L C: You have been able to tell us that these young people come to encounter us, no longer to relieve a repression, but to know what is legitimate or not, what to do or not do.

CM: Yes. Yes.

J-L C: Do people come searching for a censor who would substitute himself for the censorship of repression that is no longer operative?

CM: No, they come searching for a master of morals, who tells them what is good and what is bad. Though one finds that this is not specifically the role of the psychoanalyst. Again, there are several remarks one can make here.

For example, the young man who comes to demand of me, who comes to say to me: "Why must I desire a young woman?" A very contemporary question. The silence of the psychoanalyst in return would not be the best response. And if he has to ask the psychoanalyst why he desires young women, what can he be told? I posed this question to an audience, at Montpellier, to whom I recounted this story, and no one had the least suggestion to make. And they told me and you what you have said. I told them that I had answered this question and that that had worked. He expressed his emotion when he had a roommate, concerning how he could feel moved and not blocked in this: after all, why must I desire a young woman? They [the Montpellier audience] wanted to know everything that I had said so that this would work. What must he be told? Because you see, as bizarre as this seems, one perceives that the psychoanalyst feels himself nonetheless engaged in a duty to respond.

J-L C: Did he prefer to desire what he knew, the same thing that he himself wanted, or to desire something, or in this instance someone, who is different from him?

CM: This is metaphysical. It is true, but this is abstract. This is not to say that the abstraction is not efficacious. But I do not think that . . .

J-L C: Then what is this in the case of the promised enjoyment?

CM: Is that what you want to know?

J-L C: That is, to put it less metaphysically.

CM: But what do you know of this promised enjoyment? What permits you to credit or discredit one enjoyment with respect to another?

J-L C: We can then not even tell him that he has a choice.

CM: Yes, he has a choice. It is just that he is asking me. He is asking me, I have a choice, but tell me why I must choose one path rather than the other? I say this to you, I did not say it to them. Simply, because young women are pleasant to look at.

J-L C: Can we say then that human sexuality rests on the inclination towards the other sex?

CM: No, one cannot say that, because in reality this is a vicious circle, because if young women are pleasant to look at, they are evidently not so according to all sexual orientations. Even homosexuals, as one says, function willingly in a realm of the feminine. It is a bit more complex than that. But the response that I gave them did not aim to be at all foundational, but was purely practical and occasional.

A confused sexual identity

J-L C: Speaking of sexual orientation, which today is a question that is rather confusing, a man who is married and has two children separates from his wife and asks himself if he is not homosexual. And without going further in reflecting, he responds to this question by making it an experiment. Which is easily permitted in social networks. I found that this went with what we today call means of communication: since these are places of encounter that again directly allow this, to respond in reality. Does this mean that the processes of sexual liberation that are pursued must be enjoyed?

CM: In the case that you mention, it is entirely plausible that this inscribes itself in another determination. And which is the determination that today directs mass tourism and taste for international cuisines. Otherwise said, if I take pleasure in a relationship with a woman, I must be able to taste another enjoyment that would be that of my likeness. Why not? And what authority would be subject to a rebellion against this? And then in many cases, this manifests itself more with this type of taste for exploration and this hope of participating a bit in various existences. It takes a little bit to see what this gives, what it is worth, and if it is good. There are those who return to this being very disappointed and find that nothing there follows. There are others who will discover their true nature, etc.

One thus sees a woman pass from a lesbian activity to a heterosexual one, then return to her first inclinations to change them again, and without this subjectively having the least importance. That is to say, the body is treated like a machine that can do anything, that one can place as much in one position as in another, without this having any consequence. This is to say in a way that the atmosphere a bit changed will be out of fashion before long. This tone will seem perfectly out of date and reactionary.

J-L C: Speaking of bisexuality, does psychoanalysis, since Freud evoked psychical bisexuality, has it not contributed to making as if it were a norm?

CM: That is not psychoanalysis, but the agency of the process. It is, further, well-connected to the banality of the fact that what imposes itself is that of consumers and which from this moment on, what is about sex, for the consumer, becomes secondary, has been with regard to the enjoyment of the object that one is promised, that one has prepared for him. It little matters what is one's sex, from the moment that enjoyment will be in the rendezvous. Thus, it is not for nothing that psychoanalysis is [involved] in this adventure.

Note

1 Le Corps Sur Le Divan. Les Pathologies Minées Par L'inconscient (Bodies on the couch. Pathologies undermined by the unconscious, my translation). https://ephep.com/fr/content/texte/grande-conference-de-lephep-charles-melman-le-corps-sur-le-divan-les-pathologies-2

Chapter 7

From phobia to obsessive discourse

Gabriele Lodari

In this chapter, we refer to "discourses" (phobic, obsessive, and schizophrenic) because we want to firmly avoid reducing ourselves to the description of noso-graphic entities already defined once and for all. The medical and classificatory intention has inevitably isolated in an ontological framework in its own right, that is to say in an abstract and ideological system, what we would like to view precisely as discourses, which, although artificial, can only have as their foundations originary and pragmatic experiences. They are also at the root of the so-called normal discourses. The famous Freudian annotation in which *Zwangneurose*, obsessional neurosis, is defined as a dialect of hysteria,[1] may represent a surprising and brilliant anticipation of this approach; we must not think of it as a simple metaphor. In fact, every metaphor should be taken as originary; the metaphor is the essential starting point for any discourse and for reality itself. Freud realized – and not only in this case – that psychoanalysis cannot avoid the question of language. There is no substance underlying language.

Phobia and zoology

Freud had already spoken about the eroticization of the child's relationship with his mother; he noted in the first pages of the clinical case of little Hans (Freud, 1909a) that the onset of a phobia precisely derives from such an eroticized relationship. It is not a mere coincidence that, in the following year, with the case of the rat-man, he proceeds to a generalization of this observation, with reference to sexuality and Oedipus, extending it also to the events linked to the onset of the obsessive discourse. Then a few years later, with the case of the wolf-man (Freud, 1918), it is rather the sphere of sexuality that emerges in the foreground; no longer just the mother, as the experiences of seduction are extended to the circle of family relationships, sister, nanny, and so on.

In my opinion, what psychoanalysts have overlooked is that, in parallel to this theorematic evolution related to neurotic discourse and particularly to obsessive discourse, there is necessarily a conception of the Oedipus that can be defined as more "abstract" – that is – an accentuation of the symbolic register and a reconsideration of each function that previously seemed to connect to well-defined "real"

DOI: 10.4324/9780429432064-10

people and that now are specified as signifying functions. It is well known that this is the path taken by Lacan, who has the merit of reconsidering sexuality and Oedipus in linguistic terms, in particular by centering the father's function with reference to the signifier that he calls the Name-of-the-father. In my opinion, however, this issue is outlined precisely already in Freud, at least in clinical terms, that is to say, in pragmatic terms. Even a mother needs to be situated in the word. One is not born of a mother; each is born and finds his home in the myth of a mother, in the narrative*.

The eroticization of the relationship with the mother is possible in the absence of the paternal function, that is, more simply the 'name' function*, which is obviously not correlated with the presence or not of the real parent, that is, the person; this is not a genealogy issue at all. The father function is the name function, and the son function is the signifier function, not without the Other function, other than the name and the signifier. The Other, the Freudian unconscious, is what allows each person to dissolve as such, to reveal himself as a linguistic element. With the Freudian invention any substantial and genealogical conception of reality is dissolved. Thus, the Real is not at all a dimension separate from the Symbolic, but a dimension of the word. No encounter can happen without considering this *logic of the word*, precisely that which, unlike Hans's parents and, I would add, despite the perhaps somewhat cumbersome presence of Freud, is initially invoked by the child with his comments, which, before being engulfed by the *maternal fantasy* remain ironic and aimed at opening up. Hans's comments are in my opinion to be understood as acts of an originary word that sets the child on the path of his life. Adults, particularly Hans's father, are stubbornly intent on comprehending, and they presume an already packaged response to which they tend with each of their interventions. Sexuality and Oedipus are the key "concepts" that guide them in each of their interferences, because of total identification with the teachings of the professor. Instead, the child's naivety, that is to say, the absence of a *fantasy* of origin (in this chapter, the word fantasy is adopted for translating the Italian term *fantasma*, which traces back to the Lacanian concept of *fantasme*, in French. Please refer to the glossary of terms) and pre-ordained endpoint, the absence of any personological or social status, allows him to joke, to play with words and in this way to avoid the moralizing and normalizing codification of adults.

At first, Hans was able to preserve himself in the virtues of the originary narcissism (we can assume this is what Freud called primary narcissism). For example, Hans boasts the beauty of its genitals: "Do you know what Aunt M. said? She said: 'He has got a dear little thingummy" (Freud, 1909a, p. 23). Then he reacts to an attempt at seduction made while his mother puts the talc near his penis. Hans asked: "Why don't you put your finger there?" Mother: "Because that'd be piggish." Hans: "What's that? Piggish? Why?" Mother: "Because it's not proper." Hans (laughing): "But it's great fun" (p. 19). And here Freud reproaches the mother for having hastened the repression by rejecting the son's courtship too vigorously. Then again, the mother, who a year earlier had severely threatened the child, once discovered while playing with his penis, and had warned him: "If you do that, I shall send for Dr. A. to cut off your widdler. And then what'll you wid-dle with?" (p. 7–8). Hans, in a challenging tone: "With my bottom" (p. 8). These statements show how ironically Hans took the threat at that moment, without believing it (and we can add: as if he were rather the holder of another, uncodified, knowledge to be opposed to the moralistic one of his mother). Unfortunately, the reproach seems to become effective a year and a half later, following the accen-tuation of the fantasies of love towards the mother. The threat of castration now prevented the use of irony and openness, triggering what we can call a maternal fantasy where horror and enjoyment are confronted in an inevitable conflict. The threat of castration triggered a maternal fantasy, and at the same time the belief in the possible realization of the fantasy of incest. A paradoxical conflict begins, where Hans encounters the terror of castration, which was previously absent, fol-lowed by replacement and conversion into phobia: the fear of the horse bite.

Freud (1909a) writes:

> At the beginning of his illness there was as yet no phobia whatever present, whether of streets or of walking or even of horses. . . . His anxiety, then, cor-responded to repressed longing. But it was not the same thing as the longing: the repression must be taken into account too.
>
> (p. 25–26)

The anxiety had arisen following a dream of abandonment. Freud again: "A few days earlier the child had woken from an anxiety-dream to the effect that his mother had gone away, and that now he had no mother to coax with" (p. 118). And Freud interprets the dream as a dream of repression. The child would have wanted to sleep next to his mother, but the repression, represented by the abandonment, would have turned the libido into anxiety. The first theory of anxiety makes it dependent on repression. That is, repression would release an amount of free libido that converts into anxiety. That is Freud's first understanding of the struc-ture of phobia: an effect of repression that binds anxiety to a defensive represen-tation. Only in *Inhibitions, Symptoms and Anxiety* (Freud, 1925) will anxiety no longer be considered as a pathological effect of repression, but as what promotes its functioning in the word. With anxiety, the activity of the word begins. Lacan had understood this when he noted that anxiety is only the tip of the relationship with the *object cause of desire*, the absolute obstacle that we call the *semblant**. He added that anxiety is the sensation of jouissance and that it does not lie, that is, it indicates a relation to something real, which he called the object cause of desire. For us, anxiety is the presence of the absolute obstacle (mirror, gaze, and voice*), and only later is it represented and directed towards the object of the phobia. Just as Freud theorized in 1925, anxiety is the condition of repression and not vice versa. Yet, it is not by chance that we speak of originary repression (while in the psychoanalytic parlance the reference is always to the secondary one – just as it was for Freud, in the beginning). In relation to it we must agree that it no longer makes any sense to talk about before and after, cause and effect;

before the originary repression there is nothing, nothing itself is included in the word. Anxiety, after all, is only the perception of this nothingness, and phobia is the attempt to escape from this nothingness. The matter of anxiety inevitably leads us to the consideration of another temporality, no longer to be understood as duration, therefore no longer to be situated between a before and after; this leads us to consider the simultaneity of the semblant. The anxiety arises from the sensation of being under the gaze, crushed by the gaze (alienating), at the mercy of the mirror (falling), or overwhelmed by the voice (abstraction). Yet it is already the beginning of a phobia, because, by defining anxiety in this way, we are already representing the gaze *and* the mirror *and* the voice. The anxiety "in presence" is already a phobia, that is, it is a representation of the semblant. We can conclude that anxiety, while suppressing the simultaneity of the semblant, lies in the interval of an uncontrollable oscillation between representable and unrepresentable.

Before the phobia Hans shows that he is well established in the interval* of the word, well established in the narrative, like almost all children and, specifically, just like little Anna, Freud's daughter. One morning, after she had been forbidden strawberries because of indigestion, she woke up surprisingly excited, exclaiming: "Anna F(r)eud, St'awbewy, wild st'awbewy, om'lette, pap!" (Freud, 1900, p. 110) – thus finding in the dream, in the narrative, her revenge against the world of adults. Similarly, Hans relies on the 'name' (and its functions of abuse and growth), which opens to a narrative. For example, he recounts his fantasy of the plumber: "The plumber came and first took my behind away with a pair of pliers and gave me another one, and then the widdler". The father, no doubt about it, is very intuitive, and does not hesitate for a moment to give an interpretation that can be defined as correct: "He gave you a bigger widdler and a bigger behind. Hans: Yes. The father: Like your Daddy has, because you want to be Daddy? Hans: Yes, and I also want a moustache like yours and hair" (Freud, 1909a, p. 78).

Hans, certainly more than his father and perhaps even the professor, always relies on nomination and certainly does not let himself be guided by the concept. He aims straight at his purpose and uses the name to do it, not the concept. The function of the name is that of growth and authority, indispensable in the journey of life. This is also the path of analysis and parricide. The plumber removes his penis to give him a bigger one. Here is castration, which therefore is not at all to be understood according to current psychologism as a deprivation, but as the condition for an increase.

The story of Hans's phobias emphasizes that the sexuality and the myth of the mother, through the path of parricide, can only be reached by going through the difficulty of the word, posed by the function of father and the function of son – and not by the passage to the act of the fantasy of incest. Not with the maternal fantasy (*fantasme*). On the contrary, proceeding from the impossible, rather than from the originary of the repression or from the originary of the resistance, the belief in the realization of the fantasy imposes itself, that is, the belief that the fantasy can operate, rather than the name, the signifier or the narrative. Even *tyché* and *Kairos*, in the absence of the function of the name are made impossible, unattainable, that is, blocked in the ideal. They remain either idealized as fortune dispensed by the gods, or as inevitable fate.

No function of mother; however, the mother too can make the name work, and thus exercise the function of father, of authority. A mother and a father are not recognizable for any presumed function outside the linguistic act that determines them in the relationship, which is also originary. This teaches us the case of little Hans.

From phobia to obsession

We might say that in the following years, when he begins to deal more specifically with the obsessive discourse, Freud realizes that a mother and a father are not parents, and in particular that there is no function of mother. And that a child does not come from a mother, as the popular belief enshrines. In the past, some theologians seem to have guessed it. For example, Augustine of Hippo (1973) in the *De Trinitate*.[2] The function of father and the function of son are functions of the word. Father and son are such in the word. The same gospel message is supported on this observation, which is pragmatic and not ideal. In life, which is always *in actu*, a son proceeds from his father, but this relationship can no longer be attributed to the Platonic One, not even to God, as is still the case for Augustine. The function of father is function of the name, that is, a name that functions equivocally: no principle of identity, no reference to the *name of the name**.

The *fantasy of mastery** derives from the maternal fantasy; it is the presumption that the idea can act, that the idea is enough. How does this fantasy specify itself? It is not a mere alternative to authentic speech, between good and bad, between useful and useless. It is a question of acting forcefully in the relationship, representing it, or reducing it to an algebraic and geometric rapport. The act is also compromised. When the fantasy of mastery is in place, the act is not possible, therefore the encounter is also made impossible. Any encounter is missed; at the mercy of the misunderstanding, the encounter is continuously at risk of turning into a clash. How does the fantasy of mastery dissolve? How to ensure that there is abandonment to the relationship, a relationship of authentic speech instead of the rapport?

Based on these notes about the phobia, the thesis that I would like to develop is that obsessive speech has long since implemented what would seem to be a definitive renunciation of authentic speech, the act of speech, which would allow it to move and act effectively in the world. That authentic speech that still animates the phobia, becomes compromised in obsessional neurosis. Of course, in the obsessive discourse, the phobia remains in the background, but now it is only the support for ceremonials, cleaning practices or the fear of contamination, compulsive hand washing, scruples, procrastinations, the economy in everyday practice, and so on. The bulwarks set up to the point of paralysis by the defense have relegated the phobia to the background, in some way making it hardly perceptible and apparently harmless. In order that the phobia does not manifest itself excessively, is it not sufficient to carefully avoid the situations in which it could arise? This is the strategy of the obsessive.

The authentic and effective speech has been replaced by a formal, sometimes bureaucratic, and standardized talk, almost always obsequious, deferential, ceremonious. This attitude has caused a kind of halting of time as if the obsessive had always been on the brink of a precipice and the slightest decision implied for him a choice between life and death. Indeed, death as a *universal quantifier** dominates his/her discourse. By following this strategy, the obsessive discourse insists enormously on the rules. Ethics for him/her is replaced by morality. But a morality that is too rigid inevitably also implies a push for transgression. After holding back for a long time, the obsessive must necessarily let him/herself go. Furthermore, the obsessive also emphasizes knowledge, therefore also the 'not knowing' that in in fact at the origin of his/her paralysis. He, therefore, relies on knowledge as the cause, and it becomes for him/her a matter of perfecting him/herself in time management, implementing a mortiferous postponement that constantly puts him/her into an impasse. An impasse that is represented as an unsurmountable barrier, thus preventing its processing. As s/he experiences death as a universal quantifier, all his/her encounters are mortiferous and all of the things s/he deals with are marked by the end and always destined to fail. The obsessive's fantasy of mastery must rule everywhere.

The case of Lorenzo

On at least one out of three occasions, Lorenzo must precisely circumscribe his territory by insisting on going to the bathroom urgently. Lorenzo had been diagnosed as borderline, after four hospitalizations in mental health clinics and three suicide attempts: one for trying to throw himself off the second floor of the family home, the second again in the family home with an excess of psychiatric drugs, and the third, more serious, for an excess of psychiatric drugs, but not in the family. Later in this paper, we will need to carefully distinguish between these different attempts. Outside and inside the clinics, he had always been "cured" with lots of psychotropic drugs, as well as two electroshocks, and his diagnosis of obsessive-compulsive disorder (OCD) was enriched later (after the psychotropic drugs?) with the addition bipolar disorder.

Since knocking on my door thirty years ago, a long, difficult, but constant program of reduction of psychotropic drugs has begun (for some years now the dose has been zeroed out). He comes from a wealthy family, both his parents were university professors and his maternal grandparents were both talented musicians (it is no coincidence that Lorenzo's only interest has always been music, rock music in particular). Lorenzo likes to think of himself as a degraded son and grandson (this is the typical way for the obsessive to stick in some way to the ideal, although he almost always adheres to Ihe opposite form of deficiency towards it).

At his mother's home, where Lorenzo spends a good half of his time (he spends the other half alone in an apartment bought by his parents), the signs of a very strong medicalization of life prevail: the cabinets are crammed with all kinds of drugs. The father died a few years ago and the mother, now in her eighties, is entrusted to the care of her daughter, Lorenzo's sister and head physician in a hospital, who also takes care of treating every insignificant disorder of her brother, from a distance because she has her own family, but with great dedication.

From the window of my office, I observe Lorenzo in the street as he is coming for one of our conversations, which have been taking place twice a week for more than thirty years now. He does not walk, as he usually does, close to the walls, jumping to avoid cracks between the stones of the sidewalk. He is right in the middle of the street, and I notice that behind him a small queue of cars has formed which honk to pass. I see him with amazement turning around and raising his arm, giving the middle finger to the cars, and then continuing walking without getting away at all. He then explains to me almost crying that in this neighborhood they are all filthy and indecent: he has decided that from now on he will always walk in the middle of the street to avoid the many dogs' excrement on the sidewalk.

A week earlier I had received a phone call from him: he informed me that he could not come to the session due to severe indigestion, with diarrhea, which had forced him to bed. He pointed out that he had bought several packs of yogurt on special offer at the supermarket and when he got home, he noticed that they were expiring that very day, so he felt compelled to swallow them all. These are only two of the countless anecdotes that punctuate the story of my relationship with Lorenzo. There is in this attitude of the obsessive an overcoming of a limit (which leads to an excess) generated by compulsive behavior, which the phobic discourse lacks.

Whereas in phobia it is the writing of the *name*, what remains in the obsessive discourse is the writing of the *phrase*. The definitive, peremptory phrase, the complete sentence, the obsession; the fantasy. What fantasy? Freud says that obsessive discourse gives a lot of satisfaction to the psychoanalyst because it is consistent, docile, observant, it benefits from every gesture. So, with Lorenzo, it can happen that I get up to turn on the light or open the window and: "Ah, what a kind and aristocratic gesture!" I am immediately sanctified and I become the most generous analyst in the world! But be careful, because in order to sanctify me, I must be dead! This is the trick. As is usually the case with his mother, he must smell my death, that is, I must fall within the framework of the moral representation of every person he meets. Of course, like Aristotle for Dante (in the *Divine Comedy*) I am for him "master of those who know," but at the same time, I can only be part of the ranks of the dead. An edifying morality is always ready to overwhelm the ethics that could instead allow the faltering of his definitive, standardized sentences, that is, the precepts that escort him in every encounter. Here too the fantasy of mastery – hence the eye, the point of view – must have the upper hand over the gaze. For Lorenzo, therefore, it is necessary to search relentlessly for absolute control.

Since adolescence, Lorenzo has been a passionate record collector and has filled all the closets of his home, and that of his mother's, with the records (even thirty and more copies of an identical record!) of the British group Genesis. He does not fail to tell, inspired, the story and the various events following the day he was able to attend one of their concerts, now long gone. But can he really be called a collector? In fact, his behavior towards what appears to be an authentic hobby seems completely senseless. He goes every Saturday morning in search of new records, in all the shops and markets of the city. He carefully checks that the purchased discs are intact, but he just inspects the cellophane cover that must not bear even the smallest scratch, and he does not even dare to tear it. For some time now he hasn't listened to anything on the turntable. He then spends most of the night in a further work of careful reconnaissance by scattering the purchased discs on the bed and still examining them in the most minute detail, including the bar code. He is literally hypnotized by the bar code as if there was hidden a deep secret of its existence. A bar code, if you think about it, is unique and singular; it is impossible to refer it to the universal. It can be paralyzing for the obsessive who is forced to fantastically bring the singularity of the one, which divides itself from itself, back to the universal. The incomprehensible interest in the bar code may indicate an absolute dependence on the principle of identity, which makes him oppressed by a repetition taken as a repetition of the identical. We can say that the more Lorenzo tries to make a careful economy of resistance, renouncing to the signifier, which would lead to the next, blocking it in a definitive sentence, precisely an obsession, or freezing it in the repetition of a ceremonial, the more the resistance returns with the forced appearance of senseless ideas and ceremonials. In some way the signifier that was to be avoided therefore reappears in his manifest behavior.

The obsessive person seems to have a very good memory, but here too it is just a very worn-out personal memory bank from which to draw. A collection of memories scattered in his personal history, as evidenced by the fact that each memory is always associated with strong emotion and very often a load of aggressiveness that is sometimes still uncontrollable. No thread of memory can connect these scattered memories, which would disinvest them by dissolving them into the present dimension of emotion and storytelling. Some of the formulas of Lorenzo's speech, the obsessive speech: I have no history, but I have ideals. I have no memory, but I have an infinite series of memories. And memories of years ago still sting on the living flesh as if they were happening now. The obsessive is immersed in the time of the past, in a time that still persists, in the duration of time without interval or memory. He considers these memories to be the origin and cause of all his troubles, and experiences them with a high degree of aggression, suffering, and resentment. These (and other) feelings fail to lighten up or elevate the memories; they are the origin of all of his troubles. The obsessive suffers from the weight of memories; he feels bad for the memories. Then there is a risk that coercion will lead to occlusion.

Affective ambivalence and bipartite reality

Sometimes it happens that Lorenzo comes to the appointment loaded with representations, aggressive fantasies towards the occasional interlocutor, even just someone he met on the bus, or projections directed towards the analyst; it is almost always possible to mitigate the aggressiveness by trying, for example, to divert it towards other temporary targets. On the other hand, it happens that sometimes he appears hilarious, if not euphoric, like a river in flood, with a surprising eloquence, and a wide precise repertoire of witticisms (although quite obvious). Lorenzo seems to play very ingeniously with words, privileging equivocation and thereby wit. However, this is not the equivocation of the name, which would open up to difference and variety, but that of the phrase that therefore merely splits the world into two opposing irreducible halves: the lie and the truth in the sentence. And one can then easily exist immediately after the other. This is the origin of affective ambivalence. And then, Lorenzo's discourse can follow two opposite trajectories: from rise to fall, or conversely from deploration and lament to enthusiasm (the latter is also the path of therapy).

In my intervention with Lorenzo, I considered the importance of good-natured elusiveness and diplomatic diversion: it is useless to insist on the rules, after having once stated them. Otherwise, Lorenzo, as has often happened, immediately tends to eroticize them and in this way paradoxically opens up space for their possible transgression, since obsessive discourse tends to confuse them with ethics, therefore making of them a rigid morality. And morality can lead to success but also defeat. The obsessive discourse points to the immorality of ethics for which lying is in fact inevitable. At least apparently it glorifies morality; in fact, it is so observant of the rules that it comes to the paradox of impossible observance, the need to transgress every rule, to the point of self-degradation and self-humiliation. In the past, Lorenzo has happened to steal, with a certain level of skill and taking a considerable risk, many records in the big stores he frequents; to later degrade himself in the conversation by tormenting himself with the sense of guilt.

The question of the obsessive is about knowledge. He postulates it as a cause, as a guide, as a master of the path, so it happens that I easily become for him a "master of those who know."

For Lorenzo, every object risks becoming a fetish; not only the discs, but food and any kind of goods, any kind of furnishings, but above all his own body, to which he pays maniacal attention, which later on resulted in endless hygienic practices and the fear of contamination, infection, or contagion. In the obsessive discourse, the main fetish is the body, with its holes and their not-so-easy management. Also, in this case, we can, therefore, find the passage highlighted above from the phobia to the fetish. The isolation to which he condemns himself is an inevitable consequence. During his first conversations, Lorenzo dwelt in the heartfelt description not only of his masturbatory practices but also of the color of his urine or the consistency of his feces. The ego must be able to exercise its absolute control over the body, with all the inevitable repercussions that derive from it. In general, it is not an exaggeration to say that a body can only get sick if ethics, which is always singular and current, is replaced by a rigid morality. As Lacan (1966) reminds us, isn't it true that the century of moral conscience so much praised by Kant is also the one that gave birth to the work of Marquis De

Sade?[3] The affectation, the education, and the exaggeratedly polite behavior that stiffen his body at every meeting make it difficult for him to establish relationships that can be maintained. There is an impasse at every meeting, and Lorenzo (at least in the contingency of an occasional meeting, for example, during a stop waiting for the bus) with all his repertoire of set-phrases seems capable of perfectly managing the impasse. However, one must abandon him/herself to the impasse, without always wanting to control it with a rigid morality on the side of the ego. Each act of speech is overwhelming, free, and arbitrary, and Lorenzo can appear more skilled than anyone, as long as he remains within the confines of an institutionally well-defined, anonymous space that requires only the repertoire of conventional phrases. But the obsessive discourse does nothing but remain anchored to the name of the name, always attempting an economy of repetition which then becomes the repetition of the identical, up to mania. Compunction and apparent respect for the interlocutor end up accentuating the paradox of the lie, especially when the institutionally well-defined space is no longer recognizable as such. And this can happen in the family or the small, increasingly narrow, circle of his friendships.

Why does Lorenzo fear the gaze? Because the gaze is the point in relation to which the object escapes and becomes elusive, thus risking unbalance, together with the point of view and control that sustains it, precisely the fantasy of mastery. The point in relation to which a phrase could reveal its lying edge. In this case, the ego would no longer have any foundation to sustain itself. For Lorenzo, but for the obsessive in general, the fantasy of mastery was built to preserve the maternal fantasy. It is therefore a matter of keeping the relationship with the eroticized mother, taking a step beyond phobia. If the gaze is the condition of the phrase, of the infinite phrase in its openness, Lorenzo's fear is that the gaze may threaten the consolidated sense of his phrase (which instead should be maintained in its ambivalence, that is, in the juxtaposition of opposite meanings); in session, the phrase that Lorenzo repeats like a litany is: "Die mother, but of joy" – where the two opposite meanings exist, one after the other: mother die, mother I want you happy. The attempt is to reconstruct an oxymoron, which is now impossible because the two sentences, with the two meanings so defined, now follow one after the other and cannot be recomposed as an oxymoron. The obsessive, who primarily relies on the phrase to defend himself from the word, aims to build a sequence, but things are not in sequence. Things are in the word; they proceed from the word *in actu*. The drive, or the question, which is oxymoronic, that is, in the opening, characterized by detachment and conjunction, closes for Lorenzo in a sequence of answers, that is, in two distinct sentences that follow one after the other. Then it is inevitable that the detachment prevents the conjunction and the conjunction prevents the detachment. Here we can see a paralysis and an isolation.

Lorenzo's paralysis? Many sentences he pronounced in analysis can be summarized with the following: I know very well that I should do this and that, but I cannot. In addition to the fact that again in the foreground is the knowledge understood as the cause; indeed, perhaps precisely for this reason, in his speech in the foreground are the verbs 'must' and 'can'. This prevents the doing. "I have to, but I cannot!" is his motto. The occurrence, the doing if necessary, which would allow success, is impossible for him and therefore denied without remedy. As if there were a demon (an internal or external cause) that converts every possible occurrence into compulsion. Here is the specificity of obsessional neurosis, which Freud, since the beginning, called *Zwangneurose* – the neurosis of constriction.

The shift to the schizophrenic discourse

In fact, the world of the obsessive is divided into two distinct parts. In the internal, domestic world, he can devote himself to activities of self-reassurance and phobia management through his endless ceremonies (Lorenzo washes his hands count-less times and spends most of the day cleaning his body and the environment he lives in). In the external world, there is the risk that it will no longer be possible to maintain this program of forced behavior, at which point he is in danger of shift-ing to a schizophrenic discourse and a passage to the act. Lorenzo's relationship with death also obeys this bipartite scheme between domestic and non-domestic. Lorenzo has been diagnosed by psychiatrists as borderline personality. It has been noted several times, within the psychoanalytic field, that there is continuous complaint and a spectacular staging of suicide in the obsessive discourse, with representations of possible scenarios and preparations for suicide. But there is a widespread belief that one needs to remain calm because it is precisely a play, just a question aimed at eliciting a convincing and comforting response from the other. Therefore, in the obsessive discourse, there would be a possible but never realized suicide. In my opinion, however, Lorenzo's case requires us to correct this belief, at least partially. The first two suicide attempts had taken place in the domestic environment, almost under the eyes of the family, and certainly, they had more the appearance of spectacular staging. By the third, however, he was saved by a miracle. The environment in which it was designed was certainly not domestic (he had moved away from his family and lived alone in an attic in the city center). After swallowing an enormous dose of psychotropic drugs, he locked the attic door and lay on the bed waiting for death. His sister, who accidentally came to see him, getting no answer, had to break the door with the help of the fire-men and found him lifeless, in a coma. He then had a hard time recovering after a few weeks' hospitalization. This example proves, in my opinion, that when the obsessive discourse comes to panic, then it turns into schizophrenic discourse, and in this case, suicide can be achieved. There is no longer only the parody of a question addressed to the family member, to the other, but a parody addressed to the Other, there is identification with absolute knowledge, with knowledge of the secret of death. By now the non-domestic son can no longer play with the alternative between the outcast, degraded son and the ideal one (moreover, these are just the two sides of the same ideal), but he is forced to face an irreducible Other. And realizing, or rather remembering, that he cannot act through speech, not being able to ask any more questions, in reality being convinced that he cannot make use of the act of speech, he decides to take action. His is an extreme question now addressed to no one. Even the maternal, domestic fantasy which he could hold on to in the family, is now in the process of dissolving. In the schizophrenic discourse, paradoxically, that maternal fantasy in which death was the universal quantifier and could, therefore, be used to obtain the attention of the family members, dissolves. The bipartite world in which he had installed himself in the family, caught in the amphibology between the good people, to whom he could become attached even beyond measure, and the bad people, to be despised and rejected, dissolves and the panic that this dissolving entails can then provoke the onset of a schizophrenic discourse.

The return home and the mystical period

It is precisely when he returns to the maternal home, after this extreme confrontation with panic and death, that Lorenzo goes through what he defines his mystical period. He had always poorly tolerated the family dog, in his opinion excessively dirty, lively, and impetuous, as well as cats and any other animal. But now the dog becomes the fantasy animal that allows a point of reunion and reconciliation with the family imaginary. Not just that; he decorates his room with giant posters depicting baby animals of various kinds. He represents himself as the puppy returned to the family. For Lorenzo, the dog is now raised to the rank of authority; while before it was despised, it is now respectable and almost adored, as he himself wants to be from now on in the family. However, this new staging does not represent a simple return to the mother's nest. He returns to it after a period that we can precisely define as "schizophrenic," in which the Other had finally proved to be inaccessible, unrepresentable, foreign, non-domestic. It is clear that upon returning, the representation must somehow fall back, pinning itself to more foreign and border elements, that is, elements that are no longer directly or easily attributable to figures in the family. Far from the non-domestic world, the extreme, overflowing fear, which most likely had been at the origin of the extreme gesture, dissipates. Now, fear becomes domestic again, somehow manageable by a subject, that is, fear becomes phobia again. It is a fear that can be controlled again through ceremonials and cleaning practices. Here again is the reference to the foundation of the phobia, where the animal is raised to a fetish or despised. Lorenzo, returning to the family, therefore follows an inverse path, re-evaluating the phobia and curbing, through the fetish, panic with the relative passage to the act. There is mysticism here, that is, the harmony that has become cosmic and guaranteed by devotion to the animal.

The obsessive person, who went back to being obsessive after being schizophrenic in the estrangement of the non-domestic external environment, in the family can revamp, in a caricatured, masked way, his question, which is the question of death. The step is that of the return, from the acted suicide to the one staged and fantasized. Suicide returns to assume the appearances of a play (still today, Lorenzo does nothing but complain and rack his brain about death, his or her mother's). Once Lorenzo returned to the family context, the matter of life or death, which could be taken as an open question in the irony of the originary word, returns to what it has always been for the obsessive: a fantasmatic construction. But now with a variation: the transition from genealogy to zoology. The schizophrenic drift paradoxically served to strip him of any genealogical identification, but now he needs to replace it with the fetish, in the animal phobia, sinking back into the ambivalence that characterizes it: repulsion and attraction, eroticization, hence obsession. The ambivalence with which the family figures were once invested, now under this new mystical condition, and partly in the effort to ingratiate them, is transformed into submission. Ambivalence has become, so to speak, zoological. This second regressive, zoological, or "mystical" phase as Lorenzo appropriately defines it, which corresponds to his return to the family, suggests other general reflections regarding the legitimacy of every nosographic classification of what are called mental or personality disorders. As described above, in the immediately preceding period Lorenzo, following a violent quarrel, had moved away for a few months, and lived alone, in an attic: he necessarily had to go out on various errands and frequented some bars in the neighborhood for eating. It was an extreme period of life. He says that going out was always a shocking experience: the world seemed mechanical and frozen to him, passers-by seemed to move like puppets, the figures of the people he met had something monstrous, their faces suddenly seemed to deform into a cadaveric grimace and transmute into skulls. The world shriveled into a cold present where time froze and disappeared. Everything was too present, and he feared for the reality of his own body, now connected to a vacillating scene. Nothing was recognizable anymore and he was forced to rush back into his attic. Precisely because he feared, as in a blocked mirror, to become a corpse like the people he met, the step of suppressing himself became very urgent and unavoidable for him. The hallucination was experienced as an unbearable, but eternal and completely natural condition of his body; unreality seemed real to him. The whole world, sucked into the maelstrom of the present, was a hallucination.

The next phase, the return to the family after the suicide attempt, conserved a residual aspect of this altered perception and time, but now in a milder, sweetened way: those cadaveric faces had turned into animals, indeed into puppies, with which he could identify, in a sort of regression and without any fear. Yet the mirror was still stuck. The panic experience was turning into a mystical experience. The world in the family was pervaded by a harmonious and universal force and while retaining the feeling of an absolute, almost carnal bond with the Other (as in mysticism) he was no longer affected by any perceptual distortion.

Lorenzo's body, just like any body, has nothing substantial: it is impossible to identify any fixed point, any 'objectivity' or concrete substance to which to refer it. The events of the Other also govern our perception; hallucination is the "natural" way of perceiving reality when the Other is represented, that is, in various ways negated. In fact, there is no normal or natural perception. Moreover, the reassuring certainty of the mystic, due to the involvement of the body, is still related to the function of a blocked mirror, expunged from the word, as the great medieval mystical philosopher Ibn al Arabi (2018) reminds us. Although it refers to an Other (for the mystic it is God) still represented, the mystical perception is no longer connected to the small other, the similar person that I can meet. The latter is excluded from the combination of 'body and scene' of the word. Specular identification somehow persists. Familiar and domesticated. But now it is harmless, it is detached from all earthly identification: "God is the mirror, through which you see yourself, and you are His mirror through which He sees His names and the manifestation of their rules, and these names are nothing other than Himself."

This extraordinary observation of the mystic, based on contemplation and gaze, could, in my opinion, accurately represent the identity card of the obsessive person incarcerated in his family prison; with its dependence on a gaze that locks the mirror and therefore the function of the name. Also, the renunciations, which Lorenzo underwent again in this period, may well recall ascetic practices. In contemplation, and in general in the mystical experience, the gaze persists in latency. Although it no longer rages over the body as in schizophrenia, it returns in gentler form, partly tamed by the maternal fantasy. But under the dominion of the fantasy, the gaze is not yet a condition for an unending phrase; it calms the body but finds it difficult to initiate a story. It can only produce statements that close: these are the obsessions. The task of analysis with the obsessive is therefore to facilitate access to the narrative so that the gaze placates, and unnoticed, together and through the mirror* and the voice*, it can lead to invention. The invention that is proper to authentic life, and that alone results in the narrative.

Lorenzo still needs moral sacrifice and renunciation to preserve his body from every possible disease and contamination. He needs a body under torture and in continuous purification. And renunciation is now linked to saving, an economy of life down to the last penny.

Surely this is the way to understand the famous gloss we mentioned above, where Freud writes that the obsessive discourse is a dialect of the hysterical one. The obsessive person clings to the singularity of the phrase and the idiom, and subsequently to any object, even the most futile and singular. Also, the logic of his relationship with money then starts wavering: he pays attention to every penny (when the shop assistants of the supermarket see Lorenzo coming, they are appalled) but it can also happen that he spends all the money he has in his pocket to purchase of a record or some clothes.

To preserve the body from any backlash (from any somatic conversion) due to the ideal and the fixating of the name, the obsessive discourse makes use of the displacement offered by a phrase, a phrase that then becomes an obsession, a scruple; so, the attachment to the particular rule and the consequent renunciation. Somehow the maternal fantasy starts to rebuild itself; the maternal fantasy, which finally is nothing more than pure ideality, that for Lorenzo was in danger of cracking when going out in the world. And it is precisely the integrity of the maternal fantasy that causes Lorenzo's attention to shift to the most futile object, to the smallest detail; that is, it also allows him to preserve a certain integrity in the surrounding world. These particular objects, these details that may seem insignificant for anyone else, actually allow him to somehow make up for the object that escapes the word. But in this way, his relationship with action is obviously compromised.

Dialects are singular idioms compared to the national language. As has historically happened, a dialect can rise to a national and ideal language; the Freudian example may well suggest that for it, just as for obsessive discourse, there is no more distinction between individual and universal. And then, any nosographic classification, in general, can only be the product of an abstract ideological system. Finally, we could say that the ideological, psychiatric, or psychological system is affected precisely by the same condition that it would like to treat.

The analyst, the ideal, and religion

For Lorenzo I am the best among the many therapists he has met since childhood, I am the ideal analyst; and yet it is not really the case to imagine a quick development. On the contrary, in this way it is more difficult to avoid the representation, and therefore the negation of the impasse, renouncing its articulation. Resistance is represented, the causes are always taken for granted; that is to say, it is the ideal cause to function, to get stuck in the word, and therefore it is not a cause that escapes, which only may lead to open up to the authentic act of speech. I'm ideal because I'm already taken as dead; a substitute of the father also taken for a dead and, therefore, ideal father (moreover, Lorenzo's biological father died some decades ago). If I continue to play the role of the ideal analyst, it is more difficult for me to effectively function as an analyst. The parricide, which must occur in speech, is particularly difficult for Lorenzo because his father is ideal and already given as dead. For years now, living almost uninterruptedly with his elderly mother (alternately adored and despised), Lorenzo has undergone all sorts of renunciations that have led him to a sacrifice that would be difficult for anyone to tolerate. This includes the renunciation of food, of going out, of a partner, but more generally of anything that could lead him to an authentic life, that is, to a life to be lived through the quality of speech. Even time seems to expand until it stops. Sheltered from the irruption of the stranger, life can resume in the usual repetition of the identical. For the obsessive person, it is vital that there is always a closed place, toward which he has a special affection, as well as a torment, a place to clean up incessantly with excessive cleaning practices. It is vital to establish a dimension of daily life, within the walls of the home (which for Lorenzo has become a prison).

The juxtaposition mentioned above with the mysticism would confirm the hypothesis that the obsessive discourse is the caricature of religion. Yet Freud firmly states the opposite, namely that religion is the caricature of the obsessive discourse. I believe that Freud, a positivist and declared atheist, was (correctly) referring to religion in its institutional character, to the reformed and counter-reformed religion. This Freudian reversal, to be understood as an enhancement of this discourse, remains of extreme interest. In fact, in 1925, Freud writes that the *Zwangneurose* is

> Unquestionably the most interesting and repaying subject of analytic research. But as a problem it has not yet been mastered. It must be confessed that, if we endeavor to penetrate more deeply into its nature, we still have to rely upon doubtful assumptions and unconfirmed suppositions.
>
> (Freud, 1925, p. 113)

Ultimately, with this reversal Freud seems to notice the profound question that this discourse can spark; the question about the original way of leading life for everyone (and not only for the neurotic, isolated, and classified as such by the nosographic system). So, it seems completely misleading, albeit a common habit, to distinguish between the obsessive discourse and any other discourse, including religious discourse. When we examine the obsessive discourse – the surprising senselessness of his ceremonies, his rituals, and the constraints to which he submits – a conscious reference to the singular logic of the word becomes unavoidable. Then the confrontation with the religious discourse can only lead to the surprising observation that there is no point of view from which to start, that the point of view is only a representation of the gaze. This is perhaps the most interesting and fruitful contribution of the obsessive discourse.

Psychotherapy, with its inexperience, bases itself on the fantasy; at times to counter it, at times to sustain it. Experience has long taught me not to directly confront these fantasies, nor to face them individually, nor even to participate in them – that is, not to risk that they become even more rigid, merging into the maternal fantasy, which is ideal, with the result of making them irrefutable. It is completely useless to linger on fantasies.

To dispel the maternal fantasy, it is necessary to play on irony and wit (while avoiding sarcasm); this is possible if a narrative device can be established. Indeed, the narrative device is indispensable to avoid sarcasm and relaunch the equivocity of the name; it is essential for the doing. Only in this way can the rigid morality of the obsessive person turn into an ethics. Without a narrative, action is impossible; at best it degrades into a sterile flurry of activity and in a futile repetition of the identical, always in rituals.

If, in relation to the hysterical discourse, it is a matter of dealing with the ideal with which the Other is cloaked – unlocking the name of the name, so that sometimes a simple distraction is enough – with the obsessive discourse it is rather necessary to focus on the object, by diverting it from any ideal fixity. Regarding the obsessive discourse, it is then necessary to redirect attention away from the conservative practices and the ceremonies, and to strive to somehow reveal an object that can only persistently escape. The narrative device is also indispensable for both discourses; however, the modes of listening can differ concerning the degree of prudence and caution in the intervention, which is always unique. For both discourses, however, it is the analyst with his/her flesh, that is, with the listening acquired through his/her experience and training, which from time to time places him/her in the position of Other and of the object that escapes, to be able to lead the game.

Disinvesting the Other from the ideal can certainly generate disappointment and resentment (as frequently happens in the relationship with hysteria), but it is still easier than disinvesting the object from the ideal. The latter is certainly a more laborious and sometimes even interminable task. Then, if we accept the aforementioned Freudian reversal as an acknowledgment, and even an enhancement of the obsessive discourse with respect to the religious discourse, it is perhaps a matter of ascertaining that Christianity at least at its inception (not that of the hierarchy) is founded on the qualification of an obsessive discourse. We have said that the obsessive discourse treats the figure of the father and also that of the son as if they were dead, therefore according to a genealogical discourse, but (as is the case with Christianity) this same obsessive discourse does not want to accept this end. It is because he does not resign himself to thinking of them as dead, and to death in general, that the obsessive person insists on the ideal of both the son and the father. Of course, the obsessive discourse is a caricature of religion; it is rather an impossible religion. But it also shows the impasses in which any religion can find itself with its rites and ceremonies. That is, the obsessive discourse degrades the rite and the ceremony by transforming them into ritual and ceremonial, respectively. An impossible morality replaces the ethics that should be at the heart of any religious experience. Even charity is somewhat mimicked and counterfeited because the obsessive can be prodigal of offers and gifts (especially to the analyst) except s/he weighs, measures, and sooner or later asks repayment for them. Yet the underlying intention is precisely to establish a rite and secure it by fixing it with a ceremony. How then to understand the drift by which the rite degrades into ritual and the ceremony into a ceremonial? We can see that the ritual is precisely characterized by the relapse into the repetition of the identical, which the rite itself would like to avoid; and the ceremonial is reduced to a mere parody of the ceremony by which one would like to ensure and manifest the authenticity of the relationship with the divine, ultimately with the Other. Where does the obsessive discourse fail? It fails because it ignores the voice. The ritual is a rite from which the voice has been expunged; the ceremonial is still a ceremony in which one would like to exercise control over the gaze by seeing, and then again, the voice has been expunged. The obsessive discourse, precisely because of this renunciation of the voice, wanting to favor the control of seeing over the gaze, faces impotence both with regard to others and with regard to things.

For everyone, life is pragmatic. The obsessive always neglects the fact that the word is mirror, gaze, and voice, and that only this logic is effective and allows everyone to act in the world. The word is always *in actu*. The word does not admit being isolated, fixed, or represented in thought, at the risk of degrading into obsession (what only shows the impotence of the subject). Relationships with things, lucky encounters, harmony with others, and growth all require the voice and the narrative, whereas for the obsessive person, but also for the system of discourses that would like to cure him, there is only a world already given, predestined, and without voice.

Notes

1 To explain our attempt to find the roots of the obsessive discourse, it is useful to mention the whole context in which Freud's quoted passage is situated: "What adds so greatly to the difficulty of doing this are the resistances of the patients and the forms in which they are expressed. But even apart from this it must be admitted that an obsessional neurosis is in itself not an easy thing to understand – much less so than a case of hysteria. Actually, indeed, we should have expected to find the contrary. The language of an obsessional neurosis – the means by which it expresses its secret thoughts – is, as it were, only a dialect of the language of hysteria; but it is a dialect in which we ought to be able to find our way about more easily, since it is more nearly related to the forms of expression adopted by our conscious thought than is the language of hysteria. Above all, it does not involve the leap from a mental process to a somatic innervation – hysterical conversion – which can never be fully comprehensible to us" (Freud, 1909b, p. 156).
2 See in particular the reflections on the procession of the Son by the Father and the Holy Spirit by the Father and the Son, 15, 23, 57.
3 Lacan notes that *La philosophie dans le boudoir*, published eight years after *The Critique of Practical Reason*, completes its hidden truth.

References

Arabi, Ibn. (2018). *Unveiling the secret of the most beautiful names*. Chicago: Kazi Publications.

Augustine of Hippo. (1973). *La trinità (testo latino con traduzione a fronte)*. Rome, Italy: Città Nuova Editrice.

Freud, S. (1900). *The interpretation of dreams* (3rd Edition). New York: The Macmillan Company.

Freud, S. (1909a). Analysis of a Phobia in a five-year-old boy. In *Standard edition* (Vol. 10, pp. 3–149). London: Hogarth Press.

Freud, S. (1909b). Notes upon a case of obsessional neurosis. In *Standard edition* (Vol. 10, pp. 155–249). London: Hogarth Press.

Freud, S. (1918). From the history of an infantile neurosis. In *Standard edition* (Vol. 17, pp. 7–121). London: Hogarth Press.

Freud, S. (1925). Inhibitions, symptoms and anxiety. In *Standard edition* (Vol. 20, pp. 77–175). London: Hogarth Press.

Lacan, J. (1966). *Kant avec Sade. Ecrits* (pp . 765–790). Paris: Gallimard.

Chapter 8

Reading Freud with Lacan. Brief essay on paranoia. Or how to extricate oneself, at the dawn of the third millennium, from an impossible narration

Fabrizio Gambini

In Italy the word "narration" has recently taken on an importance and value of use that it did not have up until just a few years ago. The use currently made of this term is linked to the introduction of the concept of fake news, in turn implied by the notion of politics as invention of reality.

In order to place the meaning taken on by the term "narration" in time, I recall that in 2016 the Oxford Dictionary elected "post-truth" the word of the year, that is, the fact that people – the television audience – are more influenced by the emotion aroused by what is said to them than by reality. What to say? People are influenced by a second reality which is that of the television aquarium, that of narration made up of social networks, and that literally becomes indistinguishable from that we had been used to conceiving as unique: reality. The fact that it is the second reality implies the loss of the relationship of that reality with the world of facts, which first and foremost become television facts or divulged by Facebook, facts that are facts for the sole fact of existing in the aquarium.

Whatever post-truth is, in any event it's not upheld by a mere lie. A lie is not "fake news", as they say today in the United States of America, from which the use of the term reached us; to be straight, it's not a euphemism to indicate that resort, as old as the hills, to the option or the necessity to lie. We're talking about something else here. Indeed, from a certain viewpoint, the lie, contrasting the truth, confirms the truth itself in its laws and in its value, precisely since it is different from the lie, which when revealed loses its usefulness and its value which is that of standing in place of the truth. To get to the point, in the articulation of truth and lie pre-television – and above all, before the explosion of the social media as a communication and information tool – we are still in that type of observations on the word and on language that made Freud rejoice when he came across a linguistics essay on the presence of primal words in Egyptian that simultaneously meant one thing and its opposite: light and dark, love and hate, or precisely, truth and lie.[1]

The post-truth is something entirely different, that classifies as such above all for its effects, which are to a certain extent permanent: the mass media divulgence

DOI: 10.4324/9780429432064-11

of news simply takes the place of the news and, in a certain sense, exactly the area of that which the news is about disappears; in Aleppo what the television tells us happens is what happens.

Recently, hot on the heels of having read a good book published in Italian in 2018,[2] I found myself thinking, with certain surprise, that psychoanalysis was not free from having some responsibility in the determination of this status quo. Certainly the issue has been in the balance at least since Paul Ricoeur associated Marx, Nietzsche, and Freud, classifying them as "Masters of suspicion".[3] But it is striking in any event to read that Lacan, which Kakutani associated with Baudrillard, Derrida, and Lyotard,[4] is directly responsible for a school of thought that introduces the dimension of suspicion of the truth implied by speech, and that before all these decadent French complications you could call a spade a spade. Down this path, Kakutani seems to think that in some sense Donald Trump is also a son of Lacan. Surely the statement by Kakutani, which remains an intelligent and documented journalistic opinion, is to be reviewed and tempered, but there's no doubt that the idea of calling a spade a spade, the idea of snatching by the tail and holding on tight to the truth implied by the words we use to state it is an idea in and of itself paranoiac and therefore also not at all psychoanalytical.

The point is that if psychoanalysis were a question of content, there would just be moderate difficulties, contingent on producing a coherent narration – all in all captivating – of the psychosexual development of the child of man. Starting from this narration one could identify a fairly concrete psychopathology and formulate some sort of explanation for the folly of normality that constitutes our social bond, our being part of a polis, our being political animals. In fact, some do not avoid this pleasure and produce or adopt narration in which one loses oneself just like – first as a child and later as an adolescent – I lost myself in the universe of my readings, and like, as an adult, I continue to do so in other narrative universes.

But psychoanalysis is not its content; it is not its meta-psychology, and it isn't even its technique. This has its consequences; neither positive nor negative, but rather present, inevitable, and real. One of these consequences is that a consistent and orderly narration of the psychosexual development of the child of man is not possible. A second consequence directly concerns the technique of psychoanalysis and its relationship with its theory.

Perhaps it would be didactically useful to differentiate between the two planes and separate the meta-psychological content of the technique, but, as we will see in this brief chapter, my opinion is that not only is it not possible, but this separation in and of itself is a presage of errors, of flights of fancy, for that which concerns the content, and of simultaneous undervaluation of the technique that brings with it operational consequences of no little import.

In the seminar that Lacan dedicates to the object relation, the theme is already laid forth with great clarity right from the first lesson:

> This topic . . . [the object relation . . . Ed.] . . . could be treated, in effect, only after a certain distance had been taken on the question. We had first to

consider the structures in which Freud has shown us that analysis takes place and operates, especially the complex structure of the relation between the two subjects present in analysis, the analysand, and the analyst.[5]

Thus, I shall not address the question of meta-psychological content and the technique in two different chapters, but rather I'll seek to take on the risk of potential confusion, which I hope in any event to avoid, integrating the observations relative to the two fields between them.

To start off somewhere in the meantime, it is certain that outside the intrauterine environment many things happen. One of these is that outside people talk, there is language. But inside, too, many things happen; less, but they happen. Inside the uterus there is no gravity: the fetus floats in the amniotic fluid. There is no change in temperature, which is constant, more or less around 37°C. The mouth and nose do not let air and food go in and out: there is no inspiration since the fetus' blood, which circulates while the little heart beats, is oxygenated by the maternal respiration through the placental circulation. Even nourishment is continual, just like the oxygenation taking place through the circulation of blood that links the fetus to the mother. There is no change in light intensity and the day is not different from the night, except for that which the fetus "perceives" in the circadian rhythm variations of the mother. Substantially, it is an environment characterized by the prevalence of a homeostatic environment, free from differences; an environment in which the register of the continuous prevails over that of discontinuity, of alternation. A continuity that – as one may easily gather and as it is best to remember from now on – is first and foremost continuity with the body of the mother. Sound is an exception, which instead presents elements of discontinuity and rhythmicity: the mother's heartbeat, the transit of gastric and intestinal content in the maternal digestive system, urination, outside sounds and the voice: that of the mother and any other outside voices. From the breaking of this equilibrium, from the trauma of birth,[6] does sexual development – but as we have seen, it is a beginning that for the most part has already begun – of the little human being begin.

Here we run into the first problem that keeps us from continuing to narrate this development as if it were a linear development. In the summer of 1925, Freud wrote an essay, "Inhibitions, Symptoms, and Anxiety" in which, on Rank's idea about the trauma of birth, he says that he undoubtedly made a great effort to demonstrate the existing relationships between the child's first phobias and the impression produced in him or her by the event of birth, but that to him – to Freud – it occurs, by analogy, that, just as the most primitive anxiety, the "primary" anxiety of birth, took place with separation from the mother, so does the anxiety of emasculation whose content is the separation from a highly esteemed object which obviously is the phallus.[7] This observation is enough to challenge the same idea of chronological development, or of diachronic development, linked to the passage of time for the child of man. Indeed, it is rather the accidents of castration that grant us an "imaginarization" and the symbolization, more subjective than it is scientific, of the so-called trauma of birth. And this means that the representation of that which came before, and the meaning of this representation, objectively establish themselves at a later time. Freud called this statement *Nachträglichkeit*, and in the end it is what Lacan picked back up on in the *après-coup*.[8]

I remember a patient of mine, a very young, extremely beautiful girl affected by a serious form of catatonia. I remember her for two striking affirmations that marked my listening in the field of psychiatry and psychoanalysis forever. One day, around the mid-80s, I was in a garden of the community where Roberta was staying for an observation period. We were both sitting on a bench. She was immobile, and as a consequence, I was immobile, too, since any spontaneous movement like crossing your legs, lighting a cigarette, scratching your head, etc., seemed to me to be a sort of wrong against her tragic immobility. It would have gone on for a pretty long time had it not been that at a certain point, when it was time for me to move to go, it seemed I had broken a state of blockage, a certain tenderness of the muscles and joints. The day after, Roberta opened the door to my studio and said, "You see, Dr., I had the impression that everything moved too fast to be able to understand it, like in a play where the actors act and talk faster, not giving the audience time to understand and reflect on what's going on. So, I thought that I needed to read the script and I stopped everything, but there is no script to read". Obviously, I had read Ronald Laing and I remembered the episode where he talks about a catatonic patient, at the end of whose bed the residents used to play cards, who came out of his mutism one day to say, "Guys, you'd better stop because I see the Director coming through the window." I hadn't thought that Laing had lied, but to me it had remained a literary episode, like reading a sort of science fiction. Instead, hearing Roberta make that discourse, letting herself go to the production of that phrase, surprised me and made me fully perceive the dimension of mystery and complexity that stirs the speakers. But like I said, it wasn't the only time Roberta surprised me. One day many years later, after a session she said to me, "You see, I'd like to go upstream like a salmon, swim towards the origin, toward the meeting of the gametes that I was born from, I would like to descend into the cells, to know everything". Here, too, I was greatly surprised, but I wasn't just surprised for the literary quality of the proposition.

So, if we go back to our impossible narration and we think about the embryogenetic development of the child of man, it is clear that a scientific, magic, or literary knowledge exists that somehow seeks to answer a certain number of fundamental questions. From this viewpoint, the storks, the cabbages, the Genesis as it is told in the Bible, and the genesis of the species according to the Darwinian theory of evolution contribute, in the best-case scenario, to a harmonious evolution of answers from which every human being may draw based on age, his or her cultural tradition, and level of education. There is also something else, difficult to name, and for which I would propose to use the term "subjective", that just like age, culture, and erudition contributes to orienting our individual choices concerning the questions to ask ourselves and the answers to provide. But this reserve of knowledge isn't the only one. In fact, there is another knowledge, intimate, personal, knowledge that is at the heart of our individuality: why me? Why that day? Why mom and dad? When? In what position? Thinking what? The first kind of knowledge doesn't answer these questions and our structure of neurotics allows us to maintain the separation between the two and to thus use two different versions of the ghost to access the questions asked by the two knowledges.[9] A scientific, literary fairytale or mythological ghost steps in alongside a neurotic ghost for which my personal story is only my own, for example forever marked by the fact that mom and dad had always wanted a little girl, but I arrived, an inhabitant, unbeknownst to me, in a body that is sexed in a way that conflicts with the supposed parental desire.

This doesn't happen in psychosis. Roberta desperately seeks, literally hopelessly, to answer with the first scientific, mythological, or religious knowledge to the question placed by the second, that individual, intimate, and personal. In not telling, in not being able to tell the difference between the two, the phantasmal consistency of both is lost, and the unified knowledge becomes a thing, becomes an object that is there in its opacity and that never stops dictating – against a backdrop of anxiety – it's inevitable law. It is the script that Roberta would like to read. For her, there is a script; it's not a hypothesis, it's a certainty; it's there but you cannot get to it.

All this, this lesson that I got from meeting Roberta,[10] also means that in any event it's no use to seek a chronological or diachronic order, an order that unravels from birth to death. Despite this, our very nature of speaking beings binds us to that order.

The outcome is that psychoanalysis is a difficult exercise to practice and a tricky subject to talk about. Jacques Lacan taught a lesson that lasted for over a quarter of a century and it is a lesson organized into yearly seminars held without interruption from 1953 to 1979. The very chronology of the seminars, since there has to be one, offers up – in its rigor, its ellipticity, its striking statements, and its impasses – Lacan's take on the Freudian discovery and invention.

Put in other words, it is a faithful and unorthodox take, faithful precisely because it is not orthodox. After all, we know very well what orthodoxy is. Just think of the church that is called precisely orthodox; for example of its absolutely beautiful icons. The icons are something behind whose perfection, whose compliance with the canons, the protagonist disappears. It took Tarkovskij for us to remember that Andrej Rublëv was a painter of icons.[11] So here we're not talking about psychoanalytical canons, because a reading necessarily implies something of a subjective position and the reference to the canon, the mortification of the subjective position, is not a solution. Not even humanist individualism, glorification of the subjective reflection in the brilliance of the ego is a solution. Lacan, whose style was undoubtedly personal, however, held his lesson from a position that he said was that of the analysand, that is, a modest position, characterized by an inexhaustible debt, but perhaps here we could appropriately say interminable,[12] with the symbolic that – tied to the real and to the imaginary – determines it as a subjective position.

Despite this, that is, although psychoanalysis borders on a subjectivity of discourse that keeps it from treating the psychic as an object, and thus from becoming a psychology, the psychoanalytical path never strayed from the ideals of science, even of scientism which was the positivist kind of Freud's time. After all, as Lacan[13] points out, this is what psychoanalysis owes its credit to, despite the deviations it has made and that Freud, with unhesitating confidence and with inflexible rigor, has always opposed.

It is taking all this into account that we are addressing the topic of paranoia and taking into account the psychoanalytical position in facing the paranoia means not to put oneself up to do the work and not to let oneself be charmed – pardon the pun – by the possibility of a paranoiac knowledge of paranoia.

A paranoiac knowledge of paranoia would be that according to which an analyst, having made the diagnosis, would think he or she knows what they're dealing with; knows not like you know *of* something, about something, but rather like you know *something*. You know it certainly, exactly, incontrovertibly. To better understand, it's a good idea to proceed by degrees and once again to refer to clinical experience and its difficulties.

One day a woman around 50 came to consult me, a philosophy teacher. During the first session she told me she was harassed by her colleagues, was a victim of mobbing that sometimes got to the point of actual stalking. She has no doubt whatsoever about these behaviors. As she adamantly underscores, these aren't her impressions, but rather an absolute certainty. So, the reason she came to consult me has nothing to do with those cases where one complains they are a victim. But perhaps, she added, there is something in her that stimulates persecution, that attracts it like a magnet attracts iron. She's willing to and even interested in discussing this. Then she asked me another question, which is: many years ago, in college she fell in love with a fellow student who later died in a car accident. It was a desperate love, crazy and tragic, a love so great that it had even consumed the organ of love in her. The consequence was that she would never be able to love again. Having read that in psychoanalytical treatment a patient must go through love for one's own analyst, she asked me if the disappearance of the organ of love would have stopped her from accessing analytical treatment.

It seems to me that it's clear what we have here. The patient – let's call her Franca – has a certainty: she is harassed. This certainty of the patient can meet with the certainty of the therapist who, listening to her, says to oneself, "Diagnosis: paranoid psychosis with probable development of erotomanic delirium as a form of onset that risks repeating itself and to come back during the course of treatment". The point is: what does a therapist do with his or her own certainty? If one takes it as an object to work on, if one objectifies it as a symptom to be reduced by pharmacological, psychological, or behavioral means, then the paranoia of psychology runs up against the paranoia of the patient with null, if not outright negative and even potentially tragic, outcomes. It's a whole other story if this certainty fades into the background until it disappears, leaving room for the questions posed by the patient: "What is it about me that sparks the harassment that I am a victim of?", "Dr., do you think that I could love you?", "Dr., would you be able to handle my crazy, erotomanic love without running away and without reacting with hate?"

In this case the questions are points that open the gates to the expression of the subjective position and to addressing this position. During treatment, which lasted many years, Franca didn't hold back on developing a broad and detailed delirious ideation on her coworkers, a similar ideation on a potential suitor, and another delirious development on an erotomania that I was the object of. Specifically, she thought I was in love with her but too shy, conventional, and full of hang-ups to admit it. I should have at least had the courage to act and openly declare the situation, asking her to stop the analysis which had become unsustainable due to my emotional involvement. For years, the analysis, dotted occasionally with phone calls in the middle of the night and almost daily long letters, was carried out on the thread of the question that I answered her issues with: "Why do you need it to be me to ask us to stop? What keeps you from stopping to come regularly to my studio three times a week?" When Franca had finally given herself permission for this separation I would say that the job had substantially been done, and then some: she failed to pay me the last session and I consider this omission a real genuine piece of the real behind which, in its psychotic structure, there lay hidden, but even so neatly squared away, the recognition of a symbolic debt to which the subject could not gain access in any way.

Another clinical situation illustrates the same point on, shall we say, the flipside. Not long ago I received an adolescent kid, more or less 16 or 17 years old that came to consult me because his parents insisted after he dropped out of school; he lost the few friendships and few social relationships he had. Currently he spends almost every day shut up in his room going out a few times at night to eat something or go to the bathroom. As soon as he came in, he looked around warily and asked me to pull down the shades of the large window of the studio because he was afraid he would be seen or heard. I pointed out to him that there are curtains on the window and that the windows are closed so that light comes in but you cannot see anything or hear anything and that no one can see him or hear what he will tell me. His answer was, "No, please close everything, this way you'll make me anxious, I cannot do it, they can see me . . .". We parted with a certain pardon on my refusal to lower the shades and turn on the light. The pardon consisted in a sentence that seemed to be understood or at least graciously heard. A treatment like psychoanalysis is a treatment in words and if there isn't a minimum level of trust in the words, it is not possible to begin a treatment. If I tell you that the window and the curtains are closed and that for this reason you cannot see or hear what is going on in the room it is at least necessary to believe these words to be able to start working with those, and with other words. For the time being, I haven't seen him again, but it's possible that he'll be back, and if he comes back, perhaps it will be to start analytical work.

As is quite clear, in both cases the privilege is decidedly granted to the question and it is a privilege that soars up like an alpine peak among the hills: little or no importance granted to the medical history, no question posed by the therapist except perhaps to delve deeper into any question from the patient, no response that fills the hole of the question blocking any possible evolution. To be clear, something like: "Dr., what's wrong with me?" "It's simple, you have paranoia". The result is that a certain number of stereotypes about the doctor-patient relationship go right out the window. The right to have a certain and explicit diagnosis, informed consent to treatment, the contract entered into between two individuals with equal dignity before the law are all concepts that in psychoanalysis play out by peculiar means. A psychoanalyst would say that it's about the necessary handling of inequality, of the real of inequality, implied by the notion of transference; a detractor of psychoanalysis would say that it's about foggy, ambiguous concepts that can potentially be used by bunglers, quacks, and exploiters of others' credulity.

Obviously, I am a psychoanalyst, although of psychiatric training, and I practiced psychiatry in hospitals for over 40 years, but I never let the objectified and objectifying view, fixed in a static diagnosis, make me deaf to a question that the other person, although paranoiac, never stops posing.

It is this central point of this chapter, the fulcrum, from my point of view, around which the psychoanalytical conception of paranoia revolves. Paranoia is not recognized in a question, but rather in an object that emerges in anxiety like an answer believed completely, believed as part of reality which, however, it's best we remember, is still a psychic reality. On his reading of a text, *Memoirs of My Nervous Illness*,[14] Freud based the construction of his revolutionary concept of paranoia. One evening after having been appointed President of the Court of Cassation of Dresden, a family man, a very strict judge in a court of the Prussian Empire, son of an important and renowned pedagogue, has a bizarre thought; he finds himself thinking it and he is surprised by the presence of this thought extraneous to his own mind: "How nice it would be to be a woman experiencing sexual intercourse". His book, his *Memoirs*, is the answer to a question implied by that thought. His delirious construction is his reality, and Daniel Paul Schreber is the woman of God. His is an answer that lasts a lifetime and that bridges the gap opened by the question. After all, this also means that Freud never had Judge Schreber in front of him or on the couch, and that consequently he didn't get to address – in the melting pot of the transference – the question opened by the proposition that suddenly appeared in the patient's mind. Nonetheless, starting from the written text of the *Memoirs*, Freud founded a totally new concept of paranoia. This suffices to say that if psychoanalysis is first and foremost treatment of the question, it isn't, however, only the treatment of the question and its knowledge of the structure in the balance, for example that intrinsic to paranoia, isn't devoid of content that in some way aspires to have – and even in part certainly has – a certain objectivity. It is at this point that the Lacanian reading of the work of Freud becomes inexorable and the resorting to mathemes becomes inexorable, the resorting to diagrams that – Lacan recalls right from the first time that he resorted to them[15] – are diagrams in the real sense of the word, mathematic. Apparently, an accurate treatment of the Lacanian reading of Freud's thought is impossible here, just like it is impossible to debate the meaning of Lacan's need to introduce his topology.[16]

I will just take up the first of these patterns and to get a reading that I hope will be introductory to continuing the study of a school of thought that never ceases to open the gates for the comprehension of the clinical practice of psychoanalysis and our contemporaneity. The diagram I am talking about is that commonly called "L" from the shape of the Greek letter lambda, but that rather is in the shape of two crossing Z's (Figure 8.1).

Substantially this pattern means that every time a human being is before something, or someone, it is never a relationship between two, but rather always a four-party relationship. Let's take, for example, a concept like that of freedom. On the one hand, freedom is freedom, but we immediately realize that it is not the same thing for different people. While Giorgio Gaber was able to sing it as participation rather than a free space,[17] in 1923 to Benito Mussolini it was a Nordic divinity on whose decomposed body fascism would quite easily pass over.[18] If you can have two so radically different conceptions of freedom, it's that, behind the imaginary relationship that links the ego to that which the ego itself means as freedom, something different persists so the signification of a word is made not just by the dictionary but also by the play of the signifier, and as a consequence, of the subjective value that that word ends up having for the Other that lives in us, that is, for the subconscious. I could give an endless myriad of examples of this de facto condition, but here I'll give just one. One of my patients was committed to the psychiatric ward at the city hospital. When I called to find out how things were going they said that the patient was physically restrained to the bed

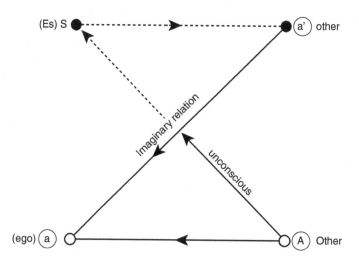

Figure 8.1 The L schema

since he had beaten the head doctor of the ward. Indeed, when I got there, the patient was in bed and when I asked what happened he answered that during the admission interview the doctor had insisted on addressing the patient using the formal subject pronoun (*Lei*) that is, using the form of courtesy with which one addresses a person you do not know very well in Italian. The problem is that *Lei* is also a feminine personal pronoun, and from that *Lei* pronounced as a sign of respect and consideration, the patient felt effeminated, accused of a suspicion of homosexuality. Before he could think, his reaction set off, that is, he slapped the unfortunate doctor who with the best intentions was conducting the patient's entry interview. So, in conclusion, what is the point concerning the diagram that Lacan offers us? It is that in interlocution, what the little other that is before us understands of what we say doesn't necessarily correspond to the intention with which the speaker pronounced the phrase. The next step, first Freudian and then Lacanian, is that each one of us is the little other that is listening, with an effect of surprise and bewilderment, to what he himself happened to say, starting from the fact that in that act of speech the subject arrogantly entered with an effect that is really *unheimlich*.[19] The term is usually, and as a rule, translated into Italian as "*perturbante*" (perturbing), but rather it should be "extraneation", a term with the merit of maintaining the reference to the Other, to the outsider, that is to whom, or to what, is and remains outside of the comfy slipper of the *Heim*, of the *chez soi*, of the domestic hearth.

Interview with Fabrizio Gambini

DB: *In 2015 you published a book all about the study of paranoia.[20] I would like to ask you, in your opinion, what's the difference between paranoia and schizophrenia?*

FG: Some training days on psychosis were held in Rome in 1999.[21] Then I was able to define schizophrenia as paranoia that fails to be such – paranoia that doesn't manage to "get organized". After all, it almost goes without saying that Lacan began his seminar on psychoses[22] stating that for Freud the field of psychoses is divided in two: on the one hand, narcissistic neurosis and schizophrenia, and on the other, paranoia. This means that somewhere there is something that links paranoia and schizophrenia to each other but that, on the other hand, the two nosographic entities are different from one another.

I picture something like a continuous line with paranoia and schizophrenia at the far ends. Nevertheless, on a continuous line there are infinite circumstances in between these two extremities. One notion that I feel is particularly useful to adopt is that we never have stasis, but rather a shifting situation capable of settling repeatedly and suddenly on points of the imaginary line that I conjure up to represent the shifts in question.

When you hear a guy in the hospital hallway yell, "Stop it! Give me my knees back, you bastard!", and when, curious and a bit worried, you ask him,

"What's wrong?", and when he says, "Nothing". Then we have a blatant case of schizophrenia. That is, we have a likely delirious hallucination, with which the ego dialogues quite neatly and the hallucination and the delirium cannot be construed as an object *of* which to speak; both are still merely an object with *which* one speaks. Contrarily, paranoia constructs the object of which to speak. The ego is free to speak of its content rather than being a slave in the interlocution itself.

The distinction I have drawn is significant, because it makes it possible to orient treatment, to help the patient construct his or her own delirious content as objects that one may speak of. From this standpoint, as therapists we could aspire to something of the sort, of a "paranoicization" of schizophrenia and to developing a quality delirium in paranoia. I do not know if we could go much farther, but the goal I set already seems extremely ambitious to me – possible, yes, but ambitious.

From a structural standpoint, differentiating the schizophrenic cases from the paranoiac cases is harder, and in this context we risk being too schematic. The hypothesis that I would still like to set forth is that the different level of symbolization, the difference between the two ways of presenting the object that I mentioned, is a function of the differences in how the paternal constellation works, which in both cases is, and remains, foreclosed. On the schizophrenia side, I think of the return into the Real of a function of the Name-of-the-Father, being an agent of castration, which is basically the Father of the hysteric, that is, an agent that symbolizes castration, weakened, which gives rise to a subjective position of frustration, that is, placement of the subject before an imaginary lack, and that fixes the object as Real. On the side of paranoia, instead I think of the return into the Real of a function of the Name-of-the-Father, still being a castration agent, which is basically the Father of the obsessed, that is, an imaginary agent of castration, not castrated, which gives rise to a subjective position of privation, that is, placement of the subject before a real lack that determines the object as being symbolic.[23] As I already said, this would partially explain why paranoia often has to do with delirium that can exist in the complete absence of hallucinations, while from the schizophrenia side we may observe an almost continuous interlocution of the subject with his or her hallucinations without the subject being able to talk about them. However, certainly this is a schematism that, if taken as a whole, is at least to me a bit difficult to digest, and that is yet to be looked into . . .

DB: *What are paranoia's connections with neurosis? Paranoiac aspects are found (for example) in hysteric discourse as well. What difference is there when comparing this to real actual paranoia?*

FG: The first chapter of *Freud and Lacan in Psychiatry*[24] is about diagnosis in psychiatry and the second is about diagnosis in psychoanalysis. The second paragraph of chapter two is entitled "the formations of the subconscious". There, in writing and fully articulated, you'll find a concept that I'll never get tired of highlighting the importance of: a "diagnosis" never refers to an individual (such and such is paranoiac, the other guy is neurotic, etc.). In psychoanalysis, a "diagnosis" refers to a structure that is always the structure of a formation and of the subject that upholds it as such. From this point, an individual (such and such) can have a psychotic formation (let's say, a hallucination or delirium), but nothing stops him or her from occasionally showing neurotic symptoms (for example, trying to prolong a session to demand respect from those in the waiting room, to be a special patient, first among peers . . .). It's important to maintain this flexibility of listening and not identify the structure of the symptom with the person . . . sometimes patients seriously afflicted with psychosis can form bits of discourse that are completely functional or completely neurotic. Everyone has had a session with a delirious, hallucinated, and even schizophasic patient, who, upon hearing the dishes on the meal cart in the hallway, he or she goes out saying, "Excuse me, doctor, is it okay if we pick up the session in a little bit? I'd like to go now, otherwise my spaghetti will get cold". It is important to recognize and treat different formations differently even when they are, shall we say, housed in the same person.

DB: *How does clinical experience help?*

FG: Basically, I'd say that clinical experience is everything, but the problem is understanding what an experience is. A habit that isn't necessarily a clinical experience. I'll tell you a story. When my father retired he bought a garden near home where he could spend his time and cultivate something. The garden was close to other gardens, many of which managed and worked by professional farmers. After about a year of "experience" my father told me, "You know the farmers are extraordinary. . . . Over time they have learned a bunch of things and they give valuable advice, but if for five generations they do the same stupid thing there is no way to get it out of their head". I think that you get what I'm trying to say. Repeating the same old way of meeting doesn't help. Many years ago I met a psychiatrist who wasn't even that old, who managed to say to me, "These patients are such a bore . . . they're all the same!" Here we have a repetition but not an experience. Perhaps we should go back to using the philosophical term "experience" and recall, with Aldo Masullo,[25] that which distinguishes signified and sense is precisely the distinction between experience (μπειρια, experientia, Erfahrung) and life lived (παθοσ, affectio, Erlebnis). "Experience" so to speak is transformation, it is surprise, it is meeting with a signifier that takes on a new meaning; it is the moment of transformation itself. One evening Copernicus did not witness the sunset but rather the Earth, which, rotating on its axis, covered it.

DB: *Tell me about a paranoiac patient with whom it was hard to start.*

FG: I remember one, he showed up one day at my studio without saying anything about himself, or at least anything I expected he would say at a first session. Rather, he started talking about a dream: there was a dark room, maybe a bed and maybe there was a corpse on the bed, it seemed to be awake in the dark, without being able to catch anything . . . perhaps some rustling. The first session got used up like this, not a word on himself, his family, his job, his problems, his friends . . . The second time he went on with his dream, as if he had discovered some other particular in the room: the color of the blanket, the shoes of the dead man, the voice of a woman . . . End of the second session. It went on like this for months, the only particular is that he often played tennis, well, with great competitiveness and aggressiveness. No one wanted to play with him; he was too good! It was hard not to give in to the temptation to find out more, for example, to want to do a sort of diagnosis. Then one day he comes in, sits down all pale and shaken and said to me, "Dr., last night I was really glad knowing that today I would come see you, otherwise I think I would've gone crazy. My son was born and – after I left the hospital where my wife had given birth – I couldn't go home because I was sure I was being followed by CIA agents. Dr., I'm not an idiot, I know that the CIA – about someone like me, who's a worker from Turin – doesn't give a damn, but they were there, I was afraid and I didn't go home so I wouldn't show them where I live . . ." I think that if I had pried more during the first few sessions, to make a diagnosis, to know whom I'm dealing with, he wouldn't have been able to run to me in his time of need ("glad knowing that I would come see you"). This means that that first acceptance, that first step back, that initial restraint, opened up an opportunity that the patient saw as entry into a safe harbor and not to a prison.

DB: *Does listening differ with psychotic and neurotic patients?*

FG: I wouldn't say so. The difference is rather between psychoanalytical listening (that you can even do in psychiatry) and psychiatric listening, or interpersonal, or friendly, or psychotherapeutic (that is, oriented towards identifying a psychopathological nucleus *on* which to intervene with psychological means). As far as what psychoanalytical listening is, I feel like we've stated that up until now in many ways, quite different from one another.

DB: *How do you make a paranoiac see that there is an unconscious underlying what he or she says?*

FG: Good question. You cannot and you mustn't. To a paranoiac, potential objects do not exist; only real objects. It is talking, letting him or her talk, urging to talk about his or her reality (delirium, hallucination) that a fabric of discourse is woven in which the unconscious subject can pop out so that the patient's narrating ego notices the breaking away. You must never question what the patient narrates: if a paranoiac turns to a professional to be protected from extraterrestrials, you, the professional, are his or her protector, not his or her analyst. A while back, a guy asked me to check him into the hospital to escape the commitment to a mental hospital his psychiatrist had suggested. At home he was pursued by aliens; the psychiatrist thought he was crazy and wanted to commit him. The bright idea was to run to the hospital and have me protect him from the aliens as well as his psychiatrist. Absurd? Yes, but that's the way things go.

DB: *How does an analyst behave when he is the object of a fantasy?*

FG: First off, the fantasies that, I'd say, are our daily bread are one thing. More complicated is, in paranoia, when they're not fantasies but rather real genuine delirious developments. Like the examples in the article about the philosophy teacher who was being followed, it's about establishing these delirations as the object of discourse, of helping patients to make them the object of discourse, of not being afraid to greet them with a "Tell me about it . . ." Of course, this implies a certain handling of the transference . . . The issue would take us a bit off track. For the time being I think we can just say that the only defense against a transference into the real, and the consequent potential passage to action, is to keep it in a web of discourse, letting it create images so that at least an initial symbolization becomes possible.

DB: *What if the essential does not get touched upon?*

FG: It really doesn't matter. Often what is essential to the therapist doesn't matter at all to the person analyzed. One will get to where one is going by one's own means, and if one doesn't, then oh well. It's a risk that you run. I especially am referring to seriously obsessive patients, which are really hard to tear away from their reveling in doubt, their own pain, their own lack, or their own limitations. Over the years I have tried, but I've ended up trying everything: interrupting a session after a few minutes, letting them roll around in their own discourse without keeping track of time for over an hour and interrupting the session due to exhaustion (mine more than theirs), giving biting and deliberately harsh readings, explaining down to the last detail the situation and the impasse that they've gotten bogged down in, giving homework in the attempt to differentiate a session from the last and the next . . . Nothing, it cannot be helped, it all runs like water down the feathers of a goose, without apparently leaving any trace . . . then perhaps a signifier, a fragment of discourse goes half-circle, a witty remark, a smile that is taken as such and not immediately reabsorbed in the suffocating web of meaning impossible to find and impossible to let go of . . .

Notes

1 Sigmund Freud, *Über den Gegensinn der Urworte* (1910), it. tr., *The Antithetical Meaning of Primal Words* in *Works (OSF)*, Boringhieri, Turin 1967–1980, vol. VI, pp. 185–191.

2 Michiko Kakutani, *The Death of Truth. Notes on Falsehood in the Age of Trump* (2018), it. tr., *La morte della verità*, Solferino, Milan 2018.

3 Paul Ricoeur, *De l'interpretation. Essai sur Freud* (1965), it. tr., *Freud and Philosophy: An Essay on Interpretation*, Il Saggiatore, Milan 1966, p. 46.

4 *Even Mike Cernovich, an infamous troll and conspiracist of the alternative right wing cited postmodernism in a 2016 interview for the* New Yorker*: "Listen, I studied postmodern theories at college. Everything is narration, so we need alternatives to the dominant narration". And he added, "I don't seem like the type who would read Lacan, huh?"* M. Kakutani, cit., p. 48.

5 Jacques Lacan, *The Object Relation, Seminar 1956–1957*, Book IV, Seuil, Paris 1994, p. 11. (It. tr. by Fabrizio Gambini)

6   Otto Rank, *Das Trauma der Geburt* (1924), it. tr. *The Trauma of Birth*, Sugarco, Milan 2018.

7   S. Freud, *Hemmung, Symptom und Angst*, (1926), it. tr. "Inhibitions, Symptoms, and Anxiety", in *OSF* cit., vol. 10, p. 283–285. See also Fabrizio Gambini, *Freud and Lacan in Psychiatry*, Raffaello Cortina, Milan 2006, pp. 46 and 47.

8   See Elena Garritano, *All in Good Time*, now being published and Alessandra Campo, *Tardivity, Freud after Lacan*, Mimesis, Milan 2018.

9   I dedicated an entire chapter, the first, of the text in which I addressed the topic of paranoia with to this distinction between the two modes of knowledge: Fabrizio Gambini, *Paranoia. Psychiatry to Psychoanalysis: Knowing How to Handle Psychosis*, Franco Angeli, Milan 2015.

10 That of Roberta, with its various consequences and implications, is a question that I have gone back to time after time and from different viewpoints. For example, see F. Gambini, *Freud and Lacan in Psychiatry*, cit., p. 12.

11 *Andrej Rublëv*, Film, 186 m., Soviet Union 1966, directed by Andrej Arsen'evič Tarkovskij.

12 S. Freud, *Die endliche und die unendliche* Analyse (1937), it. tr. "Terminable and Interminable Analysis", in *OSF*, cit. vol. XI, pp. 499–540.

13 See J. Lacan, *The Object of Psychoanalysis, Seminar 1965–1966*, Edition out of print, provided by the *Association Lacanienne Internationale*, lesson of December 1, 1965.

14 Daniel Paul Schreber, *Denkwürdigkeiten eines Nervenkranken* (1903), it. tr., *Memoirs of My Nervous Illness*, Adelphi, Milan 1974.

15 *At the end of these years of criticism, here we are armed with a certain number of terms and diagrams. The spatiality of the latter isn't to be taken in the intuitive sense of the term "diagram", but rather in another sense, perfectly legitimate, which is topological. It isn't about localizations, but rather about relationships between places, for example interposition, or succession, sequence.* Jacques Lacan, *The Object Relation, Seminar 1956–1957, Book IV, Seuil, Paris 1994*, p. 12. it. tr. by F. Gambini.

16 See Fabrizio Gambini and Mauro Milanaccio (edited by), *Why Topology. Lacan, Psychoanalysis and Topology*. Now being published at Mimesis, Milan 2019.

17 *Freedom Is Not a Free Space/Freedom Is Participation*, Giorgio Gaber, "Freedom", from the album *Pretend to be Sane*, 1973.

18 *Freedom is a Nordic divinity, worshiped by the Anglo-Saxons. . . . Fascism knows no idols, it doesn't worship fetishes. It has already passed and, if necessary, will again pass, without the slightest hesitation, over the more or less decomposed body of the Goddess of Liberty.* Benito Mussolini, "Forza e consenso", *Hierarchy*, March 1923. Cited by Antonio Scurati, *M the Son of the Century*, Bompiani, Milan 2018, p. 650.

19 S. Freud, *Das Unheimliche* (1919), tr. it., "Il perturbante", in *Opere*, cit. vol. 9, pp. 81–118.

20 Fabrizio Gambini, *Paranoia. From Psychiatry to Psychoanalysis: Knowing How to Handle Psychosis*, Franco Angeli, Milan 2015.

21 Fabrizio Gambini, "A Failed Paranoia?", in *The Other and Psychosis*, Conference Proceedings, Rome 21–22 May 1999.

22 Jacques Lacan, *The Seminar, book III, Psychoses*, Seuil, Paris 1981, p. 12.

23 See C. Calligaris, *Pour une clinique différentielle des psychoses*, Points Hors Ligne, Paris 1991, chap. III: *Différenciation des psychoses*.

24 Fabrizio Gambini, *Freud and Lacan in Psychiatry*, Raffaello Cortina, Milan 2006.

25 Aldo Masullo, *Emotional Sphere and Indifference*, Il melangolo, Genoa 2003, p. 44.

Part 3

Modern symptoms

Chapter 9

Panic as a phenomenon of modernity

Marco Focchi

The Freudian term *Gleichschwebende Aufmerksamkeit*, which is usually translated as 'floating attention', indicates more precisely the idea of a suspension, of a waiting. The German word *schweben* means in fact a slope, an indecision, a remaining in equilibrium, an uncertainty. Thus, as Freud indicates, it is a matter of activating a listening that leaves the sense suspended. Normally, listening to a person speaking to us, we try to focus on what s/he *wants* to say to us, and then as soon as his/her sentence comes to a halt that concludes it, we understand its meaning, we understand his/her intention, and we *decide* the content of the message that is conveyed to us. The decision that falls on this cut, however, allows us to grasp only the intentional value of what the speaker tells us, that is, what s/he is consciously thinking of transmitting to us. Even in a normal intersubjective dialogue a certain suspension of listening occurs, up to the point when the meaning of the sentence is determined. For example, if I say "That branch . . .", it opens up many possible meanings: I can be talking about a tree, but also about a person's professional area, an electrical circuit and many other things. But when the sentence is completed and I say: "That branch of the Lake of Como, which turns toward the south between two unbroken chains of mountains . . ." we have understood that we are talking about the opening words of *The Betrothed*, and then we know how the speech continues. At this moment we have identified the conscious intention of the interlocutor and we have grasped the meaning of his/her sentence. The interlocutor thus decides the meaning of the message starting from the cut, in consideration of the punctuation s/he perceives in the voice; in the current communication this works well and allows us to understand each other.

A listening beyond conscious intention

It is not the same with psychoanalysis. We can say that in the analytic experience an additional time of suspension is needed, because when we have understood the interlocutor's intention to mean, we have not yet taken any step within the dimension that interests us in analysis, that of the unconscious, because the unconscious does not say what the subject wants to say, but something beyond, something on which sometimes the subject stumbles – suggesting that we must pay attention to

DOI: 10.4324/9780429432064-13

lapses in the discourse – and expresses a drive need that the subject struggles to recognize, with which s/he does not identify him/herself, and that s/he feels to be in contrast with his/her conscious intentions.

For example: a patient, let us call him Enrico, who suffered from panic attacks, tells us how he was always anxious at the dining table, and how he could not stand his mother who approached his place "to cut the meat on his plate", because "Enrico – his mother said – cannot wait". Only with the subsequent associations of the patient do we understand – given the legislative position of the mother, in the absence of a father who could assert his function – the sense of castration* that assumes the otherwise innocent expression "cut the meat". Summarizing in a formula, we could say that analytic listening turns its attention not to the current referential meaning, but to the phantasmatic sense and to the level of the drive.

Clearly, it is not easy to make the patient accept the other aspect of what s/he says, or rather of what s/he says without wanting to say it, meaning what s/he says unconsciously. For this to be possible, a subjective rectification has to have taken place, which puts the patient in the position to accept a knowledge that does come from him/her, but from a place different than that of his/her consciousness. The initial attitude of the patient is usually to wait for a response from the psychoanalyst, a response that comes as a recipe. This is particularly the case with patients who are sent by medical doctors, who expect a solution resembling the pharmacological one, or advice to be applied in their daily lives. Obtaining the subjective rectification that gets the patient ready for the transference, and that therefore prepares him also to accept the interpretation, is not immediate and is not always possible either. For some patients the experience of analysis takes place as a long supportive relationship, because they cannot find within themselves the leverage needed to tune in with the subject supposed to know.

The orientation of psychoanalysis between reality and fantasy

The analysis actually starts when the patient, in a way, begins to leave the reality outside the consultation room, and let his/her own fantasy (for Lacan: *fantasme*) in. The phantasmatic dimension of the subject, unlike the symptomatic dimension that hinders life, is never immediately available. It is the most intimate intimacy, and when the subject begins to be able to bring it into play, that is a sign that it is time to move from the face-to-face position to the couch.

The moment when this transition becomes possible is not definable a priori, and there are people who spend the entire duration of the treatment in vis-à-vis because they need the visible presence of a face they can address; it is difficult for them to get out of intersubjectivity. We must not be dogmatic about this. Even in the face-to-face position there are ways to make the unconscious emerge: the important thing is that the analyst, even in a face-to-face position, does not let himself be captured by the imaginary specularity, and this is one of the fundamental aspects on which I insist more during supervisions. The transference takes place in a subjective dissymmetry, which the couch-armchair position facilitates, however the face-to-face position does not prevent it.

The difference between symptoms and panic

The expression "panic attacks" does not belong to the classical lexicon of psychoanalysis, but it has imposed itself with a strong descriptive value. Many patients recognize themselves in this phrase, which in Italy has been made manifest and socially present by the "Lega Italiana per gli Attacchi di Panico" (Italian League for Panic Attacks, LIDAP). Creating a social label allows one to create a landmark in which to recognize him/herself; it creates a pathway of identification. This is what happens with all the new forms of symptom, from anorexia-bulimia to drug addiction, compulsive gambling and so on.

The new forms of symptom constitute a field in which the symptom plays an identifying role: the subject recognizes him/herself in the symptom. Thus, there is an inverse functioning to the classic Freudian definition of the symptom, which is "a state in the state", a psychic enclave which does not reflect the Ego, and which brings needs with it that feel foreign to the Ego.

Self-help groups have fostered the growth of this new phenomenon of identification with the symptom, which may at first block the possibility of the work of the unconscious. It should be noted that Lacan also spoke of identification with the symptom, but he referred it to a final moment in the work of analysis, when the subject, having long elaborated the fantasy and the drives, no longer feels the symptom as a bearer of needs extraneous to the subject, and s/he discovers it as a sign of a jouissance to which s/he no longer feels opposed, and where the symptom no longer presents itself as an impediment to life but rather as a resource, in a manner similar to that in which the drive is invested in sublimation. There, the symptom is placed within the circuit of the drive. Here, instead, the identification with the initial symptom is placed on the narcissistic level, where the symptom is taken as a reinforcement of the identity of the subject. It is not a sign of enjoyment, but a trait raised to an ideal that forms the common point of reference in the self-help group. If everyone recognizes themselves in the symptom, this works as a social bond, as the symptom usually does, but in a segregating way, as a narcissistic block that does not allow unconscious elaboration.

As for panic attacks, in my opinion it is doubtful whether they can be considered in the category of new symptoms, because panic as such is not a symptom: it is not a sign, it does not have a symbolic value, it is the pure emergence of the dimension of the drive. In the Freudian division between inhibition, symptom, and anxiety, panic is certainly more on the side of anxiety, that is, of a real* that presents itself without symbolic connotations that make it placeable. It is important to see that the panic attack is a clinical phenomenon, but it is not a diagnostic category. It can manifest itself in different forms of neurosis by marking a threshold or an onset which, in the case of an underlying psychotic structure, can present itself as an elementary phenomenon and give rise to a subjective catastrophe, which can be followed by the structuring of a delusion.

The symptoms of our time

After the great moment of the anorexia bulimics in the nineties, there was a period when the greatest number of requests for help came from people who presented panic attacks. Today, the panic attack remains one of the major reasons to turn to a psychoanalyst or psychotherapist, together with a large increase in demands for relational problems: people in difficulty in their relationship as a couple or with children, or with difficulties resulting from the absence of relationships, for a loneliness not chosen and barely tolerated.

Both in panic attacks and in relational difficulties, and certainly also in depression, we can see a reflection of the era in which we live: strongly atomized social structures, less solidarity, declining ideals that reveal the voracious face of a techno-capitalism where profit and what Marcuse called the principle of performance make the individual feel helpless, like a tiny grain in front of an uncontrollable machine, productive and powerfully supported by spectacularization. An effective image of it is given by King Vidor's extraordinary movie *The Crowd*, which begins with a shot rotating up a skyscraper with countless windows, until it goes in to reveal an endless expanse of desks behind each of which there is an anonymous employee. The camera then frames one of them, who is the protagonist of the movie, a man of considerable ambition who feels he has a great destiny. Life, and a series of failures, will throw him back into the anonymous crowd from which he wanted to free himself, and the last image is suggestive in this sense. After having held back his wife, who is about to leave him, we see him with her in the audience of a show, where they laugh together apparently having fun. Gradually, however, the camera moves away, framing an endless audience, filled with a crowd that laughs in the same way: the crowd from which he wanted to escape has swallowed him, and as an anesthetic for the failure of his life we see him in front of a show.

This loneliness in the crowd, this 'lonely crowd', to use the expression of David Riesman, is one of the conditions underlying the ever so frequent manifestations of panic attacks. The reduction in social participation, the growing sense of isolation, the loss of networks of solidarity, ever weakening symbolic anchors, make the individual, for whom the sense of community identification has practically disappeared, feel lost in the ocean of an existence where he has no handhold to cling to.

The different experiences in the background of panic

One time a patient described to me very accurately the onset of his panic attacks: he was a student and he was in Milan, far from his hometown, a small village in southern Italy. He was shopping in a large supermarket and found himself in front of a huge amount of goods, an overabundant, overwhelming supply, that made him feel surrounded, to the point that he felt so dizzy that he fell into the typical situation of loss of coordinates that triggers panic.

The social conditions described above are the background that amplifies individual situations in which we usually find quarrelsome families, stories of aggression in relationships, sudden outbursts of anger among members of the inner circle, manifestations of violence or misbehavior between parents. But the historical background of panic does not only come from a history of aggressive experiences. There is a panic that we can define as erotic, when, for example, the sexual drive hooks up to fantasy that the subject feels are unacceptable, and it is impossible for him/her to channel desire towards the normal ways of satisfaction: emancipated women with masochistic and/or male-domination fantasies, boys strongly identified with the virile image who feel homosexual fantasy emerging, people who have embraced a religious career and are overwhelmed by neglected sensations. If there are neuroses that have gender preferences – classically hysteria affects more women than men, whereas obsessive neurosis is very rare among women and mainly affects the male gender – from this point of view panic is democratic: it affects men and women equally.

People who come to the psychoanalyst with panic attacks are generally not people who can wait. They rush in as if to an emergency room, looking for the switch that turns off the unbearable situation in which they find themselves. Of course, this switch does not exist, so it is often easier to use a drug – which, while not a solution, can be a temporary measure, a way of cushioning the sharpest points of panic, so as to allow one to conduct some psychoanalytic work. A patient once came to me with her son, who was in a sense the embodiment of her symptom, the site to which she had transferred all prospects of compensation, in contrast to the difficulties of her family of origin. For some time, she came to me to solve the problems that this created in her son, and when finally the son no longer coincided with the symptomatic position of the mother in which he was placed, the mother had a powerful panic attack. When the attempt to stop it pharmacologically failed, she came to session with a sense of alarm and urgency, telling me that it was not like the other times, that she needed an immediate remedy. In these cases, it is obviously not the use of interpretation that will allow us to face the situation. This is because, as we said above, the phenomenon of panic does not have the structure of the symptom; it is not carried by a symbolic vector. In this case, it was particularly evident: at the very moment when the symptom had dissolved, freeing the son, the panic that the symptom had previously contained within the symbolic coordinates given by the acquired family, as a compensatory replacement for the family of origin, was also released. The symptom clearly had the function of acting as a dam to the anxiety, and without it the panic manifested itself without mediation. It is therefore a question of reconstructing a symbolic framework that works as a limit to the panic overflow of anxiety. The intervention in this case does not consist in the interpretation that gives meaning. Rather, it is a question of raising a bastion, marking a boundary, using the signifier not as a bearer of meaning but to draw a line of demarcation, a threshold. And that's what I did that day: bring the panic, which was nameless and without a cause, back to situations that were recognizable by her that she had lived in the past, making it possible for her to frame what was otherwise without representation and without a face. I reminded her of past situations she had told me when she had found herself in front of her father, a violent man who had locked himself in a room with her to punish her and beat her. It is a scene that clearly justifies the fact of feeling terror, and that reframes the present, seemingly indecipherable moment in light of something that justifies the fact of feeling fear.

The antithesis between panic and sense

Paradoxically, if in neurosis it is usually a question of deconstructing the suffering side of the symptom by dismantling it, without suppressing it, in panic it is a question of re-establishing the function of embankment that the symptom is not playing. In a way, it is a question of constructing a symptom so that it can be worked on. Is this not what we do with the transference? Is the transference not a sort of emotional laboratory in which we reconstruct the most complicated relationships in the patient's history and rework them in a controlled situation? There is something similar about panic: we need to build a laboratory symptom that can stem the rampant anxiety, so that we can work with it in a controlled manner. This means that panic has no sense; rather, it is antithetical to sense. It is a real, as it is not subject to interpretation. The effect of panic is to open a senseless hole in the existence of the subject, and we cannot revert to a *restitutio ad integrum* [restoration to original condition, Ed.], as in medical therapies. There is no integrity that can be restored in the life of the subject, because subjectivity is formed from what Freud had called trauma, meaning the senseless hole of the encounter with the real. This hole is not to be sutured; it is the heart of subjectivity. It is usually concealed by the imaginary screen, but the moment this screen is torn, there is no reparation possible, because the human imaginary is torn *ab origine* [from the beginning, Ed.], as an effect of that premature birth studied by Louis Bolk that Lacan has described in the formation of the mirror stage.

Panic is therefore, in a way, the effect of a revelation. It is not the production of an *ex novo* (anew, from the beginning, Ed.) clinical effect, but a phenomenon generated by the failure of imaginary compensations that have held up to a critical breaking point. In stories of people with panic attacks there is almost never a particular reason why the attack occurred at that time rather than at another. Circumstances can be reconstructed: the supermarket overloaded in the case of which I reported above, sometimes a trip, other times the death of a loved one, the sense of pressure due to excessive proximity in an emotional relationship. There are never events that we could define as "traumatic", or causative; there is simply a shift or a redefinition of the balance within the psychic economy of the subject, which brings to light the hole of origin. It is a matter of constructing symbolic ramparts around this hole, as a sort of signaling; a system of coordinates; a cartography that allows the subject to approach the critical zone without falling into the abyss. The analytical work in these cases is not of interpretation or sense, but of delimitation, of mapping. It is like constructing an artificial phobia. Little Hans knew where not to go: where there were horses. The horses – or rather, the phobic signifier that for him was the horses – were like the guardians of an area he should not enter. In phobia this geography is, so to speak, external, it belongs to reality. In old Vienna, horses were a real presence that had assumed a symbolic function for Hans. With panic attacks, it is about creating an "inner" geography.

Distinguishing between panic and anxiety

In this regard, it is perhaps interesting to distinguish more precisely between anxiety and panic. Anxiety is a classic theme of psychoanalysis. Freud sees it as a warning sign indicating a drive need that is unacceptable for the Ego. Lacan explains the difference between anxiety and fear by pointing out that anxiety is not without an object. This seems to contradict the classical conceptions of anxiety, which distinguish it from fear. Fear is always described as a feeling arising in front of some danger, whereas anxiety arises without anything recognizable, concrete, visible. In fact, the object to which Lacan refers is not an object of the world, an empirical object, that we can identify, but an object that is, as it were, expelled from the representation of the world so that the world can have consistency.

In that window on the world that is the fantasy, an empty box remains, to make sure that everything else holds, that it is consistent. The psychoanalytic experience shows that this empty box is the phallus, index of symbolic castration. Without its inscription in the subjective structure, everything collapses into psychosis. The fantasy, in its psychoanalytic definition, includes the desiring subject who vanishes in front of the emergence of the object of desire. In the formula in which Lacan defines it, there is never coexistence between subject and object; there is not a subject in front of the spectacle of the world, as it is in classical philosophies. The subject in the analytical sense does not coincide with the contemplative subject; it is rather a desiring subject, which moves towards an object that constantly withdraws, and when the object emerges, as in the moment of love, it is the subject's turn to bar her/himself and fade through a *fading** movement. I can never grasp, seize, stop the object that is the motor of my desire, and that is why in the formula of the fantasy the object is marked by the negativized phallus, that is, by castration. What, then, is this object that I can never take, in front of which I can never place myself in a specular way, and that when it emerges in a specular image, it disintegrates the coherence of my image with effects of estrangement, or of depersonalization or, in the case of psychosis, with elementary phenomena that are the prelude to delusional formations? This object is ultimately me in my naked bodily existence, the one subtracted from the mirror image; it is me outside the imaginary representation in which I recognize myself as I, it is the 'me' in excess of 'myself'. Many patients report the alienating experience of looking at themselves in the mirror, staring intensely into their eyes to the point where the reflected image eclipses as otherness and they feel the gaze emerging as a pure and disturbing presence. The more the presence is felt, the more this experience becomes distressing, to a point where it becomes unbearable. What emerges in this experience is the perception of the body not as a mirror image but as made by those objects that have no place in it, like the gaze, the voice. These are bodily objects separated from the body image that indicate the *real* presence of the body. When Lacan says in *La Troisième* that the experience of anxiety is the experience of feeling reduced to one's own body, he has in mind this real body made of objects without a mirror image.

It is in relation to this experience that we can distinguish anxiety from panic on the basis of a temporal modulation. The anxiety, as a signal, lets the subject feel the imminence of danger, draws attention to the immediate future, to what is about to present itself, to what is perceived but not yet there. It keeps the subject in an anxious tension, making him/her feel the imminence of the real. His or her glance is towards the future, however imminent, and the subject expects what s/he fears, but is precisely in a situation of waiting, however often unbearable. In panic, what was expected comes with all its devastating power. The fact that often times the phenomenon of panic is described as a bolt from the blue indicates that there are no recognizable triggers for the subject, and not that there is no creeping anxiety. The anxiety may have been silent for a while and suddenly emerge resulting in panic, but the subject who falls into panic is certainly a subject of anxious temperament, someone who has not yet experienced panic breaking in, rather than one who is first serene and then, suddenly, falls into panic. The experience of panic is therefore the actualization of the threat announced by the anxiety; it is a situation from which there is no shelter, in which the subject finds himself helpless, without footholds. What initially agitated him has come true, what was expected is now present and inevitable, and that is why when he comes seeking help, he does not have time to wait for the work of analysis; he needs an immediate remedy, as the catastrophe is not around the corner, it is already here. This makes the therapeutic situation difficult with this type of patient, who have a particularly high capacity for emotional contagion, into which one must not be dragged, in order to present them with a fixed point to cling to. In the early stages this is the most important manoeuvre: they must be given a foothold in the presence of the analyst as a figure who does not lose his mind and on whom they can lean. Panic is an invasion of the real, and the work on the symbolic must be able to arrive little by little, when some props have been set up. For example, one day a patient calls me, as she is caught in a sudden panic crisis that surprises her. I see her as soon as I can and she tells me: "Today is not like the other times, I immediately need something to block this nightmare in which I find myself". People with these panic crises tend to hold on to someone next to them, as those who are about to drown cling to those who try to save them at the risk of drowning them too. The contagion of panic comes from the feelings of urgency and helplessness that it transmits together. With my patient I had to appear calm, making her sit down, asking her questions, holding the situation until my calmness infected her instead of her infecting me with her panic.

It is interesting to see these phenomena in relation to another clinical manifestation, depression, which illustrates another temporal modulation, that of the past. If anxiety is the waiting, the imminent sense of catastrophe and panic is the moment when this has come, depression corresponds to the time when the catastrophe is felt to be irreparable, and facing it is superior to one's own strength, which leaves a sense of renunciation and resignation. For this very reason, however, the depressive transition is essential for the re-elaboration of the panic crisis. If panic is in fact the moment when the catastrophe is felt as inevitable and hit the subject, the depressive elaboration, which must not remain stalled on the sense of renunciation and resignation, helps the subject, as a time of mourning, to rework the loss, to symbolize it.

Two modes of treatment: phobic-geographic and affective temporal

We have proposed in these brief notes two possible ways of treating the phenomenon of panic attacks. One is, so to speak, *phobic-geographic*: it involves building a symbolic dam around the hole to avoid falling into it. It is a mode of treatment similar to that which, by constructing a phobic object, determines the geography of the subjective world by indicating areas that should not be approached. Phobia in this perspective is not considered in the light of pathology, but as a determination of the limits: the world is livable when we know how to travel through it, when we know what to avoid. In a way, it is a phobia that is made active, in the same way that in the treatment of neurosis, in the perspective of the late Lacan, the problem is not suppressing the symptom but making it productive, stripping it of neurotic suffering in order to make it appear as the function of a sign of enjoyment.

The other possible mode of treatment that we have tried to outline is what we can define as *affective-temporal*. Where panic is felt as the load, the over-investment of an unsustainable excess, it is a question of re-establishing a place for a lack that allows the subject to reactivate the way of desire. This is made possible by a transition to depressive affect, to the extent that this is not limited to a passive, stagnating renunciation, but constitutes a time of re-elaboration of the loss that reactivates the possibility of desire.

You will notice that in the first mode, the phobic-geographical one, we mentioned the need to circumscribe a *hole**. In the second, the affective-temporal one, we referred to the opportunity to re-establish the place of a *lack** so that it is possible to reactivate desire.

Hole and lack are very different concepts in Lacan's teaching. The hole is the index of a real in the subjective structure; it is what remains irreducible to the symbolic structure, what cannot be framed in a structure of order. If the contours are not indicated by a symbolic construction, it remains a loaded cannon that can manifest in the phenomenology of panic as a bolt from the blue, or in psychosis as the trigger of psychotic onset.

Lack refers instead to the symbolic structure and is in relation to an order, that is, it must go to the right place; it must be recognized not as a lack of something that escapes us and leaves us powerless, but as a lack as such, because only in this way does it work as the activation of desire rather than as a frustrating relapse.

These two modes are both necessary in the treatment of panic disorder. The first concerns the emergency situation that panic imposes; we can indeed use the plural, the emergency situations, because one cannot divide it into phases, as if there were an emergency moment, after which the problem can be treated symbolically through the interpretation of desire. In subjects with panic attacks we always find ourselves with alternating moments of urgency and moments in which it is possible to work on symbolic structures, and it is up to the sensitivity of the analyst to understand what is necessary in a given moment for the patient.

Chapter 10

Anorexia, bulimia, binge-eating and obesity. An interview with Domenico Cosenza

Domenico Cosenza and Diego Busiol

In this chapter, I present an interview with Dr. Domenico Cosenza, psychoanalyst with many years of experience working with anorexic patients, not only as a clinician, but also as a director of institutions in the field. I asked him a few questions on how to understand anorexia, bulimia, binge-eating, and obesity, what the underlying issues may be, and what steps the treatment involves.

DB: *Dr. Cosenza, I have the impression that when it comes to anorexia, bulimia, binge-eating, and obesity, many people (and among them also many therapists and counselors) focus too much on food. The very label of "eating disorders" reinforces the idea that the problem lies in the field of nutrition. But what do we really mean when we talk about anorexia, bulimia, binge-eating, and obesity?*

DC: These are subjective conditions of a pathological type in which there is something visible and also something invisible. What appears clearly to the eye is the unregulated behavior that these patients have, first of all, towards the food object; that is to say, what they do with food at the level of radical restriction in anorexia, binge-vomiting in bulimia, and binging without evacuation in obesity. But it is not limited to this. On a visible level we also see other phenomena, which are particular and that also international descriptive psychiatry highlights: the relationship with body image, for example, which assumes a particular distortion in anorexia, even though some authors would argue that this is also present in cases of obesity and binge-eating but in different forms. We also have some behaviors that tend to occur quite frequently. For example, a tendency towards isolation and social withdrawal in anorexia; or certain effects on the body that are also found in medicine, such as the body mass index (BMI) below a level considered to be normal in anorexia and bulimia, and on the contrary significantly above this level in the binge-eating and especially in obesity.

Now, however, the question is: what can we name as the causative factor of this type of condition? This is where differences begin to be introduced. We can make a distinction between purely descriptive approaches, such as those that the DSM advocates, particularly in the last three editions; and then, there

DOI: 10.4324/9780429432064-14

are other perspectives with which to look at what is at stake at the root of the so-called eating disorders. At this point a bifurcation is created, between a perspective centered on the disorder, which is that of the DSM and descriptive psychiatry, of neo-Kraepelian paradigm; and another perspective, that of the symptom, which is closer to the tradition inaugurated by Freud. If we understand the eating disorder simply as a distortion of behavior or cognition, we imply the fact that from the therapeutic point of view the work to be done consists in an orthopedic operation of the distorted conduct or the false, erroneous cognition. Clinical practice with these patients would then consist, in this perspective, of a treatment aimed at "orthopedicising" their disorder and restoring it to normal functioning, in the sense of a statistically given normality, such as the one on which the DSM is based. The perspective that is instead proposed on the side that has its roots in Freudian teaching is much more complex and supposes that what happens to these subjects cannot be reduced simply to a distortion of so-called normal behavior, but assumes a symptomatic value, that is to say, what happens to these subjects is something that represents them, without them realizing it. It is a solution they have found with respect to a condition of life in which the alternative would most likely have comparable to falling off a cliff. So, in this sense, from the perspective of psychoanalysis, it is preferable to speak of symptomatic solutions found by subjects who have not been able to find any other more effective anchor to go through a critical moment of their existence so fall into this type of disorder. Let me give a concrete example that concerns most of the cases of anorexia and bulimia, namely the fact that most of these cases are triggered during puberty and concern in particular, and in the great majority of cases, girls. In most of these cases we find a particular problem that is linked to going through puberty; many young girls find it difficult to go through this crucial stage of existence, which is when they are called to assume a sexual role, that is to say, to make a drive choice that allows them to orient themselves in the life of desire and enjoyment. Then, in many respects, the anorexic or bulimic onset becomes a solution to a failure of the girl, or in some cases the boy, to enter the dialectic of love and sexual life. It is like a substitute solution for a step that has proved unsustainable. We could say something similar for drug addiction, more on the male side, which is another pathology that represents an elective form chosen by many young people during the passage of puberty as an alternative to an actual inscription within the dialectic of love life. These are considerations that we make in the light of contemporary clinical phenomena, but they have very ancient roots. We find traces of this framing, well before Lacan, in the founding authors of psychoanalysis (Freud, Abraham) who have read in a certain way the drive matrix of addictive pathologies. Therefore, it is important to observe that in this field there are heterogeneous and in some ways irreconcilable perspectives because there are perspectives that tend to reduce the problem at the level of deficit or behavioral and cognitive disorder – a disorder to be straightened – and perspectives that instead insert the eating disorder within the framework of the subject's experience and make it a particular solution that they have found when faced with something unsustainable for them, beginning from a certain moment of their life.

DB: *How is the refusal of food linked with the difficulties in the relationship?*

DC: It is a fundamental link, if we consider that for humans the first encounter with the other coincides with the first encounter with food. That is to say, the object of nutrition is an object eminently at play within the relationship. After all, the mother's body through the breast becomes the embodiment of a complex articulation between the relational and the nutritional plan, which is at the origin for any subject. Freud himself, presenting the foundations of psychosexual theory in the famous *Three Essays* of 1904, basically tells us that (sexual) drive leans on the biological need linked to nutrition. This relationship of structural support in which the drive is intertwined, for the human being, to the need from the very beginning, in fact makes the alimentary act something irreducible to a pure nutritional act. Nutrition is, for the human being, structurally related to the drive. That is, it is taken as part of a structural relationship with the Other who offers food, with the desire at stake in this offer that we receive, and with the enjoyment that it entails. This takes place to the point that it is difficult to distinguish between these different levels involved in the same act.

DB: *In many cases there is a phase of refusal of food which then results in the opposite, in binging.*

DC: Yes, this happens very often in the phenomenology of anorexia-bulimia. The subject's problem is that s/he is unable to stay within the gradation of the experience, whether this be alimentary or not: either s/he eats nothing, or s/he has to eat everything. This is the problem of the bulimic subject. As to say: if s/he eats a little, s/he must eat everything. S/he cannot remain, with respect to oral satisfaction, in a satisfaction that is limited to something. The moment something enters the body, the urge to binge is triggered. It becomes something irremediable. In bulimia, it can only be remedied through evacuation practices: vomiting, compulsive exercise, laxatives, etc.

DB: *Often, these binges involve junk food, sweets, biscuits; everything that is sweeter, fatter, worse.*

DC: This happens often, but the clinic surprises us. A very important point that is rarely emphasized is that even these practices, if you examine them through psychoanalytic listening, that is a listening that focuses on the particular plot of the subject's speech, reveal a singular construction, and thus they can be reduced to homogeneity only until a certain point. This means that there are patients who make, during their binge, an undifferentiated use of food (I open the refrigerator and eat whatever I find); other patients make instead a very selective and ritualized use of food, that is to say, the moment of the binge becomes a ritual moment, a constructed moment, which must follow a series of steps, almost as if it were a religious ceremony. It is very interesting for the clinician to be able to reconstruct the *subject's alimentary rite*, because the construction of the rite leaves traces of the subjectivity that produces it; it tells us something important. It leaves the imprint of s/he who has produced it which is beyond his/her intentions. In saying this I partly contradict a sort of procedural standard of the analytic approaches with these patients, which encourage one not to pay attention to the patients' relationship with food but to focus only on something else. I agree with the basic idea of this, but not with neglecting the dimension of construction that comes into play in the singular way in which these patients build their ritual of enjoyment. This construction bears their signature, even if they don't know it. Rather, the problem is how to subtract this rite from its isolation and bring it in the treatment within the history of the subject.

DB: *You practice in a clinic, so you probably see more extreme or difficult cases. An anorexic is generally perceived as someone in danger of dying, or who is letting him/herself die. However, people we see in the consultation room bring us issues relating to anorexia, without being at risk of dying. How can we understand these different levels of anorexia?*

DC: it is useful to distinguish different levels. There is a phenomenological, descriptive level which concerns the *behavior* of the anorexic person, and that is visible. Then, there is the level that concerns the anorexic *position*, which is something more solid. It is possible to have subjects, particularly women, who for a certain period of their life rely on practices, behaviors, or ways of treating the body that veer towards being classed as an anorexic condition. However, in many cases it is something transitory, and this is very common in the female experience. It is common for many women, for example after difficult moments in life, especially loss of a loved one, to respond to this loss with (especially at body level) renunciation, or deprivation. What differs here is the anorexic position that is structured as an unconscious decision that has the value of stability for the subject; it is a lifestyle choice that goes beyond transitory responses and becomes a libidinal economy that permeates existence and works in a very specific way. A further level to consider is the relationship between anorexia and the subject's structural functioning; here, we enter into an even more complex discourse because anorexia can present itself in different forms that respond to structural needs that are different from each other, heterogeneous.

This is why what I have tried to say in my books on anorexia that it is very important, namely that as clinicians, when faced with an anorexic patient, we always ask ourselves the question: what is the function of anorexia for this subject? This question is important because depending on how we respond, starting from the patient's speech, we will have heterogeneous forms of anorexia that respond to different reasons and, therefore, must be treated taking into account these different reasons. They cannot all be treated in the same way. One form is hysteric anorexia, which occurs in response to a certain difficulty that the subject encounters in the dialectic of the relationship with the desire of the other; different from this, for example, would be psychotic anorexia, which has a delusional basis, in which the subject refuses food based on a persecutory type of certainty, for example that someone is poisoning it. Thus, not eating food becomes for the subject a condition of survival before a threatening 'other' who wants to eliminate him/her. This is just to give two possible examples. Anorexia is not a monolith, but it must be thought of in its various possibilities of functioning. I will add one thing in response to your question: anorexia certainly has a level of functioning that goes towards the infinitization of the symptom linked to weight loss due to the refusal of food, and these are the situations in which we meet the maximum risk. Faced with these situations, we find ourselves intervening in the real to put a limit in place, since the subject lacks this limit. The patient is unable to stop by her/himself, s/he has not incorporated that internal limit that allows her/him to say "stop". So, either there is another who stops the patient when s/he is in the grip of this infinitization that makes her/him run towards death, or there is the risk that death occurs in reality. And it is no coincidence that mental anorexia is, among the psychiatric pathologies, has one of the highest mortality rates. This must be kept in mind. At the same time, it is one of the psychiatric pathologies with the highest rate of possibility of cure over time, that is, the cure rate among anorexic patients is high after many years of treatment. Many patients resume their lives, they have a family, a job; however, only after years of treatment.

Then, there are two sides of anorexia that strike: one is this drive towards death, and the other is that for many patients, anorexia can be a solution that offers stability, and is built to last over time. It works as a system of daily practices that the subject somehow follows in order to persevere in this condition. Things that accompany her/his daily life: small rituals around food, body, calories. Attempts to organize daily life, so as to avoid encountering something unexpected. Practices aimed at controlling the body, the other. Clearly, these are practices that are condemned to failure, because it is impossible to have total control over life; because what is unpredictable in life, comes from within rather than from the outside. It is the drive itself that is uncontrollable. Then, we are talking about a practice (anorexia) that is very powerful – very often fueled by a megalomanic ideal – producing effects of euphoria, but at the same time, a practice condemned to failure.

DB: *It is difficult to involve these people, who are so focused on substance, in a talking cure.*

DC: This is one of the problems we have with this clinic, which I prefer to call the 'clinic of the excess'. It is a clinic in which the subject does not present himself to us as a divided subject, who has questions, who articulates a transference towards the therapist, but on the contrary tends to present her/himself as undivided, having no questions or with a weak question, and as being little inclined to establish a transference, and at the very best, establishes one entirely played in the imaginary relationship with the therapist. It is not surprising that all of this makes treating these particular symptoms very difficult.

These symptoms are different in structure from the analytic symptom as understood in the Freudian sense, which is a symptom that is enigmatic, divides the subject, causes sufferance but also enjoyment, and pushes the subject to ask someone who is 'supposed to know' something about it for help, in order to read it and be able to understand what it means. The problem is that this type of articulation, which we find in the neurotic and that is at the basis of the analytic treatments of neurotics right from the preliminary interviews, in this new clinic is not a starting point but rather a point of arrival. That is to say that initially, when anorexic patients come to us, they do not arrive with an open attitude; they arrive in a closed condition. Usually they are not the one who has asked for treatment. This demand comes from family members, doctors, those who bring these patients to us, so that they can be helped in some way. To be helped, first of all, to recognize that they are in a difficult condition, which is not obvious and indeed problematic, as there is in these patients, as in drug addicts, an absence of recognition of the disease. That is to say that they do not consider what happens to them as a pathological condition: it is the others who see the pathology – the family members, friends, and loved ones – but not them. For them, it is, on the contrary, a condition that is in some ways fortunate, a condition that has more the characteristics of a solution than those of a problem, and in the case of anorexia (and also drug addiction) it assumes the characteristics for the subject of lifestyle, rather that of pathological condition. This is why it is very difficult to work with these patients, because they do not recognize that what is happening to them is something symptomatic. Therefore, the problem we have in their treatment is how to produce the symptomatization of this condition which initially is not recognized as a symptom for the subject, but is a symptom for society, for the family, for the other. It is a social symptom, in the beginning. When we work with these patients, we try to transform this social symptom into a subjective symptom, but this transformation operation requires a time that can be broad. Hence the difficulty these treatments have from the very beginning.

DB: *Now you are talking about the cases you see in the clinic, if I have understood correctly.*

DC: Not necessarily. Definitely about those in the clinic, but it is also of the case for those we see in the consultation room, as they too are referred by parents, partners, friends, doctors. On this regard, there is not a significant difference when comparing patients we see in the clinic and those we see in private practice. What differentiated them is rather the psychopathological intensity, that is to say that we hardly see some of the cases that we see in the clinic in the consultation room and here it is only with great difficulty that we can treat them. These are extreme cases in which, for example, sometimes the intensity of the symptom is so strong that the patient is unable to even come to consultation room. They are patients who need to find another place where they can live for a certain time of their life and heal themselves within this place. Not all cases with this type of problem benefit from a treatment which is limited to the use of speech (psychotherapy, or group therapy). The majority of these cases can find many benefits from it, but there are cases in which the symptomatological severity is such that it cannot be treated, at least not immediately, In settings where speech is the only dimension of cure. They really need another place where they can live: another daily ritual, another way of life, an alternative cohabitation, meeting another Other than the family one, and so on. These are the cases we encounter in the clinic, in the therapeutic communities, in the hospital.

DB: *I understand that it is not easy for them to develop a transference to treatment. How about the transference to the analyst or the therapist?*

DC: It depends on the type of anorexia we are dealing with. For example, if we are dealing with a hysterical anorexia it works in a certain way, because basically hysterical anorexia is hysteria, and therefore the problem is how to bring the passion for anorexia back to the fundamental passion of the hysteric, which is a passion for the enigma. Basically, in an analytically oriented treatment of hysterical anorexia, we try to make the passion for the enigma play against the passion for anorexia, and if the subject is hysteric, generally there will be a change from the passion for thinness to the passion for the enigma as a condition in which the subject can get closer to what fascinates the hysteric, that is, uniqueness. The need to be unique for the other, to be the phallus for the Other, inevitably comes into play in the clinic of hysteria. Anorexia is a state that can give one the feeling of being special for a certain time, but in the end is by no means so unique; it is a serial response in the contemporary world, but not the only one. The more a subject is attracted by something that concerns his/her singularity, his/her most enigmatic dimension, the more his/her desire will take shape. Then, at a certain point, the treatments of hysterical anorexia become treatments of hysteria, but it takes time to dissolve the rigid armor that the anorexic symptom has built.

It works differently in cases of true or mental anorexias, where we are not dealing with a divided (neurotic) subject; we are dealing with something more complicated, for which the process of separation of the subject from the other has proved to be precarious and problematic, in many cases since the loss of the object that occurs in weaning. This is why the young Lacan defined mental anorexia as a "refusal to wean", a refusal of the process of separation, which is not only separation from the other but also the separation of a part of oneself, a part of one's own body. Something in this process has remained frozen. And in puberty, when the subject (especially the female subject) finds her/himself exposed to the question of desire – starting with the body that becomes pulsionalized to enter the dialectic of desire of adult life – here, the same issue arises yet again. That is to say that if the subject has not lost the object in the time 1 of weaning, this failed loss will be felt in time 2 of puberty. Time 2 is the period in which the subject is called to assume something of his/her own sexual position, to come into play as an adult desiring subject, to take his/her own position in relation to the desire of the other.

There is something in this passage that usually turns out to be highly problematic. The encounter with the desire of the other, at the level of sexuality, turns out to be something unsustainable for the subject, also for reasons related to the quality of the experience of satisfaction. After all, these are subjects who have not really experienced a loss of enjoyment, so their relationship with satisfaction remains a complete relationship, not a partial one. What the exposure to the life of desire and love life offers them is a distressing dialectic in which the other is sometimes there, sometimes not, subject to a variation of presence and absence that is unbearable for these subjects. This reveals to us the failure of their inscription in the field of the Other, and their finding themselves disarmed in the face of the unexpected and the encounter with the traumatic Real*. Being in this regime of satisfaction is something that feels like a torture to them. Then, it becomes much more preferable for them to remain in a regime of satisfaction that can give them the sensation of full enjoyment, without loss, without rest, and this full enjoyment in mental anorexia is experienced starting from the repeated and systematic refusal of food.

However, the repeated and systematic refusal of food is not only a refusal of food: it is refusal of the body as sexed (the subject experiences the loss of the secondary characteristics of the body), and refusal of the social bond, this being a dimension in which one experiences a loss of enjoyment (this is what Freud tells us in *Civilization and Its Discontents*, that is, in order to enter the social bond, one has to pay a price, and has to lose a share of his/her freedom. One cannot do what one wants but must comply with what civilization imposes on him/her as a precondition to social life. Only in this way one can find his/her role within the collective bond).

So, we can say that in the anorexic condition the subject prefers to preserve a full enjoyment rather than accepting to enter the field of the Other and experience a loss of enjoyment. This is why Jacques-Alain Miller says that in mental anorexia, and more generally in the new forms of the symptom, what is at stake is the rejection of the Other. Other authors (see Augustin Menard) say something similar when they argue that what the anorexic refuses to eat is the signifier; that is to say that the subject refuses to eat (food) but also refuses to accept what (the signifier) introduces a loss into their experience of enjoyment and what prevents him/her from becoming One with the object, One with the other. The entry into the field of language produces the loss of enjoyment as a structural effect. In this sense, the anorexic refuses to eat pieces of the signifier; s/he rejects the Other to preserve the mirage of a full enjoyment.

DB: *What type of intervention is most effective with anorexia? How does this differ from a more classic clinic? And what modalities do you adopt with these cases, in your practice?*

DC: What I have tried to argue in my books on mental anorexia, starting with *Il Muro dell'Anoressia* [The Wall of Anorexia] of 2008, is that we have entered a new age of the unconscious within which analytic practice can no longer be presented, with these cases, in the form of a hermeneutics of the unconscious sense, as was partly the case for the Freudian clinic of classical neurosis. This is because patients are deaf to the dimension of sense; giving a semantic interpretation to an anorexic patient, or to a drug addict, is an act that fails completely, in the sense that the subject does not perceive it as something that concerns him. Therefore, the whole endeavor of psychoanalysis as an interpretive art that through the symbol allows us to grasp the unconscious meaning is not effective with these patients (making the necessary exceptions for the hysterical-neurotic forms). In fact, if we exclude the neurotic forms (which are not the majority) in cases of true or mental anorexia, the psychoanalyst's intervention becomes decisive if it is operated not so much on the signifier/meaning, or symbolic/imaginary axis, as on the signifier/object axis, on the border that unites, in Lacan's registers, the Symbolic and the Real. The work to be done is not so much of interpretation of the unconscious sense underlying the symptom, as much as naming of the Real of out-of-sense jouissance at play in it, which allows for a singular localization tailored to the case. Or it is a cut, an intervention aimed at marking a loss, a detachment, a fracture line in the subject's relationship with the jouissance that pervades him/her. Thus, this practice of analytically oriented intervention is pragmatics more than semantics. It is the pragmatics of the act that operates in the border dimension between the Symbolic and the Real of subjective experience. It is a completely different practice of psychoanalysis to that of past decades. And on this regard, it must be said that Lacan, especially in his latest teaching, orients us in this direction; not only for these cases, but also in the analysis with the neurotic. Even if the neurotic needs to go through a work of disidentification that also brings sense into play, to undo the identifying stratification that s/he has built up over the course of his/her life. The fundamental orientation of the treatment, even in neuroses, will aim at detaching the subject from his relationship of subjection to the libidinal object that causes it. Lacan's latest teaching helps us a lot to grasp the specificity of this clinic, a clinic in which meaning has already been removed by the patient who, as Lacan says, is "unsubscribed" to the unconscious [*désabonné à l'inconscient*, in French], devoid of a belief about the unconscious sense of his symptoms. And therefore, from the beginning we find ourselves having to come into play at another level of clinical experience, which no longer relies on the semantic virtues of the transferential unconscious as a meaning-producing machine.

In the case of an anorexia patient that I have been seeing for about a year in the consultation room, after months and months where the patient regularly comes to the sessions to say that what drives her to minimize her eating is the ideal of the flat stomach, an ideal that every evening as she stands in front of the bathroom mirror of her house she sees as unreachable, a breakthrough is suddenly made. The young woman, anorexic for more than 10 years, has a symptomatic onset in puberty after two impositions by her mother, which re-emerge as memories. First, she comes to the conservatory exam knowing she is not ready (and not wanting to apply herself) but unable to say no to this maternal demand, and she fails the exam. Then, four years later, through the effect of a second blade who intervenes to sever her by now precarious condition, she bows to the maternal injunction to call a schoolmate, seen as a role model by her mother, on the phone to congratulate her on her excellent high school graduation grade, which is a few points higher than her grade that the mother devalues. Shortly thereafter, this girl's anorexia breaks out. "An unbearable question", I limit myself to saying, underlining what emerged in the two memories of the patient as a girl. From the excess of the belly that is never flat enough, a passage now opens in the naming that moves the excess into play at the level of the maternal demand and the superegoic enjoyment that holds the patient in a relationship of subservience to this demand. Anorexia becomes a way of responding to this excess with another excess that the patient believes she is able to control on the surface of her body. The naming of excess in relation to the unruliness of the maternal demand introduces a break that shifts the axis of the patient's analytic work onto her relationship with the unregulated demand of the Other, to which up until now, she has not been able to put a limit except through the anorexic solution. Evidently, giving in to anorexia and abandoning the symptom reopens in this woman the anxiety of falling back completely into the jaws of the unruly demand of the Other from which she somehow tried to escape. Hence her attachment to anorexia, which for some time has kept her on the threshold between losing her menstrual cycle and her recovery.

This is a general guideline that I have been trying to support for some time with respect to the treatment of anorexia, in particular starting from my book *Il muro dell'anoressia*. Later, I extended it to a broader psychopathological horizon that I defined as the 'clinic of excess', in particular starting with the revised edition of my book *Il cibo e l'inconscio. Psicoanalisi e disturbi alimentari* [Food and the Unconscious. Psychoanalysis and eating disorders, Franco Angeli, Milan 2018]. It is clear that this clinic, however, due to the particular effects that the symptom has on the body, is a clinic that in the most serious cases requires networking, that is, there is also the need for a doctor for the treatment, someone who can intervene to monitor the condition of the body because these subjects do not have an internal limit, thus when they enter a symptomatic infinitization they need someone who can intervene promptly. Otherwise, they risk reaching death, without wanting to. One of my theses about this is that they are not suicidal subjects. These subjects do not want to commit suicide; they want to experience as much enjoyment as possible, which is different. And so it happens that they die because they enjoy too much. This is an aspect that Lacan teaches us: full enjoyment coincides with the death drive. And these cases prove it to us: drug addiction, anorexia show us precisely the relevance of this axiom of Lacan. This is why it is important that a doctor is included as part of the treatment of these patients, because there is a need for someone who can act as a sentinel of the bodily condition, preventing the patient from going adrift. Because these patients literally drift away. They enjoy themselves so much that a subjective eclipse occurs in them at the moment of enjoyment. It is something that they recognize the moment they are out of these conditions, and then they realize that when the symptom takes hold of them, they are not present. They have irresistible fits. This is also what the binge patients say after a binge; when the urge to binge comes, it is something stronger than them.

DB: *Episodes of binge-eating can also occur in patients who use substances, borderline patients, and patients who do not primarily have eating disorders.*

DC: Variability is a characteristic of this symptomatology of the last decades. We have gone beyond the paradigm of monosymptomaticity, that is to say, fewer and fewer cases remain with the same symptom throughout their life. What happens mostly is that particular montages are produced that hold the subject together. It is quite common. For example, bulimia is often associated with the abuse of substances or drugs or alcohol.

DB: *Obesity is rarely mentioned. It is rarely thought that it could be a psychological symptom.*

DC: There is a great debate going on in contemporary psychiatry about this. Presently, obesity as such has no place in psychopathology; it is a medical syndrome. However, some authors, especially Hilde Bruch, the great pioneer of studies on eating disorders, indicate very effectively that there are relational conditions that determine the development of obesity since childhood. Obesity frequently occurs since childhood, while anorexia and bulimia occur more at pubertal onset. The problem with obesity is that there is indeed a great silence around this syndrome. There are very few contributions from psychoanalysts on the subject of obesity, whereas we have entire libraries dedicated to anorexia and bulimia. There is a silence of psychoanalysis, and not only of psychoanalysis, but also generally around the theme of obesity, which contrasts with the enormous spread of obesity around the world. That is to say that the real progressive pathology is not anorexia or bulimia, but obesity, which has been defined by the WHO as the new pandemic of the 21st century. And yet, with respect to obesity we are in an epistemologically backward condition. It is still not clear how to frame this problem, who should deal with it, what is the etiology underlying this symptomatology. But something similar also happened for mental anorexia until the mid-sixties. It was not clear whether it was a neuroendocrine, psychiatric, or other pathology. There are still many steps to be taken regarding obesity, because in my opinion we are still in a pre-scientific condition from the point of view of its classification. We have not put together the elements that allow us to read it. Something has happened in recent years, which has also partly affected the structure of the DSM V, namely the fact that with the invention of the category binge-eating disorder, some of the cases that can be traced back to the framework of obesity have already been recognized in psychiatry as psychopathology. But this is only some of them; those in which this type of problem is associated with what in the DSM is called 'a feeling of loss of control', usually characterized as a secondary effect of a depressive mood. The problem is that only a fraction of obesity cases fall within this framework. There are obesities that are characterized, from the dynamic point of view, by a very different functioning. There are forms of obesity of a more hyperphagic type, in which obesity functions as a control system, in which the subject tends to program his/her moments of the day in a ritualistic way, including eating moments. The whole range of cases of obese subjects is not yet part of a dynamic and psychopathological consideration, but it will likely be part of it in the future. There was already a lot of debate before the 5th edition of the DSM in which some American psychiatrists, like Devlin, questioned whether there is a place for obesity in the DSM. It is a book yet to be written. It is a pathology that will perhaps find a first possible clarification of its dynamic and psychopathological dimension by the end of the 21st century.

Chapter 11

Depressions

Franco Lolli

The depressive phenomenon

The depressive phenomenon is a symptomatic archipelago consisting of psycho-pathological manifestations of different intensities and severities and character-ized by the inflection – more or less pronounced – of mood tone. The depressed person describes him/herself as lacking vital momentum, uncomfortable in social relations and, for this reason, tending to withdraw; deeply suffering from the sense of estrangement that defines his/her relationship with the world, crossed by negative and catastrophic thoughts, and unable to make people around him/her understand the depth of their pain. His/her speech is, in general, occupied by repetition of a few thoughts, which obstinately reaffirms the lack of perspective in an existence now considered (by them) dramatically unchangeable. The ineluc-tability of the present is projected into the future and also colors the past: time seems paralyzed in a today without end or beginning, which blocks the subject in an apparently insurmountable despair.

Sometimes the intensification of this experience results in a silence that no longer recognizes speech as a possible catalyst for change: these are extreme situations, in which the opposition of a radical disenchantment takes the form of an explicit refusal to enter into an exchange with the other. The feeling of self-devaluation is particularly intense: the so-called depressed person doubts his/her own value and interprets the smallest sign from the other as the confirmation of his/her (pre-sumed) irrelevance. From this characteristic aspect of the phenomenon, it is pos-sible, in fact, to make an initial diagnostic distinction of extreme importance.

Psychic pain in neurosis

In neurotic subjects, the question of personal value focuses on the dimension of exchange: the lament, in fact, focuses on the feeling of not being worth anything *for the other*. This lament, as Sigmund Freud observes in *Mourning and Melan-choly*, contains within itself an accusation addressed to the other, to the insuffi-ciency of his/her attention, care, interest: self-criticism, then, veils and mitigates the attack on the other, protecting the subject from a possible reaction of irritated

DOI: 10.4324/9780429432064-15

retaliation. Upstream of this neurotic posture, there is the devastating effect of an event of loss, of an unresolved loss (most of the time, not consciously perceived) that keeps the subject in a condition of unfillable lack. An effect that Jacques Lacan (2012) describes as such: "We carry on mourning and we experience the devaluating effects of mourning in so far as the object that we are mourning for was, without us knowing it, the one which had become, that we had made the support for our castration*. Castration returns to us; and we see ourselves for what we are, in so far as we would be essentially returned to this position of castration" (p. 75). This – one might say – is the Lacanian theory of 'psychic pain': when the beloved object (which, with its presence, recognition and gratitude, concealed the castration of the subject, even attributing to the subject the narcissistically relevant value of irreplaceability) disappears, the experience of helplessness and powerlessness returns, associated with feelings of devaluation, on which germinates, precisely, the depressive feeling. The loved object was the support of our castration, Lacan says its disappearance puts in the foreground the condition of 'poverty' of the ego, of misery, of lack; in other words, it brings the subject back to its incurable division. The potentially depressed person thus feels that he is losing not only the situation (emotional, working, relational) through which s/he was able to deny his/her existential precariousness, but also – and this is the point of greatest metapsychological interest – a part of himself, that part which, fantasmatically illuminated by the gratifying contact with the object, shone with a special light. The future depressed person encounters a sort of amputation of his/her own desirability, a mutilation of the sensation of being important to someone, an eclipse of a representation of him/herself, and a decline in the loving and 'wanted' self that the admiration of the other guaranteed. The shadow of the object – Freud writes in *Mourning and Melancholy* – falls on the ego: the ego returns to feel for what it is, that is "poor thing". Psychic pain – to be more precise – consists of this feeling of being reduced to $, with no escape, no possibility of finding shelter in the fantasmatically vitalizing relationship with the object.[1] The problem that the depressive phenomenon (in a neurotic structure) poses in the foreground is that this psychic pain is – unconsciously – rejected by the subject: the rejection of mourning – it is important to reiterate that this is an unconscious rejection – can be considered, therefore as the psychodynamic process at the bases of the symptomatic constitution.

From the loss of the object to identification to the loss

In this sense, the depressed person is someone who turns the loss of the object into the new (and inevitable) object that can symptomatically allow him/her to regain the lost consistency. Particularly intense and appropriate in this regard are the reflections that Roland Barthes (2010) notes in his notebook (which would become the splendid book *Mourning Diary*) following the death of his beloved mother: "henceforth and forever I am my own mother" (p. 36), he writes in the darkest and most depressive phase of his grief. In this poignant passage, one can clearly see how in depression the lost object tends to occupy the entire subjective scene, and to invade the psychic activity of the subject who, in some ways, finds himself engulfed by the absence of the object. The pain for the loss of the mother is 'faced' by the son by becoming mother himself, in a kind of endless commemoration of the loss: in this poetic expression we can see how affirming 'I am my own mother' is equivalent to saying 'I am the lost object', or even better, 'I am the loss of the object'. Depression, in this sense, could be defined as the endless prolongation of this initial phase of mourning, in which the subject is literally invaded by the absence of the loved object.

Depression, therefore, opposes the process of mourning: it is, in other words, a form of unconscious rebellion to the inevitability of loss that, instead of being assumed, fixes itself as an indelible immanence, permeating the whole existence. In depression we see a kind of resistance of the unconscious to separate from the lost object due to the fact that when the object disappeared, it took away with it a part of the subject, the part that was made to feel special by the object. The difficulties that the depressed person faces, it might be said, are how to separate from this part of him/herself, how to mourn him/herself, and how to accept the castration that the loss evokes. The depressed subject lives pressured by a pain of loss that never ends because it is always current; a pain that is renewed every day as if it were the first day. Nothing changes, nothing evolves, everything seems paralyzed. Their words and thoughts are always the same. Indifferent to any future perspective, the depressed person spends all his/her time preventing the loss from spreading its effect; the lost object continues to fill life with its absence, a life that revolves entirely – I repeat – around the event of the disappearance of a previous condition whose nostalgic load prevents any other form of libidic investment.

The impossibility of mourning

This attempt to deny the loss – which occurs through fixation to the moment of loss – aims, in fact, to reject the state of subjective mutilation that the loss entails; this aspect is particularly visible in cases where, for example, those who have suffered the loss of a loved one are unable to dispose of their clothes, their toothbrush, their hat left on the hangers, the slightest signs of what was their presence. Everything must remain as it was before, emptiness cannot be tolerated because it evokes greater pain. The refusal of the unconscious to process the loss – a refusal that results in the unforgettableness of what is no longer there – expresses, therefore, the difficulty the depressed person faces in dealing with the attack of the traumatic event on his own integrity.

Considered from this perspective, it is possible to define depression as the mortifying freezing of the subject to the loss, that is, the subject remains chained to the loss in thought, so as to evade the question of one's own condition of lack that the loss of the object implies. What is avoided is the strenuous work of psychic reorganization that, after all, characterizes the period of mourning. In mourning, the real traumatic event triggers a necessary reorganization of the affective and existential dynamics, to progressively restore the possibility to desire again. To be even more explicit, in mourning, the subject must take back his own desire after the event of loss has stressed the precariousness of satisfaction and the risk of mortification to which he/she is inevitably exposed. In depression, this work is prevented by the immobilizing effect of humiliation of desire that occurs when its satisfaction is interrupted by the loss of the object to which the desire tended to; this remaining obsessively anchored to the moment of loss basically reveals the obstinacy of the unconscious not wanting to realize the subjective vulnerability to which the dialectic of desire exposes the human being.

Viewed from this perspective, depressive fixation allows the human being not to return to risk anything in the relationship with the other, remaining in a solitary and exclusive defensive stance. To go back to the previous example, as long as the closet is filled with the lost person's clothes, there will be no space to accommodate those of a new partner.

Depression, then, can be defined as a mourning that has never begun and which, paradoxically, never ends. In mourning, as we know, the reality principle demands the subject to abandon the previous libidic position, renewing this way the incidence of castration in the life of the human being. The work of mourning consists in having to do without a piece of enjoyment* and accept this subtraction which, only if accepted, can give rise to a new libidic investment: just like the paternal metaphor, it plays, in this sense, a mortifying function, which is necessary, however, for future vitalization. It affects what is most dear to the subject and demands that the subject detach itself from this, in view of the possibility of a reward to come. In the work of mourning, as well as in the Oedipic process, the subject comes to terms with the need for renunciation and, in some ways, submits to the relentless law of castration. As observed by Kusnierek (1989) "In other words, the work of mourning relates to the work of castration; because of the mourning, the necessary mourning of the phallus is mobilized" (p. 147. My translation).

Depression and rejection of castration

Depression, conversely, is configured as a rejection of the work of mourning, therefore, a rejection of castration: this has at least two consequences. The first, and most obvious, concerns the effect that this rejection has on the subject's level of desire. Desire is, logically, the result of a lack. Greek mythology teaches us that Eros is the son of Penia. There is no desire without experience of lack, poverty, indigence. The desire and its incessant research movement (and the consequent subjective activation) are driven by the aspiration to fill the void that causes it. The real object of desire – Lacan will specify – is that which is behind it, that from which it originates, that towards which it tends to and which, by definition, it will never be able to reach: the object of desire is the loss of the original fullness. The nostalgia of a time when one's own compactness had not yet been undermined by the experience of loss is at the core of the neurotic myth. It is from this ambition, which is structurally destined for failure, that the desire arises. Its attempt to return to the supposed condition of full satisfaction will be in vain: what it will encounter (the multiplicity of objects towards which it orientates itself), in fact, can never be what caused it. But it will be precisely from this impossible coincidence of the object-cause with the object-aim (to use a successful theorization of Jacques-Alain Miller, who distinguishes in this way the inconsistency of the object by which desire is provoked and the material and illusory consistency of the innumerable objects towards which desire is directed) that the tirelessness and vitality of its action will derive. In depression, then, the rejection of castration has mortifying consequences on the level of desire. The rejection of the experience of lack turns off the libido, drains any vital momentum, and confines the subject in anhedonia and apathy typical of his/her morbid condition.

But the refusal of castration can also be understood as the inability of the subject to let go of a part of himself, as the inability to separate himself from the imaginary identification to the phallus that constitutes – as we have already seen – a foothold for the subject. The lost object cannot be replaced, nor does the subject seem to be able to recover its phallic value elsewhere. The narcissistic disaster concerning the subject uncovers the subject in his radical vacuity. Having always tried to adhere to the phallic ideal, when this falters, an unmasking of the identification which shakes the subject in its ontological foundations is caused. This determines his detachment from the reassuring phallic significance. The consequence of this narcissistic wound is the emergence of a void, therefore, that concerns both the subject and his Other: the emptiness of the world thus coincides with the emptiness of the subject, and vice versa. Things in life lose their sense, fade emotionally, fade in intensity until they flatten out into total indifference. The light is off, and in the dark, everything is dark.

Exposed to the lack-of-being that the absence of the object (support of castration) produces, the subject of the unconscious will try to defend itself with a 'too much-of-being', with a negation of castration, turning the loss of the object into the new object through which to reconstitute its own compactness. In this sense, the depressed person presents him/herself, to all intents and purposes, as an apparently undivided subject: s/he replaces the lost phallic enjoyment – the splendor of feeling indispensable for someone – with a superegoic form of unconscious enjoyment (denied on the conscious level) that pushes him, incessantly, towards the compensatory (and clandestine) satisfaction that the new object (the loss object) assures him.

Depression in psychosis

So far, the depressive phenomenon in a neurotic structure. If we consider, instead, what happens in the psychotic structure, in the foreground there is an experience of self-devaluation with a completely different configuration: the self-accusation, in fact, is not an implicit attack on the other (considered guilty of having 'revealed' his condition of lack) but a bleak finding of one's own ontological inconsistency, a clear confirmation of the vacuity of the being and the groundlessness of one's own existence, which is independent of the outcome of the relationship with the other. The depressive trait of psychosis (which would be more correct to call melancholic) consists of, firstly, a feeling of insurmountable derilection, and secondly, a feeling of radical unjustification of one's own being in the world, which can take the form of identification with the waste object, reification of oneself, the guilt of existing, the total absence of recognition of value to one's own 'being there', the libidinal emptying of the body, or the rejection without appeal of any compensation. The subject feels that he is worth nothing, not to someone, however (as in the case of neurosis) but in absolute terms: indeed – one might add – what is missing is precisely that 'someone' for whom to feel important. No accusation is implied in the self-accusation, therefore, but only the clear acknowledgement of the structural void which, in some ways, paradoxically coincides with an inverse experience of maximum psychic congestion. Not a symptom reactive to the event that evokes, in the present, the trauma of castration, but a freezing in a state of helpless indefiniteness that a problematic mirror stage has deposited as constitutive data.[2]

Two profoundly different logics distinguish, therefore, the development of the depressive feeling in psychotic structures from that which can be observed within neurotic structures: in the former, an original and unresolved sense of abandonment permeates the whole of existence, whereas in the latter, the current experience of loss reactivates and expands a previous (and not elaborated) suffering towards the 'phallic downsizing'.

To have or to be: neurotic declensions of depression

This phallic downsizing – it should be pointed out – may present different nuances, depending on whether it concerns what Lacan defines as the subjective dimension of being rather than the subjective dimension of having. On the side of being, which is generally more frequent on the feminine side, the stability of the bond with the Other of desire is affected, a bond for which the subject is ready to give up any good, possession, and power.[3] The love of the partner – it could be said, gives the subject self-value: its loss, as a consequence, represents a loss that undermines its own consistency. To be nothing for the Other means the very impossibility of being. Depressive affection lies in this special contingency. The loss of the emotional relationship negativizes, in fact, the representation of oneself, shakes the sense of dignity, erases all pride, and devastates one's being in the world. The world empties out, and with it goes its own being.

In the logic of having – not necessarily reserved for the male – the subject feels obliged to continuously give proof of his 'alleged' having, in order to confirm his own value. In fact, not only must he prove that he has it, but he must also protect it from possible loss; he is affected, in fact, by the anxiety of the owner, well described by Jacques-Alain Miller in his seminar, *The nature of the semblants.*

Performance and defense: the more one is performant, the more s/he protects him/herself from loss and consequently, the stronger and more reassuring the identification to the phallus will be. The phallic having is directed towards a plurality of objects: certainly, towards 'owning' a partner capable of making the subject shine with reflected light. But, as the clinic teaches, there may be countless objects that satisfy such a phallic need; professional success, a good social position, an enviable status, the accumulation of goods, a huge wealth, and so on. What matters is what the object gives to the subject in terms of phallic power and narcissism. The event of loss that triggers the depressive dynamic has to do, then, with an 'attack on capital', on the dimension of the *having*: the threat is felt at the level of the solidity of the recognition of one's own phallic power, guaranteed by the possession of special qualities, status, and *performances*. The loss of a job, the deterioration of one's social position, the end of a relationship with a partner admired and desired (by others), the fear of poor performances (sexual, sporting, social, etc.), all heavily affect one's own consideration of oneself. The ego is wounded on the level of the having, marked by a castration that has dealt a hard blow to the image of someone who has always thought him/herself in possession of amazing assets and abilities and, as a result of such having, has not been obliged to ask and not been forced to pass through the 'humiliating' funnel of raising a question.

The phallic trauma and the construction of the symptom

In some ways, the distinction between these two neurotic depressive dynamics can reasonably be considered comparable to that which distinguishes hysterical neurosis from obsessive neurosis. In the first, in fact, depression presents itself as a consequence of feeling rejected, not finding a place in the desire of the other, not feeling recognized, and the failure of the attempt to dig into the other that lack to be filled with one's own sacrificial voluntarism. In the second, depression presents itself as a consequence of the presentification of one's own lack and the revelation of one's own misery, which belies the narcissistic imagery on which the previous identifications were based. In both cases, phallic trauma is at the origin of the depressive slope that the existence takes, although – as already mentioned – it declines in different ways: the feeling of decaying from the position of privileged object of the other's desire is thus sustained, on the one hand on an experience of devaluation of one's own being, and on the other hand on the experience of devaluation of one's own having. Two dialects of the same language, in essence, which – as the clinic often points out, however – tend to mix and intertwine, rather than oppose each other.

It should be made clear in this regard that the issue of phallic trauma is central both in terms of diagnosis and treatment. Its appearance in the plot of the patient's account provides the clinician with one of the decisive criteria for differentiating neurosis from psychosis: what s/he must pay particular attention to when listening to the analysand's speech is, in fact, the presence of elements that indicate a discontinuity in his/her history, a fracture between before and after, between a past time (with almost mythical outlines) in which 'everything was fine', and a present tormented by suffering. It is fundamental, in order to formulate a diagnosis of neurotic depression, to identify in the patient's words the incidence of an event of rupture, due to which nothing is as it was before and nothing will ever be as it was. The importance given to this type of statement lies in the fact that it reveals (in the *apres-coup*) a wound that has interrupted the linearity of her/her history: which, therefore, appears marked by a loss, evoked – without the subject's knowledge – by a current event (which reactivates the unelaborated core). The typical depressive experience of a neurotic structure is therefore constituted in two stages: in the first stage – which is, generally, the time of childhood or first puberty – the child finds himself involved in an event of loss (the death of a loved one, the transfer to another city, a strong disappointment that undermines the ideal image of a parent, the disintegration of the family unit, the birth of a brother who ousted the child from a special position, an event of strong social humiliation, etc.). This event of loss – and this is the salient fact – does not find a possibility of symbolic elaboration, is not 'put into words', and remains encysted in psychism forming a sort of hypersensitive core that is ready to resonate in situations of similar affective tenor. In a second stage, any event that has to do with the experience of loss – and that may, as often happens, not be perceived as such – reactivates what has remained 'in storage'. What had not been signified thus returns to be felt, but, this time, on the symptomatic level, in the typical form of 'psychic pain'. The depressed person suffers, in fact, from an intense and persistent pain that s/he cannot locate, a pain that does not have a somatic seat but that colonizes every moment of his/her existence. Unlike anxiety – which, as Freud had pointed out, is discharged along the body's pathways, that is, it is felt in certain areas of the body – depression has a purely psychic, aleatory, and, for this reason, arbitrary character: the subject 'hurts', but s/he does not know where and why. The sense of loneliness that derives from it originates from the impossibility of making others understand the intensity of one's own suffering, which – as we often happen to hear – risks being dismissed by relatives and friends as a whim or indolence.

Depression and refusal to know

The neurotic subject who suffers from depressive experiences is, therefore, a subject for whom a childhood event of loss that has remained unprocessed is later repeated in an occasional contingency: the peculiarity that we find in these cases is the unconscious refusal to know about it. Lacan (1990) writes in this regard:

> For example, we qualify sadness as depression, because we give it soul for support, or the psychological tension of Pierre Janet, the philosopher. But it isn't a state of the soul, it is simply a moral failing, as Dante, and even Spinoza, said: a sin, which means a moral weakness, which is, ultimately,

located only in relation to thought, that is, in the duty to be *Well-spoken*, to find one's way in dealing with the unconscious, with the structure.

(p. 22)

Lacan's explicit reference to Dante and Spinoza is clarifying and clears the field from possible misunderstandings of moral nature; it is a matter of understanding the depressive dynamic, says Lacan, starting from the Spinozian assumption that putting one's ideas in order – formulating clear and distinct concepts – has always the effect of dissolving passion, and therefore, of attenuating the suffering. This means that the condition of malaise is closely related to knowledge, to be precise, to the refusal of knowledge. The subject – one could then say – suffers psychically when he cannot or does not want to know the reasons for his own evil. Here Lacan's statement is clarified: the moral cowardice of the depressed person consists of him/her retreating when faced with the knowledge that, although it does not promise any joy in itself, it is able to procure that pleasure, that 'erotic' and libidinal reactivation that is the effect of the research itself. This means that depression is configured as an impasse of the subject when faced with the task of going to the bottom of his/her own issues. The subject closes himself in a kind of debility, a refusal to know (about his/her issues and him/herself), which translates into *tedium vitae*.

The responsibility of the subject, to whom Lacan, in clear countertendency to the 'welfare' approach of modern psychology, calls the reader, is that of knowledge, of *bien dire* ['to say it well', Ed.]; the subject has the ethical duty to seek the reasons for his/her suffering, to discover his/her own implication in the symptom of which s/he complains, to identify the extent to which the unconscious is satisfied with his/her symptom. The subject has the responsibility to know all of this and cannot leave it to anyone else to heal him/her.

Clinical considerations: from the complaint to the question

This notation by Lacan has undoubted clinical value; what is actually observed in the treatment of depression is an evident stagnation of the subject with respect to knowledge. Most of the time, s/he seems disinterested and doesn't readily get involved in the search for the causes of his/her pain. When encouraged to talk about him/herself, s/he seems annoyed by the request, and indifferent to a possible work of reconstruction of his/her own history that does not propose the usual refrain to which s/he delegated the task of representing him/her. Often disenchanted and disillusioned about the power of speech and knowledge, the depressed person asks not to suffer anymore and to get out of the tunnel into which s/he feels s/he has entered, without bothering, most often, to try to understand how he may have ended up there. Closed in his lament, he tries to escape from the truth that concerns him, covering it with the exasperating theme of abandonment and self-criticism, in a sort of unconscious maneuver of masking the real reasons for his suffering. The clinic shows that when a work on knowledge is started – that is, when the patient begins to take an interest in the reconstruction of his story and to seek in it the reasons for his discomfort – an extraordinary effect of 'lubrication' of the psychic gear is produced; the visible and immediate result is a significant attenuation of the feeling of suffering, discouragement, and apathy, which testifies to the formidable antidepressant power of the research work of the unconscious. In Lacan, the definition of moral cowardice is, therefore, an attempt to bring depression back into the sphere of analytical psychopathology and, at the same time, to subtract it from the pressing dominion of neuroscience, which tends to reduce it to a pure neurobiological fact; depression, seen from the psychoanalytic perspective, consists of a (unconscious) self-betrayal, that is, in the development of a "not wanting to know" that takes on the symptomatic forms of the typical humoral collapse and the existential disaster connected to it.

The task of the analysis is to pull the subject out of the hole he unwillingly entered which seemed to him/her like a perfect hideout but actually posed the most threatening danger; the analytical cure must push the subject to get back in touch with his own story, to highlight the ambivalences, contradictions, shadows, or grey areas, and to find his own 'signature' even in those decisive passages in which the subject thought he had not played any role.

Mortification and transference: the analyst's position

The analyst's first task – one could say – is to re-engage the depressed patient with the use of speech: in other words, it is necessary to support the establishment of a transference on the signifier which, most of the time, appears to be reduced to the rancorous or disconsolate reiteration of the lament. The difficulty of the treatment of a depressed person lies precisely in his mistrust of the 'therapeutic' power of speech. The shock of loss freezes his speech, confining it to a repetition of contents that progressively tends to drain the analytic sessions: it is typical, in these cases, that the patient, after having briefly described the situation in which he finds himself, by the fourth or fifth session, claims to have said everything. How is it possible – one wonders – that an entire existence can be 'said' in five-six sessions? Yet such content seems to impose itself on the speech of the depressed person. What is lacking is a depth of reflection on experience, the three-dimensionality that only the supposition of an unknown knowledge introduces into the signifier chain. Life – as already mentioned above – appears discolored: a few discouraged considerations merely describe a stagnation of existence.

As Roland Chemama (2012) keenly observes, the depressive experience produces a disconnection between the subject and his own story: where there is the story (with its unprocessed traumatic load) there is no subject, and where there is the subject there is no story.

The mortification that characterizes the being in the world of the depressed person tends, in this way, to spread also in the analytical setting: mistrust, disenchantment, pessimism, skepticism. When this is not explicit closure and negativism, all this describes the transference climate that generally inaugurates the analytical path. The demand for healing is not supported by a question of knowledge: the desire to feel better does not include the desire to know the reasons for one's own discomfort but is limited to a request for indications (medical or behavioral) on how and what to 'do'. This, in all respects, can be considered the most frequent way of presenting a demand; to which the analyst has to respond by considering, on the one hand, the impossibility of satisfying it in the terms in which it is explicitly formulated, and, on the other hand, the need to accept the dimension of appeal that is manifested in it. The difficulty faced by the analyst with these kinds of demands lies in knowing how to balance, on a case-by-case basis, the share of the inevitable frustration of the demand for reassuring advice, with the acceptance of the request for help that is expressed in disguise in the lament.

This type of request for help, so strongly marked by a general libidinal mortification and a mistrust in the power of speech and transference, necessarily calls into play the analyst's posture: when he sees a person whose symptom manifests, on a phenomenal level, the penetrating power of the death drive, the psychoanalyst must be willing to reconsider his own way of being in the therapeutic relationship, to make sure that his (classical) aptitude for silence, neutrality, passive listening, abstention, and waiting does not enter into a dangerous resonance with the desertification of the psychic life of the subject whose request s/he receives.

Technique updates

The traditional psychoanalytic *setting* does not seem, in other words, to be the most suitable for the preliminary treatment of the depressed person: the possibility that the psychic 'maceration' in which the patient spends his/her existence encounters in the analyst's position what the patient would imaginarily experience as a 'torpor' and an indolence similar to his own, risks plunging the encounter itself into a stagnant atmosphere from which, defensively, the patient will keep his/her distance. In a libidinal economy marked by a withdrawal of erotic investments from the world and which, paradoxically, aims to make of loss and failure the object of the inevitable confirmation of its 'being there', the analyst has the responsibility to offer the patient (and, moreover, in the limited time of the first sessions) the opportunity to come into contact with a revitalizing relational dimension. To put it more clearly, in cases which are so refractory to psychotherapy, the task of the analyst is to ensure that the interview the patient has agreed to attend (often under pressure or to the limits of constraint of a friend) is transformed into an experience of awakening, regenerating the desire to know. This entails a revision of his posture: in line with Freud's reflections on the possibility of extending the analytical treatment to a wider number of people (originally excluded from the rigid conditions that Freud himself imposed at the beginning of an analysis), the psychoanalytic technique must be updated. In a 1904 text – *Psychotherapy* – Freud (1953) stated peremptorily that "patients who do not possess a reasonable degree of education and a fairly reliable character should be refused" (p. 263). The method – he continued – is not suitable for those who undergo treatment "only because they are forced to by the authority of relatives". To these indications, he will add, as a requirement for the acceptance of a patient, that the latter "possess a normal mental condition", which automatically excludes "psychoses, states of confusion and deeply-rooted (I might say toxic) depression". When the analyst decides to work with depressed people (a decision that questions these considerations of Freud), it is obvious that his therapeutic attitude cannot be exempted from a radical revisitation, which Freud (1956) himself – as already mentioned – had foreseen: "the application of our therapy to numbers will compel us to alloy the pure gold of analysis plentifully with the copper of direct [hypnotic] suggestion. . . . The task will then arise for us to adapt our technique to the new conditions" (p. 402). We will then have to face the task of adapting our technique to the new conditions that will be created. This is the theoretical-clinical work that the father of psychoanalysis has urged us to do: we must 'adapt' the technique to the new morbid situations that, unlike the psychoanalysts of the first generations, we are willing to accept in the studio.

Necessity and risks of the imaginary transference

I believe that, when dealing with cases of depressed people, a first (but fundamental) update of the classical analytical method consists of foreseeing (and acting) a quota of imaginarization of the transference, in order to avoid the conversation plunging into the desolation of a psychic despair that finds no echo in the person who receives it. It is necessary that, in the short time of the preliminary interviews, the depressed subject finds himself confronted with an unexpected, surprising, unforeseen situation, even irritating or stinging, but nonetheless a vitalizing situation: the analyst must come forward, introducing into the device of the interview significant elements that emphasize his presence. So, for example, in front of a patient who, during the first interview, told me about his previous experiences of psychotherapy, describing his failures as the inevitable effect of the severity of his condition (disguising, in this way, the fierce criticism directed at the helplessness of the various psychotherapists he had met), I answered, with a deliberately (and jokingly) exaggerated tone: "Oh no! You don't want to put my head in your private gallery of psychotherapists' trophies!" To the heaviness of a list of personal failures (which hid – I repeat – the most insidious of the attacks on the Other), I chose to respond with humor, with a sort of early interpretation of a coercive mechanism (of premeditated destruction of the Other), with an act of 'survival' that signaled the strength of my desire not to succumb and to fight – with him – to overcome the unconscious compulsion to repeat the worst. Or, at the end of a first session with a woman who had repeatedly declared her total disbelief in analysis and the conviction that she could never get rid of the evil that was asphyxiating her existence (bringing, moreover, highly dramatic and painful autobiographical content), I intervened exclaiming with great vehemence (also in this case, with a benevolent smile as a background to the statement) that really we could not have started better than this, that there could not have been a more promising start, and that all she had said was exactly the material that will allow us to do a great job. Or again, when, during his third session, a man with a rather important "depressive career", who was treated for decades with antidepressant drugs and had a series of psychotherapeutic failures behind him, affirmed that he had now said everything, that he no longer had 'secrets', and that in his story there were no more 'mysteries', I noted the repeated denial of the signifiers that revolve around the unsaid: to his previous therapists he'd 'confessed' everything – he told me – and then he really didn't know what to talk to me about. I clearly felt that he was dismissing me with kindness, reaffirming his candor and his innocence. I decided to grasp and underline the sense of that repeated denial and I asked him point blank to talk to me about any childhood memory that had to do with the body and his pleasure: games played, things seen, thoughts or fantasies. He would open the following session with a series of memories of which – he will tell me – he had never spoken to anyone, experiences of early encounters with an intense, invasive, perverse enjoyment of the body, which from 3 or 4 years old had influenced his sexuality and his fantasies: the unexpected intervention of the analyst had evidently produced a sudden mobilization of his unconscious material which will give the psychotherapeutic treatment the necessary impulse to get out of the state of inertia to which it seemed destined. Or again, at the end of the second session in which a young man complained more and more self-aggressively of how unworthy and guilty he felt for doing nothing but causing harm to the people who loved him (through his indolent and passive position of rejection of life), I intervened with a false solemn tone and saying: "Well, then you will say two Hail Mary and three The Our Father!", indicating, also in this case with a good-natured and amused look the game of fiction (the sinner who he asks to be "forgiven" by his father-priest) in which his speech tended, in an endless repetition, to fall in. The surprise and bewilderment of the end-session would become, in the following session, a pressing question on the motive of the intense search for punishments that has always characterized his life and, above all, a renewed desire to understand the reason for his will to expiate.

Transference neurosis

As can be seen from these quick examples, it is a question of introducing vital elements into a significant chain that is condemned to spin in circles. A sort of challenge, therefore, a bet, a gamble that intends to cause effects of dynamism in a situation that, by definition, points to an opposite condition: a strategy, however – it should be noted – that is at risk of dangerous transferal inflammation. It is necessary to take into account that if, on the one hand, such an 'energetic' posture of the analyst – as already mentioned – responds to the need not to let the therapeutic relationship slide into a cadaverization of the setting, on the other hand, it exposes the relationship itself to the danger of its excessive incandescence on an affective-libidinal level. If, on the one hand, the analyst must take in consideration the difficulty of his patient to "hook up" to the analytical device (as it is not supported by a question that guarantees its development), on the other hand, he must be aware that his departure from the classic neutral and wait-and-see position is likely to trigger a possible intensification of transferential feelings. Against the background of these technical reflections, however, we are guided by the extraordinary observations that Freud (1914) presents in his writing of *Remembering, Repeating and Working-Through*. In this important text, which composes one of the three parts of the essay "Further recommendations on the technique of psychoanalysis", the father of psychoanalysis supports the idea that transference should be seen as a "playground" in which "it is expected to display to us everything in the way of pathogenic instincts that is hidden in the patient's mind" (p. 153). Freud, in this way, theorizes an "almost complete freedom" of expansion of the transference, through which to reactivating the dynamism of the libido which, now directing itself on the figure of the analyst (its new target), will cease to attribute to the symptom the special value of unconscious enjoyment. It is so, then – says Freud – that the transference is to be considered as "an intermediate region between illness and real life": the libido detaches itself from the symptom and gives life to what Freud calls "transference neurosis", from which the patient "can be cured by the therapeutic work". Otherwise said, transference becomes the most powerful therapeutic tool available to the analyst to the extent that it is configured as an "artificial illness which is at every point accessible to our intervention". To return to the question previously raised, the inflammation of the transference promoted by the analyst – in order to counteract the deadly power of the morbid condition – becomes an instrument to make a possible detachment of the libido from the pathogenic mechanism (thus affecting the unconscious enjoyment ensured by the subject's fixation to the loss) and release it into circulation. This happens through attracting the libido onto his own person. The next step (to be carried out as soon as possible) will be to 'attack' this 'artificial disease' that the transference itself has become, to symbolize its fundamental elements, to elaborate its repetitive nodes, and to order its logical scansion. This special dynamic of the cure, of which Freud describes the importance of the treatment of neurosis as a whole, appears to be particularly effective in working with so-called depressed patients, in whom – as Freud himself specifies in *Mourning and Melancholy* – the libidinal withdrawal within the ego results in little interest in the other. This withdrawal, of which, moreover, the symptom of hypochondria represents one of the most evident and frequent signs (in a kind of narcissistic retreat on the body that takes the form of a constant concern about his state of 'health'), must be taken into account by the analyst: he, in fact, cannot count on the patient's spontaneous investment in the relationship, taken, as the clinic shows, by the need to stem the internal libidinal hemorrhage – as Freud defines it – produced by the event of the loss. The analyst must, therefore, 'provoke' the relationship, 'impose' it as a libidinal object alternative to the stupefied contemplation of the loss. Through doing this, he attacks his patient's economy of enjoyment, in an attempt to scratch his autarchic trait and cause its desirable failure. In other words, in the treatment of depression, the analyst must make himself a 'symptom' for the patient, that is, take the place of the inert and mortiferous one (symptom) that blocks his/her patient's existence: the activation of a transference in which the analyst offers himself as the subject of an unexpected question, not at all numbed by the hypnotic strategy of the mortifying depressive reiteration and alive in his being desiring, constitutes in my opinion a risk which, if well calculated, cannot but be run. Once the symptomatic libidinal balance has been shaken and the libidinal economy put back into motion (having until then been in total stagnation), it will be the analyst's ethical responsibility to free him/herself from the position the imaginary transference has placed on him/her. In fact, the psychoanalyst must know that s/he lends him/herself to being the object that reactivates a drive dynamic without ever being able to believe that s/he is the true recipient. His/her function is simply to rekindle in the patient an 'erotic' interest in the world, from which, however, s/he must, as soon as possible, vanish: his/her task is limited to triggering a process of reactivation of desire which, however, must be oriented as soon as possible on new 'object investments'. It is here, then, that the transference is configured as the most powerful antidepressant available to the psychoanalyst, whose initial willingness to 'impose' him/herself as an enigmatic and agalmatic transferal object must find the right counterweight in the subsequent orientation of the transference itself towards knowledge, towards *bien dire*, towards putting one's own thoughts in order.

Depressive logic and contemporary social discourse

It is clear, however, that such a posture from the analyst does not automatically guarantee the activation of a course of treatment: the most severe forms of neurotic depression can show a resistance to treatment that, at times, makes the helplessness of the analyst himself visible in the face of the overwhelming power of unconscious enjoyment. Moreover, it is necessary to take into account that the individual psychic condition is evidently amplified (and, in part, justified) by the contemporary socio-cultural context that, as is known, scotomizes the theme of loss: the capitalist discourse, in fact, excludes the dimension of lack, triggering and reinforcing a process that, in the endless circularity of the production and consumption of objects, promises the restoration (illusory but not for this reason not sought after) of the lost fullness. In some ways, the depressive dynamic reveals one of the constitutive traits of the social discourse in which it unfolds. There is a surprising homology between the rejection of castration that grounds the depressive phenomenon and which characterizes neoliberal societies. In other words, what is found at the collective level seems to take shape at the individual level: the impossible symbolic elaboration of what has to do with lack, with failure, and with death. The essentially tanatophobic context of contemporary society prevents the taking into account and the subjectivation of the experience of finitude: this, symbolically rejected, returns in the symptomatic forms that depressive phenomenology show well. In such a conjuncture, therefore, the occasional experience of loss not only – as already seen – reactivates ancient unprocessed nuclei encysted in the psychism of the subject, but also triggers an individual process that seems to translate, on a subjective level, what happens on a collective level: rejection of the loss and its transformation into a new object to identify with. In this sense, the negation of castration unites the psychic functioning of the individual with that of his/her social group, in the non-random coincidence of a refined avoidance of the hard work of mourning. This is probably why depressive affection seems to be so widespread and expanding in age groups (I am thinking in particular of puberty) that were spared until a few decades ago (from this perspective the rampant phenomenon of social withdrawal of adolescents can be understood).

Final considerations

The depressive phenomenon, in conclusion, obliges the analyst to deal with two issues that are only apparently distinct: one, more clinical, which has to do with the psychoanalytic treatment in general, and the other, theoretical, which addresses and examines the close correlation of the symptom with social discourse. From their delicate (and inevitable) interweaving, derive both the necessary reconsideration of the setting and how the analyst is required to stay within it, and the constant commitment of psychoanalysis to identify the psychopathological effects caused by the new forms of 'discontent' of civilization. The unconscious enjoyment of the depressed subject can, then, be considered as the implication (in the shadows) of the maniacal enjoyment of neoliberal capitalism: both devoted to the disavowal of the loss, both pushing the subject/ citizen to avoid the painful work of mourning, one making the absence of the object a new (inevitable) form of presence, the other relentlessly replacing the object, in the illusory promise of a definitive fullness. When the analyst agrees to work with a neurotic subject suffering from depression, he is called to update his technique, adapting it to the crypto-consumerist logic that, inevitably, will guide the patient's conduct during treatment: he must, therefore, revitalize the setting without transforming it into a comfortable supermarket whose products (advice, indications, prescriptions, drugs, explanations, etc.) are stubbornly requested by the patient to elude the difficult processing of the loss. His intervention must be able to frustrate such a request, but at the same time should indicate the additional meaning contained in his demand. The analyst, in fact, aims to give depth to a speech flattened on the 'here and now', to release it from the immanence of the chronicle and the lament, to project it into a significant transcendence that gives depth to the words, and to emancipate it from its reduction to simple causal determinisms.

Notes

1 In this sense, one could think of depression as a perturbation of the subjective phantasm, which Lacan, as we know, writes with the matheme $\$\diamond a$. The divided subject, the crossed subject, the subject lacking-of-being (wanting-to-be) would no longer find support in the object a, which, because of the 'mournful' event, would have lost the status of cause of the desire of the Other and, consequently, its logical consistency: this is the thesis of Jacques-Alain Miller (2001) that in "Ironic clinic" writes: "And why not oppose to it, as the formula of depression, the a-logical consistency of the object, an object which is then no longer cause of the Other's desire?" In depression, the object a – "foundation of the illusory unity of the subject", adds Miller himself – is no longer the cause object (that is absent at the level of reality) but coincides with the object that has disappeared, degraded, that is, to the object of reality whose loss is fixed as unforgettable.
2 In this regard, I find Marie-Claude Lambotte's observations on the gaze of the Other of the melancholic subject insurmountable. See Lambotte, M. C. (1999), *Il discorso melanconico: dalla fenomenologia alla metapsicologia*. Borla: Rome. In particular from page 209 to page 395. Original book in French: Lambotte, M. C. (1999) *Le Discours mélancolique: de la phénoménologie à la métapsychologie*. Anthropos: Paris.
3 The story of Medea is the most clarifying representation of it.

References

Barthes, R. (2010). *Mourning diary*. New York: Hill and Wang.

Chemama, R. (2012). *La depression, la grande névrose contemporaine*. Toulouse: Erès.

Freud, S. (1914). Remembering, repeating and working through. In J. Strachey (ed. and trans.), *The standard edition of the complete psychological works of Sigmund Freud* (Vol. 12, pp. 147–156). London: Hogarth Press.

Freud, S. (1953). On psychotherapy. In J. Strachey (ed. and trans.), *The standard edition of the complete psychological works of Sigmund Freud* (Vol. 7, pp. 257–268). London: Hogarth. (Original work published in 1904).

Freud, S. (1956). *Turnings in the ways of psychoanalytic therapy. Collected papers* (Vol. II). London: Hogarth Press.

Kusnierek, M. (1989). A proposito di Amleto. *La Psicoanalisi, 5*. Astrolabio.

Lacan, J. (1990). *Television: A challenge to the psychoanalytic establishment*. New York and London: Norton.

Lacan, J. (2012). *The seminar of Jacques Lacan, Book X (Anxiety 1962–1963)*. Trans. Cormac Gallagher, from unedited French manuscript. Unpublished. Retrieved from www. lacaninireland.com

Miller, J. A. (2001). Ironic clinic. *Psychoanalytic Notebooks of the London Circle (NLS), 7*, 9–24.

Chapter 12

Addictions

Toxicomania and others

Jean-Louis Chassaing

Situating the question

It would be more chronologically appropriate to start with the chapter on toxicomania [rather than that on limit states or borderline, Ed.] which is complex because it is multidimensional and of multiple interests. It is an interdisciplinary field. Although recent, it is historically first in nosology. The French term addiction arrived later, at the start of the 1970s. It is more general, comprising different behaviors, which is why we will start with it.

Addiction

A reminder of historical context is indispensable if we want to understand the importance of the word in the language of origin, Latin, and its use in the clinic today. The English *drug addiction* has helped us understand this term, *addiction*. It was a synonym for toxicomania in France. At the beginning of the 1970s, a French-British psychoanalyst, Joyce McDougall (1990) brought the word addiction to the French language, finding its origin in the Roman Law. It means "enforcement by committal for anyone who has not paid their debt". Enforcement by committal is a juridical term which means imprisonment, slavery. A man who is a debtor must pay with money or goods. If they do not pay, a specific judge with a powerful hierarchical position, the praetor,[1] sentences them to enslavement by their creditor. This means that they are in debt and they pay with their body, physically, instead of paying with money or goods, objects. We can transpose this by saying that a person is in debt, symbolically, in relation to language and its history, in relation to the surrounding language and to the familial, social history which preceded them. In Freud and Lacan's psychoanalytical theory, there is a loss of enjoyment in regulating this debt towards language and history, loss of which the part that is given is a particular object, the object *a*.

In the case of addictions, we would have to deal with an insatiable enjoyment, "endless" if not for death. Overdoses in toxicomania are an example of this.

DOI: 10.4324/9780429432064-16

The philosopher Michel Serres (2009) has consecrated a powerful and pertinent chapter about this term "addiction". A Latin term. *Said to*: it's the present theory of addictions: said slave to so-and-so, it's in the register of the Gift: gave in slavery, but also in the reflexive: giving oneself to. *Ad/dictus*: addiction = addition of *say* and *gift*. "Being said" or "giving oneself" in slavery, without protest; being obliged to reimburse one's debt with one's body if not with one's goods. We could say "without any other metaphor" than one's real body.

Michel Serres clarifies the context, that of the Roman Law, as well as the signification in Latin. Contrary to the English word, *addicted*, the Latin word, *addicere* unveils the said. Quoting him, "as if the addicted person could be given to something other than language". And further, "Can an experience of the given be reduced to its utterance? With this question comes that of drugs – lingering around the body, around language, around the group and the world, lurking in the very knots that bind them together" (Serres, 2009, p. 96).[2] Even though we have retained the phrase 'enforcement by committal' [*la contrainte par corps*], we have forgotten about the unpaid debt and the speech. It's *a tripod*. The speech as we have evoked it, is that of a high placed magistrate from the antique Rome, the praetor. *Said to*. His spoken word does not tolerate any doubt being cast on what he is saying. "The praetor approves and confirms the will of each party . . . the essential thing is to enter into language and assess its weight, to give it its full force. Which proves that before the praetor we were outside of language . . . the law cannot be spoken before his arrival. He gives everyone the right to speak. First, originary, he initiates the time of law" (Serres, 2009, p. 97). The force of law, the force of language. The praetor owns the *Imperium*, the supreme power; he is in liaison with the divine. Michel Serres evokes his power to consult the auspices, that of reading the signs indicating the Gods' will. This accomplished, further down in the history, in the world from before our world to "the addiction to birds", to the reading in the sky of that which makes signs. Nothing can be instituted *nisi aves addixissent* "without the addiction of birds" (Livy). Question: who is this Imperium nowadays? Who is the praetor of law today? Who imposes this enforcement by committal? What is the "choice" of this payment? The drives? A social discourse?

It's in the clinical practice that the French-English psychoanalyst Joyce McDougall introduced the word, in 1972. She limited it to 'psychosomatic' clinical practice, with sexuality as a non-deviant, non-perverse drug. Her friendly frequenting of a certain Robert Stoller, a psychiatrist who studied deviant sexualities, is certainly not for nothing. We owe to the latter the notion of 'gender'. Not only did McDougall introduce the word, she offered a Freudian clinical approach, speaking for example of 'action-symptoms'.[3] She evoked bulimia and toxicomania. This enlargement of toxicomania to other clinical fields under the "label" of addiction is not new. And today, talk of 'drug addiction without drugs' or 'behavioral addictions' is psychoanalytically unfounded. This is merely naming things on the basis of observed behaviours, which is hardly adequate to psychical reality and subjective history.

Freudians and post-Freudians

Freud's contemporaries and the post-Freudians were very much alive to addictions, even though the word here evoked did not yet exist in French. Thus, Otto Fenichel (1897–1946) was the first to discuss "toxicomania without drugs", in 1945. That covered classifying research but also a base for the current clinics, different from the usual psychoneuroses of defense. Karl Abraham, in turn, wrote on alcoholism (in 1908). He mentions a similarity with the perverse acts that appear secondarily to alcohol excesses. He also notes the ability to "obtaining pleasure without trouble" (Abraham, 1927, p. 88). Sandor Ferenczi (1911) describes a case of alcoholic paranoia with delusions of jealousy. He believed that alcohol destroyed sublimation, although he was not the first to say so. Otto Juliusburger (*German Psychoanalytic Association*,1912), and Leon Pierce Clark (USA, 1919) underline the homosexual and sadistic tendencies of these behaviors (with alcohol), as well as the permanency of depression. Later, anticipating the discovery of 'burnout', the Swiss psychiatrist Paul Kielholz compared alcoholism to a narcissistic neurosis linked to manic-depressive psychosis. He also mentioned the frequency of perversions in alcoholics. Sandor Rado was a great inventor of concepts in this domain. We will return to him for the clinical part.

Other Freudians have worked on the question of "addictions". Ernst Simmel, neurologist and a German-American psychoanalyst, and much later Herbert Rosenfeld thought there was a parallel between addictions/toxicomania and the psychosomatic illness, obsessional neurosis, equally with the manic-depressive states and perversions. We found that the domain is large. But it is worthwhile to revisit historical conceptions, seeing that this clinical approach has been subsequently abandoned and rejected. The other major analysts are Hans Sachs and Edward Glover; they helped to decipher this clinic.

Freud (1897) also, in his letter from 22 December 1897 to Fliess wrote: "The insight has dawned on me that masturbation is the one major habit, the 'primary addiction', and it is only as a substitute and replacement for it that the other addictions – to alcohol, morphine, tobacco, and the like – come into existence" (p. 287). The solitary pleasure, without the other's body but with a consumption object, the object *on hand*. It is all an important work to read Freud on this subject (Chassaing, 1998), but this other phrase of Freud, in a letter of 11 January 1897, reveals again the interest. He speaks about a perverted man, dipsomaniac (with alcohol): "His dipsomania arises through the intensification or, better, substitution of the one impulse for the associated sexual one. (The same is probably true of the gambling mania of old F.)" (Freud, 1897, p. 222).

Nowadays the term addiction is used for everything. It has replaced the word *dépendance*, and hardly brings us any more precision about the role of the body, even though this means forgetting the strength of obsession – tyrannical, persecutory obsession, in the words of Charles Melman. Let's leave the history and the language to each one's appreciation; to each his or her own addictions.

Toxicomania

The term 'toxicomania' is more modern and does not exist in every language. It was first used in the medicine and psychiatry of 19th century France (Chassaing, 1998, 2011). According to the great clinician Emmanuel Régis (1914), student of Benjamin Ball (1855–1918), it was Charcot's secretary, Charles Féré who coined the *generic name* 'toxicomania' in order to group together different types of dipsomania (alcoholism). Generic is opposed to specific, it is in the public domain. *Toxicon* is the poison and therefore no longer a product in the pharmacopoeia (Petit, 2019). Toxicon-mania is an addiction to a toxic substance or poison! But it is also possible to talk on a wider scale about a passion for *Pharmakon*. The words *Pharmacy* and *Pharmakon* are linked through etymology to a furnace, a fire, a crater, the action of mixing things for a long time in a mortar before transforming them, producing new substances that are more or less unexpected.

Faced with an increase in these types of behaviors (which have nothing to do with analgesic prescriptions that happened during war-time in the years 1905–1913; see Chassaing, 2011) and alongside numerous studies on psychiatric hospitals, psychiatrics, doctors in France and even in Europe, in a moralistic world of medicine that will be short-lived, speak about toxicomania and drug addiction like it's a plague on society. Are they ill or delinquents? Ill and delinquents? Or just delinquents? The debate is either there or avoided.

Everyday clinical realities

Addictions cover a range of behaviors. Why? These behaviors are not a symptom in the usual sense of the term as the latter is linked to language. Indeed, if we look at this from a classical angle, a symptom is linked to the repression of certain signifiers from its history. Some repressed elements emerge under the form of a symptom. In these addictive behaviors, we have more to do with the immediacy, the non-mediated, with enactments. Behavior, the body, acts committed, or even passages to the acts, are the most common. Language is impoverished here and does not seem like a favorable medium in this relationship. It's more direct; taking the object that is within easy reach and having it to hand. What are these behaviours? Of course, toxicomania, eating disorders (anorexia, bulimia), pathological gambling, which we can associate with certain acts of violence, often impulsive.

Addictions in Joyce McDougall

As we have already said, this psychoanalyst allowed the term to resurge in Roman law: *ad-dict*. She was referring to two clinical situations: psychosomatic medicine and non-perverse sexual addictions. It is in the preface and the chapter titled

"Masturbation and the Hermaphroditic Ideal" that the author takes a look at Freud's letter to Fliess from 22 December 1897. She brings up "the narcissistic economy as such, and its eventual permutations in those who struggle ceaselessly to preserve their feeling of subjective identity" (McDougall, 1990, p. 12). She talks about addictive escape in this state of slavery, bringing up here the difficulties of this creative physical act, that is to say "maintaining the object, in its absence, within oneself" (McDougall, 1991, p. 30. My translation). This is what needs to be discussed if we want to correctly ascertain the tyrannical permanence, not only of the object itself but of its effects! Without a doubt, there is a problem, pathos, with this permanence, in this "harassing" upkeep. It has a crude state which is psychologically non-elaborated. A phrase from Freud explains it very well. This phrase is found in the minutes of the Vienna Psychoanalytic Society (scientific meeting of 20 January 1909): "Certainly, there are quite extensive interactions between the somatic and the psychic. But here a new problem arises: is there a theory that would permit us to conceive of a toxic stimulus being transformed into a psychic one, and, similarly, of psychic activity detoxifying the toxic stimulus? Whoever could show us that all toxic substances become poisonous if the psyche does not digest them would render us a great service" (Numberg and Federn, 1967, p. 115). Here we detect the impact a psychoanalyst and psychoanalysis can have on this "detox": linguistics processing. Nonetheless, Freud is prudent and analytical as he adds nuance to the fact that treatment is only concerned with a physical detox!

Joyce McDougall insists on narcissism (here we find clinical questions from borderline states, especially among North American authors like Kohut and Kernberg) in conjunction with anxiety and difficulty with psychological and linguistic processing among these subjects. We could say these modern subjects. Finally, this realistic note from McDougall (1990) is important: "When it falls to the soma alone to find its (inevitably) biological response to psychic conflict and mental pain, its inventions by definition are uncountable in words. Here the analyst finds himself listening to something ineffable, an unspeakable nothingness, rather like a metaphor of death" (p. 17). It is necessary to listen to this silence, these absences and difficulties, without "stifling" the relationship with haste as they say, or with interpretations that are made too quickly or harmfully for the person in question. These types of patients pose to us questions of commitment, keeping to their word and attending their sessions and appointments. In a text for which the publication dates back to 1987, Jean Clavreul (1987) remarks that "in this regard, the psychoanalyst has a lot to learn from these men and women from whom he must first ask himself if he can actually expect a word" [My translation]. He writes that one must put up with the failures of the session, the "forgetfulness", the time that passes without seeing, the absence therefore, and then the unexpected returns, and a relationship to temporality that does not appear in neurotic cures. "Psychoanalysts pay little attention to problematic nature of commitment" he says. This is less true – clinical practices considered – today as in 1987(!): "With alcoholics and addicts this difficulty is constant. This is one of the reasons why it is in a psychoanalyst's best interests to be more interested in these types of patients, as long as they understand that it is just as impossible to impose upon them the necessity to come to their sessions with a functioning regularity as it is to ask them to commit to stopping drinking or taking drugs". This game of presence and absence can take various forms. Clavreul insists that we have difficulty "accepting that it is so hard for the other to keep to his commitments, or more precisely that he plays with us like a baby plays with his bobbin". In our opinion this does not necessarily indicate a disregard of the transference, sometimes the contrary, but more often, this indicates a certain anarchy in these peoples' lives, a tendency to give in to impulse and other unexpected events.

For Clavreul, there is something to learn from these patients; "there is a chance to question our least-disputed certitudes" and for psychoanalysts this clinical practice constitutes one of the most decisive stages in their learning.

Freudians and post-Freudians[4]

We will only take a few examples, added to those from the presentation, for which clinical interest is always present. Sandor Rado (1890–1972) talks of "alimentary orgasms" (Rado, 1926, p. 408) and "oral erotism" (p. 407) even when drugs are taken through places other than the mouth. This is a question of oral fixation which has a lot to do with incorporation. According to Rado, a comparison between toxicomania and anorexia and bulimia is obvious. In "The psychic effects of intoxicants" (1926), he wrote: "The whole mental personality, together with the drug, then represents an autoerotic pleasure-apparatus" (p. 405). According to the author, drugs have two important functions: they act as a shield against outside arousal, and they are necessary when a large arousal exceeds the pain threshold. We can ask the question of interior arousal: are drugs a barricade to enjoyment? Or as Freud says in his letter to Fliess: Would the effect of the drug replace this enjoyment, the excitement, in an illusion of mastery? Drugs bring about sensations of tension at the same time as reducing existing tensions. The author speaks of 'pharmacothymia' This is a "*pharmacological* euphoria"[5] relating to narcissistic discord that provokes a break-up of the natural organization of the ego through artificial means. It also evokes masochism and perversion. Drugs cut off sensations. The author insists on these artificial aspects. He talks of 'meta-eroticism': intoxication becomes a sexual goal. After the alleviation of suffering through drugs there is a "pleasure beyond" that can also identify with mania.

Hans Sachs (1881–1947) describes a case of perverse reaction and exhibitionism in a neurotic person following a trauma during their first sexual relationship. This case has been mentioned by Lacan. The influence of drugs is mentioned. Hans Sachs considers drug abuse an intermediate link between neurosis and perversion (an artificial perversion in a way).

Edward Glover (1932) insists on drugs having a function of cutting things off (see also S. Rado, and further, Lacan). "By cutting off the body (i.e. sensory perceptions) the drug appears to have obliterated instinctual tension or frustration. . . . By cutting off the external world (see Freud), the drug can obliterate not only actual instinctual stimuli from without but stimuli due to projected instinct" (p. 326).

Later on, Simmel and Rosenfield claimed that a drug addict is incapable of using their psychic apparatus to cope with stimuli; the body therefore replaces them and reacts in an auto-erotic way to the tension and stimuli. Drugs take the place of all objects.

And finally, a female analyst, Thérèse Benedek was of the first people to describe a case of alcohol addiction as a way of fighting "polyphagia" (or bulimia).

Lots of these authors, even up until today, recognize easy spirals into such passages to the act or acting out.

Freud and the Cocaine Episode

In a work that speaks about psychoanalysis and toxicomanias, a brief note on "The Cocaine Episode", as Ernest Jones calls it in his biography of Freud, should not escape us (nor should the Freud's addiction to cigars right up to the end of his life). The Cocaine Episode is shorter (Chassaing, 2006)! After reading some medical articles on indigenous people from the Andes and others on German soldiers, Freud studied the active outcome of this extraordinary plant, the outcome of the coca leaf. He carried out work, offering coca to people including himself and his fiancée Martha. He puts forward a very sharp and concise clinical analysis that is devoid of any moralism of the effects of this alkaloid in this "Episode" which lasts from 1884 to July 1887. Later he would put forward his own version of this episode in "My life and psychoanalysis" in 1935.

His work wants to appear scientific: it is ahead of its time but he was not the only one to produce such work. However, unlike his few colleagues, his interest does not lie so heavily in the local anesthetic that would be discovered (*xylocaine*) as in the general effect of cocaine. But the lack of consistency of its effects, which differ according to the person, the place, and the moment, did not allow him to pull from this a universal scientific theory. He uses formulas and letters to attempt a method backed up by figures but one that also considers clinical aspects of the subject. There is too much variation, which he discovers after with the hysterics at the *Salpêtrière* by Charcot. For a more detailed history, refer to our work from 2006 and Freud's letters to his fiancée Martha (Clavreul, 1987; Freud, 2005).

Freud and 'Civilisation and Its Discontents'

This is an important text, edited in 1929. In it, Freud cites three sources of suffering for man: our body, the outside world, and relationships with other human beings. He also describes the three ways in which man can alleviate this suffering, "the sedatives", "auxiliary construction" (*Hilfskonstruktionen*): first of all, strong diversions, then replacement satisfactions, and finally narcotics. He considers the latter as "the most brutal and the most effective of methods intended to exert such an influence on the body." We can also read in this a particularly fine clinical analysis.

Lacan and his definition of drug

We will now look at a conference held by Lacan at the Salpêtrière in 1966 in which he puts forward an original viewpoint and psychoanalysis on the invasion of drugs on our environment. Here in the *Lettres de l'Ecole freudienne de Paris*, in a discussion with a colleague about Little Hans, Lacan talks about "enjoyment of castration". Castration* is considered making a cut in the organ to pass to the phallic signifier and language, and no longer to the natural. He says that castration relieves one of anxiety. Little Hans' realization that his "widdler" (*Wiwimacher*) does not exist on his sister and can therefore be absent is the source of his anxiety. The transition to language and mobility of the phallus as a signifier of the lack relieves him of his anxiety; anxiety "of being married to his sexual organ, his penis" says Lacan. Here he suddenly gives this definition: "*everything which permits the escape from the marriage is clearly welcome, hence the success of drugs, for example; that is no other definition for drugs than this one: it is what permits to break the marriage to the widdler*". In this way, castration, a symbolic operation, helps the transition from the penis to the phallus. In Hans' failure in castration, phobia somehow comes to play this role, to escape the marriage, except for the symptom. And drug use comes to replace this, castration – a cut therefore, but in the real of the effects of the object – drifting on another path which will certainly not spare the subject from another sort of anxiety, that of obligation: that of the real permanence of this object. For more on this read Charles Melman's excellent study, "Les sexolytiques" (Melman, 1998).

Reflections and actions to be taken

Distinctions

It is first important to distinguish between different addictions. We do not distinguish between addictions with and without drugs. This means focusing on the materialized object, even though according to psychoanalytic theory, the object is the psychic object. In gambling is there no object? In eating disorders there is no object? Is the object purely a drug product? What is an object? Followers of behavioural science/cognitivism have a simple and pragmatic definition for this, in a negative sense of the term; it is a tangible object to hand, "concrete" as they say according to a utilitarian viewpoint! But this same object can be used or not used in different ways according to the person, their history, or the moment. Claude Olievenstein, one of the pioneers covering toxicomania in France, defines toxicomania as "an encounter between a personality, a product and a moment". Even if it is not specific, this approach quite rightly complexifies the difficult clinical problem!

The object is psychic; it is not necessarily the tangible product itself but rather its effects. They are variable. Addiction to gambling (which type?) or to heroin does not have the same causes or the same consequences. A hashish smoker is not always dependent on hashish. Being addicted to heroin does not mean being addicted to hashish.

That being said, it is clear that there is a necessity to keep account of the real chemical effects of different products. Dangers can differ from product to product but also their effects can change according to the person. In the same way, the family, environmental, and cultural contexts are different and must be taken into consideration.

Clinical practices should not dwell on the question of licit versus illicit, but many relatives either do not take the law into account or are obsessed with it and with cracking down. Clinical practices include those of the body and spoken word. But the law and its rules are an outside reality that is important for everyone.

Finally, biological, biochemical, and physiological research are fascinating. However, it is the expansion of synthetic products, analgesics, and consciousness modifiers which have allowed drug addiction to develop. Or rather, these are the instruments that have been diverted from their original function. *Pharmakon*, these products relieve suffering and create addiction, both at the same time. One AND the other.

The diversity of clinical situations

As we have said, the term *toxicomania* not only covers a number of varied situations but its unit reference is disputed. What is an addict? Here we try to give an overview of some practical situations which present themselves, without being exhaustive.

Mr. X 1 presents himself/he is addressed to us/he is in the emergency room. A *heroin addict*, he is in an obvious state of despair.

What are the emergencies?

Usually everything is presented – by the subject, his entourage, or his health workers – as an emergency. The emergency, the "everything straight away", this immediacy, paints the picture of addiction. In actual fact, these emergencies are for the therapist:

Medical: an overdose, comas, cardiac decompensation, the consequences of superinfection and AIDS.

Psychological, or even psychiatric: states of delirium and their consequences.

Legal: It is often useful, especially for families, to remember that these types of behaviours are subject to the law.

Social: It may be necessary for the patients to have someone with them following a loss of identity papers of when dealing with undernourishment, which is often made worse by infections, etc.

Individual history: The account of products taken (associated drugs, legal and illicit); personal (surgical, psychiatric, and family medical history); social insertion; contact and the environment. Often the product taken and its emergency mask the possibility to undertake a true examination. These are illnesses to examine, like in every ill person!

A deep examination: Medical, psychiatric. It is necessary to take one's time with this clinical, or even paraclinical examination, not to let it pass by as an "emergency" as if it does not exist and not to give in to this common "symptom".

Mr. X 2 is *taking drugs* (according to himself, his family, and others). The term "taking drugs" is commonly used by the family; it requires a precise examination. Which "drugs"? What relationship does he have with the product? What does he (or his relations if he is a minor) want from it? With a fascination for the product, "taking drugs" prevails over reason: But what does this mean exactly?

After a medical or psychiatric consultation or an interview, Mr. X 3 tells us that he "takes products". Which ones? This story needs to be explained. Does he know the risks: legal, medical-psychiatric . . . ? This being said, what sort of place does this "taking products" occupy? Does he feel dependent on them or is it occasional? A psychological or even medical examination is necessary anyway.

Mr. X 4, aged 40, has been *sent by social, or even juridical or police services*. He was "caught" with heroin or cocaine that after years of addiction followed by abstinence, he does not "consume" but takes only on New Year's Eve and on his birthday (it is a rare case but can exist). He would say that he is not addicted. A psychological examination and a discussion are needed. If there is no identified pathology, this occasional drug taking is his responsibility and "the door is open" for him to come back. There is no need to force support upon him outside of legal order.

Mr. or Mrs. X 5 comes to see us *"to give up (drugs)"*. We offer some meetings, as regularly as possible (knowing that this will be difficult and that the therapist will have to adapt to the intensity of the relationship, as well as to difficulties opening up and absence at sessions). It is necessary to "deal with this" and try to maintain the relationship, while also claiming responsibility, depending on the mental state and personality of the patient.

Who is talking? Who is acting?

We have already said that toxicomanias and addictions can refer to different disciplines. The therapist must not think and act *like* the policeman and vice versa. Yet, these types of "mix-ups" are not rare. Economists have the greatest influence today; they look for solutions to drug trafficking, working on the question of supply and demand, and their propositions, legalizations or controlled distributions, clash with politicians who find themselves unable to apply unpopular initiatives. This depends on the country, its history, the products, and agronomical as well as intellectual and artistic culture.

Materialistic organicists only think about the product. It is clear that we must medicalize the handling of addiction, but we also need to recognize that the definition of *toxicomania* is very wide – sometimes too wide. In any case, it is the most seriously ill who need the most care. Some people are labelled addicts while only being occasional users. The action to be taken should be reviewed case by case, and it is clearly important to take into consideration, or even give psychotherapy to the families of the addict. So, it is important not to work alone. As with anorexia patients, help from a general practitioner and an internal medicine doctor or even an endocrinologist is often necessary, just as the relationship with social services sometimes turns out to be required. In the same way as for serious addictions, controlled distribution of a product such as Subutex or methadone bring about a life-saving sedation, while maintaining a significant dependence. However, this was an undeniably welcome progress. Therefore, it is a whole team who intervene. Each one has their own role to play in these difficult and complex pathologies.

Individual and social

If taking drugs is to always exist, that is to say that plants have put themselves ahead of man and the industrialization of products has brought about a surplus of possibilities. Chemists shift some groups – OH or others in a parent drug, and a new drug is created which for some time escapes the international classification of drugs.

But the accessibility to all sorts of enjoyment today is another factor in the development of addiction and the immediate *dominance*, the seizure at will and in the presence of tools of pleasure and enjoyment are gradually accompanying and replacing linguistic processes. One does not have to look far to see the devaluation of "speaking well", the loss of vocabulary and the little interest given to syntax rules.

In his conference in the Salpêtrière in February of 1967, Lacan questioned the position of a doctor in the world, and the displacement that the latter had undergone and would undergo in terms of his status. He described the influence of techno-science and the filling or our space with voices and looks, curious prolongations of the body that have nothing to do with the dimension of enjoyment of the body. And he also spoke of, in addition to the ubiquitous voices and looks, the overflow of psychotropic drugs in our world. All techno-scientific productions, made for the progress of man, and *pharmakon*, heal and poison at the same time, are carriers of death. Addictions, new subjects to think about, set the tone for clinical practices that will be in the future, but are already here.

Notes

1 In Latin *prætor* "chief", from *præire* "precede, walk ahead".
2 Binding, or lashing, begins by securing the rope to one of the pieces of wood, usually with a capstan knot or a wood knot. In French, the term "brêlage" (binding, lashing) refers to two different things:

   - a technique of assembling pieces of wood using ropes;
   - straps used to carry a firearm.
        The French term "brêlage" and the verb "brêler" mean "to assemble with ropes". They are also used to express the action of strapping boats (canoes or kayaks) on a trailer hitched for this purpose.

   There are several types of lashing:

   - square lashing, which allows fixing poles at right angles (it is also called "right lashing");
   - diagonal lashing, which allows fixing non-perpendicular sticks;
   - shear lashing, which is used to juxtapose two timbers in parallel.

3 Linked to a "deficit of psychic structure and a lack of symbolisation", (McDougall, 1974, p. 162).
4 All the references can be found in: Chassaing (1998).
5 Euphoria is enjoyment, an almost mystical elevation.

References

Abraham, K. (1927). *The psychological relations between sexuality and alcholism. Selected papers* (pp. 80–89). London: Hogarth Press.

Chassaing, J. L. (Ed.). (1998). *Écrits psychanalytiques classiques sur les toxicomanies.* Paris: Éditions de l'Association Freudienne Internationale.

Chassaing, J. L. (2006). Freud et la coca: un "allotrion" bien plus qu'une erreur de jeunesse. Pour une analyse détaillée de cet "épisode". In J. L. Chassaing, J. Béraud, O. Bézy, & P. Claveirole (eds.), *Cocaïne, aphasies: études des textes préanalytiques de Freud* (pp. 13–43). Ramonville Saint-Agne: Erès.

Chassaing, J. L. (2011). *Drogue et langage. Ducorps et de lalangue*, Ramonville Saint-Agne: Erès.

Clavreul, J. (1987). Alcoolisme et toxicomanies: d'une parole aux limites. In J. Clavreul (ed.), *Le désir et la loi: approches psychanalytiques* (pp. 231–292). Paris: Denoël.

Ferenczi, S. (1911). Le rôle de l'homosexualité dans la pathogénie de la paranoïa. *Œuvres Complètes, 1,* 172–188. Paris: Payot, 1968.

Freud, S. (1897). Letter from Freud to Fliess, December 22, 1897. *The complete letters of Sigmund Freud to Wilhelm Fliess, 1887–1904.* Cambridge: Harvard University Press.

Freud, S. (2005). Un peu de cocaïne pour me délier la langue . . . [Textes de Freud sur la cocaïne]. Trans. The German by Marielle Roffi. Foreword by Charles Melman. Preface by Jean-Louis Chassaing. Paris: Max Milo.

Glover, E. (1932). On the Aetiology of drug-addiction. *International Journal of Psycho-Analysis, 13,* 298–328.

McDougall, J. (1974). Le psyché-soma et la psychanalyse. *Nouvelle Revue de psychanalyse, 10,* 132.

McDougall, J. (1990). *Plea for a measure of abnormality*. London: Free Association Books.

McDougall, J. (1991). De la sexualité addictive. *Psychiatrie française, 22*, 29–51.

Melman, C. (1998). Les sexolytiques. In J. L. Chassaing (ed.), *Écrits psychanalytiques classiques sur les toxicomanies*. Paris: Éditions de l'Association Freudienne Internationale.

Numberg, H., & Federn, E. (1967). *Minutes of the Vienna psychoanalytic society. Volume II, 1908–1910*. New York: International Universities Press Inc.

Petit, P. (2019). L'événement De Quincey. In P. Petit (ed.), *Être toxicomane ? Psychanalyse et toxicomania* (pp. 27–47). Ramonville Saint-Agne: Erès.

Rado, S. (1926). The psychic effects of intoxicants: An attempt to evolve a psycho-analytical theory of morbid cravings. *International Journal of Psycho-Analysis, 7*, 396–413.

Régis, E. (1914). *Précis de psychiatrie*. Paris: Doin.

Serres, M. (2009). *The five senses: A philosophy of mingled bodies*. London: Continuum.

Chapter 13

Limit-states or *borderline*[1]

Jean-Louis Chassaing

Translation from the French by Sam Warren Miell

On atypical forms in a symptomatic network

As with all concepts (hysteria, paranoia, etc.) history, context, semiology, and nosology are important and even fundamental. But here, a particular situation arises because imprecision and difficulty in conceptualizing, grasping, and defining are part of this concept of the limit state, which is a concept "borrowed" from modernity, conceptual evolutions, and styles of living.

It is difficult to give a precise clinic if it is not for a few current benchmarks, linked to society! Difficult because this clinic is characterized by its vagueness, by a certain evanescence. Contrary to the criticisms which have been made, it is not only a question of "the limits of the psychiatrist", but of a variable polymorphism borrowed from the times: narcissism, depression, instability, inhibition, risky behavior . . . structural instability in fact. Perhaps it is also a question of finding adequate expressions to hear this difficult clinic as closely as possible.

Clinical case

A young woman has a dream. She reports many dreams indeed, in a surprising manner. Is it because she has difficulties speaking – a constant theme with her? Head down, without looking, her hand in front of her mouth, she whispers in between long silences. We are face to face; she refuses to lie on the couch. I do not insist on it. Diagnosis of structure is not straightforward. She has an intellectual job and is intelligent, sharp in her remarks. Her complaint is above all that of devaluation, of herself and of her parents, which is ambiguous because, as much as she hates her mother, she admires in her a woman who is 'unsurpassable', albeit cold and distant. She herself is something of a tomboy. She is the only daughter between two brothers, one elder and one younger, and she is very close to the latter, as if they were twins. She is at bottom depressive, and displays great, uncontrollable surges of anxiety.

The dream: It is brief, unlike the previous ones. *A letter – blank – I am there (the patient), you are also there (the analyst) . . . the letter is stamped and valid (or, it will be sent) whatever its weight.* That's all.

DOI: 10.4324/9780429432064-17

Analyst: *Is there an address?*

Her: *No, no.*

Analyst: *Ah, no address . . . so blank but stamped.*

Her: *Yes.*

Analyst: *And it hasn't been sent; it's awaiting delivery [*en souffrance*]* (a pun on a letter which 'remains stuck', which is not sent or which stays in the cupboard, and on 'suffering' [*souffrance*]. One says that such a letter that is not sent is 'suffering' [*en souffrance*], in waiting to be sent.)

Her: *You could say that, yes.*

The analyst: *Yes. It is stamped [*affranchie*], with a postage stamp. Stamped . . . do you know what that means?* (This word [*affranchie*] also means 'freed from slavery, emancipated, free', in relation to slaves, for example. One also uses it to say that one is free to do what one wants, what one has decided.)

Her: *Oh yes, that's true . . . that's funny!*

Analyst: *So this letter would be ready to go but would not. For that matter, it's missing an address . . . one wonders why?*

Her: *I don't know . . . I think I hadn't paid attention; it's now, while speaking, that perhaps, as I have difficulties speaking, it doesn't come out, it's perhaps this, the words don't come out, they don't leave . . .*

Analyst: *That's a good thought, the words . . . the letter . . .*

Her: *Yes, I'm afraid of not saying what I must; one must choose the right words . . .*

Analyst: *Ah . . . 'one must' . . . But how do you know if they are good ones . . . or bad? And for whom must we choose them? Who asks it of you?*

And then . . . no address to send it to . . . but the analyst is present . . .

Do you know this short text by Lacan on 'The Purloined Letter'? A letter which, whatever its contents, which we do not know – Lacan refers to Edgar Allan Poe's tale – always arrives at its destination. After a journey in which it transformed the bearers of this letter! The letter is purloined and it passes from hand to hand. Perhaps you are afraid of giving it an address . . . of addressing it?

Her: *Yes, I know a bit about it – I discuss psychoanalysis with a friend (the analyst knew about this patient's interest and reading in psychoanalysis).*

Discussion

This young woman – shy, intelligent – who displays a great inhibition, who has difficulties speaking, choosing her words, who has barriers, without for all that being dissociated or diffluent, and so without symptoms of the register of psychosis, is very anxious before coming to consultations, anxious to the point of depersonalization. She is represented in this dream by the letter that is almost ready but has not been sent. Stamped [*affranchie*], free, with all the content that would assure its departure, it stays in place. The stamp, the postage, is of the right value but here the value is independent of the content. One could think of a neurotic inhibition, but the intense anxiety and also the massive transference, this close-up anaclitic support, described by all the authors, makes me think of an ill-organized personality, of a *borderline* personality. Moreover, in our interviews she was taken to speaking of the sexual and of sexuation, in an uncertain way: what is a woman especially?

What is a borderline personality?

Abstract

This is a clinical category that is difficult to define and recognize, but it would appear to correspond to several cases of the *contemporary clinic* in Europe, the USA, Latin America, and in fact around the world.

During my discussions in Jean Bergeret's group in Lyon – a theoretician who has written extensively on this subject – it was a question of *a-structure*, with a privative 'a'. An ill-established, unstable psychical organization. The conjunction with the ways of life of our contemporary societies was also highlighted. Sigmund Freud's 1908 text *'Civilized' Sexual Morality and Modern Nervous Illness* is a good example of this kind of thought, as well as the manner of responding to it.

Limit-states, *borderline*. These entities, which are quite poorly established in their definitions and even contested in their nosological[2] reality, have as their clinical 'origin' three main sources:

* North American psychoanalysts – mostly psychiatrists, or else psychologists – discomforted by a clinic that was variable and in which transference was difficult to manage.
* French psychoanalysts, who noticed an evolution in the demands of patients, with little mentalization and more frequent acting out [*passages à l'acte*], as if 'doing' had replaced 'speaking'.
* French paediatric psychiatrists, often psychoanalysts, who also noticed changes in the attitudes, especially of adolescents, but also of children, with significant 'disharmonies' between different areas – intellectual and behavioural, emotional – even mismatches within the same area (for example, a large 'advance' in an affective, sexual, or behavioural domain, or the assumption of stereotypical professional responsibilities, and a stasis in the same domain, most often for example a significant dependence on the familial environment; these disparities are accompanied by *anxieties*, which are difficult to put words to, on account of these quasi-discordant associations).

Definitions: atypical clinical forms

Terms vary according to the time and the reference: *limit-states, borderline, borderland, borderline personality, borderline personality disorders, borderline personality organizations*. These states, or syndromes,[3] or symptoms, are likewise contested in their nosological (i.e. classificatory) existence (even as nosographic, i.e. descriptive entities). In effect, these variations in description give the impression of a *melting pot*[4] of clinical traits, both neurotic and psychotic. This, then, would not amount to a unified nosographic and nosological entity. It is therefore necessary to give a brief review of the relevant history of psychiatry and psychoanalysis, in France and the United States.

The creation of this clinical category is also linked to difficulties in the care of certain patients by North American psychiatrists and psychoanalysts, and more particularly in this case related to the confrontation of so-called *narcissistic* personalities, often depressive and reactive, sometimes manifested in *acting out [passage à l'acte] rather than in speech and language.*

Some trace this notion of the limit-state, of *borderline* personality, to the years 1966–67, owing to high-impact communications in the international scientific community, publications by North American psychiatrist-psychoanalysts. These publications announced particular psychopathological developments in certain patients, whom psychiatrists could not classify on the axes of neuroses and psychoses. Symptoms belonging to both categories were described in the same patient, but, above all, other criteria intervened more seriously, eclipsing the classical registers of nosology. These psychiatrists speak therefore of 'borderline personality organization' and insisted on other clinical criteria: narcissism and depression.

The clinic described is verbose, imprecise, and associates the most diverse clinical signs, but some overlaps exist. These psychoanalysts, psychiatrists, and psychologists describe these various scattered signs, announce the difficulty of grouping them in a unified way, and try to establish a more or less autonomous entity.

The interpenetration of signs of the classical neurotic order with signs identified with psychotic states suggests that it is a matter of a class *between* neurosis and psychosis. It seems more satisfying, if we want to preserve this rather vague unity, to posit that there are groups of signs other than neuroses and psychoses, and that limit states exist not *between* but *beside* neuroses and psychoses.

This unit-entity is contested by the proponents of the conservative position of three classical structures: neuroses, psychoses, and perversion. This last category, *perversions*, presents some affinities with limit states, which are defensive arrangements with a particular object relation. The bringing together of border-states and perversions with certain states of addiction, such as serious drug addiction, is also evoked. These are behaviors which can refer to classical structures – neuroses, psychoses, perversions – or approach 'a-structures', with a privative *a*, such as limit-states.

In the 1930s, French psychiatrists and psychoanalysts had already described series of entities whose contents remained problematic, because signs borrowed from neuroses and psychoses were also identified in patients without the personalities described falling into only one of the two known categories. These were 'neurotic mechanisms in psychoses', 'polymorphic pseudo-neurotic forms of simple schizophrenia', 'mixed states and transitory schizoneurotic states'. The terms employed thus describe the clinicians' difficulties.

In fact, classical French and German psychiatry in the 19th and early 20th century had already described *atypical forms*, as exist in all medicine. But it was a North American psychiatrist, Charles Hamilton Hughes, who in 1884 proposed this term, *borderland*, to describe his difficulties in classifying certain patients, in particular those whose pathology corresponds more often to 'the madness or phobia of touching with delirious manifestations', without being, for all that, psychotic. It is amusing, in reading this article, to note that he borrows this term *borderland* from a French alienist psychiatrist, Benjamin Ball. Border states? Limit states? *No man's land?*[5] This clinical reality overwhelms classical conceptions.

Clinical development; psychopathology

We have seen that these variations, both of clinicians and of patients, are therefore included in the clinical picture of these states, these organizations that are poorly organized or close to disorganization. That is to say, they will make up part of it, via relational 'movements' that are difficult to determine and more or less unforeseeable given the fragility of these patients.

This *transferential relationship* is most often established in the context of an object relation which is 'against, up against [*contre, tout contre*]', in both senses of the word. The word *anaclitic*[6] has often been proposed. It describes a relation of support from the other, which can evoke a mirror situation, a situation of particular dependence in which the gaze is significant in relation to a mistrust arising from the *fragility* of the barrier between the patient and the other. This 'need' can turn into aggressiveness.

Clinically, this relation with the other is displayed in alternations between pressing demands, which are rarely satisfied, and violence, not only in words but also in acts (slamming doors, repeated episodes of running away and making dramatic returns with significant emotional demands). We could speak of 'intolerance towards frustration,' and evoke this narcissistic aspect whereby the patient's fragile ego is dependent on the gaze of the other and requires from them a solid but 'true' support. 'True' meaning, most often, what accords with the patient's own ideal, to the exclusion of anything different. This is 'unbearable' for the patient and can also be in relation to the therapist who experiences it. This is why it has often been said, in the face of the difficulties of definition (variability), and in the face of this 'unbearable', that 'limit-states are the limit of the psychiatrist'!

However, these real elements intervene to determine a *course of action*. These patients are generally young people and one finds here aspects of the adolescent clinic. Silence is part of their speech, as are difficulties in maintaining regular schedules. In other words, the therapist must endure absence. And persist. The treatment is carried out in fragments, a situation which we must above all accept, even if respect must be invoked, firmly but without reproach. On the other hand, the anaclitic aspect is distinctive. One must expect a massive *transference*, demanding and even tyrannical. An unconscious recourse to acting out [*passage à l'acte*] is not uncommon. Disillusion is constant, alternating with requests for a response that is immediate and adequate to the demand. Patience, flexibility, and firmness are necessary. Sometimes the therapist is caught in what used to be called 'neuroses of failure'. Vigilance is essential.

We have talked about the history and the birth of this entity. We can consider there to be a current, 'contemporary' aspect to it. The significance of the gaze, the importance of the invasive presence of the other, the multitude of information, the virtual, screens, the incessant and tyrannical mode of dissemination of objects, leads to a consideration of the importance of the impact of the social in psychical functioning. Where the traditional family was well-established, with its storefront set out on the street, it is today the street itself that dictates its influence, news, trends, which dictates 'what one must have, must be, must seem'.[7] We can circumscribe these changes by studying the significant, immediate object relation to an object 'at hand'. For example, see, under the heading of 'addictions', drug-taking, or bulimia – in short, the pathognomonic and specific relation to immediacy and excess. Another aspect is the evolution of the relation to language, be it diminution of vocabulary or indifference to syntax.

There are, however, semiological points of reference. We have already suggested the importance of narcissism, the identificatory fragility of these patients, the lack of egoic protection in their relationship to the other, which soon appears invasive, translated into a distinctive depressive state, even a veritable melancholy.

The clinic reveals moments of *depersonalisation*, more or less episodic or background, an impression of 'not being present', of 'being in the dark . . . as if wrapped in cotton'. These 'impressions' are difficult to describe, evanescent, intangible, but are a source of social and individual embarrassment, of worry, of *an intense anxiety*. Piercing anxiety, not referring to anything in particular, is a major symptom. It is distinctive because it is linked to 'feelings of imminent disappearance . . . of psychical death'. We could speak of the death of desire, how these states have often been identified as depressive. Depression is in fact another primary symptom. It is distinctive because it arises and solidifies with respect to this feeling of disappearing, of this vulnerability especially 'in the face of others', this obligation to 'play an artificial role'. Hence the connections with what has been accurately described as '*as if* personalities'. This obligation to 'play a role in front of the other' is obviously evoked by personalities of a neurotic structure, but here, in these fragile organizations, the associated anxiety is severe, and far from being simply 'embarrassing'. Listening carefully to these patients reveals their anxiety of disappearing, an anxiety that can sometimes be transmitted to the therapist.

The clinic bears witness to behavioural disorders, subjective impressions, and a particular relationship to language.

- Behaviours are privileged over verbal expression, which will be weak and deficient ('It's pointless', 'It doesn't say what I feel').
- Addictions are frequent (drugs, gambling, computer screens, eating disorders).
- Violence, used as a means of connection, is also frequent.

- Repeated impulsivity is present.
- Apathy, with loss of desire, disinterest, withdrawal, systematic aggression towards the other.
- Intense anxiety, accompanied by a feeling of annihilation, is debilitating; the more or less successful installation of unstable and varied phobias can also indicate this clinical picture.
- There is no shortage of suicidal tendencies, and episodes of acting out and self-harm are also indicators. The apprehension of certain repetitive behaviours raises the question of masochism. 'Abandonmentism' [*abandonisme*] and the reiteration of failures are also observed. But behaviours alone cannot determine the whole of borderline personality organization.
- Serious difficulties in verbal expression, accompanied by dissatisfaction and discouragement in the face of language's inadequacy to the thing expressed. Nor does this exclude, at times, ruminations of thought, even obsessional behaviour. One can also hear precious scouring of vocabulary, which can even go as far as neologisms.

Discussion

As we can see, the semiology lacks precision, or rather, is profuse. There are not only forms of passage but conjunctions with signs identified with neuroses and psychoses, as well as the variability of presentations in the same subject.

Does an 'a-structure' amount to a structure? *This stability in instability appears, to us, to be linked to the contemporary world.* For the psychiatrist Binswanger, depression was linked to the American way of life! The references have changed, the possibilities have increased, the relationships themselves bear witness both to an avowed or suffered individuality and to a dependence, a need for assistance. The world of objects at hand ends up preventing, even encompassing, the smallest lack, and enjoyment [*jouissance*] has become the norm. This profusion, this tumult, is the predicament in which we are swept up – the news included – and the almost compulsory seizure of the elements of this dizziness is coupled with the apprehension of a lacking [*manquer*].

In the introduction, we mentioned Freud's text on 'civilized sexual morality'. His students returned from the United States and reported on the developments of North American society, which had generated a new psychological illness, neurasthenia (after Beard). But in response Freud took up the psychoanalytic concept of libido. What became of this unalterable aspect of living which was transmitted beyond the death of the individual? The question of desire and of enjoyment [*jouissance*] arose, on the basis of reported social and clinical transformations. Does it arise in the same way today?

Lacan alludes to this term, *borderline*, in the session of 19 December 1962 of the seminar of 1962–1963, 'Anxiety'. He evokes, regarding 'the wolf man', this 'borderline case' – this as he is defining the fantasy, and more precisely the frame of the fantasy. He gives an example to compare and distinguish this case – that of a schizophrenic patient for whom the frame of the fantasy seemed not to have been constituted. In the dream of the 'wolf man', there is, beyond the window, the tree with its branches. At the end of the tree's branches, in the window frame . . . the wolves . . . and their bright eyes, their gaze. In the case of the schizophrenic woman, a case that Lacan borrows from Jean Bobon, there is a drawing, 'which can be found in any collection of psychiatry,' according to Lacan. Here, there is also 'a tree'. At the end of the branches, what is there? 'What, for the schizophrenic, plays the role that the wolves play in the *borderline* case that is the wolf man? Here, a signifier; it's beyond the branches that the schizophrenic writes the formula of her secret: *io sono sempre vista*, "I am always in view" and/or "I am always . . . the view" '.[8] Lacan points out that both *vista* in Italian and *vue* in French have an ambiguous meaning. There is the past participle but also the function of viewing in the objective and the subjective sense: the function of viewing and being in view, he says. A question of the gaze, therefore, which Lacan here places after the drawing of the vase and of its image, bearing this *unheimlich*, this 'déjà vu' of anxiety. This distinction supposes the frame of the fantasy for 'the *borderline* case' ('the fantasy is always framed'), and not for the schizophrenic, for whom the gaze object is collapsed into its being ('I am', '*io sono* . . .', viewed and view [*vue et la vue*]). In addition, it is 'beyond the branches' that is situated, not wolves, but, directly, words, signifiers. Should we see this as a deficit of the imagination for the 'benefit' of the 'directness' of language? But also, what would serve to distinguish the fantasy for the 'borderline case' and for the neurotic?

Notes

1   [Translator's note: the words 'borderline' and 'borderland' appear in English in the original, throughout.]
2   *Nosology* is the classification of illnesses in coherent groups, depending on their description. *Nosography* is semiological description.
3   A syndrome is a group of symptoms.
4   [TN: In English in the original.]
5   [TN: In English in the original.]
6   Anaclitic, from the Ancient Greek *anaklitos*, 'leaning', to rely on . . . It is a question of the psychology or psychoanalysis of a particular object relation. This word was coined in 1946 by a North American child psychiatrist and psychoanalyst of Hungarian origin, René Spitz (1887–1974), who worked closely with children. Sandor Ferenczi, a psychoanalyst close to Freud, sent Spitz to the latter for an analysis.
7   [TN: this is a play on the phrase '*avoir pignon sur rue*', which means, literally, 'to have a gable on the street', and figuratively, 'to be well-established.']
8   [TN: Chassaing's text, corresponding to the text established by the Association lacanienne internationale, does not exactly match the one published by Seuil, which does not include the term 'borderline'. See Lacan, *Le Seminaire livre X – L'angoisse*, ed. by Jacques-Alain Miller (Paris: Éditions du Seuil, 2004), p. 89; *The Seminar of Jacques Lacan, Book 10: Anxiety*, ed. by Jacques-Alain Miller, trans. by A. R. Price (Cambridge: Polity Press, 2014), pp. 73–5.]

Part 4

Transversal questions

Chapter 14

The relationship with the mother

Renata Miletto

Even though nowadays a demand for a cure is not very often motivated by difficulties in the relationship with the mother, it is quite common for this difficulty to emerge during the course of the treatment. Despite the fact that the person is now an adult with a life of their own, and that the symptoms they are complaining about seem to relate to their working or sexual life, at some point the relationship with the mother comes up and reveals itself to be central to their issues. This is the case for a young man who talks about his impotence, describing episodes of great anxiety that lead him to interrupt sexual intercourse or to end it prematurely. It would only be when the patient stopped dismissing his relationship with his mother in his speech as a banal "visit now and then" and started viewing it as more serious that he could begin to consider his "impotence" as a tool used until that moment to keep his distance from a "dangerous" relationship. This is not surprising if it is true that, as Freud argued, it is the infantile neurosis that repeats itself in the adult one, and that the former developed from the child's first significant relationships, precisely the family ones: "in spite of all the later development that occurs in the adult, none of the infantile mental formations perish . . . and in appropriate circumstances can emerge once more" (Freud, 1913, p. 184).

The mother and the family complex

We speak of family relationships because the relationship with the mother, although primary in the development of the child, is constituted within other (pre-existing) relationships that the mother has: first of all with the father – a relationship that determines the place that the child will find in the couple – and then with her family of origin. But most important, it is a relationship immersed in language and organized in culture. Thus, a much less unique and exclusive relationship than one may think. The family, and the function attributed to the mother nowadays, are certainly not the same as in the last century; further, they are not the same in the West, as in Arab or Asian countries. If we can try to identify invariants, it is true, however, that an analytical treatment must take into account also the specificities of the country in which it takes place, the language and culture of those who demand it.

DOI: 10.4324/9780429432064-19

Freud studied the mother-child relationship through placing it within the Oedipus complex, that is, the basic triangular structure of the child's psychic development and subjective constitution. Freud situates the structure of the Oedipus in the actual relationships that the child has with his parents and identifies the trigger of the man cub's vital development, and the psychic evolution that accompanies it, in seeking the return of those first moments of care and the satisfactions that helped his total helplessness when faced with the demands of life. The desire for the mother therefore persists, as imperious and urgent as the vital necessities. The father constitutes an obstacle to the desired exclusive relationship, but a healthy obstacle, to the extent that he introduces a law, a regulation to that privileged and tendentially exclusive relationship, and therefore opens it up to something else, to the world.

Lacan takes up Freud and defines, from the beginning of his elaboration, "family complexes" as the complexes through which the formation of a subject passes – namely, the weaning, intrusion, and Oedipus complexes – whose elements, social and cultural, therefore essentially of language, form a structure in which the individual is articulated with the social. This passage, more or less successful or difficult, gives the child access to his identity, to the bond with others, to sexuality. The value of this approach is, among others, to place, at the basis of subjective development, the encounter and vicissitudes of the relationship with the Other, distinct from the real people who have occupied its place.

The mother as first 'Other'

The mother is therefore, for the majority of human beings, the first Other – the upper-case letter indicating that she is an other who introduces into the field of the Other of language – towards whom, due to a state of immaturity at birth, which is much more severe than for animal cubs, the child finds himself in a total and irreducible dependence with regards to the satisfaction of basic vital needs. And it is an encounter with a similar alien Other who on her own initiative, moved by her desire, the mother intervenes to help and makes the experience of satisfaction possible. I will not dwell on the element of extraneousness, which may not always be integrated into an experience of tolerance of otherness, but which could return as an element to be expunged and canceled in favor of a relationship strictly between similar persons: the Other is a stranger. I must stress instead that this first encounter is with the desire of the Other. The enjoyment that accompanies it is what engages the child, where he finds a home [Heim] and pacification of the tension of need, and to which he responds. This is what the amazement of a girl in session made me think of, when she explained that during a very difficult moment during her vacation, she had a thought: "I wish I could go back to my mother", thinking immediately after that it was very strange, given that her mother would certainly not be the first person she would go to for help, consolation, or to find rest. So, "mom" meant: home, lack of conflict, protection, or . . . ?

The investment of the maternal Other in the child is indispensable. We know that a newborn who is nurtured and cared for anonymously, by ever-changing personnel, without physical or emotional contact, without words for him, can let himself die. Lacan (1990) says "what is irreducible in a transmission . . . is of a subjective constitution, implicating the relation with a desire that is not anonymous", and speaks of the function "of the mother: in so far as her needs bear the mark of a particularized interest, even should this be so by the path of her own lacks" (p. 8).

The first satisfactions do not distinguish between reality and non-reality. If the object of satisfaction is present there is no experience of reality, but if the object is missing, the satisfaction can only be hallucinated within certain limits. Absence, lack burst into the continuum of experience, when the subject finds him/herself faced with the pressure of need. Thanks to this lack, the first opportunity for an active moment of research also arises. It is starting from here, and therefore from a lack that inaugurates a cycle of presence/absence in an experience of discontinuity, that the constitution of the subject and his first Other begins. The relationship to the mother is therefore marked from the outset by some discordance, and this is what makes Freud say that the first object is lost, to which Lacan adds that, if it is lost, it is because one has never had it. We have already mentioned that the first encounter is with the desire of the Other, with another desire, which the child will try to fill, with which he can alienate himself in identifying, but which, for the most part, the child will find himself insufficient to saturate.

Das Ding

What do we think supports the unconscious permanence of this desire, this nostalgia? The encounter with the first Other and the perceptions linked to it are divided, says Freud (and Lacan later takes up this idea), into "two components, of which one makes an impression by its constant structure and stays together as a thing [als Ding], while the other can be understood by the activity of memory" (Freud, 1895, p. 331). The Thing is what remains unrepresentable of the encounter, the first, with the Other. And, says Lacan, it reaches the notion of an unforgettable primordial Other. But the Thing is not attainable and is present only in the Real* of its absence.

The encounter therefore leaves traces on the body, memory traces of the movements and perceptions linked to those first satisfactions. These are traces that, through comparison, will or can be invested into research work for an external object capable of representing them, starting the psychic activity of judgment and recognition: that's it! But the object found will never be the one sought; we can only find traces of it: "The world of our experience, the Freudian world, assumes that it is this object, das Ding, as the absolute Other of the subject, that is supposed to be found again. It is to be found at the most as something missed. One doesn't find it, but only its pleasurable associations" (Lacan, 1992, p. 52). The object will therefore be rediscovered through the recognition of signs, elements of the symbolic system of language, but it will only be a representation, therefore a substitute, of that first Other. A subject's constitution can get stuck at that point, unable to start reanimating those traces. Not being able to question what the Other really wants from him, he remains "spoken" and totally taken, enmeshed in the enjoyment of the Other that accompanied those traces. It is starting from this point that we can try to understand the most serious cases of psychic failure, such as mental debility, autism, and some psychoses.

Mother is a signifier

The relationship with the first maternal Other, in neuroses, can be thought of as the relationship with the object which, following those traces, can represent that first encounter, and constitute a substitute for it as in a return. This relationship can orientate the subject in drive enjoyment, love, and desire, but it cannot create for a human being, that is, a speaking being, a direct relationship with the first object. This relationship remains inevitably mediated by the words that revive those traces and name them, bringing them into existence through the imaginary reflection that gives shape to them. This is what gives value to the object, makes it attractive, and is also what differentiates objects in terms of attractiveness to us, unlike animals. It is a relationship that develops in the field of the Other of language and is therefore denatured. There is no possibility of a "natural" relationship, which follows the certain and preformed guidelines of instinct, which can therefore be assumed to be harmonious and fully realized. But when we think of a mother, we think instead of the closest possible relationship to this, which only the contingencies of individual histories can have distorted. This is the meaning of the lament that we often hear, in women who reproach themselves for not having been good mothers, of children who say: my mother was not a mother.

If there is one thing that clinical experience teaches us very early on, it is that we should not assume that the patient's speech pertains to the real person but rather what this person represents, which may be due to real characteristics but above all is determined by the meaning they have for him. And this is what counts in the treatment: it is his/her truth, which is also affirmed through distortions of reality. Freud distinguished psychic reality from external reality, and with the method he forged he did not intend to rectify the first in favor of the second, for the purpose of adaptation, but instead aimed to bring out the discourse or repressed desire which prompted one to represent it symptomatically in this way.

For a long time, a young woman spoke of her mother in a radically negative way. Her figure loomed in her words as that of a tough person, devoid of emotional impulses, unable to grasp her discomfort as a "strange" child, and capable only of efficiently carrying out the duties of caring for the family and inflexibly demanding a similar execution by the children. Only later in the course of the treatment did her discourse noticeably change, bringing out a less negative understanding of the figure of her mother and the existence of attempts, which she herself rejected, to get closer to her daughter: another person.

Mother was for her the signifier of the one who gives life, the Real of her origin, her enigma, sexuality, which all her heavily symptomatic conduct rejected. The work done by the word in analysis, long and often interrupted, in a back and forth between past and present, between personal history and "philosophical" reflections, has allowed her to reconstruct a meaning, a plot, within which her mother has found a place other than to represent a monster. For us, therefore, mother is a signifier that an analytical treatment can mobilize, going through the imaginary fantasy it conveys, transforming the relationship, making it livable, and disinvesting those traits that persist by repeating themselves in many situations.

The presence of the incest taboo in all cultures signals for psychoanalysis; more than the possibility of a sexual relationship with the mother, the presence of the incest taboo in all cultures indicates for psychoanalysis the impossibility of direct access to and a complete grip on the object of desire and all the attempts to circumvent, deny, and recusal of this impossibility.

The mediation of language and speech is therefore a matter of structure, and it is on this that psychoanalysis was born and based its method of treatment. For this reason, when we listen to a patient we listen to signifiers, that is to say linguistic elements that do not have a univocal meaning, which have a meaning well beyond what they intend to denote according to the intentions of the person speaking. The analyst's intervention then aims to question these signifiers, to shake the certainty of signification, to open up the discourse to something else.

Mother is a signifier of welcome, caring, unconditional love, which accepts you as you are, always and however: it is on the maternal side that the "everything", the "limitless" is situated. A lady comes to ask for help, distressed by the discovery that her youngest son, who is in his early twenties and still lives with her, has started to use drugs. In the same period, her ex-husband has asked her to leave the apartment belonging to him as the judge only granted her to live in the apartment until their two sons were of age. Does she have to fight with his lawyer to keep the boy in distress from moving homes? Does she have to find a new apartment for the two of them? Should she believe the boy's father who claims it would be better for him to start fending for himself? This is also what the son says, who refuses any help, avoids her presence, and claims he wants to live his own life. She describes herself as a mother who has done everything for her children, giving up a love life of her own, without spoiling them, encouraging them to become autonomous, but she recognizes that the youngest has always been more problematic, or rebellious or very dependent. What should she do as a mom? Then she begins to talk about the loss of her mother, of whom she is still inconsolable even today, after almost 20 years. A courageous mother who lived a hellish life raising two children and trying to protect them from a psychotic husband and father, who was hospitalized several times and whom she tried to remove from the home for mistreatment, but then was always welcomed back. She describes severe depression upon her death; this is when her marital crisis began. Even today, the presence of her mother is constant, as is the pain of her difficult life and that of her own. And from there she developed a discourse in which she ordered otherwise what she lived – the choices she did or didn't make, out of solidarity with her mother's choices, and loyalty to her – and what had literally prevented her from letting her mother die. And this allowed her to think more calmly about what she could do to help her son.

Mother is the signifier of the one who gives life, in a dimension of certainty – *mater certa est, pater incertus* [the mother is certain, the father is uncertain] – linked to the Real of the body, to its presence, which not only establishes the guarantee of belonging and bond, but the existence itself. Body that has not only been involved in pregnancy and childbirth, but also subsequently, in the necessary care. In this sense, the mother really differs from the father, and the relationship with her can make one particularly resistant to a cure, as it is founded in a hand to hand without words that one may want to maintain at all costs. Isn't perfect love the one where words are not needed to express oneself? And some silences are not only difficulties in expressing oneself, in taking the risk of speaking, but the enjoyment of a bond that is wanted to be perfect, without the misunderstandings of language, without distances.

A young patient recognizes that the torment of his first important relationship with a girl was linked to the desire to finally be able to realize the love he had for his mother, completing it with the intimacy of sex, the only real lack in that happy relationship. He does not allow the discourse to turn to any shortcomings or errors on his parents' side during his growth, which have led to the big problems and the great suffering that prompted him to come to me: "I do not authorize them to take any responsibility towards me, he says". Nor is he too surprised when he associates the experience of that impossible love with the experience he has at rave parties, "feeling one's body in the vicinity of bodies that share the same enjoyment, a certain and silent presence, being an element of the thing, from within, not like someone who is looking for it". Mother is the signifier of that ideal relationship between two people, which makes every real relationship (including that with the real mother) seem lacking. But at the same time, it is a signifier of a relationship to be abandoned in order to grow, whose persistence is the cause of many disturbances in adult life.

The pre-Oedipal mother of contemporaneity

It is true that in some cases the pre-Oedipal relationship between two people persists, and the triangulation of the Oedipus either does not end or it fails. That is to say, a relationship remains in which the third element is not constituted by the intervention of the symbolic Law of the father, but by the imaginary object with which both try to saturate the desire of the other: this leads the mother to reintegrate her product, making the real child the child of her desire, without those gaps between the real and the imaginary child that would allow her to recognize his otherness/subjectivity; and for the child to totally identify with the object that fulfills the maternal desire. That being said, it still may not be a peaceful relationship at all, but rather a struggle for mutual imposition and conquest.

The father is the function that takes the imaginary object out of two's hands and that poses himself, for the mother, as the one she desires more than the child, and for the child, as a symbolic reference for a symbolic identification. This is a function of separation that has relied for a long time on the real father as the agent of an operation, castration, which substitutes a name for that imaginary object. The symbolic nomination is ordered according to the law of culture and language, and thereby symbolizes the lack of being. This is what Lacan names the Name of the Father and it is a function that today, following the great changes that have taken place in culture, has become fragile, so much so as to speak of a decline, evaporation of the Name of the Father, and disappearance in the psychic structuring of the normalizing efficacy of Oedipus. The contemporary clinic testifies to this with the reduction of traditional neuroses and the increase of limit states, phobic symptoms, perverse behaviors, substance addictions, eating disorders . . . Someone today speaks of a culture that tends to incest and of a clinic that expresses symptomatic elements that can be defined as incestuous, because they have to do with the lack of separation, otherness, discrimination of affects, elimination of time.

Abandoning the mother

So, what is the "mother" to abandon? It is not often the mother of reality, but everything that allows a direct, immediate, and certain enjoyment of the object, an enjoyment that finds no limits except in the exhaustion of the body, a relationship that excludes Other, the otherness of the similar other and a bond based on the laws of word and language, in favor of a communication of signs. In analytic work. "abandoning" the mother does not come as a result of indication or advice, but as a result of the introduction of the possibilities of the word and its articulations, which can slowly give some air to petrified signifiers and introduce something else, when the enjoyment "beyond the pleasure principle" linked to that relationship allows it.

Today it is more difficult to listen to a discourse that recognizes the existence of the unconscious, accepts to be questioned, does not demand quick "technical" solutions, and does not privilege the enjoyment of a language where the thing directly corresponds to the sign. It is therefore more difficult to follow "the discipline of the signifier", which is what Lacan said the direction of the cure consists of. In many cases it is a question of: offering an address to the patient's words, putting a symbolic articulation that has broken down back into operation, supporting the subject in remaining suspended on his points of loss, discreetly but explicitly representing that third party who accompanies him/her on the journey, who underlines and constitutes the memory of what has been said and that if not registered, slips unheard, immediately forgotten.

In general, it is not advisable for the analyst to directly engage in a detachment operation, especially when the relationship appears to be stuck. This could also be a defense against the danger of being abandoned by that Other whose encounter has introduced us to the world as human beings; a mortal danger to subjectivity.

The child does not always find "the desire of a child" (i.e. of another capable of recognizing him/her as a subject and of allowing the movement of separation) in the place Other that has welcomed him/her. Perhaps instead the desire, as in the mother of this patient, is to recover, through "a son", a more solid identity, a more dignified social status, compensation for how life has hurt her. And the child may have responded, in the silence of a humiliated father, with the offering of himself as an object, in the renunciation of a life of his own, the zeroing of all his desires, playing dead in order to continue to exist. A cover memory reconstructs his position: his mother holds him asleep in her arms at night while she is chatting animatedly with the neighbors. It's up to him, feeling himself slipping away, to try to hold on to her. This man always knew he should get away from his mother, but to do what? And he has always known that it was up to him to be "her interface with the world", even though she was a woman capable of taking care of herself and who had never asked him for anything: she didn't see him, he says, but took for granted that he was there. The reason why he asks for an analysis, now in his fifties, is that following a rapid senile deterioration, his mother hardly recognizes him anymore, she gets lost, she is no longer his mother. It is she who is leaving. And the anguish for her end is the same as for his own end; it is his own death but also the anger for the silent waiting for a recognition that can no longer take place, for the meaning of his life which is made useless by this death and the inability to imagine that it will continue. The analysis is allowing this person to perceive how the Other abandons only in the imaginary register. The Other as a symbolic field of articulation of the word mobilizes and enlivens the bonds with others, brings to light a question and stimulates a recognition that it is worth, because it did not arise from a game of mutual enjoyment.

References

Freud, S. (1895). Project for a scientific psychology. In *Standard edition* (Vol. 1, pp. 283–397). London: Hogarth Press, 1966.

Freud, S. (1913). The claims of psycho-analysis to scientific interest. In *Standard edition* (Vol. 13, pp. 165–190). London: Hogarth Press, 1955.

Lacan, J. (1990). Note on the child. *Analysis*, 2, 7–8.

Lacan, J., (1992). *The seminar of Jacques Lacan. Book 7, The ethics of psychoanalysis: 1959–1960*. Milton: Routledge.

Chapter 15

Listening to perversion

Sergio Benvenuto

Note from the Editor:

Although perversion is normally distinguished from neurosis and psychosis, in clinical practice the boundaries between them are not so clear-cut, and it is not uncommon to listen to neurotics who have perverse traits (or who are perverse with neurotic traits). Interestingly enough, for Freud children have a "polymorphously perverse disposition", and "a disposition to perversions is an original and universal disposition of the human sexual instinct and normal sexual behaviour is developed out of it" (Freud, 1905, p. 231).[1] Indeed, perversion presents some "transversal" issues and has been included in this section. Sergio Benvenuto has written extensively about perversion. I asked him to talk about his clinical experience, in particular with respect to listening to perversion, and the direction of treatment with these patients. What follows is his contribution.

It is quite rare for a psychoanalyst to work with a pure pervert, someone who does not complain also about neurotic traits. Neurotics and psychotics seek therapy, since their symptoms are egodystonic, but very rarely do perverse subjects, since they usually experience perverse acts as being egosyntonic. For this reason, the most exhaustive descriptions of perverse subjects are given mostly by psychologists or psychiatrists working in the forensic field, when they must report on subjects accused of criminal sexual acts, or when a judge condemns, so to speak, a pervert to undergo psychotherapy.

An analyst may indeed have neurotic or psychotic patients who also exhibit perverse symptoms and behaviours. For this reason, there is no specific recommendation when following analysands – I will use this term instead of 'patients' – who present perverse desires. No serious psychoanalytic school recommends specific techniques for the psychoanalysis of perverse subjects.

Moreover, psychoanalytic practice tends to specify its own tactics and treatment strategies in relation to each analysand, each clinical case being a case in

DOI: 10.4324/9780429432064-20

itself. We may say that each therapy is the encounter between two singularities – which cannot be reduced to school standards – that of the analysand and that of the analyst. Faced with the same case, two analysts may have completely different approaches; and it is not possible to say that one is right while the other is wrong. There are no Neurotics or Perverts, there are subjects who display neurotic symptoms and wish to perform perverse acts. For this reason, I will not talk here about a specific technique to treat perverts – perversion per se does not exist – but about a single case of perversion in a neurotic context. Neither will I do this in order to draw overall indications on how to operate with perverts, but only to highlight the role of psychoanalytic listening in a specific case.

Fabio's case

Fabio is a man over 50 years old who began therapy for a series of neurotic problems – so many he once said, "My life is one big symptom". He was constantly anxious about his own fragility. He had gone through more or less long depressive phases, from which he had emerged, he said, thanks to antidepressants; however, after a couple of years these stopped working. He had had other analytical experiences, which he had either interrupted prematurely or had not brought significantly changes. Hence his pessimism with regard to the therapeutic potential of psychoanalysis – indeed he continuously considered interrupting treatment. In his opinion psychiatric medication was effective, antidepressants in particular, which he had been taking almost uninterruptedly for decades, and which he himself, with the complicity of some doctor, administered on his own. In general, we may say that he suffered from what today one calls the "impostor syndrome": when he achieved brilliant results in his career or in his love life, he felt they were not deserved, that he had been successful only out of luck. In general, he possessed all the traits of the "as if personality" as defined by Helen Deutsch (1942), even though throughout his life he had pursued specific and unchallengeable ideal goals. It is as if a certain ironic (or sarcastic) distance separated him from who he appeared to be to others.

Sexuality and women

Among the main symptoms that, according to him, had devastated his life was his relationship with sexuality and women. After a few months of idyllic romance – also erotic – with a new woman, very soon he would experience a remarkable decline in sexual desire: "The woman I am with becomes like a sister to me", and "as sexually attractive as a hen". Hence the need to find other sexual partners, in a never-ending cycle. He may have loved some of these women tenderly, but it was in fact impossible for him to have sex with them again, unless he imagined he was having sex with other women while making love with them. He could also remain in a sexual relationship with a woman for years as long as she was far away, perhaps living in another city, so in a situation in which, so to speak, the relationship could not be "taken for granted": in fact, he always had to win her back or almost, so his desire was rekindled. It is as if erotic desire were ignited only in relation to sexual courtship, and once he had conquered a woman his desire disappeared. He called this a "Napoleonic kind of sexuality". Routine sexuality made him cringe, yet he would also have liked a "comfortable" sex life, that of a stable couple, and his Don Juanism was to him a sort of life sentence. A never-ending race.

He had only one way of keeping the flame of desire burning with a woman he somehow loved: to be betrayed by her. He was affected by what I would call negative jealousy. At first, like Sacher-Masoch, he organized meetings between his male friends and the woman he was with to "hand her over" to them. Later, he gently pushed his woman into the arms of someone she liked, trying to witness, in some way, their sexual intercourse. But over time masochistic enjoyment became more elaborate: not being able to see the sexual encounter of his woman with another man was also a source of pleasure. The suffering caused by being excluded, also visually, from his woman's relationship increasingly became a source of enjoyment. Once he encouraged the encounter of his woman, for whom he felt an intense erotic attraction, with a tinsmith, with someone from a social class clearly inferior to his own. Fabio began to finance his woman's meetings with the man and went as far as posing as their driver in a seaside resort, where the couple spent a few days in a five-star hotel, while he stayed in a cheap hotel nearby, ready to satisfy all their wishes – he drove them to dinner in the evening, for example. To be treated as a driver by the couple, and to masturbate miserably in his hotel room while thinking of their pleasure, was for him a source of prolonged enjoyment, in which the experience of humiliation was continually reversed and experienced as the possibility to taste a sweet-and-sour kind of enjoyment.

Although he was basically heterosexual, Fabio occasionally indulged in homosexual fantasies, which he sometimes acted out – though only of one type: being sodomized. In a relationship with a man, only the passive, "feminine" position excited him. It would have been unthinkable for him to penetrate a man. It soon became clear that he viewed passive sexual intercourse as a masochistic experience: he enjoyed the humiliation of being treated "like a female". After all, he believed that all normal women were "masochists" simply because they are passive during sexual intercourse, which is why the humiliations he sought were "masochisms inflicted by she-masochists", as if his were a sort of exponential masochism.

Some time earlier he had formed a relationship with a slightly younger woman, and together they experimented some "games" he had never tried before. He did not value this woman, he considered her stupid and pettish. In fact, he had a lasting but chaste relationship with another woman whom he highly esteemed and respected, and a very strong erotic attraction towards this "stupid" woman. What this was is indeed an emblematic case of what Freud described as a form of degradation of love life[2]: a man who proves to be impotent with the woman he loves and respects, and instead experiences arousal and enjoyment with prostitutes or women from lower social classes or who are intellectually inferior. One of his favorite sexual games was to tie her and himself with a chain and a bolt and spend the whole day together (they could not free themselves not even to use the toilet).

She liked this double constraint because she experienced it as an acted-out metaphor of an inseparable couple (she was in love with Fabio, and was faithful to him, even though she knew he was promiscuous); Fabio's enjoyment, on the other hand, consisted in self-inhibition, in the humiliation of not being able to untie himself from her. He also began to have her urinate on him, in particular on his face and also in his mouth. Once he did not hesitate to lick her vagina while she was menstruating. I repeat, according to him all this was not proof of strong love for her, but "pure lust" as he said. He once took a small inflatable boat to her place, the type people use at the beach, and asked her to fill it with her urine: he spent the night immersed in this urine, while she slept in the bed next to the rubber boat.

All this could be viewed as being mere libertine play, given that his partner actively participated in these games and was amused. This may indeed be the case if these masochistic acts had not been performed in a more complex setting, which I would call asymptotic removal of women. It is as if, in essence, he wanted to bring about the total disappearance of women, of every woman, but never reached this goal, thus experiencing a sense of failure and of desperate defeat. What he wanted was to distance women as much as possible from himself but still remain in control of them. Like moving closer and closer towards the edge of a cliff but never falling into the precipice of pure absence.

Childish fantasies

During analysis we found that masochistic fantasies had started when he was very young. He remembered that as a child – perhaps at the age of eight or nine – he saw a film in which the hero, "a hunk" as people said then, was tied and, bare-chested, was whipped: he liked the scene. He imagined that he too, as an adult, would have stood naked while being whipped. As a child he also saw a film in which the protagonist was seriously injured in a duel, and was cared for by a young woman, for months, and finally fell in love with her: he imagined that a similar story could happen to him. The idea of being hurt and cared for by a woman lulled him into a slimy kind of sweetness. I was particularly struck by a specific behavior that I would call self-fetishist. As a child, he read a children's story that almost corrupted him: *The Prince and the Pauper* by Mark Twain. Two children who are identical in appearance meet by chance in sixteenth century London: one is the heir to the throne of England, the other is a beggar. They swap clothes for fun, so the tramp is mistaken for Prince Edward, while the real Edward embarks on a long and tortuous journey in the poor and infamous slums of England. The ordeal of the prince-pauper fascinated him, and there was one detail in particular that attracted him: the boy was barefoot. The prince's odyssey among sixteenth century rascals and tramps, in fact, allegorized his twisted relationship with the world: he was forced to live in a universe that he viewed as being aesthetically and ethically degraded, but without being part of it, possessing the aristocratic soul of a prince, and to render his dejection bearable it was necessary to eroticize the misery of life. From then, his entire sexuality – he said – had always been like the bare feet of the prince, who – he imagined with delight – walked the lurid streets of London: the *humiliation of the nobleman* gave him unspeakable pleasure. And he had always felt, even as a child, he was a nobleman, even though his family was not rich.

As a child, he began to imitate Twain's little hero. When he was about 11 years old, and was left alone in the house, or went out alone, he took off his shoes and ran along the street barefoot. He often met a small group of kids, some of whom were barefoot – at the time he lived in a third-world country. Today we can say with certainty that what he was experiencing was an erotic sensation: meeting with the street kids, he trembled both with excitement and fear, of being "discovered", as if he were an infiltrator, because he was "*travestito*", "dressed up", as he said, (indeed it is possible to dress up also by taking one's clothes off). He did not want his erotic enjoyment to be discovered: his being barefoot had to appear to others as casual. Like the prince in Twain's story (he belonged to an esteemed local family), he dressed up as a poor man.

He was quoting what everyone said at the time in Rome about Julius Caesar: that in Rome he was every woman's husband, and every man's wife. He felt himself as an emperor, who can afford passivity and humiliation. To a nobleman nothing is forbidden.

Contact and distance

Today, when Fabio takes off the trousers of a woman he has just started to date, he has a very similar feeling to when, barefoot, he used to set foot, trembling, outside. Being barefoot certainly did not provoke the same pleasure when he was in the house or at the beach: this happened only in public spaces, in a crowd of people wearing shoes. It was the enjoyment of transgression. In a "shoed" universe – a neologism of his – his feet would pace the transgressive antiphrasis of a naked and dirty little piece of flesh.

In summer, he would walk around barefoot, like Socrates, enjoying the excessive contact with the city. Walking around with no shoes on, he realized our cities are not built for our skin, but only for leather and rubber. "Soles isolate us from the bark of the earth, we walk on stilts, a few inches from the ground".

Things were made easier by the fact that it became fashionable for people, for a few years, to go barefoot in the Western metropolises he now lived in: some young people, particularly girls, walked around the city barefoot. Fashion made his "podo-maso" transgressions more practicable. For this reason, some friends of his were not that surprised when he took them on a tour of the city barefoot. He has vivid memories of how observing a famous monument of the city, he could *also* feel the ground, "I-was-there". As he felt his eyes touching the marble of the statues, the skin of his feet could feel the rough roundness of the porous pavement, with one foot he touched a damp puddle, perhaps of dog urine, while the other pressed against a peanut on the ground. He felt his whole body, from his eyes to his toes, as if flayed, thrown into the sharp space of things.

In short, the nakedness of his feet compensated, with this excessive contact with the earth, for his spiritual "as if" distance. There was a gap, an ironic one, separating his consciousness, which was relegated behind the invisible glass of his profession, from the life he was semi-living. "My podiatric sensuality", he said, "is a dose of anti-venom against my exile from the present."

Childhood trauma

We went on to reconstruct, piece by piece, his childhood history. He recalls that a crucial period of his existence was between the age of 6 and 8. At the age of 6 a little sister was born, and he felt betrayed by the fact that his mother now focused all her attention on the newborn. He seemingly loved his newborn sister, in fact, he became anxious every time she fell ill with one of the typical maladies of her age. There is a dream he can remember very clearly, from when he must have been 7 or 8 years old. He dreamed his sister was sitting naked in the bathtub, his mother was washing her. At a certain point, however, he realized that the body of his little sister was made up of a myriad of cubes of meat stuck together, and some of these began to come off and fall into the water. Her whole body was about to tear itself apart. In a state of anguish, he and his mother tried to put her back together again, and then he woke up. My idea was that the dream was about castration* anxiety: in the bathtub Fabio could see that his little sister didn't have a penis, hence the idea that it had fallen off. But a more in-depth interpretation led me to these conclusions: the dream staged his aggressiveness towards his sister, the desire to crush her. Over time, his sister's fragility became something that belonged to women in general: he was afraid of hurting them, of taking them apart, because of his resentment. The resentment towards his little sister who had "stolen" his mother from him became the model for an unconscious attitude of hate towards women. Moreover, since puberty, he has always harbored a sort of resentment towards his mother, a sort of contempt, which he was not able to explain. "What has my mother done to me?", he wondered.

One day, almost certainly after the birth of his sister, he was playing in the loft with a girl the same age as him and proposed a game to his friend: they should undress each other. He does not remember going beyond this striptease and remembers how the pleasure of transgression had a clear erotic quality that he would experience again as an adult. Their game was discovered by their parents, who, having very conservative ideas concerning sexuality, punished him. From then on he became an extremely prudish child: when he washed in the bathtub he kept his underwear on. He even forgot the anatomical difference between male and female.

In that same crucial period, he began experiencing some disorders he can remember, which we were gradually able to trace in a chronological order. In fact, just before the erotic game with the girl, he had had an obsession with a delirious quality. He was convinced that his hands swelled, that they became as big as the hands of adults, and that they turned yellow-green, a color that is typical of smokers' skin (his father was a heavy smoker). He would hide his hands behind his back, also when he was alone. At the table, he would take food with his mouth without using his hands, "like a dog". It lasted a few days, but it impressed his parents enough to send him to be treated by a child psychologist. He remembers almost nothing about the psychotherapy, which ended soon because he thought it was boring. He did not however go back to suffering from the previous anxieties.

In that same period, he also met a boy the same age as him in the synagogue (his family was Jewish) and fell in love with him. Falling in love seemed to him the right term, because he experienced all the feelings he would have had later, as a teenager, for the girls he loved. Intimidated by this, he didn't dare talk to the child, whom he saw often, and thought of him all the time, planning to spend hours together . . . He also imagined sleeping with him and embracing him almost naked. The crush lasted a few weeks. Yet he says he was certain that at the time, at a very early age, he was experiencing all the symptoms and the suffering of being in love, something that usually does not occur before puberty. A certain feeling of shame associated with this precocious infatuation reminded him of the shame he felt when his parents discovered him playing striptease. One might ask: is there a link between being punished for sexual games and falling in love with a boy? Probably, at the time, under the impact of his change in status – he was no longer an only child, but one of two – he had become an adult very soon: his hands were as big as those of adults, he had sex like adults, he fell in love like them . . . as if becoming the sibling of a little sister had forced him into an adult position.

Attracted to feet

As an adult Fabio did not become a female-foot fetishist, however, and this attraction for his own bare feet, which re-emerged in adulthood, was a form of narcissistic fetishism, so to speak. In fact, feet are, together with the anus, the most humble part of the human body. Feet however, unlike the excretory organs, are exiled from the erotic sphere. Foot fetishists, fixated with feet and shoes, are, in certain way, acting a Nemesis, executing revenge: "feet, which always come last, will be the first thing I love". With feet and shoes the lower part of the body touches the ground in its most dirty, humble form. It is no coincidence that almost all expressions and metaphors of humiliation involve the feet and the anus: to kiss someone's feet, to kneel at somebody's feet, "I'm not worthy of tying his shoelaces", "being trampled on", "as useless as an old pair of boots", "kiss someone's ass", "to be treated like an old shoe", etc. Moreover, it is no coincidence that among the shoe, socks, and feet fetishists there are plenty of fantasies and discourses revolving around the anus: obviously the feet and the anus are organs linked to humility. In Fabio's case, this humiliation was connected to anatomical but also socio-political aspects: the attraction for the world of the poor and underprivileged. It later became clear, though, that from childhood he himself had felt poor, rejected, humiliated. Or rather, he had the feeling he was a disinherited and impoverished nobleman. Probably he had been disavowed following the birth of a "castrated" sister who had deprived him of maternal love.

His father was a very ambitious man, he dreamed of becoming famous as a writer. However, he had opted for the life of a family man and was dedicated to his profession; he had indeed written something, but without success. His greatest ambitions were therefore focused on his firstborn son, he exalted his qualities and was proud of him. For instance, he highly praised Fabio's school compositions.

Evidently, Fabio felt precociously *marked* by his father's ambition: he had to become a great person, already at the age of seven. In his imagination, however, he had to become not a great writer, but a politician. He dreamed of becoming a great politician, perhaps even the president of the Republic. Starting in childhood he constructed what H. Kohut (1971) termed Grandiose Self, compared to which, however, he always felt inferior. On the one hand there was the belief "I cannot live if I do not become a great politician", on the other hand a destiny of failure and ruin that made social and professional successes appear as not real, phony, fake.

A trivial cause

The birth of his sister, his fall from the position of only child, played a crucial role in pushing him towards masochistic desires and feet self-fetishism. The birth of a little sister: what a trivial event! Millions of children have siblings but do not become neurotic or perverts. For decades, not only psychoanalysis, but also the various experimental or cognitive psychologies have tried to understand this mystery: how is it possible that an event, a trauma – such as the birth of a little brother or sister – is completely accepted and dealt with by certain children, while with others it becomes a structuring cause of deep spiritual distress, or of extraordinary perverse enjoyment? Research and theory try to find the answer by looking at the personality and attitude of the mother, a sort of *deus ex machina* of the psychological or psychiatric destiny of a subject. This line of research has not produced very convincing results so far. Unavoidable individual differences – whether congenital neurological differences or purely personal historical elaborations of events – ultimately constitute an independent variable, a cause which is not itself the effect of any other cause. His relationship with his mother was of course, as much as possible, questioned, in order to identify something else, something beyond her being "guilty" of having given birth to a second child. Why did Fabio's psychoanalysis reveal a sort of stubborn resentment, like a kind of dormant contempt, towards his mother? As a young person, he had experienced conflict with his father, though not with his mother – yet a closer glance revealed a sort of inaugural, dense, cumbersome disappointment caused by his mother, which seemed to occupy a dominant position in his detachment from the world. Hence his belief that his mother had treated him like "*una pezza da piedi*" (foot-wrap) – exactly what he asked women to do to him, to walk on him, to excite him.

What had his mother done to him? We will never know. When he was a child, no psychologist observed their relationship in detail. But the turning point was precisely the birth of his little sister.

It is as if during his childhood Eros was dominated by primordial humiliation. Not because his mother or father had explicitly humiliated him – on the contrary, he was treated, so to speak, as a prince, like Prince Edward in Twain's novel. But this condition – which made him feel he was always some meters above ground, as in his recurring dreams – corresponded to the sole of his feet, a painful but also blissful counter melody of his handicapped superiority.

Fetishism

It is possible to say that not all fetishists are masochists, that many are excited by woman's shoes not because they are trampled on, humiliated, or dominated. It seems to me that the fetish is, paradoxically, a narcissistic object: a beautiful female shoe is a sort of bold and unrecognizable metaphor of the subject itself. "*Sono una vecchia scarpa*" (I'm an old shoe), could be said by an old professor who wishes to be acknowledged as a well-known and established personality. The love for shoes is, to quote Kleinian psychoanalysts, a form of reparation: the object that a woman separated from herself is now a subject itself, which can be virile, that is, offer its own penis to a woman, only because she is connected to the very humble object that has been thrown away, that is humiliated, and the subject feels he is this object. The shoe is no longer an appendix of a woman: the woman is herself an appendix of this shoe. In any case, Fabio was not a female shoe or foot fetishist: he was a fetishist of his own feet. Also, this self-fetishism was secondary. His real "fetish" was women's infidelity, their enjoyment with other men. This way, by means of women, he satisfied his homosexual impulses, placing the penis at the centre of the sexual act. Exactly like male homosexuals.

Treatment

In Fabio's case the devaluation of himself was the other side of an overwhelming exaltation of himself. He had a very strong professional ambition. He was quite successful in his scientific career, but this meant nothing to him: he would have liked to achieve much more. For instance, to be awarded the Nobel Prize. His professional ambition had drained other desires: for example, he had no interest in having children (he had got some women pregnant and had urged all of them to have an abortion). He had a very high intellectual opinion of himself, his arrogance had no limits; also, it is interesting to note that his close friends were arrogant people as well, they all believed they were real geniuses. The sphere of friendships was characterized by this shared conviction, which obviously led to comparison and rivalry and, sometimes also to dramatic rifts. But at the same time, in a cyclothymic oscillation that was in some ways also synchronous, he considered himself a failure, an empty promise. This is narcissism according to psychoanalysis: it is never only idealization of oneself, but also always a failure of this idealization. By narcissism, one should intend not so much one's own grandiose self-image, but the fragility of that image, that is, the fact that the subject oscillates between a self-exaltation and considering himself a failure. The narcissist's self-idealization is at the same time excessive and fragile, and Fabio's self-esteem always depended on external feedback, on confirmation of his "success". His self-esteem did not come from inside but from outside: it was the effect of social recognition. Any kind of defeat was debilitating. Because to be defeated, to fail, was not an accident but a revelation: failure revealed how insignificant he actually was. However, he himself described himself as "a papers-producing-machine". Fabio had, in fact, worked to become the war machine of his father (who died when Fabio was still very young), with the aim of succeeding in order to satisfy him. His professional commitment, as well as his sexual commitment, were extreme: and in both cases what counted was "success". Fabio's manic-depressive oscillation mirrored what he felt towards his analyst; Kohut spoke of mirror transference. We have already said that Fabio did not believe in psychoanalysis; this means that he did not have a very good opinion of his analyst. He told me clearly that he sort of pitied me, that I was attempting to toss off some brilliant interpretation because I had no idea where to turn. Any shortcomings in my studio – a broken door handle for instance – were signs of my economic difficulties and, in short, of my professional failure. How to establish transference in this context? It was evident that, contrary to what Lacan says – transference is linked to the analyst as *subject supposed to know* – Fabio did not suppose I had any particular knowledge. Yet he came for years, and he was able to overcome his main problems. How was this possible?

A complex system of contradictions is visible here. On the one hand, his father greatly overestimated Fabio, who took upon himself his father's Ideal Ego. On the other hand, however, the birth of a little sister, who became the centre of the attention and concerns of his mother, created a stark contrast to this "great" stature of his: a fragile child, always about to decompose, seemed to be more important than him. Hence the temptation to take upon himself also feminine fragility, to "act as a woman", but limitedly to humiliation, subjugation, and passivity. After all, although he said he was a feminist, his image of women was that of inferior beings.

Like most perverts, at the bottom of his existence Fabio was experiencing what I would call a radical disenchantment. He cultivated no explicit ideal, apart from a brilliant scientific career, and for him social and individual life was a pattern of illusions and hypocrisy, and psychoanalysis was part of this. Fabio defined himself as an "absolute materialist": what counts in life are the more or less carnal pleasures, eating, drinking, defecating, fucking, having fun, etc. In this context, the somewhat ethical aura surrounding psychoanalysis irritated him and made him smile. In his view, positive feelings represented an infantile aspect of humanity. It is clear that with such a subject I had to avoid any kind of attitude that could have been seen as edifying, preaching; above all, I had to be careful never to act as if I were the source of some kind of knowledge. It was immediately clear to me that I should not attempt any interpretation with him, that is to say, I should not present myself as the carrier of a type of psychoanalytic knowledge. It was evident that in the eyes of Fabio all expressions of knowledge were signs of imposture. He especially hated transference interpretations, which he derided and viewed as application of a psychoanalytic routine, a clumsy attempt on the part of the analyst to "put himself at the centre of the patient's life". However, from the very beginning I positioned myself as "he who does not know": I didn't know what advice to give him, I didn't know how to help him . . . I showed a certain impotence, mostly sincere, because if I had faked it only to satisfy his demand, he would certainly have noticed and would have exposed me. I didn't have to *pretend* I was powerless, I had to acknowledge it and admit it. All the positions adopted by a subject supposed to know fail with perverts, or rather, with narcissistic subjects who possess traits of perversion. The true pervert does not suppose anyone to know. So again, how was transference to occur? It is clear that a therapy continues only if there is transference, but how to build it in the event of such a radical rejection of all authority, be it moral or scientific?

His psychoanalysis continued, I think, simply because I showed interest and, I would say, compassion towards him. In short, transference was not based on the subject supposed to know but on the subject supposed to love, which in this case was equivalent to a subject supposed to feel compassion. After all, Fabio wanted to be loved in some way, not *in spite* of a certain exhibited cynicism, rather, I would say *because of it*. He had an extreme hunger for love, even though it was denied by an exhibited "materialistic" and nihilistic cynicism. The less "human" he was, the more he wanted to be accepted humanly. It was transference based on the commonality of ignorance and impotence, certainly not on knowledge and power. Fabio was looking for the *proof of love* his own way. And he obtained it from my tenacity.

Interview with Sergio Benvenuto

DB: *What did this case teach you, as an analyst?*
SB: It taught me one thing in particular, and that is to deal with patients who are skeptical about psychoanalysis, that is, who do not believe in the effectiveness of speech. In fact, Fabio had always preferred to take antidepressants. I have seen, with him as with others, that you can also make words work with subjects who do not believe in words. With these analysands it is not the contents of the interpretations that count, what counts, I would say, is the transferential position they occupy. Which I called *supposed love*. In short, Fabio needed a travel companion who saw him as he saw himself, a kind of defeated warrior.
DB: *Do you remember any particularly successful interventions, or something that had a particular effect? I am particularly interested in understanding*

how we come to invent in the session: an allusion, an interpretation, an insight . . . something that makes the analysand ponder.

SB: I remember saying: "You think you know almost everything essential about yourself. So why do you keep coming? What do you expect to learn?" He couldn't answer. Finally, a question with no answer.

DB: *You reported here several dreams, fantasies, and memories of Fabio. So, Fabio could associate? Was he interested in the unconscious, and in his own lapses? What interested him most about analytical work?*

SB: Apparently Fabio was a very good analysand. He knew how to associate, interpret, he was interested in slips, dreams. He did this because "it's what a patient is supposed to do". He was playing a game, he was curious to see where it would lead. But he was a non-believer. After all, he was looking not for truth but for love. Because his life was taken up by enjoyment, there was no space for love. In his eyes love was like the upholstery of sensual enjoyment. The psychoanalytical relationship initiated him to the dimension of love.

DB: *What was Fabio's relationship to his own enjoyment? What troubled him?*

SB: Unlike the neurotic position, the perverse position is one of perfect awareness of enjoyment, indeed, enjoyment is precisely what is deliberately pursued. What struck Fabio, on the other hand, was the *frozen* nature of his own enjoyment: the need to pursue enjoyment always in the same way. The repetitive, almost ritualistic character of his perverse games. At one point, he decided to experience the "impossible" adventure of a non-perverse sexual desire. What happened, though, is that he invested this adventure as a perverse experience. For a certain time, he had a normal relationship with a woman: frequent sexual intercourse, no masochistic fantasies, or excretory games. He enjoyed this very much, for a certain period of time, as if it were a new sex game. Not to *be* a normal lover, but *act* as a normal lover. However, it was a hetero-syntonic way of acting. What in fact renders a sexual act a perverse act is its hetero-dystonic nature, the fact that there is no true consideration of the sexual desire and enjoyment of the other.

DB: *It seems that Fabio often complains, particularly about the analysis and the analyst, and yet he continues to come. How did you understand these complaints/devaluations about the analysis and the analyst?*

SB: Psychoanalysis was discredited because, in his view, it had no effect on his mechanisms of enjoyment. He was addicted to *jouissance*. As a young man, in fact, he had used some drugs (Indian hemp, alcohol, occasionally also cocaine . . .). He was skeptical the way an addict is skeptical about psychoanalysis: the enjoyment deriving from psychoanalysis will never replace the enjoyment an addict derives from a substance. My patient kept coming because psychoanalysis amused him, in short, it provided enjoyment. To enjoy was essential for him, a neutral life was not possible, a life that was neither painful nor entirely dedicated to *jouissance*. If he didn't experience *jouissance*, he suffered – there was no middle ground. Fortunately, psychoanalysis was perceived not as work, but as fun.

DB: *Did you somehow pick up these complaints in session? Have you made any interventions (more or less indirect) that would allow Fabio to say more about his continuous complaints?*

SB: His complaints were not continuous, we could say they had an ironic nuance. He didn't so much complain about psychoanalysis, rather he derided it. In fact, he pitied it. And he wanted to prove to me that I was a lousy analyst, a naive person, a "poor soul". Which was how he felt, despite his social achievements. In his case transference was a Mirror Transference: the psychoanalyst was like a twin brother, slightly more stupid, a loser like himself. I didn't attempt to deny this position, and this set things in motion.

DB: *I found your staying in the transference as the one 'who does not know' very interesting; it seems to me a useful indication for working with these analysands. What was Fabio looking for in the analyst?*

SB: Fabio was very good at expressing himself outside psychotherapy. He didn't need an analyst to find words of his own, frank words. We may say that he saw the analyst as someone who listened and was interested in understanding him. He appreciated the analyst's effort to understand something about him, even though he actually thought I was not understanding much about him. The analyst was not the subject supposed to know, but the subject supposed not to know, like Socrates ("I know that I know nothing"). The subject needed this impotence to be acknowledged in order to respect it. He was attracted by my acknowledged ignorance.

DB: *Based on this case, it seems to me that you (similarly to many Lacanians, I would say) do not openly interpret the transference. Analysts of other orientations tend to interpret the transference much more frequently, and indeed some base their entire intervention on the interpretation of transference. What use do you make of the transference, and why do you make this of it?*

SB: Unlike Lacanians, I believe that transference should sometimes be interpreted. What I avoid is abusing it: that is, believing, like James Strachey did, that the only important interventions ("mutative interventions") are those that concern the analyst-analysand relationship. I believe that many analysts fall victim to a certain megalomania: they think that whatever the analysand does or says, it always concerns the analyst! I think this borders a sort of referential delusion.

As I said, this patient was particularly irritated by transferential interpretation. His reply was, "You adhere to the school, you interpret by the book!" So I almost never interpreted with this analysand, since, as I have said, he didn't suppose me to know anything. He essentially needed someone to witness his tragedy, someone who, like Virgil with Dante, would accompany him into the Hell of suffering and *jouissance*. A fellow traveler, not an interpreter.

DB: *It seems to me that in perversion there is a remarkable indulgence in fantasy (perhaps with more intensity than in neurosis). I am thinking of the elaborate staging of Fabio, or of the Marquis de Sade in his writings, or of some analysands who report that they are unable not to indulge in a whole series of fantasies of greatness. Why is this?*

SB: As you say, there were fantasies of grandeur behind this. The most unspeakable, because they were improbable. Also, the perverse fantasies of abjection were basically fantasies of greatness: Fabio felt greatly abject. It was hard for him to live without this procession of fantasies of grandeur. He also had fantasies about his dead father, in which he acted as a guide for this dead father. He was imagining himself as the father of his father. So, he began to guide me too, to lead me on tours of his unconscious, in short, he tended to act like the psychoanalyst of the psychoanalyst. He was convinced, in fact, that he would maybe not cure me, but make me a better analyst. "You're lucky to have encountered such a difficult patient, you will be strengthened and become a great analyst". He also told me I should have been the one paying, not the other way around: his case was allowing me to improve.

DB: *Listening to the stories of people with narcissistic/perverse traits like Fabio, we often find this dichotomy: on the one hand, a rich social life, where they often find themselves at the centre of the scene, and on the other hand a deep sense of loneliness and sadness. The fantasies of greatness are counterbalanced by the fantasies of abandonment and exclusion, of falling from the pedestal, of a "fallen nobleman". Is this a common trait in narcissistic/perverse people?*

SB: If you are referring to this underlying sense of melancholy, the answer is certainly yes. Fabio often dreamed of being alone in a foreign city: he had not found a girl to be with, his friends would leave, go to meetings or parties he was not invited to . . . they were real nightmares of loneliness. Whereas, in fact, he had a rather intense social life, which, however, did not prevent him from feeling lonely, as you say. I think it's something like what we call the loneliness of kings. He felt he belonged to an aristocracy that isolated him from the "masses", yet he needed friends, women . . . he needed his Falstaff. But the Falstaff's he found were never the right ones.

Notes

1 Freud, S. (1905). Three essays on the theory of sexuality. In J. Strachey (ed. and trans.), *The standard edition of the complete psychological works of Sigmund Freud* (Vol. 7, pp. 136–243). London: Hogarth Press.
2 Freud, S. (1912). The most prevalent form of degradation in erotic life. In J. Strachey (ed. and trans.), *The standard edition of the complete psychological works of Sigmund Freud* (Vol. 11, pp. 179–189). London: Hogarth Press.

References

Deutsch, H. (1942). Some forms of emotional disturbance and their relationship to schizophrenia. *The Psychoanalytic Quarterly, 11*(3), 301–321.

Freud, S. (1905). Three essays on the theory of sexuality. In J. Strachey (ed. and trans.), *The standard edition of the complete psychological works of Sigmund Freud* (Vol. 7, pp. 136–243). London: Hogarth Press.

Freud, S. (1912). The most prevalent form of degradation in erotic life. In J. Strachey (ed. and trans.), *The standard edition of the complete psychological works of Sigmund Freud* (Vol. 11, pp. 179–189). London: Hogarth Press.

Kohut, H. (1971). *The analysis of the self: A systematic approach to the psychoanalytic treatment of narcissistic personality disorders*. New York: International Universities Press.

Chapter 16

Clinic of the void. An interview with Massimo Recalcati

Massimo Recalcati

Massimo Recalcati has published numerous books on a wide variety of clinical and social issues, including Lacanian theory and practice, transformations in the contemporary psychanalytic clinic, the so-called new symptoms, and more in general about discomfort in our society. I asked him to present here some of his theses, and he agreed to build a sort of interview based on his previous publications. This interview[1] is based on three of his books (Recalcati, 2002, 2010, 2011), which describe very well what he named the 'clinic of the void'.

DB: *Dr. Recalcati, the classic psychoanalytic clinic distinguishes quite clearly between neurosis and psychosis. In particular, you observe that the classic clinic of neurosis is a "clinic of the lack". What do you mean by clinic of the lack, and why, in order to understand the "new symptoms" (anorexia, bulimia, obesity, drug addiction, panic attacks, depressions), do you suggest instead to think of a "clinic of the void"?*

MR: The clinic of the lack is a clinic of the unconscious desire, repression and return of the repressed, symptom, and division of the subject; it is a clinic that finds its ground in the formation of the unconscious. . . . The thesis of the existence of a 'clinic of the void' is not intended to define a new structure but is a crucial aspect of the contemporary psychoanalytic clinic. The so-called new symptoms (anorexia and bulimia, drug addiction, panic attacks, depression, alcoholism) actually appear as irreducible to the logic that governs the neurotic constitution of the symptom. The clinic of the void refers, first of all, to this irreducibility. In this sense, although it does not refer to borderline personalities, it is itself a *borderline clinic*, as it assumes positions of the subject that are difficult to decipher by resorting to the neurosis-psychosis binomial, and because it faces a declination of the symptom that is irreducible to the classic scheme of the metaphorical return of the repressed.

DB: *The clinic of the lack developed on the cornerstone of repression. In rigid societies (such as Freud's Vienna) desire was repressed from consciousness because it was impossible, forbidden, unspeakable. Repressed, however, does not mean erased; desire still operates on an unconscious level. Listening to*

DOI: 10.4324/9780429432064-21

hysterics and obsessives it is not difficult to find traces of the desire, since it "oozes out at every pore", as Freud says. Nowadays, in many societies this strong censorship or prohibition is missing. Quite the opposite: everything seems possible, the offer is unlimited. Yet, we see many subjects that are lost, depressed, empty. Where did the desire go?

MR: The experience of the lack is connected to that of desire; one desires what one lacks. In this case, it is the lack that causes the desire. . . . The experience of the void is instead the experience of a lack dissociated from desire; the void is not a lack that activates desire, because void rather signals the extinction of desire, its fall, its eclipse. . . . Void is not associated with desire but rather with anxiety. . . . The clinic of the void is oriented by binomial anxiety/defense, and desire seems absent to the subject who is caught in anxiety and the desperate search for an adequate defense. . . . At the center there is no longer the conflict between law and desire, but a lost subject who experiences the absence of desire, its freezing, its extinction (in this sense we can also represent it as a *subject without an unconscious*). From this perspective, neurosis is no longer the clinical figure capable of framing this new version of the subject as "unsubscribed to the unconscious" [this is an expression used by Lacan: *désabonné à l'inconscient*, in French], but rather, for example, the subject with panic disorder, who lives his life taken by the urgency to defend himself from an anxiety that haunts him and that prevents him from living.

DB: *The demand for cure has changed a lot since Freud's time. These new symptoms often make no sense to the subject. They are not something that provokes questioning in the subject. Sometimes these people do not even know what to ask when they come to us.*

MR: The new symptoms do not seem to be defined based on the metaphorical, enigmatic, ciphered character that assumes the return of the repressed as an agent of the division of the subject, but rather from a problem that radically affects the narcissistic constitution of the subject – in the sense that it indicates a fundamental defect of it – and from enjoyment practices (as is evident if one thinks of bulimia and drug addiction) which seem to exclude the very existence of the unconscious.

DB: *Can we describe what differentiates the new clinic from the classic neurosis clinic?*

MR: 1) *The new symptom is no longer configured as a metaphor, that is to say that it is no longer established on the centrality of the pair repression-return of the repressed.* . . . The consequences for the practice are manifold: the subjects of the new clinic do not pose to the analyst a problem related to the enigmatic meaning – therefore to the truth – that the symptom would contain but, if anything, the distressed need to find a regulation of the more functional symptom, more ego-syntonic. In this perspective, a bulimic subject can simply ask the analyst to recover his anorexic strength without wanting to know anything about the meaning of his bulimic symptom;

2) *The new symptom implies a solid identification (accentuation of aliena-tion) or a drive compulsion (accentuation of separation) to the detriment of their articulated conjunction.* . . . If the accentuation of alienation restricts the identity of the subject – this is the case, for example, of the idealizing identi-fication of anorexia – the accentuation of separation unleashes him from the Other, pushing him towards the dead sea of an enjoyment without desire – this is the case, to take another example, with drug addictions;

3) *The field of new symptoms is the field of anti-love*: the subject does not move the lost object into the field of the Other, he does not pose himself as a subject inhabited by a lack of being.[2] . . . the only possible (wild) transference object is the very object of pathological addiction;

4) *In the new forms of the symptom the object is not a cause of anxiety but a remedy for anxiety.* . . . The new symptoms are attempts to resolve anxiety rather than manifestations of anxiety as the foundation of desire;

5) *In the new forms of the symptom, the symptom does not tend to express the irreducible particularity of the subject but rather attests its alienation to social semblants.* . . . The symptom is no longer an index of the subjective division, nor of the incompatibility between the program of desire and the program of civilization, but it is what tends to smooth out any form of divi-sion. It is not what shakes and undermines the narcissistic identification of the subject with his own ego, but it appears as a strengthening of his own ego, an essential condition of his imaginary solidity.

6) *In the new forms of the symptom, the symptom is not the index of a sin-gular invention, of an uncommon symbolization, of a work of the subject of the unconscious, but tends to be an indication of a repetition of the Same, the common.* . . . This becomes clear in the clinic of pathological addictions: the subject is a slave to a blocked temporality, equal to itself, of a time fixed to the uniform repetition of the Same enjoyment.

7) *The new forms of the symptom are characterized by what we provoca-tively define "in the absence of the unconscious".* . . . The subject of the unconscious as a subject of desire is annihilated by the rising tide of an enjoy-ment without satisfaction that imposes itself at the command of an inflexible Sadian superego.

DB: *The clinic of the void goes well beyond the field of neuroses. What other ele-ments can we find in the clinic of the void?*

MR: In the clinic of the void we can find elements of the clinic of perversion, narcissism, and psychosis: 1) perversion: the clinic of the void illustrates a whole series of cases where the subject protects himself from the encounter with castration through a list of non-human objects that function as a barrier to castration: the bottle, the drug, the image of one's own body in the mir-ror, food, psychotropic drugs. These objects constitute a list of non-human partners of which the subject makes a fully fetishistic use; 2) narcissism: for the subject protagonist of the clinic of the void, the problem is not how to enter into a dialectical relationship with the Other, but how to have an identitary consistency that can be independent of the Other. In the classic clinic of neurosis, for the hysteric, for example, the fundamental problem of the subject is how to be the one, the only one, and the irreplaceable for the Other. In the clinic of the void, however, the main question of the subject is how to exist, how to have a sufficient feeling of one's own existence. In fact, we are talking about an empty subject, therefore, a subject who has a weak narcissistic constitution, who lives his life as superfluous, senseless, vulnerable, uprooted, without desires, and without meaning. With respect to this narcissistic fragility, the symptom (anorexia, drug addiction, bulimia, etc.) functions as a sort of injection of narcissistic cement of identity. More than a problem, the symptom becomes a solution to strengthen an extremely precarious identity. . . . These new symptoms tend to isolate the subject, to place the subject as a monad closed in its own enjoyment, in an enjoyment without the Other; 3) psychosis: there is a psychotic background of the new clinic to highlight how it is not organized on the basis of symbolic, metaphorical symptomatic constructions, but through passages to the act. . . . It is a clinic of acting without thought, of evacuation, beyond repression, it is no longer a clinic of desire in its constitutive relationship with the symbolic law but of drive discharge.

DB: *Can we say that the clinic of the void it is a pre-Oedipal clinic? What is the social framework behind the clinic of the void?*

MR: For Freud, Oedipal identification is what gives meaning to life, what gives meaning to drive renunciation, qualifying in this renunciation the only possibility for an authentic humanization of life. It is only by renouncing the immediate and primarily incestuous enjoyment of the drive discharge that human life separates itself from animal life and can receive meaning. The Oedipal ideal was what allowed the organization of social ties through the deferral of drive enjoyment.

In the current program of the hypermodern civilization, we cannot fail to record a generalized crisis of the paternal function. . . . What changes primarily with respect to the classic Freudian framework? . . . Currently, the dominant social Super-Ego is sustained by the commandment of enjoyment, on making enjoyment an obligation, on the imposition of enjoyment as a Law, on making the urge to enjoy become a new Law. More precisely, the current metamorphosis of the Super-Ego means the emancipation of the Super-Ego from the place of the moral Law and its presentification as an imperative of unlimited enjoyment. It is no longer the rigorism of the Kantian ought-to-be that regulates social ties, but Sadian libertinism which sustains a will for unlimited enjoyment. This means *raising enjoyment to the level of a must.* . . . The meaning of life no longer stems from the ideal identification with the Oedipal Father but from the affirmation of an enjoyment without Law, without constraints, an enjoyment that only seeks to increase itself. Hence a constant inflammation of the drive activity and the idea, related to it, that an immediate and not deferred satisfaction of the drive is possible.

DB: *What is the cause of this change? How can we describe this discourse that runs through our societies?*

MR: The system that feeds the illusion that it is possible to offer integral and immediate satisfaction is what Lacan, in a famous conference delivered in Milan in May 1972, titled *Del discorso psicoanalitico* [*On Psychoanalytic Discourse*], defines as "Capitalist Discourse".

The discourse of the capitalist is a conceptual category that Lacan formulates, trying to identify the new law that governs social ties after the 1968 contestation and after the historical affirmation of capitalism as the dominant economic system, at least in the West. . . . What is the specific cunning of the capitalist's discourse? The object that the market makes indefinitely available is not what satisfies the demand, but what produces it artificially, urges it, activates it infinitely. In the age of the domination of the capitalist's discourse, the object is no longer in relation to the needs of the subject, much less to his desire. The object, instead of satisfying or aiming to satisfy, always generates new pseudo-lacks so that the demand for objects continues to reproduce itself infinitely. The capitalist's discourse opens up artificial holes in the subject and, at the same time, offers the illusion that there are objects capable of saturating these holes. . . . What we call the clinic of the void fits into this context: in the passage from Freud's psychology of the masses to Lacan's capitalist discourse.

DB: *Nowadays, many people report feeling disoriented, adrift. They seem unable to find their place in the Other. When they speak of their life and their childhood, they often describe an Other (in most cases maternal) too present, cumbersome, from which there has never been a clear separation (they were rather the 'appendages' of the other), this is also thanks to the weakness of the Father. You often speak of "evaporation of the Father".*

MR: The "evaporation of the Father", to use one of Lacan's successful expressions, constitutes the social background of the profound transformations that have affected psychopathology. . . . Without the protective umbrella of the Father, the insecurity of existence emerges without any more defensive schemes. The hypermodern age is then not only the age of lightening life from the cumbersome weights of ideals, but it is also the age of life adrift, chaotic, disoriented, devoid of reference points, destabilized, lost, vulnerable; of life that takes refuge in solid identifications or that dissipates in liquid binds with the object of enjoyment.

DB: *The clinic of the void is also a clinic of the image and gaze. I am thinking about Lacan's L schema: in the absence of the dimension of the unconscious, the imaginary axis prevails. These are subjects at the mirror, without realizing it. All is limited to the dimension of the (their) ego. In fact, they report many experiences of shame, humiliation, embarrassment, low self-esteem, fear of the judgment of the other, and aggression.*

MR: The dimension of narcissistic issues is at the center of the clinic of the void. . . . Senses of unreality, anaffectivity, futility, non-existence also define the personalities "as if" by Helene Deutsch and "false self" by Donald Winnicott: social adaptation takes the form of a desubjectivized acting of a role that seeks to compensate or mask a fundamental void in the narcissistic constitution of the subject. In this sense, the clinic of the void is also a clinic of masks.

DB: *But these are masks with which the subject is unable to play. There is none of the playful aspect of playing a different role. The mask here is a prison. Nowadays, we hear a lot of talking about "impostor syndrome". Many people accuse themselves of being a fake and not deserving of the successes they receive. They fear that sooner or later they will be found out. Somehow, they feel they are playing someone else's game.*

MR: In the clinic of the void, the importance of the mask is not in relation to the hysterical game of identifications. If the clinic of the lack – as the hysteric position of the subject in particular teaches us – is a clinic that elects the mask as a subjective modality for making the desire of the Other exist, the clinic of the void finds how the mask is rather aimed at making the subject in its being exist. The mask does not function here as a phallic covering of the subject but as establishment of the subject that does not exist, as a cover, in fact, of its fundamental void.

In the case of the hysterical mask, the subject plays with the mask, escapes identification, and at the same time produces infinitely new ones to act as the cause of the Other's desire and to compensate for the defect of embodiment of his own body that marks it, whereas the function of the mask in psychosis serves to support the very being of the subject. . . . Hence the fundamental studies of Helene Deutsch on personalities "as if" and of Winnicott on the "false self" as social masks that allow a subject without its own stability of being – a subject on the edge of psychosis, empty, without the support of a symbolic identification – to be able to identify with a role, a character, an artificial identity.

In the field of neuroses, the use of the mask is always based on the difference between the being of the subject and his social semblant. In this way, while the obsessive subject's spirit of seriousness can try to compact this hiatus, the hysteric maximizes it by playing with truth and with their own identifications. . . . In fact, one can play with the mask only if the mask does not coincide with the being of the subject. [. . .] The contemporary clinic actually tends to be configured as a mask clinic. Deutsch and Winnicott, in particular, highlight the defensive nature of the desubjectivized adhesion to the mask. . . . In order to verify this clinical incidence of the mask, one can think as a paradigm of certain new drug addictions: the subject uses the substance as a maniacal tonic to guarantee the seal of the egoic mask that allows him to stay in the world. The contemporary use of drugs is less and less of an extreme criticism of the civilization program, but rather reveals itself as a pure chemical artifice to validate the identity of the social mask. In these cases, drug use no longer corrodes the being of social semblants but aims to adapt the subject to the new "performance principle" imposed by the dominant social discourse.

DB: *In the classic neurosis clinic, Freud recommended a sort of neutrality (actually, the German term 'Indifferenz' used by Freud was translated by Strachey as neutrality) in listening. Can the analyst's neutrality/indifference wait and silence be used to engage the subjects of the contemporary clinic, or should the treatment be reconsidered?*

MR: For there to be an application of psychoanalysis, there must be a preliminary subjectivation of the demand for treatment, with an additional problem that the contemporary clinic imposes because the new symptoms appear more as *solutions to the problem* than as *problems that require a solution*. Consequently, in the application of psychoanalysis to the therapeutics of new symptoms, it is necessary to produce a transition from the hypothesis that there is a demand for treatment to the need to carry out a preliminary treatment of the demand in order for a cure to truly develop. . . .

The preliminary treatment in the classic clinic of neurosis consists of carrying out a *double transformation of the demand*. The first is defined in the formula of the "rectification of the relationship of the subject with the real", the second in that of the *hysterization of the discourse*. . . . The ethical transformation of the demand consists in indicating to the subject the role that he plays in producing and preserving the conditions of his suffering, that is, in recognizing him as a subject involved in his symptom. . . . The second consists in transforming the demand for help into a demand for knowledge about the truth of one's own unconscious desire. *The will to know must subvert the will to heal.*

DB: *I think we can say that the clinic of the lack is a clinic of (unconscious) conflict: there is a desire that cannot be verbalized, but that insists in the unconscious, and that returns in the form of slips, forgetfulness, etc. Perhaps this is why it is easier for a question to arise. In the clinic of the void, which seems to me a clinic of jouissance rather than desire, it is more difficult for a question to emerge. The patient may request to get rid of a symptom or substance (food, alcohol, drug), but it is relatively rarer that s/he wants to know more about what is happening to him. What kind of question do we encounter in the contemporary clinic?*

MR: The clinic of contemporary symptoms manifests itself as a clinic beyond repression, with a symbolic deficit, as a clinic of the passage to the act rather than a clinic of the unconscious cipher of the repressed. . . . The new preliminary question imposes itself primarily as a reflection on the *contemporary status of the demand for treatment.* The *convulsive demand* that inhabits the capitalist discourse no longer seems like a demand that is maintained in relation to desire. This kind of demand is not animated by the lack of being that inhabits the subject, but it is the capitalist's discourse that generates it by producing both the void of the object (creating infinite pseudolacks) and the object capable (illusory) of filling it. . . . We can also isolate another fundamental configuration, that of the *melancholic demand . . .* which is an insistent demand of the impossible, absent object. It is a stubborn demand of the object that is not there, the lost, vanished object. This stubborn insistence, however, ends up dissolving the world of objects, showing his ghostly ephemeral face. It is a fading that drags the subject with it. In the convulsive demand, the power of the consumer object, the shape of the gadget-object, and the artificial multiplication of the offer explode. In the melancholic, demand for the subject disappears and the whole reveals itself as nothing.

DB: *In fact, when these subjects bring their experience of void to the session, it is not uncommon for them to complain that the analysis "is useless", that nothing works for them, and that they are not going anywhere. If this nothing prevails, it is also difficult to establish a minimum of transference, which is necessary to begin an analysis.*

MR: In the new clinic, the symptom is no longer on the side of the division of the subject but seems to be placed on that of the identifying sign, therefore on the level of a non-hysteric identification, not linked to the dialectic of desire. This identification is rather an identification that solidifies the subject who becomes his symptom. It is precisely this kind of identification that makes both the operation of subjective rectification and the hysterization of the discourse difficult. . . . This new characterization of the symptom has the major effect of preventing the development of the transference. If the symptom is not what destabilizes the subject's homeostasis but is what ensures it, it is difficult for the movement of the transference to be animated by the symptom as an appeal to a subject supposed to be able to decipher the enigmatic meaning of symptomatic suffering. . . . The only transference that matters is that to the ideal value of symptomatic identification or to the object of enjoyment, as shown, by way of example, in the clinic of anorexia-bulimia. There is no transference on the subject supposed to know because the transference is captured by the ideal of the slim body or by the power of the object-food. This wild transference obstructs the possibility of a symbolic transference and imposes a new strategy of the preliminary treatment.

DB: *How can we operate in this new context?*

MR: The new clinic ruthlessly points out the limits of semantic interpretation in the treatment process. What is basically an element of structure – that is, the differentiation between the symbolic level of the signifier and the real level of jouissance – in the new clinic is radically amplified by imposing an inevitable rearticulation on the therapeutic application of psychoanalysis. This rearticulation must first of all involve a particular enhancement of the so-called therapeutic relationship with respect to the semantic action of interpretation. It is a question of separating the conditions that can make an interpretation effective: it is necessary to make a preliminary *rectification of the Other instead of the subject*. . . . With the expression "rectifying the Other" I suggest defining the analyst's preliminary task in terms of an incarnation of an Other that is different from the real one that the subject has encountered in his history and that presents himself as an Other unable to operate with his own lack. If the practice of preliminary interviews in the classic clinic of neurosis insisted on emphasizing the rectification of the subject's position, hence a radical change in demand as the effect of an assumption of subjective responsibility, the new clinic imposes on us a radical change in the offer: what Other are we able to offer the subject? . . . In the hypermodern age where there is no Other capable of symbolically supporting the weight of existence, we must try to reintroduce the subject in a livable dialectic with the Other. It is no coincidence that Winnicott's theory of holding – which indicates an analytic operation irreducible to that of semantic interpretation – develops precisely in the context of clinical work with severe, schizoid or so-called borderline patients, who are however eccentric to the classic clinic of neurosis. . . . This development requires, in the new clinic, a "yes!" preliminary to the subject that can introduce an Other different from the Other (traumatic, due to excessive presence or excessive absence) that the subject has encountered in their history.

Notes

1 Not reviewed by the author.
2 "want-to-be" (*manque a'être*).

References

Recalcati, M. (2002). *Clinica del vuoto* [Clinic of the void]. Milano, Italy: Franco Angeli.
Recalcati, M. (2010). *L'uomo Senza Inconscio. Figure della nuova clinica psicoanalitica.* [The Man Without Unconscious. Figures of the new psychoanalytic clinic]. Milan, Italy: Raffaello Cortina Editore.
Recalcati, M. (2011). Breve sintesi dei fondamenti della Clinica del vuoto [Brief summary of the foundations of the Clinic of the void]. In M. Recalcati (ed.), *Il soggetto vuoto. Clinica psicoanalitica delle nuove forme del sintomo* [The empty subject. Psychoanalytic Clinic of the New Forms of the Symptom]. Trento, Italy: Edizioni Erickons. Retrieved from www.erickson.it

Chapter 17

Good and bad encounters with jealousy

Paule Cacciali

A mother comes to be seen about her 4-year-old daughter: "My daughter hasn't been eating since her sister was born in July (it is now October)". This is the worried mother's way of saying that her daughter has lost her appetite since the birth of her little sister.

A father is questioning himself about the issue of his son's jealousy: "No, he's not jealous of his sister, they get on well and are inseparable, but they continuously argue and fight with each other . . . like siblings". This last remark is true when referring to the father's complaints about his eldest's outbursts against his sister but can also say a lot about the son's aggression and violence beyond the family setting.

The issue of jealousy between siblings sometimes worries parents to the point that they ignore it when it is accompanied by hateful notions: "My brother, that idiot!" a boy, otherwise very reasonable and intelligent, will say. It is true that this feeling that can manifest itself very early challenges the myth of infantile innocence and is what made Saint Augustine write in *Confessions* (book one, chapter VII) that the child is a sinner: "Then, in the weakness of the infant's limbs, and not in its will, lies its innocence. I myself have seen and known an infant to be jealous though it could not speak. It became pale, and cast bitter looks on its foster-brother. . . . May this be taken for innocence, that when the fountain of milk is flowing fresh and abundant, one who has need should not be allowed to share it, though needing that nourishment to sustain life?" (Augustine, 1876, p. 9). Religious and literary texts and varied facts are full of stories on the theme of jealousy and its consequential covetousness.

However, observation of the child and the work of psychoanalysts have updated the role of jealousy in the origin of the sociability of a very young child. Jealousy in this pre-Oedipus stage does not represent an essential rivalry, but rather a mental identification. Similar to the experience of a mirror where the child recognizes his image (mirror stage), when the young child meets someone similar, he links this to the mirror experience, in other words, to both the structure of the body itself and its relationship functions, as he is now separated from the maternal body.

Let us remember that meeting one's reflection in the mirror and meeting a similar child are silent mirrors but both speaking ones. To realize this, one only has to

DOI: 10.4324/9780429432064-22

watch small children in action, able to parade around, charm another child, show themselves as domineering, only to aggressively snatch away the toy that this other child was playing with, then even imitate them in his gestures.

There is almost always a conflicting relationship present in each child: love and imaginary identification, a conflict between two opposing and complimentary attitudes: to give a spectacle to the other or to be lovingly captured and follow them with one's gaze. An active or passive attitude, both in turn . . . this does not happen without cries, sometimes without tears and the benevolent intervention of the adults present.

This entirely imaginary identification clearly shows the recognition of another but also of a rival. The emergence of jealousy in relationship to feeding mentioned by St Augustine must therefore be interpreted with great caution. In fact, jealousy can manifest itself in cases where the subject, who has been weaning for a long time, is not in a situation of vital competition with a sibling. Therefore, we can speak of a certain identification with the state of the brother: this is the case with the four-year-old child will take up the bottle again at the birth of a newborn. It is aggression towards the younger child that dominates the affective economy of the jealous child, but this is both suffered and acted upon, underpinned by an identification with the other, who is also the object of his jealousy. The image of the non-weaning sibling is of no relation to the struggle for life and evokes special aggression only because it recounts for the child the experience of separation from the mother at the time of weaning.

In any case, the ego in its constitution will keep the traces of this structural passage through jealousy since it is constituted at the same time as the other in the jealousy drama. In fact, jealousy implies the introduction of a third object. The young child's commitment in his identification with a fellow child, through jealousy, leads to an alternative in which the fate of reality is played out for him: either he finds the maternal object and clings to the refusal of reality and to the destruction of his rival, or he welcomes him as someone who is not a stranger, but a "competitor" which implies both a rivalry and an agreement with him in a socialized relationship.

When jealousy takes a pathological turn, it manifests itself in the child, when personal identification in this child still falters. It can take mytho-manic turns, but can be transitory. It can also take a paranoid turn when the ego regresses to an archaic stage where something like "or him or me" is played out.

This question of jealousy which never ceases to torment children remains the basis for the possible or impossible encounter with the O(o)ther as a third party separating the child from his mother, just as the paternal function can do at the symbolic level.

Reference

Augustine, S. (1876). *The confessions*. Edinburgh: Clark.

Index